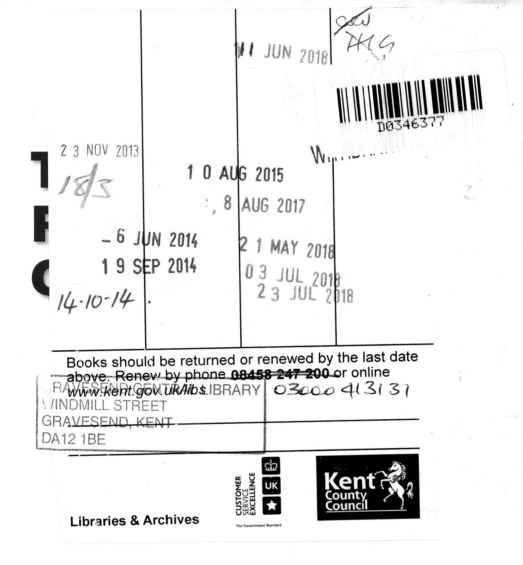

27TH EDITION

The Good Retirement Guide

Everything you need to know about health, property, investment, leisure, work, pensions and tax

Edited by Frances Kay

KoganPage

LONDON PHILADELPHIA NEW DELHI

The information contained in this book is for general guidance only and does not constitute professional advice. Users should consult with a professional adviser concerning any specific issues, and their impact on any individual or entity, before making any major financial decision.

This 27th edition published in Great Britain in 2013 by Kogan Page Limited.

Kogan Page Limited
120 Pentonville Road
London N1 9JN
United Kingdom
www.koganpage.com

British Library Cataloguing-in-Publication Data

A CIP record for this book is available from the British Library.

ISBN   978 0 7494 6817 0
E-ISBN   978 0 7494 6818 7

Typeset by Graphicraft Limited, Hong Kong
Print production managed by Jellyfish
Printed and bound in Great Britain by CPI Group (UK) Ltd, Croydon, CR0 4YY

Contents

12   Voluntary work   323

13   Health   341

14   Holidays   375

15   Caring for elderly parents   409

16   No one is immortal   449

Chapter One
Are you looking forward to retirement?

The first 40 years of life give us the text; the next 30 supply the commentary. **ARTHUR SCHOPENHAUER, QUOTED IN THE *OBSERVER***

It's official ... old age has been postponed! The age at which we consider ourselves to be old is steadily moving upwards, and even at 80 years old, 20 per cent of us say we do not feel old (source: European Social Survey). So maybe 60 years old is the new 40, and 80 years old the new 60? Whatever you think, something that should not be postponed is acquiring a copy of the latest edition of *The Good Retirement Guide*. This book contains everything you need to know about retirement. Each year (and this year's publication is the 27th edition) it is updated to give advice on matters relating to all aspects of retirement – from planning your future through finance, pensions, work, home and health to leisure activities and holidays.

Over the last century retirement has changed dramatically. Not so long ago life expectancy was shorter and many people who stopped working at 65 enjoyed a retirement of less than 10 years. Now it is very different. Recent figures released by the Department for Work and Pensions predict that more than a quarter of children currently aged 16 and under can expect to reach their 100th birthday. The statistics reveal that as many as 11 million people alive now will become centenarians: 3.3 million are aged 16 and under; 5.4 million of them are between 17 and 50; 1.4 million are 51–65, and more than 900,000 are already over 65. This situation has been described by the International Longevity Centre as 'a huge societal success' but it comes at a price. Indeed there is a real risk that increased longevity will generate serious intergenerational tensions, where there is a clash of needs for resources between young and old.

There are regular reports in the press about people working beyond retirement. One enthusiastic author was delighted when his paintings went on display in the same week that his debut novel was published – at the age of 92. In agriculture it is not uncommon to find men and women working well into their late 70s and 80s. More than a quarter of farmers in the Highlands and Islands are aged 70 and over, according to Scottish Agricultural College research. You might think that if you are in your 80s, forgetting to put your teeth in before going out is not too serious an error. But one octogenarian farmer from the Isle of Skye recalled trekking into the hills to round up his sheep only to realize that he had left his dentures at home. Without his teeth he could not whistle commands to his sheepdog. As a result the dog and sheep went everywhere except in the right direction. Defeated, he had to return home to retrieve his dentures and get back up the hill to round up the sheep. He retains his sense of humour when recounting the story and remains committed to his working life on his 150-acre holding (*BBC News Magazine*: 3 May 2012 – Meet the UK's oldest farmers).

But what about those of us approaching retirement now? Since it can last up to 25 years, perhaps we should embark on some radical rethinking when planning for the future to ensure it is a positive experience. Work–life balance is important at any age, and whether we intend to carry on working to some extent or enjoy our retirement in a leisurely way, we need to give it serious thought. If we do not spend time now concentrating on 'the work of growing old' we won't have the right things in place when we need them. With a healthier, more energetic group of older workers, lots of people wish to continue working after retirement age, so that they remain active. For example, older individuals make huge contributions to local communities through volunteering – 51 per cent of volunteers are aged over 60 (British Household Panel Survey/Future Foundation).

Interestingly, fewer than one in five retired people now feel it is their responsibility to leave an inheritance to their children, since so many are already helping their children and grandchildren with education and housing costs. It is a fact: pensioners are becoming harder to recognize and retirement now means different things to different people. A large percentage of 60- to 70-year-olds continue to work in some capacity; not necessarily because of financial constraints, but because they are fit and healthy and enjoy it.

With lots of older people being young in attitude, tastes and energy, the majority of those coming up to retirement are concerned about two things:

living well on a reduced income and maintaining their feelings of self-worth once the status that went with their job has ceased. Retirement is a major lifestyle change, and the closer people come to retiring, the more they should be thinking about the kind of retirement they want. When you consider what standard of living you want, and how much money you'll need, this can be viewed by some with apprehension. This varies from person to person, but the possible lack of sufficient financial resources, coupled with the loss of social life on giving up work affects most retirees to some degree. The things that few people miss are the stresses, tensions, deadlines, targets and watching the clock that accompany life in the workplace.

Planning for a meaningful life after work ends cannot start too soon. There is far more to it than putting together a financial portfolio. Even before ceasing to work, it is sensible to stop working at weekends, make sure you take care of your health, keep an open mind and be curious about new things and ways of doing things differently. If you want to continue working, think about what you could do which might be fun. Develop friends outside the workplace and keep old friendships in good repair: true friends will last a lifetime. Learn how to handle freedom – consider going self-employed for a time before you retire. Remember that money can buy many things to make life comfortable but it cannot buy happiness. Take all of your paid holiday before you retire so that you can get used to leisure time. For some who are not used to their own company, spend some periods of time alone, so that you learn to enjoy your solitude and can distinguish between it and loneliness.

Top tips for enjoying retirement are to travel as much as you can in the pre-retirement phase. The wider your outlook the more likely you are to enjoy the opportunities for travel once you have ceased working. Also, do not allow your identity to be tied into your job. Should a pre-retirement course be offered to you by your employer, check that it deals with personal issues and not only financial issues. Well designed pre-retirement courses should dispel fears and anxieties and enable you to look forward with confidence to a happy retirement.

Readers of *The Good Retirement Guide* will find pages of sound, sensible advice and suggestions to help them overcome any retirement angst. It is just as important to be organized in retirement as it was during your career, and you should aim to develop a routine that suits you once you stop working. If you plan your days and weeks in advance, you will find it possible to fit in all the things you want to do, secure in the knowledge that you don't have to ask someone's permission first.

Friends and former colleagues who have recently retired may well be happy to be consulted for their advice, to share experiences and offer tips on 'dos and don'ts'. One golden rule many agree with is to resist the urge to make lots of changes early on, or to fill your time in the first few weeks with activities of all sorts. Wait a while before committing yourself in all directions, because decisions reached in haste may be regretted later.

Research is always useful: seeing what the options are opens up new horizons for the newly retired and now people are literally spoiled for choice. Whether you are interested in continuing to work part-time in some capacity or are relishing the prospect of having leisure time in abundance, each individual should think hard about what will best suit his or her circumstances. For some people part-retirement is a way forward. It has the advantage of maintaining some of the status quo by working a few hours a week, while having plenty of leisure time as well. Staying fit, active and having enough social activity are also important. This prevents isolation, which can lead to depression in some cases.

The Good Retirement Guide is packed with information, suggestions and advice on every aspect of retirement and beyond. It aims to inspire you to do things you've never thought of, and help you to sort out the practicalities should you not already have explored the opportunities available. It is an invaluable resource book which will help you enjoy your retirement to the full.

A number people in their 50s and 60s are prepared if necessary to work for longer to improve their pension pot, but this depends on each individual case. Generally everyone over the age of 55 should know what their needs are. They must ask themselves whether they have enough to be able to live in the same way as when they worked. If not, they should plan their budget. Most people need less money in retirement – broadly speaking that is around two-thirds of their pre-retirement income. With the present cash-strapped economy, everyone has to take steps so that they can live within their means, and for many that requires some degree of compromise. So when thinking about your finances, look at your current income, outgoings and assets and make sure you've done everything you can to boost your income for retirement. It is vital when planning to retire that you know how to make the most of what you've got.

Chapter 2 of the *Guide* deals with money in general. Chapter 3 is all about pensions and Chapter 4 relates to tax matters. Whatever aspect of retirement concerns you most, the first step is of course to do some figure work. Chapter 7 of the *Guide* contains a very practical budget planner.

Working through this is time well spent, if you haven't already carried out such a financial exercise. Everyone needs a clear idea of how much they spend and on what. Until you have done this, how can you work out how much you will need to live comfortably in retirement?

In the course of your preparation, you will want to assess your likely savings, including lump sums from your pension or any insurance policies you may have. The more accurate the picture, the more detailed the plan can be of how to maximize the value of your assets. Chapter 5 deals with investments and the many types of investments on offer. Should you be considering whether or not to buy an annuity and what tax planning should be considered, professional advice is essential. Chapter 6 is all about financial advisers and how to find a reputable person to assist you in this complex field.

For a number of people retirement offers the opportunity to start a new career. Finding paid work over the age of 55 may not be easy but it is something worth considering. Working beyond retirement is satisfying in more than financial terms. Some individuals turn their talents to something entirely new, while others go freelance or become consultants in their existing area of expertise. There is a growing number of recruitment websites designed especially for retirees. Chapter 11 has a number of suggestions for looking for paid work and contains plenty of useful leads and sources.

Should you be interested in becoming a mature entrepreneur, Chapter 10, Starting your own business, provides good advice and suggestions to help you decide whether this course of action is right for you. If you have specialist skills or have always wanted to try running your own business, becoming self-employed in retirement is something to contemplate. Being your own boss at any age is exciting and should this be one of your so-far unfulfilled ambitions it can be tremendously rewarding. Entrepreneurs are often very successful and – whether you are aiming high or not so high – extra money always comes in useful.

As already mentioned, more than any other group in society, older people are the social glue of most communities. They are often the linchpins of local clubs and societies. Hundreds of over-65s make valuable contributions to many different types of work. Giving back to society increases feelings of self-worth and adds greatly to a sense of fellowship. Whether you can spare only the occasional day or can help on a regular basis, Chapter 12, Voluntary work, has an abundance of suggestions you might like to consider. If you feel like joining the army of volunteers in your neighbourhood and devoting some of your energy to local good causes, there are literally scores of opportunities for retired people.

Your health is the subject of Chapter 13, which contains information and advice on how to keep well. The key ingredient to a happy and fulfilling retirement is good health. Without it, energy is lacking and many activities are restricted. While a number of people have the misfortune to contract unexpected illness, good health as you grow older is largely in your own hands. Taking regular exercise is vital, as well as paying attention to your weight, giving up smoking and drinking in moderation. Obesity and associated health issues have a huge impact on life expectancy. In real terms there is a big gap between those who look after themselves and those who make little or no attempt to follow healthy lifestyle choices.

When it comes to leisure activities, there are opportunities throughout the country for almost every kind of sport and hobby, many with over-55s especially welcome. There are hundreds of specialist bodies, and although the lists are by no means exhaustive, Chapters 9 and 14 give details. The choice of leisure pursuits is enormous and many recently retired people often wonder how they ever found the time to work. Whether you are sporty, scholarly, hands-on or sedentary, you will find an interest that caters for your enthusiasm.

One of the opportunities offered by retirement is the chance to move home. Some people can't wait to up sticks and relocate to another area. While this works well for some, it can be a lengthy and costly business in the current economic climate. New retirees should think hard about such things as proximity to family and friends and how easy it will be to become integrated in an entirely new community. If, however, you have been living in a place which was expedient while you were working and now it is no longer advantageous, a move may be sensible. Make sure you consider carefully all the pros and cons. The big advantage to not working is that decisions do not have to be made in a hurry. It may be that downsizing is the answer, but weigh the options before taking the plunge.

While moving home can be good, for many the preferred option is not to move but to improve. There are plenty of ways of adapting a house to make it more convenient and labour saving. Lots of possibilities are explored in Chapter 8, Your home. If you are caring for elderly parents the range of organizations that can provide you with backup is far more extensive than you might realize. For single people especially, who may feel that they have no choice but to give up a career, knowing what facilities are available could prove a veritable godsend. These are listed in Chapter 8 and other options are found in Chapter 15, Caring for elderly parents.

Retirement today is full of opportunity and choice. The 2013 *Guide* is thoroughly updated to reflect recent changes to tax, pensions and opportunities. Planning for retirement can be hard – this book makes it easier.

Pre-retirement courses

If, as previously suggested, 60 is the new 40, then 80 is the new 60. Whatever age you are due to retire, taking advantage of a pre-retirement course will help you plan well for the next stage in your life. Maybe you are lucky enough to have worked for a company that provides pre-retirement courses for its employees. Some companies run in-house courses, but if your organization doesn't offer such help, or if you are self-employed, there are a number of independent organizations that can help you. When would be the best time to attend such a course? One or two years before retirement, or earlier? Some people like to prepare for retirement in stages. It is important that some financial decisions, such as those affecting company or personal pension planning, are taken as early as possible. Others, like whether or not to move house, could wait till much later on.

Courses are designed to address the main subjects: finances, health, activity, leisure, housing and the implications and adjustments needed to be made when you retire. The most useful for individuals rely less heavily on the amount of factual information the course contains but the extent to which it helps to focus and stimulate your own thoughts on the various issues ahead for you and your family. If your pre-retirement studies stimulate discussion with your partner and others in similar situations, it will have achieved its objective.

Here are some websites with loads of information and advice to those planning retirement. They offer good pre-retirement courses, including some online courses:

Laterlife Learning provides the most comprehensive approach to retirement in the UK. Pre-retirement and mid-life planning courses available across the UK. See their website for full details: **www.laterlife.com** and **www.retirement-courses.co.uk**.

Life Academy is a charity that enables people to learn about managing the changes in their lives through life and retirement planning and financial education. In both finance and health the importance of adequate forward planning is essential given increased longevity. Website: **www.life-academy.co.uk**.

Millstream helps senior people make the most of new opportunities when they leave their main employment. Two-day residential courses offered. Website: **www.mill-stream.com**.

PRIME (The Prince's Initiative for Mature Enterprise) is the only national organization dedicated to providing everyone over the age of 50 with support to achieve financial, social and personal fulfilment. Website: **www.prime.org.uk**.

Retirement Counselling Service (RCS) has been helping individuals with retirement planning for over 30 years with courses and seminars throughout the UK. Website: **www.the-retirement-site.co.uk**.

Retirement Education Services hosts regular one- and two-day retirement planning open courses at venues throughout the country, open to all individuals and couples approaching retirement, covering money, pensions and lifestyle issues. Website: **www.retirementeducationsers.co.uk**.

Scottish Pre-Retirement Council is a charitable organization providing pre-retirement courses to help as many people as possible enjoy a fruitful and happy retirement. Website: **www.sprc.org.uk**.

New focus for the retired

There are many organizations and websites representing the interests of retired people. The over-50s are an increasingly large and important section of the population, so it is not surprising to find numerous sources of advice and information on issues that affect their lives at both national and local levels. Here are some useful websites:

Age UK is the largest charitable organization providing information, advice, products and services to people to improve later life: **www.ageuk.org.uk**.

Gov.UK is the UK government's website for all issues relating to pensions and retirement planning: **www.gov.uk** – Pensions and retirement planning.

National Pensioners Convention is the campaigning voice for UK pensioners – for dignity, financial security and fulfilment for all older people: **www.npcuk.org**.

Retirement Expert offers expert advice and information on all issues related to retirement: **www.retirementexpert.co.uk**.

Retirement Links provides users of the site with current, meaningful and relevant retirement- and pensions-related articles and publications: **www.retirementlinks.co.uk**.

UK Retirement focuses on planning, enjoying and making the most of retirement: **www.ukretirement.co.uk**.

An excellent way of having fun and collecting good advice and information about retirement and everything related to it is to visit **The 50 Plus Show**. This is Britain's biggest exhibition for the active over-50s focusing on positivity, activity and creativity. You can have a fun-packed day out and pick up a lot of useful information as well. An annual event, it takes place in three locations across the UK: Manchester, Glasgow and London. See website: **www.50plusshow.com**.

Chapter Two
Money in general

Money can't buy you happiness but it does bring you a more pleasant form of misery. **SPIKE MILLIGAN**

Retirement is the reward for a hard-working life – you've worked for years, saved for your pension, perhaps you've managed to pay off your mortgage; now is the chance to take it easy and spend time doing the things you enjoy most. Maybe this is when life really begins? But while you may be ceasing work, you should not allow your money to retire as well. It is important that it continues to work hard for you, so that you've got the financial flexibility you need. There are many money-related decisions to be made when you retire: get them right and your income could increase year by year. If mistakes are made, or you fail to plan, you might be faced with making personal cutbacks at a time when you should be relaxing and enjoying yourself.

With people living longer, final salary pension schemes fading fast and state pension age rising, more pensioners are open to the elements of inflation (be it CPI or RPI), annuity rates or stock market performance. Aviva (the insurance provider) suggests that over three-quarters of pensioners are worried about the rising cost of living and having to continue working to make ends meet. Obviously one way of increasing the problem is to bury your head in your hands and do nothing. Failing to work out how much you are actually worth will simply postpone facing reality.

So what steps can you take to avoid being strapped for cash once you leave your job? Whether you are close to giving up work or you are several years away from retirement, the most important thing to do is carry out a serious review of your retirement plans. This will help you work out what options there are for maximizing your future income. The worst thing is to be an ostrich and ignore the situation in the hope that it will never happen. Whatever the state of the world's financial markets, smart people leave nothing to chance regarding their own pockets. This is Money (**www.thisismoney.co.uk**) the financial website of the year, suggests eight simple steps to achieving perfect personal finances. This applies generally whatever age you may be, but is particularly important for those coming up to retirement:

Step 1: Make a will.

Step 2: Pay off debts.

Step 3: Get term life assurance.

Step 4: Fund your company pension to the maximum.

Step 5: Buy a house you can afford.

Step 6: Put six months' worth of outgoings in a cash ISA.

Step 7: Any money that is left can be invested in more ISAs.

Step 8: Find yourself a fee-based financial planner.

There is so much advice about how to recession-proof your finances that it's almost impossible to open a paper, turn on the news or look at the internet without seeing or hearing something on the subject. The first step should be to focus on your personal circumstances and take a look at ways to plan your finances. If, for example, you are coming up to retirement and have a stable job with a strong company, you are fortunate. Should redundancy be a distinct possibility, the right preparation is crucial. Where possible, while still working, everyone should build up a cash emergency fund (provided you have no debts – apart from a mortgage). This means saving roughly enough money for six months of bills (living expenses): you could start an ISA, and save as much as you can.

Should your income be likely to drop, it makes sense to cut debt costs as much as possible. This could mean paying off credit cards or, if you still have a mortgage, overpaying it so that you can save money while interest rates are low and there is continuing economic uncertainty. (The rationale behind this is that it is currently almost impossible to get a decent return on your savings elsewhere.) Before doing anything, you would be well advised to check with your mortgage provider or financial adviser. If on the other hand you have savings, remember that the government guarantees £85,000 per person per UK-regulated financial institution. If you've more than this, you can spread it over multiple accounts. If you have a financial problem that you cannot resolve, there is a free service set up by law with the power to sort out problems between consumers and financial businesses. It is called the Financial Ombudsman Service and there is more information about this in Chapter 6.

To ensure you have a comfortable retirement, you will need to carry out a full financial health check. Its purpose is to give you a clear view of your current financial position. You should get a state pension forecast, then contact the pension trustees of your current and previous employers. Once you've done that, work out how much income you are likely to need in retirement. Be as realistic as you can – for example, how much you are likely to save once you are not travelling to and from work. Remember to factor in holidays and any debts you might have. If you have lost track of investments or previous pensions, it is worth spending some time in tracing these.

Money matters are on many people's minds at the moment. With the current economic climate causing difficulties for many, the ability to manage your money and know how to budget is important. Knowing how much you spend is essential, so you can work out what's left and that it really is yours. A tip some people recommend is keeping track of your expenditure by means of a 'spending diary'. Whether you use a notebook or a spreadsheet, the result is the same. Put down everything, so you can see how much you spend; it's then quite easy to see if you are spending too much. Don't forget that there are some 'retirement freebies' which are well worth taking advantage of: various things you become entitled to once you've passed a certain age. These include travel concessions, some health benefits and help with fuel bills. It's surprising how much these small things add up to.

The key to managing your retirement well is to know how to make whatever money you have go as far as possible. There are many useful websites brimming with information on retirement issues. It is an excellent investment of your time to do some thorough research in this regard. Details of some of the better ones are listed later in this chapter. Since getting a grip on your finances is vital, depending on the standard of living you want to have, you should do this as early as possible.

Doing the sums

How do you get an objective view of your financial affairs? One sensible way is to draw up a budget showing your income and outgoings. To make a proper assessment, you need to draw up several lists:

1 expected sources of income on retirement;

2 essential outgoings;

3 normal additional spending (such as holidays and other luxuries).

The following should also be considered:

4 possible ways to boost your retirement income;

5 spending now for saving later.

You should also try to factor in some of the variables and unknowns, which are much more difficult to estimate. The fluctuations in the world's economies do not help, but two of the most important items to consider in retirement planning are tax and inflation. Things like stocks and shares, property prices and energy costs go up as well as down and all these affect retirement finances. Emergency situations can arise, the most likely being illness, so, if possible, special provisions should be made. The big question (which no one can answer) is how long you, your partner or any dependants might live.

If you base your calculations on current commitments and expenditure, remember your lifestyle and spending habits may change considerably. To get the figures into perspective, think how you will live in retirement. You should spend some time working out what items will still represent a significant percentage of your budget, and which will no longer be so important. There will be a number of areas where savings can be made, and there will be others where extra outgoings need to be included. The most practical way of using the list is to tick off the items that will definitely apply to you and, where possible, write down the expenditure involved (see Budget planner, Chapter 7). While this will be no more than a draft, the closer you are to retirement the more sensible it is to do this exercise. Repeat it as often as necessary, and certainly update it each time you obtain more facts and information.

Possible savings

Once you stop working you could save quite a lot because there will be a number of expenses you no longer have. These include travelling costs to and from work, meals out, business clothes, and other work-related incidentals such as drinks with colleagues, staff collections and entertainment. Other costs like National Insurance Contributions cease on retirement, and unless you choose to invest in a private plan, your pension payments will also stop. It is important to check (once you retire) what your tax coding is because you may well move to a lower tax bracket.

If your children are no longer financially dependent on you and your mortgage is almost paid off, you could begin to feel quite good about things. Retirement age is changing: state pension age is expected to be equalized at 65 by 2018 and reach 66 for all by 2020. Retirement benefits include: concessionary travel and free NHS prescriptions, as well as cheaper theatre and cinema tickets (usually matinees), reduced entrance charges for exhibitions and a wide choice of special holiday offers. Lots of benefits apply to both men and women from age 60, but at present you have to wait till you're 75 to qualify for a free TV licence.

In addition to the foregoing, many insurance companies give discounts to mature drivers, some of which apply from age 50+. Other companies restrict eligibility to those aged 55 or even 60. This scheme could be terminated when the policy holder reaches 75, but a number of companies extend the cover to a spouse or other named person with a good driving record. The discount for people over 50 years old ranges from 10 to 15 per cent. There are considerable extra savings for drivers who have a five-year claim-free record. You should approach your existing insurance company first and ask what terms it will give you. Purchasing online is becoming more popular and many insurers offer discounts if you are prepared to do this.

Extra outgoings

If you are spending more time at home once you retire, your utility bills will increase. You may also find you spend more on outings, hobbies and short breaks and holidays. There is so much choice in retirement these days that as long as you budget well in advance you should have enough money to do all you want. Looking ahead, home comforts become increasingly important and you may want to think about paying other people to do some of the jobs that you previously managed yourself. Anticipating such areas of additional expenditure is not being pessimistic; actually it is the surest way of avoiding future money worries. Once you've worked out your retirement income and expenditure in detail you should be able, with a bit of adjustment and compromise, to manage well.

Expected sources of income on retirement

Your list will include at least some of the following. Once you have added up the figures in the Budget planner (Chapter 7) you will have to deduct income tax to arrive at the net spending amount available to you:

basic state pension;

State graduated pension;

SERPS;

State second pension;

occupational pension;

personal pension;

stakeholder pension;

State benefits.

Additionally, you may receive income or a capital sum from some of the following:

company share option scheme;

sale of business or personal assets;

investments (stocks and shares, unit trusts, etc);

other existing income (from a trust, property, family business);

bank/building society savings;

National Savings & Investments bond or certificate;

endowment policy.

Unavoidable outgoings

No one will have the same list as another, since one person's priority is another's luxury. For this reason, the divide between 'unavoidable outgoings' and 'normal additional expenditure' (see section following) is likely to vary considerably with each individual. For example, pet owners would consider pet food and veterinary bills an essential item of expenditure. If you do not have, or intend to get, a pet, such costs can be disregarded. Almost everyone will want to juggle some of the items between the two lists or add their own particular requisites or special enthusiasms. Whatever your own essentials, some of the following items will certainly feature on your list of unavoidable expenses:

food;

rent or mortgage repayments;

council tax;

repair and maintenance costs;

heating;

lighting and other energy;

telephone/mobile and internet connection;

postage (including Christmas cards);

TV licence/free-to-air or digital subscriptions;

household insurance;

clothes;

domestic cleaning products;

laundry, cleaners' bills, shoe repairs;

miscellaneous services, eg property maintenance, such as plumber, window cleaner;

car, including road tax, fuel, insurance, roadside assistance (RAC/AA or similar), servicing;

other transport;

regular savings and life assurance;

HP/other loan repayments;

outgoings on health.

Normal additional expenditure

This could include:

gifts;

holidays;

newspapers/books/magazines/CDs/DVDs;

computer expenses (including broadband);

drink;

hairdressing;

toiletries/cosmetics;

entertainment (hobbies, outings, DVD purchase/rental)

miscellaneous subscriptions/club membership fees;

charitable donations;

expenditure on pets;

garden purchases.

Work out the figures against these lists. Then, to compare your expenditure against likely income, jot them down on the Budget planner (see pages 145–49).

Possible ways of boosting your retirement income

Are you expecting to win millions on the lottery, or benefit as a 'lost heir' inheriting untold wealth from a hitherto unknown relative? If so, you may feel the following section is of limited interest. For most of us, however, a bit more money is always useful. Few people can afford to turn away extra income these days, yet there are really only three possible ways to give your retirement finances a boost: these are from your home, work and investment skill.

Your home

Your home offers several different options: moving somewhere smaller, taking in lodgers or raising money on your home. (All the possibilities are explored in greater detail in Chapter 8, Your home).

Moving somewhere smaller

You could sell your present home, move into smaller accommodation and collect a capital sum at the same time as reducing your running costs. You will need to do your sums carefully as your profit might not be huge. Moving home is always an expensive business, with lawyers' fees and removal costs. You should allow for some decorating expenses and a possible period of overlap when sorting out payments for telephone rental, extra electricity bills and so on.

If you are planning to buy, remember to add stamp duty. SDLT, as it is known, is currently between 1 and 5 per cent, depending on the value of the property up to £2 million, payable on the whole purchase price. Moving may well be an excellent decision, but if money is the main criterion you need to be thoroughly realistic when calculating the gains.

Transferring an existing mortgage to your new property or getting a new one might be another option. Mortgages are available to people over retirement age. Whatever you are considering, you must obtain professional advice from an accountant or solicitor, who will help you work out the details.

Taking in lodgers

Older people often have the advantage of owning a property which can be used to earn money. If you have more space than you need in your current home and you don't mind sharing with other people, have you considered taking in a lodger? There are more people looking for somewhere to live than there are places to rent. If you think a paying guest or, if your property lends itself to the creation of a separate flatlet, a tenant in part of your home could work, do bear this option in mind. When assessing the financial rewards, it is wise to assume that there will be times when the accommodation is empty – so you will not be receiving any rent. The good news is that you may be able to keep more of any earnings you make.

Under the government's Rent-a-Room scheme, if you let out a *furnished* room in your home you can earn up to £4,250 a year without paying income tax. (£2,125 if letting jointly). Any excess rental over £4,250 will be assessed for tax in the normal way. The scheme does not apply if you let *unfurnished* accommodation in your home. You don't even have to be a home owner to take advantage of the Rent-a-Room scheme, but if you are renting, you will need to check that your lease allows you to take in a lodger. You can also use the Rent-a-Room tax-free allowance against bed-and-breakfast earnings.

If you're paying a mortgage, it is best to verify the mortgage lender's and insurer's terms too. The relief applies only to accommodation that is 'part of your main home', so take care if you are thinking of creating a separate flatlet. You must ensure this qualifies and that it is not at risk of being assessed as a commercial let. An architect or other professional adviser will be able to help you with the technical requirements.

Raising money on your home

You could contemplate part-selling your home for either a capital sum or regular payments under an equity-release scheme. This way you can continue to live in it for as long as you wish. If this course of action sounds attractive, check carefully. There are some drawbacks and you would be strongly advised to discuss the matter with your solicitor.

Work

How about continuing to work? There is plenty of scope here for earning money, even in the current economic climate. If you don't mind the idea, one of the simplest solutions is to talk to your employer to see what options there are for you to remain with your present organization. Age discrimination legislation helps since it strengthens the rights of individuals who want to postpone their retirement. Carrying on working gives you the option of deferring your pension or, if you prefer and the scheme rules allow it, you could start drawing your pension benefits. Lots of people now choose this way of boosting their income by easing down to part-time work.

Retirement for you may offer the chance of a job switch or setting up on your own. When you do the figures, it is as well to err on the side of caution with regard to any additional income this will provide. Becoming self-employed or setting up a business may sound attractive but there are start-up costs to be considered. It is the exception, rather than the rule, for a new enterprise to make a profit during its first two or three years. If you have skills and time available, spread the word among friends and colleagues. You might be surprised at the scope of work opportunities. There is a lot more information on work, and how to get it, in Chapters 10, 11 and 12.

Investment

If you think of investing as being the preserve of the rich, this is simply not the case. Everyone has to start somewhere. What is most important is to get good advice from a trusted professional to help you find the most suitable investment opportunities for you. There is a mind-boggling array of financial products and if speculating is something you haven't done before, it can be fascinating and rewarding. You will learn in Chapter 5 the various forms investment can take. There are so many options you should find something to suit your situation whatever the amount of risk you are prepared to take.

Maximizing your income in retirement is essential if you want to have money in your pocket. The rules on buying an annuity changed on 6 April 2011. Up until then you had to buy an annuity by your 75th birthday, guaranteeing you an income for life. Since then the age limit has been removed. If you have a lot of money in your pension pot, you don't have to buy an annuity at all. But certain conditions apply. If you don't have all that much money, you still have to get one. There are other changes too, such as gender equality rules, brought in by the European Court, which may be bad news for men, and (possibly) good news for women. Annuities are explained in more detail in Chapter 5, Investment. But the one thing you must do before buying an annuity is to shop around to find the very best one for you.

Spending now for saving later

Do you enjoy spending your hard-earned money? Perhaps you consider very carefully before committing yourself? You may be surprised to know that many people when making retirement plans find they need, or want, to make certain purchases. These could, for example, include paying off all outstanding commitments. Most people's basic list – at least to think about – includes one or more of the following:

expenditure on their home;

the purchase of a new car;

the termination of HP or other credit arrangements.

In addition to these there might be some general domestic or luxury items that you have been promising yourself for some time. The question is simply one of timing: that is, determining the right moment to buy. Ask yourself these questions: Can I afford it more easily now – or in the future? By paying now rather than waiting, will I be saving money in the long run? This is something you will need to work out before you can complete the figures for your retirement planning.

Though it involves a few minutes' paperwork, a worthwhile exercise is to jot down your own personal list of pros and cons under the headings 'spending now' and 'spending later'. If still in doubt, waiting is normally the more prudent course.

Home improvements

With the housing market still struggling, many people have taken advice and been told: 'Don't move, improve.' If you plan to remain in the same property, would making some changes or improvements be sensible now? These could include installing double glazing, insulating the loft, modernizing the kitchen or converting part of the house to a granny flat. Any significant expenditure on your home is best undertaken when you can most easily afford it. Some people find it easier, and more reassuring, to pay major household bills while they are still earning. Others specifically plan to use part of the lump sum from their pension to create a dream home. What would make best financial sense for you?

Of course, if you intend to stay in your present home for a long time, investing a fortune in your property is fine. But should plans change and you need to move after a couple of years, you will be lucky to recoup your expenditure on a property you've modified to your own taste.

Purchasing a car

Would buying a new car cheer you up? If so, there are two reasons for getting one ahead of your retirement. Perhaps you have a company car that you are about to lose or your existing vehicle is getting old and is beginning (or will probably soon start) to give you trouble. Should either of these apply, then it probably makes sense to buy a replacement vehicle sooner rather than later.

Company car owners should first check whether they are entitled to purchase their present car on favourable terms. A number of employers are quite happy to allow this. Also, in terms of reducing carbon footprints, two-car families should think seriously about reducing to one vehicle come retirement, when it is possible that having two vehicles is no longer necessary.

Paying off HP, loans and similar

This is, generally speaking, a good idea, since delay is unlikely to save you money. However, one precaution is to check the small print of your agreement to make sure that there is no penalty for early repayment. A further exception to the rule could be your mortgage, and on this matter you will need to ask your accountant's advice. If you are thinking of moving (and the issue is really whether to transfer an existing mortgage or possibly acquire a new one), include this among the points to raise with your solicitor.

Money – if you are made redundant

With job losses still continuing, and many people fearing being made redundant, much of the information in the earlier part of this chapter is equally valid whether you become redundant or retire in the normal way. However, there are several key points with regard to redundancy that it could be to your advantage to check.

From your employment

You may be entitled to statutory redundancy pay

Your employer is obliged to pay the legal minimum, which is calculated on your age, length of service and weekly pay. To qualify, you will need to have worked for the organization for at least two years, with no age restriction. Redundancy pay is 1.5 weeks' pay for each year worked if you are over 41 years, up to a maximum of £430 a week.

Ex gratia payments

Many employers are prepared to be more generous. As long as it's not more than £30,000, statutory redundancy pay is not taxable. Any payment over this limit is subject to tax and National Insurance.

Benefits that are not part of your pay

Redundancy may mean the loss of several valuable benefits such as a company car, life assurance and health insurance. Some insurance companies allow preferential rates to individuals who were previously insured with them under a company scheme.

Holiday entitlement

You could be owed holiday entitlement for which you should be paid.

Company pension

Company pension scheme members normally have several choices. See the 'Company pension schemes' section in Chapter 3, Pensions.

Your mortgage

Your mortgage lender should be notified as soon as possible and might agree to a more flexible repayment system. Check whether your mortgage package includes insurance against redundancy. There is help available from the state if you are claiming benefits, such as income support or income-based Jobseeker's Allowance. Those claiming these benefits could have their interest payments covered for two years if their mortgage is below £200,000. However, no help is available to pay off the capital of your mortgage.

Other creditors/debts

Any creditors that you may have difficulty in paying (electricity, gas, a bank overdraft) should be informed as early as possible in the hope of agreeing easier payment terms. There could be an argument for paying off credit card bills immediately, even if this means using some of your redundancy pay.

Jobseeker's Allowance (JSA)

Even if you are hoping to get another job very soon, you should sign on without delay. Your National Insurance Contributions will normally be credited to you. This is important to protect your state pension. To qualify for JSA you need to be under state pension age and must either have paid sufficient Class 1 National Insurance Contributions or have a low income. You must also be both available for and actively seeking work.

Current information about JSA and other possible benefits can be found on the **Gov.uk** website (the gateway for government advice): **www.gov.uk**.

Redundancy Help can provide answers to queries on all aspects of redundancy; website: **www.redundancyhelp.co.uk**; and another useful agency is **The Citizens Advice Bureau** advice guides; see website: **www.adviceguide.org.uk**.

Money left unclaimed

It is estimated that there are over £15 billion unclaimed assets in the UK. During the course of this year millions of pounds of unclaimed money will be handed over to the Treasury because there are no clues as to who it belongs to. That means there are hundreds of thousands of people who do not even know the money is theirs. Some funds are in unclaimed benefits and entitlements, others are unclaimed lottery prizes, the remainder is money such as legacies from wills, funds from pensions and insurance policies where there is no next of kin to claim them. (The beneficiaries are possibly no longer alive or have moved and are difficult to trace.) More than one in 10 people think they may have forgotten assets and many people do not know how to begin to trace their money.

There are now a number of useful websites to help you. Experian's Unclaimed Assets Register (UAR) has lots of helpful information: **www.uar.co.uk**. For lost building society accounts, see The Building Societies Association website: **www.bsa.org.uk**. Try **www.mylostaccount.org.uk**, which aims to reunite savers with lost or dormant bank accounts. *Which?* magazine also gives information and advice on how to track down missing accounts and unclaimed money: **www.which.co.uk**. You could also look at **www.moneyexpertise.co.uk**, which has facts and information about unclaimed money, or **www.yourmissingcash.co.uk** and **www.findersuk.com**.

Extra income

The number of state benefits and allowances available to help many pensioners that are not claimed is staggering. Many pensioners live on low to middle incomes and have been hit hardest because of falling interest rates, the rising cost of living and public spending cuts. Despite just under half of all pensioners being entitled to pension credit – a top-up for people on low incomes – a third of people don't claim it; 1.8 million pensioners live in poverty yet millions of pounds of pensioner benefits go unclaimed each year. Age UK (Britain's largest charity dedicated to the needs of the elderly) suggests the reasons for this are that many pensioners are unaware of the range of benefits available, or don't realize they are eligible. They also think the process too complicated and intrusive or are simply too proud to claim.

According to Age UK, the top five myths that prevent pensioners from claiming benefits are:

'I don't think I'll be eligible for Pension Credit.'

'I'll get so little it's not worth me claiming.'

'I have some savings, so I won't get anything.'

'I've been turned down for Pension Credit before. It's not worth applying again.'

While many of these benefits are 'means tested' some, such as Disability Living Allowance, are not dependent on how poor or how wealthy you are. Moreover, even when means testing is a factor, for some of the benefits income levels are nothing like as low as many people imagine. Because this information is not widely enough known, many individuals – including over a million pensioners – are not claiming help to which they are entitled and for which in many cases they have actually paid through their National Insurance Contributions.

A number of voluntary organizations, benevolent societies and charities also provide assistance to individuals, sometimes in cash or sometimes in the form of facilities, such as special equipment for disabled people. Details are given in the relevant chapters.

For further advice and information on benefits check the following websites:

Department for Work and Pensions: **www.dwp.gov.uk**;

Jobcentre Plus: **www.gov.uk** – search 'Benefits'

Citizens Advice Bureau: **www.citizensadvice.org.uk**;

Age UK: **www.ageuk.org.uk**.

Making your money go further

If you enjoy browsing the internet and this chapter has whetted your appetite for research on the matter of retirement planning, the following websites cover a broad range of topics relating to your finances and retirement:

www.adviceguide.org.uk;

www.everyinvestor.co.uk;

www.financingretirement.co.uk;

www.litrg.org.uk;

www.moneyadviceservice.org.uk;

www.moneyexpertise.co.uk;

www.moneyweek.com;

www.thisismoney.co.uk;

www.which.co.uk.

Useful reading

The following publications are especially for those coming up to retirement and the recently retired.

Your Guide to Retirement – Making the Most of Your Money is a comprehensive guide to help you manage the transition from work and make decisions that will improve your financial security throughout retirement. It is published by the Money Advice Service; website: **www.moneyadviceservice.org.uk**.

Wise Guide – Life-improving Advice for the Over-65s is the practical pensioners' handbook to benefits, debt help, discounts and lots more. You don't have to be retired to pick up great tips. It is published by Independent Age; website: **www.independentage.org**.

An excellent book for those wanting detailed information about planning their finances is *Talking about Retirement* by Lyn Ashurst, published by Kogan Page. The author is an authority in her field and gives a comprehensive and detailed study of a careful and planned approach to the retirement process, based on about 50 case studies. For more information and other recommended titles on retirement and associated issues published by Kogan Page, see **www.koganpage.com**.

Chapter Three
Pensions

What looks like tomorrow's problem is rarely the real problem when tomorrow rolls around.

JAMES FALLOWS, QUOTED ON THEMOTLEYFOOL.COM

'Work harder and longer... for less.' This message (or words to this effect) has been a familiar headline across the media regularly over the past year or more. Hard times ahead, we might think. Much continues to be written on the 'UK pensions crisis' with warnings of great hardship for many up-coming retirees. But surely there must be some green shoots or signs of optimism somewhere? Let's look back at history for a moment: when the state pension of five bob a week (25p) was introduced by Lloyd George in 1909, it was awarded to the needy – but only those who were deemed to be of 'good character' actually received it. That amount of money could, in those days, have bought you 30 pints of beer – but you wouldn't have received any money at all if you were habitually drunk. And your retirement wouldn't have lasted anything like the 25 years or so which most of us expect today. So some things have improved.

Leaving that aside for the moment, we read that many people of retirement age today are stuck at work because their personal savings and pension pot are inadequate. This comes as a shock, particularly if their friends retire while they themselves have to keep on working. So what's happening? In essence, as life expectancy increases, society isn't putting enough aside for its old age. If we're not saving enough yet living longer, then this trend is surely set to continue.

A report from the Office for National Statistics (ONS) warns that soaring energy bills, rising food costs and low interest rates have squeezed pensioner finances. Figures were released showing that in the UK 12.5 per cent of women workers and 10.1 per cent of men did not leave the 'labour market' until they were between the ages of 70 and 75. Just a third of the private sector workforce in Britain have company pensions, with the average 'pot' buying a pension worth just £1,400 a year.

The reality is that our own experience of retirement is far removed from that of our grandparents, and way further removed from those in the 1900s mentioned above. We are living *much* longer than they did. In 1981 a man of 65 could expect to live to 78, whereas today a teenage boy's life expectancy is around the age of 91. The Institute of Directors (IoD) recently made a study of Britain's pension architecture and described it as 'unattractive' and 'confusing'. It reported that faith in pensions is 'dwindling'. Currently the UK has a workforce of 29 million people, yet fewer than 19 million people work in the private sector. The latest ONS statistics indicate only 3 million are active members of occupational schemes (down from 8 million in 1967), as opposed to 5.3 million active members in public sector schemes (up from 4.1 million in 1967). Of the 3 million active private sector scheme members, two-thirds are members of defined benefit schemes (source: *Workplace Pensions: Challenging Times* – final report of the Association of Consulting Actuaries (ACAs) 2011 Pension Trends Survey, published 3 January 2012).

According to reports last year, final salary pension deficit swelled to record levels, reflecting the pressure these schemes are under. UK gilt yields have reduced, forcing cash-strapped businesses already struggling to keep these pensions going to find more assets to fill the deficits. Poor investment returns coupled with increasing life expectancy have made these schemes unaffordable for employers. More than 90 per cent of these once-envied schemes are now closed to new workers, and soaring numbers are shutting down to existing workers, who are switched to a cheaper scheme. The slump in gilt yields has also cut the retirement income for hundreds of thousands of workers retiring with standard, stock market-linked pensions, as insurance companies have reduced their annuity rates.

One consequence of Britain's failing pension schemes is that millions of people are turning to tax-free ISAs to save money. Figures from the ONS show Britons put £22.9 billion into pension schemes in 2009, down from £24.9 billion in 2008, compared with the £44 billion invested in ISAs.

In an effort to ease the situation, the government is increasing state pension age to 66 for both men and women by 2020, and raising it to 67 between 2026 and 2028. The IoD suggests that if the state pension age were raised to 70 by 2044, this higher state retirement age would encourage private saving for those wishing to retire earlier. But one thing is for sure: we are simply deluding ourselves if we adhere to the belief that state or private pension schemes were ever designed to support a potential 30-year retirement from an effective 35-year working life. Only last year plans for a flat-rate state pension were unveiled by the government in the Queen's Speech (May 2012), which would represent the biggest overhaul of the system for decades. This would affect only new pensioners on reaching state pension age, not the millions of existing pensioners, and thus create a two-tier system of state pension which would exist for some considerable time. The debate continues.

Now, do you know what NEST is? And did you know that less than one-third of the UK population do not have a pension, and 48 per cent of the population say they cannot afford to pay into a pension scheme at the moment? The government has recently developed its own system to encourage low-to-middle wage earners to contribute to a personal pension plan. This is the National Employment Savings Trust, the not-for-profit, low-cost workplace pension scheme into which employees can be entered. It's new, and from October 2012 about 8 million employees up to state pension age began saving into this company pension scheme for the first time. This auto-enrolment scheme has been introduced for all companies who employ more than 50,000 people and it will be extended to all companies from 2013. This scheme promises to provide some income for several million people who previously would have had nothing beyond the state pension. As encouragement, employers are given tax breaks if they do not opt out. Automatic enrolment, the government hopes, will start a savings revolution, but first people will need to understand the value of saving for their future (see **www.nestpensions.org.uk**).

But there is room for optimism for up-coming retirees, despite the fact that the 'Baby Boomers' retiring now are regarded as a golden generation leaving the workforce, with a quality of pension never to be seen again. With auto-enrolment in pensions, greater awareness of the need to save, an expectation and desire to work for longer, increasing housing assets, a skills shortage and equity release (the medium- or high-value property which pensioner households will use to support their retirement) – all these promise to improve the circumstances of those expecting to retire within the next decade. Coupled with employers wanting workers to remain in their posts for longer and a desire among employees to continue working, it is likely that this group will be better prepared for retirement and ageing than might previously have been thought.

But the antidote to an impoverished old age is obvious: we all must save like mad as early as possible. Easy enough to say (or write), but how can we stash away cash if we don't have much left at the end of the month? A rule-of-thumb guide (provided by This is Money website: **www.thisismoney.co.uk/pension-plan**) is to take things a step at a time, decade by decade:

In your 20s you should focus on clearing your debts, open an ISA and save what you can afford.

In your 30s reassess your debts and outgoings, join your company pension scheme and think long term with your investments.

In your 40s if you haven't started saving, do so now. Keep adding to your ISAs and as your earnings peak, dedicate some to a pension.

In your 50s maximize your contributions, remove risk from your pension investment plan and consider using a SIPP (Self-Invested Personal Pension) for greater control.

In your 60s check that all your debts, including mortgage, are in order. Decide whether you'll buy an annuity immediately or take drawdown and, most important of all, talk to an IFA (Independent Financial Adviser) before you take any action.

Now that wasn't too painful, was it?

The state pension

First, let's consider the state pension. The earliest you can claim it is at state pension age. Retirement age should not be confused with pension age. Retirement age is when you choose to retire. You can still work when you reach state pension age. Currently, if you are a man born before 6 April 1959 your state pension age is 65. A woman born on or before 5 April 1950 has a state pension age of 60. Women born on or after 6 April 1950 will find their state pension age increasing to 65 between now and 2018, to equalize with men. By 2020 both sexes will have a state pension age of 66. Further increases can be expected so as to avoid a pensions black hole, which means state pension age will have to rise along with life expectancy.

Since October 2011 the default retirement age of 65 has been scrapped. Employers are no longer allowed to dismiss staff just because they are 65. But as the state pension comes under increasing pressure, it is important to make private pension savings and not rely on the basic state pension to finance your retirement.

Your right to a state pension

There are two types of state pension – basic and additional. The amount of basic state pension you may get depends on the number of qualifying years you build up using your National Insurance Contributions (NIC) record. If you have paid, been treated as having paid, or been credited with NIC for a certain number of years during your working life, you may get a basic state pension. The earliest you can get it is from state pension age, but you have to claim it.

On 6 April 2010 the number of qualifying years needed to get a full basic state pension was reduced to 30 years for women and men (before this it was normally 39 and 44 years respectively). If you are an employee, your employer will have automatically deducted Class 1 NIC from your salary, provided your earnings were above a certain limit (2012/13: £146 a week – the 'earnings threshold'). If you are self-employed, you will have been paying a flat-rate Class 2 NIC of £2.65 every week and possibly the earnings-related Class 4 NIC as well. You may also have paid Class 3 voluntary contributions at some point in your life in order to maintain your contributions record. If you are over pension age you do not pay NIC. There may have been times during your working life when you have not – either knowingly or unwittingly – paid NIC. If you have gaps in your NIC record, you may qualify for a basic state pension of up to 60 per cent of a full basic state pension based on your spouse's or civil partner's record, when he or she has reached state pension age.

Since 6 April 2010:

married men and female civil partners will also be entitled to a pension based on their wife's or civil partner's record – but their wife or civil partner must have been born on or after 6 April 1950 and have reached state pension age;

any pension for a wife, husband or civil partner will be payable whether their spouse or civil partner decides to claim or to defer his or her own state pension;

the earliest date a male civil partner will be entitled to this is 6 April 2015 because that is the date that a man born on 6 April 1950 reaches pensionable age.

Lived or worked outside Great Britain?

If you have lived in Northern Ireland or the Isle of Man, any contributions paid there will count towards your pension. The same should also apply in most cases if you have lived or worked in an EU country or any country whose social security is linked to Britain's by a reciprocal arrangement. However, there have sometimes been problems with certain countries, so, if you have any doubts, you should enquire what your position is at your pension centre.

Home Responsibilities Protection (HRP)

If you were a carer for a child or a disabled person throughout any tax year after 1978 up until 5 April 2010 and you were not doing any paid work, or you had low earnings and did not get credits, you may have got Home Responsibilities Protection. HRP reduces the number of years you need to have paid, or been credited with enough contributions, to get a full basic state pension. HRP was awarded automatically if you got Child Benefit for a child under 16. But if you were caring for a disabled person or you were a foster carer, you usually had to complete an application form for it.

There are two important points to note. First, if you are a woman and were claiming Child Benefit, HRP should have been credited to you automatically, whereas a man staying at home to care for a child would have needed to arrange the transfer of Child Benefit to himself. Second, HRP is available only for complete tax years in which earnings were less than 52 times the lower earnings limit. Although HRP can be claimed by both sexes, it predictably applies more frequently to women.

Since 6 April 2010 Home Responsibilities Protection has been replaced with weekly credits for parents and carers. You can receive these credits for any weeks you are getting Child Benefit for a child under 12, you are an approved foster carer, or you are caring for one or more sick or disabled people for at least 20 hours a week. If you reach state pension age on or after 6 April 2010, any years of HRP you have been awarded before April 2010 will have been converted to qualifying years of credits up to a maximum of 22 years.

For more information about the changes introduced by the Pensions Act 2007, see website: **www.gov.uk** – Working, jobs and pensions.

Other situations

If you have been in any of the following situations you will have been credited with contributions (instead of having to pay them):

> you were sick or unemployed (provided you sent in sick notes to your social security office, signed on at the unemployment benefit office or were in receipt of Jobseeker's Allowance);

you were a man aged 60–64 and not working;

you were entitled to maternity allowance, invalid care allowance or unemployability supplement;

you were taking an approved course of training;

you had left education but had not yet started working;

since April 2000, your earnings had fallen between what are known as the lower earnings limit and the primary threshold, ie between £107 and £146 a week (2012/13).

Married women and widows

Married women and widows who do not qualify for a basic pension in their own right may be entitled to a basic pension on their husband's contributions at about 60 per cent of the level to which he is entitled.

Since the introduction of independent taxation, husband and wife are assessed separately for tax. As a result, a married woman is now entitled to have her section of the joint pension offset against her own personal allowance, instead of being counted as part of her husband's taxable income. For many pensioner couples, this should mean a reduction in their tax liability.

Reduced-rate contributions note: many women retiring today may have paid a reduced-rate contribution under a scheme that was abolished in 1978. Women who were already paying a reduced-rate contribution were, however, allowed to continue doing so. These reduced-rate contributions *do not count* towards your pension and you will not have had any contributions credited to you. If you are still some years away from retirement, it could be to your advantage to cancel the reduced-rate option, as by doing so you may be able to build up a wider range of benefits without paying anything extra. This applies if you are currently (2012/13) earning between £107 and £146 a week, ie between the lower earnings limit and the primary threshold. If you are earning above the primary threshold (£146), to get the same extra benefits you would have to start paying extra contributions. For advice, contact your local tax office or see the website: **www.hmrc.gov.uk**.

How your pension is worked out

Anyone trying to decide whether they can afford to retire should get their state pension forecast from **The Pension Service**. It is worth getting an early estimate of what your pension will be, as it may be possible to improve your NIC record by making additional Class 3 voluntary contributions. See website: **www.gov.uk** – Working, jobs and pensions.

Basic state pension

The full basic pension for a man or woman (April 2012/13) is £107.45 a week, and £171.45 for a married couple. These are the maximums available. If you do not have the maximum qualifying years to qualify for the full basic state pension, you will be entitled to a lower amount based on the number of qualifying years on your record. State pensions are increased in April each year. All pensions are taxable other than one or two special categories, such as war widows and the victims of Nazism.

The amount of basic state pension you receive at state pension age is based on your National Insurance Contribution record over your working life. The rules for the state pension have changed and the number of qualifying years you need for a full basic state pension now depends on when you reach state pension age. Those reaching state pension age on or after 6 April 2010 require 30 qualifying years to get a full basic state pension. Each qualifying year of paid or credited contributions will be worth 1/30th of the full basic state pension up to a maximum of 30/30ths.

Since April 2011, the basic pension is increased annually by the highest of price inflation, earnings or 2.5 per cent. But if you retire abroad, you only get these increases if you live in a European Economic Area (EEA) country, Switzerland or a country with which the UK has a reciprocal agreement that includes state pensions.

Due to improvements in service arrangements, you only need to claim a state pension two months before your state pension birthday date. You can check your state pension age using the calculator on the **Gov.uk** website: **www.gov.uk** – State pension.

If you do not qualify for a full basic state pension you may be able to pay Class 3 NIC if you have gaps in your National Insurance record. Paying them would mean that years that would not normally be qualifying years would count towards your basic state pension. Your forecast letter will tell you whether or not you can do this. There are time limits for paying Class 3 NIC and you must normally pay them within six years of the end of the tax year for which you are paying.

If you need help deciding whether you need to pay extra contributions, you can obtain help from the **National Insurance Contributions Office** (**www.hmrc.gov.uk/nic**) or **The Pensions Advisory Service** (**www.pensions-advisoryservice.org.uk**).

Additional state pension

If you are (or have been) in employment, you may have been building up an additional state pension, known as the State Second Pension. (This was formerly known as SERPS – the State Earnings Related Pensions Scheme but was re-named State Second Pension in April 2002.) The amount of State Second Pension (S2P) you get depends on your earnings and your NIC record. There are other means of entitlement to some S2P: for example if you earn below a certain amount set by the government, if you cannot work through long-term illness or disability, or if you are a carer.

The S2P is not available to the self-employed, for whom the alternative pension choices are either a personal pension or a stakeholder pension. If you are an employee, you are automatically included in S2P unless you decide to contract out, or you are a member of an employer's occupational pension scheme that is contracted out. If you decide to contract out, you stop building up your S2P entitlement and build up a replacement for it in your own pension. You will continue to be contracted out of S2P unless you decide to contract back in.

For more information about contracting out, or if you have any queries regarding the S2P scheme, you can obtain help from this website: **www.gov.uk** – Working, jobs and pensions.

Deferring your pension

When you reach the state pension age, you decide whether or not to start drawing the state pension. Retirement does not have to start on any particular date or a single day. Many people prefer to stop working gradually by reducing hours or shifting to part-time work, so you might not need your entire pension straight away. By deferring your state pension, you can have a bigger pension when it does start, or alternatively a lump sum. Your state pension is increased by 1 per cent for each five weeks you defer it, ie an increase of 10.4 per cent a year for each year you defer. But this is only worth considering if you can live without the pension for now. You can continue deferring your pension for as long as you like. The extra money will be paid to you when you eventually decide to claim your pension. The lump sum is worked out as if your deferred pension had been invested and earned a return of 2 per cent more than the Bank of England base rate.

There is no upper limit on the extra state pension or lump sum you can have. You have to defer your state pension for at least five weeks to qualify for extra pension or at least one year for a lump sum. As with all state pensions, the extra is increased in line with inflation each year (or more in the case of the basic pension since April 2011). The amount you get counts as taxable income.

If you opt to receive a lump sum, this also counts as taxable income, but special rules limit the tax due. However large, the whole amount is taxed at the top rate of tax you were paying before the lump sum was added. For example, if your top rate was 20 per cent, the whole lump sum is taxed at 20 per cent. You can start your pension but put off the lump sum until the next tax year. This is useful if your tax rate will be lower in the next year – for example, because you will have stopped work.

If you plan to defer your pension, you should also defer any graduated pension to which you may be entitled – or you risk losing the increases you would otherwise obtain. More information can be found on The Pension Service website: **www.gov.uk** – Working, jobs and pensions.

Adult Dependency Increase

This is an increase in the state pension for a husband, wife or someone who is looking after your children, as long as certain conditions are met. Since 6 April 2010, you are no longer entitled to claim an Adult Dependency Increase. If you were already entitled to this increase on 5 April 2010 you will be able to keep it until you no longer meet the conditions for the increase, or 5 April 2020, whichever is the first.

Income Support

If you have an inadequate income, you may qualify for Income Support. There are special premiums (ie additions) for lone parents, disabled people, carers and pensioners. A condition of entitlement is that you should not have capital, including savings, of more than £16,000. A big advantage is that people entitled to Income Support receive full help with their rent and should also not have any Council Tax to pay. See 'Housing Benefit' and 'Council Tax Benefit' in Chapter 8.

Pension Credit

Pension Credit is an income-related benefit for those who have reached the minimum qualifying age and live in Great Britain. You do not need to have paid NIC to get it. There are two parts to Pension Credit.

Guarantee Credit may be paid to you if you have reached the minimum qualifying age. It tops up your income to a guaranteed minimum level (for the year 2012/13 it is £142.70 if you are single, or £217.90 if you have a partner). The age at which you can get Pension Credit Guarantee Credit is gradually increasing from 60 to 65 between April 2010 and 2020. To find out the age at which you can apply for Pension Credit, you should use the Pension Credit calculator at **www.gov.uk** – Pension Credit calculator.

Savings Credit is for those who have saved money towards their retirement. You may be able to get it if you are aged 65 or over. You may be able to get Savings Credit as well as Guarantee Credit. You may still get Pension Credit if you live with your grown-up family or own your own home.

If you wish to apply for Pension Credit, you can do so up to four months before the date from which you want to start getting Pension Credit. If you were born before 6 April 1950, the earliest age you can get Pension Credit is 60. If you were born after this date, use the state pension age calculator to find out the first date you can get Pension Credit. The longest Pension Credit claims can be backdated is three months. You do not have to pay tax on Pension Credit. If entitled to it, you may get Savings Credit (for the year 2012/13) of £18.54 a week if you are single or £23.73 a week if you have a partner.

The age from which you may get Pension Credit – the qualifying age – is gradually going up to 66 in line with the increase in the state pension age for women to 65 and the further increase to 66 for men and women. To find out when you reach the qualifying age for Pension Credit, visit **www.gov.uk** – State pension.

If you apply for Pension Credit, you may also apply for Council Tax Benefit and Housing Benefit at the same time. The age at which people can get Housing Benefit and Council Benefit for pensioners is also increasing from 60 to 65 between April 2010 and 2020. *Housing Benefit* is to help people on a low income pay some or all of their rent. *Council Tax Benefit* is to help people on a low income pay some or all of their council tax. If you are on a low income, you may be entitled to these, but how much you get will depend, among other things, on your income, savings, rent and council tax. Your local council deals with these benefits, and you can claim them even if you don't get other benefits. You do not have to pay tax on them.

If you apply for Pension Credit, you will be helped to claim Housing Benefit and Council Tax Benefit at the same time. Visit the **Gov.uk** website to find out more information: **www.gov.uk** – Heating and housing benefits.

Other sources of help

Don't be ashamed to claim.

New research has uncovered stigmas around claiming benefits. A recent survey commissioned by Turn2Us (part of the national charity Elizabeth Finn Care) has uncovered some of the stigmas and negative perceptions of welfare benefits held by over-55s on low incomes who could be in need of financial help. The results were released last year, when the charity launched its second annual Benefits Awareness Month (April 2012). It was aimed at encouraging people in financial need to check their potential entitlements.

The research found that only just over a fifth of over-55s on low incomes believed that those claiming means-tested benefits have a right to do so. Nearly two-fifths held the opinion that claimants needed to help themselves and remain independent, rather than relying on the state for support. Shockingly, over one in 10 of the over-55s on low incomes revealed they would prefer to cut back on essentials, such as food or heating, rather than claim benefits. Seven per cent said they would be too ashamed to tell friends and family if they were claiming.

According to Age UK's 'Let's Talk Money' campaign, around 1.97 million pensioners are failing to claim Council Tax Benefit worth £1.7 billion a year to which they are entitled. Every year as much as £5.5 billion of benefits that older people are entitled to go unclaimed, despite many of them struggling to make ends meet. The main reasons for their failure to claim are the complicated claims process and those who are too independent and proud to claim benefits. One of the results of research carried out by these charities shows that much needs to be done in terms of raising awareness of welfare benefits available and reducing some of the negative perceptions against claiming when times are tough.

For help relating to benefits, **Turn2Us** (website: **www.turn2us.org.uk**) is a charity set up specifically to identify potential sources of funding for those facing financial difficulty. Individuals can log on to this website for free and in confidence.

Also look at **AgeUK**'s website, Britain's leading charity for older people: **www.ageuk.co.uk**.

Community Care Grants, Budgeting Loans and Crisis Loans can all help with exceptional expenses if you are facing financial difficulties. These are all dealt with through the **Gov.uk** website. See **www.gov.uk** – Jobseeker's Allowance and low income benefits for the widest range of online government information for the public, covering benefits, financial support, rights, employment, independent living and much more. For information for disabled people, see **www.gov.uk** – Disability benefits.

Early retirement and your state pension

Because some people retire early, they can mistakenly assume it is possible to get an early pension. While the information is correct as regards many employers' occupational pension schemes, as well as for stakeholder and personal pensions, it does not apply to the basic state pension. If you take early retirement before the age of 60, it may be necessary for you to pay voluntary Class 3 NIC to protect your contributions record for state pension purposes. Your local tax office can advise you about NICs.

How you get a state pension

You should claim your pension a few months before you reach state pension age. The Department for Work and Pensions (DWP) should send you a claim form (BR1) at the proper time, but if this doesn't arrive it is your responsibility to contact the DWP. If you have moved recently, make sure it has your current address. After you claim, you are told in writing exactly how much pension you will get. You will also be told what to do if you disagree with the decision. See website: **www.gov.uk** – Working, jobs and pensions.

How your state pension can be paid

Pensions are usually paid direct into a bank account. This can be a bank or building society account or, if you prefer, a Post Office Card Account. Individuals who prefer to receive their money every week have the option of receiving a weekly cheque, which can be cashed at the post office or paid direct into a Post Office Card Account.

Other situations

Pensions can be paid to an overseas address, if you are going abroad for six months or more. See website: **www.gov.uk** – Working, jobs and pensions (see section 'State pension if you retire abroad').

If you are in hospital, your pension can still be paid to you and you will receive your pension in full for the duration of your stay, regardless of how long you have to remain in hospital. For advice contact either The Pension Service or the Citizens Advice Bureau.

Christmas bonus

This is paid shortly before Christmas to pensioners who are entitled to a qualifying benefit. For many years the sum has been £10. The bonus is combined with your normal pension payment for the first week in December.

Advice

The Pension Service provides information to current and future pensioners so that making informed decisions about pension arrangements is straightforward. The Pension Service plans for everyone to have more independence in later life by tackling pensioner poverty and reforming the pension process. If you need help with your retirement plans it can assist you. It will explain what the state will provide when you retire and let you know what pension-related benefits you may be entitled to.

If you have any queries or think you may not be obtaining your full pension entitlement, you should contact the Pension Service as soon as possible. If you think a mistake has been made, you have the right to appeal and can insist on your claim being heard by an independent tribunal. Before doing so, you would be strongly advised to consult a solicitor at the Citizens Advice Bureau or the Welfare Advice Unit of your social security office. Some areas have special Tribunal Representation Units to assist people to make claims at tribunals. If you are contacting the Pension Service with a query, you should quote either your National Insurance number (or your spouse's) or your pension number if you have already started receiving your pension.

For further information about pensions, there is a booklet full of advice entitled *Pensioners' Guide* obtainable from **The Pension Service**, part of the Department for Work and Pensions. See website: **www.directgov.uk/en/ PensionsandRetirementPlanning**. Other useful sources of information include:

The Pensions Advisory Service: **www.pensionsadvisoryservice.org.uk**;

The Service Personnel and Veterans Agency: **www.veterans-uk.info**;

Citizens Advice: **www.citizensadvice.org.uk**.

Private pensions

At the beginning of this chapter mention was made of the UK press reports about the pensions crisis, or black hole. The situation has arisen because there is not enough money in private companies' pension funds or the government's coffers to guarantee a comfortable retirement for the entire working population. There are three main reasons for this. First, the post-war baby boom means there is an unavoidable surge in numbers recently retired or coming up to retirement age. Second, this ageing population (the over-60s) are living much longer. According to government figures, just under one million people will turn 65 in 2013 and this figure is increasing yearly. Third, the stock market has been more volatile over the past few years. This hasn't just affected payouts from company pension funds; it has seen many companies close the doors to their previously generous pension schemes for any new employees.

The result of all this is the unwelcome news that everyone has to save more, as the financial responsibility for ensuring a comfortable retirement falls firmly on our own shoulders. According to the Wealth and Assets Survey (WAS), membership of pension schemes is closely related to socio-economic status. In general, the higher an economically active person's socio-economic classification, the more likely they are to be a member of a pension scheme. So if you have been saving into a private pension, you need to find out what the money will amount to in terms of your final pension pot, and then work out how many years it will last you.

The government has now swept away the complex rules relating to how much money you can pay into a pension fund each year. The annual allowance now stands at £50,000 a year for everyone. This yearly contribution should be more than adequate for most people. For those who have taken a break from contributions, there will be the useful option to potentially carry forward up to three years' annual allowance. Those who are in final salary schemes or those with employer, employee and individual pension contributions over two consecutive tax years which combine to over £50,000 will need to be particularly aware of the limits. It would be wise to check with your pension provider when your current 'pension input period' (the accounting period for your pension scheme) ends.

There is a limit on the value of retirement benefits that you can draw from approved pension schemes before tax penalties apply. That limit is called the Lifetime Allowance and in the 2012/13 tax year this has been set at £1.5 million. While these changes do set a cap on the amount of pensions tax relief individuals can obtain, they still permit significant tax-free savings into a pension and are far simpler than the restrictive regime they replaced. It is important to bear in mind that tax rules and tax reliefs can and do change and their exact value depends on each individual's circumstances.

Despite a certain amount of apprehension, pension savings are still one of the most tax-effective investments available because you receive income tax relief on contributions at your highest tax rate and the growth in your pension fund is totally exempt from income tax and capital gains tax. Another advantage is that part of the pension can be taken as a tax-free cash lump sum when you retire.

Company pension schemes

Types of company pension schemes

There are four main types of pension. The pension that your employer offers may be 'contributory' (you and your employer pay into it) or 'non-contributory' which means that only your employer does. If the scheme offered is a group stakeholder pension scheme, your employer doesn't have to contribute, so you alone may be putting money in.

Although you don't have to join a pension scheme offered through your job, it's usually a good idea to do so because not only does your employer contribute, but you often get other benefits as well as a pension. These could include life insurance, which pays a lump sum and/or a pension to your dependants if you die while working for that employer. It could also include a pension if you have to retire early because of ill health, and a pension for your spouse and other dependants when you die.

Final salary

These are the Rolls-Royce of pension schemes because they promise a known proportion of your pay when you retire. How much you get is worked out from how many years you're in the scheme and your salary when you either leave it or retire. They are a type of defined benefit scheme. You build up a pension at a certain rate – 1/60th is quite common – so for each year you've been a scheme member, you receive 1/60th of your final salary. For example, if you were in the scheme for 10 years and your final salary was £30,000, you'd receive a £5,000 a year pension – that is 10/60ths of £30,000.

Final salary schemes are costly for employers to run and have all but disappeared. In the private sector only 1.3 million workers are in a final salary scheme and few schemes are open to new employees. More public sector workers (such as teachers, police, NHS and local government workers) pay into a final salary scheme, but this is still only 5.3 million out of 29 million employed people in the UK. If you work for one of the few remaining employers with a final salary scheme, you should join it. The average employer contribution to a private sector final salary scheme in 2007 was equivalent to 15.6 per cent of each member's salary a year.

Career average

These are another type of defined-benefit scheme, because the benefit (your pension) is worked out using your salary and the length of time you have been a member of the pension scheme. The pension you receive will be based on an average of your earnings in the time that you're a member of the scheme (often averaged over the last three years before retirement). What you receive will depend on the proportion of those earnings that you get as pension for each year of membership. The most common are 1/60th or 1/80th of your earnings for each year of membership.

The benefits of such schemes are that the pension is based on your length of membership and salary, so you have a fair idea of how much your pension will be before retirement. Also, your employer should ensure there is enough money at the time you retire to pay you a pension, and you get tax relief on your contributions. Scheme investments grow generally free of income tax and capital gains tax. Your pension benefits are linked to your salary while you are working, so they automatically increase as your pay rises. Your pension income from the scheme will normally increase each year in line with CPI instead of RPI.

Is there a risk? If a salary-related occupational scheme or the sponsoring employer gets into financial trouble, the Pension Protection Fund can provide some protection. You can normally get a pension of up to 90 per cent of your expected pension, subject to a cap. (See the **Pension Protection Fund** website for more information: **www.pensionprotectionfund.gov.uk**.) Your employer may close a salary-related pension scheme to new or existing members and offer a money-purchase pension scheme. The scheme trustees will give you information about your options.

Money purchase

These are also known as defined-contribution schemes. The money paid in by you and your employer is invested and builds up a fund that buys you an income when you retire. Most schemes offer a choice of investment funds. The amount paid in varies, but the average employer contribution in 2010 to money-purchase schemes was 8 per cent of salary.

It helps to think of money-purchase pensions as having two stages.

Stage 1. The fund is invested, usually in stocks and shares and other investments, with the aim of growing it over the years before you retire. You can usually choose from a range of funds to invest in. (Remember that the value of investments may go up or down.) The **Pensions Advisory Service** (TPAS) has an online investment choices planner to help you decide how to invest your contributions (see **www.pensionsadvisoryservice.org.uk/online-planners**). For information in print, get a copy of **The Pensions Regulator**'s guide *Making Pension Fund Choices: Think before You Choose*; see **www. thepensionsregulator.gov.uk**.

Stage 2. When you retire, you can take a tax-free lump sum from your fund and use the rest to secure an income – usually in the form of a lifetime annuity. A lifetime annuity is an income you buy with your pension fund when you retire. The amount of pension you'll get at retirement will depend on: how much you pay into the fund; how much your employer pays in (if anything); how well your invested contributions perform; the charges taken out of your fund by your pension provider; how much you take out as a tax-free lump sum; annuity rates at the time you retire – and, the type of annuity you choose.

The benefits of money-purchase schemes are that you get tax relief on your contributions; your fund grows generally free of income tax and capital gains tax; you may be able to choose the funds to invest in; and your employer may contribute, if it's a work-based pension.

Group personal/stakeholder

If you've decided on a private pension, you can shop around for either of the above. These are also money-purchase schemes, ie the pension you get is not linked to your salary. Your employer offers access to either a personal or stakeholder plan, which you own, and can take with you if you get a new job. Your employer will choose the scheme provider, deduct the contributions you make from your salary and pay these to the provider, along with employer contributions. There are some differences between them.

Stakeholder pensions must have certain features. Some of these include limited charges; low minimum contributions; flexible contributions; penalty-free transfers; and a default investment fund – ie a fund your money will be invested in if you don't want to choose one yourself. If your employer offers a *group stakeholder* pension, it doesn't have to pay into it.

Personal pensions: these are similar to stakeholder pensions, but they usually offer a wider range of investment choices. If your employer offers a *group personal* pension scheme, it must contribute at least 3 per cent on your behalf. Personal pension charges may be similar to stakeholder pension charges but some are higher. High charges deducted from your fund by the pension provider can reduce the growth of your fund (and high charges do not necessarily mean better performance). You can compare stakeholder and personal pensions from different providers on the website **www.moneyadviceservice.org.uk**.

Self-Invested Personal Pensions (SIPPs)

If your company pension is likely to be worth less than you expected, owing to inflation and poor stock market performance, one way to redress the balance is to start a Self-Invested Personal Pension. SIPPs enable you to take control of how part of your pension pot is invested. And the good news is that the government is so eager for you to save via a SIPP it will even give you tax back. You can either pay a lump sum to a pension provider or drip feed in monthly amounts. The latter can be made via a scheme into which both you and your employer pay. But instead of your employer directing where your money goes, you get free rein over where it's invested. You can buy a range of asset classes, from stocks to bonds to gold bullion (though you can't buy residential property or fine wines). Monthly contributions can be as low as £50. You can pay in amounts equal to 100 per cent of your annual salary up to a current ceiling of £50,000 per year. You can access your SIPP from age 55 and you can normally take up to 25 per cent as a tax-free cash sum with the balance being used to buy an annuity. SIPPs are not suitable for everyone; broadly they are for people with larger pension pots. As SIPPs are fee-based arrangements, the smaller the fund the more expensive they are. If you are someone who finds the idea of investing your own money daunting, a SIPP may not be for you. For advice talk to your financial adviser or look at the website **www.moneymadeclear.gov.uk**.

Flexible drawdown

The introduction of 'flexible drawdown', effective since 6 April 2011, allows pension investors to take money from their pension as and when they want it. You could, therefore, take your pension pot as a lump sum (taxed as income). By taking money out of your pension you would, however, be removing it from a tax-free environment, so you would probably leave funds in the pension until you needed them, at which point you could draw out however much you needed.

Leaving funds in the pension makes tax-efficient sense because the fund growth is free from UK income and capital gains tax (tax deducted from dividends at source cannot be reclaimed). You will still normally be able to draw up to 25 per cent of your pension tax free when you take retirement benefits. (Don't forget tax rules and tax reliefs can change and their exact value depends on individual circumstances.)

Some of the requirements you will have to meet to be eligible for flexible drawdown include being over 55 to start drawing a pension; also receiving a secure pension of at least £20,000 per annum. This can include the state pension, final salary pensions and pension annuities. The reason for this requirement is so that even if you draw your entire pension out and spend it, you are unlikely to fall back on means-tested state benefits.

Other requirements are if either you or your employer makes contributions to a pension scheme; this could mean that you are prohibited from using flexible drawdown until the start of the tax year after those contributions are made. After you have moved into flexible drawdown, you will be effectively prevented from accruing any more pension benefits, so it is only worth considering once you have finished building up pension benefits.

Family pensions

Another change to pension rules is that you now have greater scope to pass your pension on to your heirs. Until recently options had been very limited, but you can pass your pension on to beneficiaries of your choice as a lump sum, even if you are older than 75 when you die. This will be subject to a 55 per cent tax charge. While this may still sound like a high level of taxation, remember that assets outside a pension are potentially liable to inheritance tax of 40 per cent when you die, as well as income tax and capital gains tax while you are alive. Part of the plan is that the government wishes to recoup the tax relief it has paid before the pension is inherited. The tax charge is designed to claw back the tax relief already provided. The government is keeping the current provision which generally allows you to pass your pension on to a beneficiary as a tax-free lump sum if you die before 75, provided you have not started drawing retirement benefits.

For those who have taken benefits and die before age 75, the new tax charge of 55 per cent will represent an increase in tax from the current rate of 35 per cent. (Encouragingly, however, statistics show that a healthy man aged 65 has just a one in 10 chance of dying before age 75.)

If you have a small pension pot

If the value of your pension rights is below a certain level, it may be possible to give up those rights in exchange for a cash sum. From 6 April 2012 the link to the Lifetime Allowance has been removed. The threshold is announced each year by the government: for the year 2012/13 the limit is £18,000. An important point, if you have more than one pension plan, is that the 'exempt' amount of £18,000 does not apply to each of them but is the total aggregate value of all your plans.

Minimum retirement age

The minimum age at which you are allowed to take early retirement and draw your pension has been 55 since 6 April 2010. It may be possible to draw retirement benefits earlier if you are in poor health and unable to work.

Becoming self-employed

If, as opposed to switching jobs, you leave paid employment to start your own enterprise, you are allowed to transfer your accumulated pension rights into a new fund. There are two main choices. The most obvious solution is to invest your money with an insurance company, or to take either a personal or a stakeholder pension. An alternative course of action, which might be more attractive if you are fairly close to normal retirement age, is to leave your pension in your former employer's scheme. Before making a decision, take professional advice from your Independent Financial Adviser.

Questions on your pension scheme

Most people find it very difficult to understand how their pension scheme works. However, your pension is a valuable asset, especially as you approach retirement, and it is important that you should know the main essentials, including any options that may still be available to you.

If you have a query or if you are concerned in some way about your pension, you should approach whoever is responsible for the scheme in your organization. If the company is large, there may be a special person to look after the scheme on a day-to-day basis. This could be the pensions manager or, quite often, it is someone in the personnel department. In a smaller company, the pension scheme may be looked after by the company secretary or managing director. The sort of questions you might ask will vary according to circumstance, such as before you join the scheme, if you are thinking of changing jobs, if you are hoping to retire early and so on. You will probably think of plenty of additional points of your own. The questions listed here are simply an indication of some of the key information you may require to plan sensibly ahead.

If you want to leave the organization to change jobs

Could you have a refund of contributions if you were to leave shortly after joining?

How much will your deferred pension be worth?

Should you want to move the transfer value to another scheme, how long would you have to wait from the date of your request? (This should normally be within three to six months.)

If you leave for other reasons

What happens if you become ill – or die – before pension age?

What are the arrangements if you want to retire early? Most schemes allow you to do this if you are within about 10 years of normal retirement age, but your pension may be reduced accordingly. Many schemes operate a sliding scale of benefits, with more generous terms offered to those who retire later rather than earlier.

If you stay until normal retirement age

What will your pension be on your present salary? And what would it be assuming your salary increases by, say, 5 or 10 per cent before you eventually retire?

What spouse's pension will be paid? Can a pension be paid to other dependants?

Similarly, can a pension be paid to a partner, male or female?

What happens if you continue working with the organization after retirement age? Normally, any contributions you are making to the scheme will cease to be required and your pension (which will not usually be paid until you retire) will be increased to compensate for its deferment. Since April 2006, provided their scheme rules allow it, members of occupational pension schemes can draw their pension benefits, if they wish, without having to wait until after they leave.

What are the arrangements if you retire from the organization as a salaried employee but become a retained consultant or contractor?

If you just want information

Are any changes envisaged to the scheme? For example, if it is a final salary one, is there any chance that it might be wound up and a money-purchase one offered instead?

If there were a new money-purchase scheme, would the company be making the same contributions as before or would these be lower in future?

Is there any risk that benefits – either members' own or those for dependants – could be reduced?

Is there a possibility that members might be required to pay higher contributions than at present?

Should I transfer my long-lost fund?

Are there any benefits to transferring old pensions into one new scheme? One benefit is the saving on fees. However, you should assess the performance and fees for the new scheme into which you want to transfer the funds. Watch out for transfer charges. These are punitive fees which act as a sneaky deterrent for savers trying to integrate their pensions and keep matters simple.

Other help and advice

Previous schemes

In addition to understanding your current pension scheme, you may also need to chase up any previous schemes of which you were a member. This is well worth pursuing, as you could be owed money from one or more schemes, which will all add to your pension on retirement day. According to the This is Money financial website, an amazing £1.4 billion is estimated to be forgotten and hidden away in accounts worth less than £5,000. These 'stranded' pots are left behind when workers move between jobs, particularly at the start of their careers. As retirement approaches, many face problems tracking down small-sized funds, a problem which the Pensions Advisory Service (a government-sponsored advice body for those about to retire) warns can be 'painfully slow'. Government figures suggest that 4.7 million additional small pension pots will be added to the system by 2050. This is thanks to auto-enrolment – the new government-backed pension scheme compelling workers to save, plus a 'high job churn' as workers jump between different employers and careers.

At the moment around 70,000 people get in touch with the DWP for help in finding a lost pension. Hundreds more queries are fielded by the Pensions Advisory Service. At a time when pensioners are facing the full effects of the 'granny tax', bottom-of-the-rung saving rates and slashed annuities – the income paid out for life in return for your pension pot – reuniting people with lost funds has never been more important.

For free help tracking down a pension, contact the **Pension Tracing Service**, which assists individuals who need help in tracing their pension rights. See website: **www.gov.uk** – Working, jobs and pensions and choose the link to 'Workplace and personal pensions'.

If you have any queries or problems to do with your pension, in addition to the Pension Tracing Service there are three main sources of help available to you. These are the trustees or managers of your pension scheme, the Pensions Advisory Service and the Pensions Ombudsman.

Trustees or managers

These are the first people to contact if you do not properly understand your benefit entitlements or if you are unhappy about some point to do with your pension. Pensions managers (or other people responsible for pensions) should give you their names and tell you how they can be reached.

The Pensions Advisory Service

The Pensions Advisory Service provides members of the public with general information and guidance on pension matters and assists individuals with disputes with personal, company and stakeholder pensions. See the **Pensions Advisory Service** website: **www.pensionsadvisoryservice.org.uk**.

Pensions Ombudsman

You would normally approach the Ombudsman *only* if neither the pension scheme manager (or trustees) nor the Pensions Advisory Service is able to solve your problem. The Ombudsman can investigate: 1) complaints of maladministration by the trustees, managers or administrators of a pension scheme or by an employer; 2) disputes of fact or law with the trustees, managers or an employer. The Ombudsman does not, however, investigate complaints about mis-selling of pension schemes, a complaint that is already subject to court proceedings, or those that are about a state social security benefit, or disputes that are more appropriate for investigation by another regulatory body. There is also a time limit for lodging complaints, which is normally within three years of the act, or failure to act, about which you are complaining.

Provided the problem comes within the Ombudsman's orbit, he will look into all the facts for you and will inform you of his decision, together with his reasons. There is no charge for the Ombudsman's service. The Pensions Ombudsman has now also taken on the role of Pension Protection Fund Ombudsman and will be dealing with complaints about, and appeals from, the Pension Protection Fund. He will also be dealing with appeals from the Financial Assistance Scheme; see below and the **Pensions Ombudsman** website: **www.pensions-ombudsman.org.uk**.

If you have a personal pension, the **Financial Ombudsman Service** (FOS) could help you. Since last year, the maximum award that the Financial Ombudsman can make has increased from £100,000 to £150,000. See website: **www.financial-ombudsman.org.uk**. It is possible you may be referred to the Pensions Ombudsman, but if so you will be informed very quickly.

Protection for pension scheme members

New rules have been introduced to protect pension scheme members in the event of a company takeover or proposed bulk transfer arrangement. There is now also a **Pension Protection Fund** (PPF) to help final salary pension scheme members who are at risk of losing their pension benefits owing to their employer's insolvency. Members below the scheme's normal retirement age will receive 90 per cent of the Pension Protection Fund level of compensation plus annual increases, subject to a cap and the standard fund rules. See website: **www.pensionprotectionfund.org.uk**.

There is more help too for members who lost pension savings in a company scheme before the introduction of the Pension Protection Fund. The **Financial Assistance Scheme** (FAS) offers help to some people who have lost out on their pension. It makes payments to top up scheme benefits to eligible members of schemes that are winding up or have wound up. Assistance is also payable to the survivor of a pension scheme member. It is payable from normal retirement age (subject to a lower age limit of 60 and an upper age limit of 65). See website: **www.pensionprotectionfund.org.uk**.

Pension rights if you continue to work after retirement age

When you reach normal retirement age you will usually stop making contributions into your company pension scheme even if you decide to carry on working. Your employer, of course, would have to agree to your continuing to work but, thanks to the age discrimination legislation, this should not normally be a problem if you are under 65 and are physically and mentally capable of doing your job. Even if you are over 65, you may find that your employer will be only too happy for you to stay – and, even then, if your employer wants you to leave, they will have to give you at least six months' notice in writing. If you are facing such a decision, here are some points to bear in mind:

You can continue working, draw your company pension and put some (or possibly all) of your earnings into a separate scheme.

You can leave your pension in the fund, where it will continue to earn interest until you retire. In most private schemes you could expect to receive in the region of an extra 8 per cent for every year that you delay retirement. If you continue working, say, for an additional five years, your pension would then be 40 per cent higher than if you had started taking it at the normal age. You will also have been earning a salary meanwhile, so you are likely to be considerably better off as a result.

You can leave your pension in the fund, as described above, and additionally contribute to a personal or stakeholder pension, provided your contributions do not exceed the annual allowance (2013) of £50,000.

Provided your scheme rules allow, you can continue working for your existing employer and draw your pension benefits, as opposed to – as previously – having to defer them until you left the organization.

Equal pension age

Employers are required to treat men and women equally with regard to retirement and pension issues. This means that by law they must have a common retirement age that applies equally to both sexes. Similarly, they must also have a common pension age, and pension schemes must offer the same benefits to their male and female members.

Divorce, separation and bereavement

Divorce

Pension sharing became legally available in respect of divorce or annulment proceedings commenced on or after 1 December 2000. While an advantage of pension sharing is that it allows a clean break on divorce, many experts believe that it may well have the effect of so diminishing the pension scheme member's retirement fund that he or she may not have sufficient left to rebuild an adequate pension. The situation could apply to men or women. Although women usually benefit most from pension sharing, recent legislative changes equally allow an ex-husband to have a share in his former wife's pension rights.

The question of pension sharing is a subject to raise with your solicitor if you are in the process of divorce proceedings. But however much in favour your legal adviser may be, in the final analysis it is up to the court to decide on what it sees as the fairest arrangement – and pension sharing is only one of several options available.

Divorced wives

If you have a full basic pension in your own right, this will not be affected by divorce. However, if, as applies to many women, despite having worked for a good number of years you have made insufficient contributions to qualify for a full pension, you should contact your pension centre, quoting your pension number and NI number. It is possible that you may be able to obtain the full single person's pension, based on your ex-husband's contributions.

Your right to use your ex-husband's contributions to improve or provide you with a pension depends on your age and/or whether you remarry before the age of 60. As a general rule, you can use your ex-husband's contributions towards your pension for the years you were married (ie until the date of the decree absolute). After that, you are expected to pay your own contributions until you are 60, unless you remarry.

If you are over 60 when you divorce, then whether you remarry or not you can rely on your ex-husband's contributions. If you remarry before the age of 60, then you cease absolutely being dependent on your former husband and instead your pension will be based on your new husband's contribution record. The same rules apply in reverse. Although it happens less frequently, a divorced man can rely on his former wife's contribution record during the years they were married to improve his basic pension. A divorced wife might have some claim to her former husband's occupational pension benefits.

Pension sharing

As previously mentioned, provisions to enable the court to share occupational or personal pension rights at the time of divorce or annulment came into law on 1 December 2000. The legislation now equally applies to the additional state pension. Sharing, however, is only one option for dealing with pension rights and would not necessarily apply in all cases.

Separated wives

Even if you have not lived together for several years, from an NI point of view you are still considered to be married. The normal pension rules apply including, of course, the fact that, if you have to depend on your husband's contributions, you will not be able to get a pension until he is both 65 and in receipt of his own pension.

If you are not entitled to a state pension in your own right, you will receive the dependant's rate of benefit, which is about 60 per cent of the full rate (or less if your husband is not entitled to a full pension). In such a case, you can apply for Income Support to top up your income. Once you are 60, you can personally draw the wife's pension without reference to your husband.

If your husband dies, you may be entitled to bereavement benefits in the same way as other widows. If there is a possibility that he may have died but that you have not been informed, you can check by contacting the **General Register Office** website: **www.gro.gov.uk**. The indexes to all birth, marriage and death entries in England and Wales are available from the **National Archives** website: **www.nationalarchives.gov.uk**.

Widows

There are three important benefits to which widows may be entitled: Bereavement Payment, Bereavement Allowance and Widowed Parent's Allowance. All are largely modelled on the former widows' benefits (Widow's Payment, Widow's Pension and Widowed Mother's Allowance). It is important to note that all the above are now equally applicable to widowed men or those who have entered a civil partnership. To claim the benefits, fill in form BB1, obtainable from any social security or Jobcentre Plus office. You will also be given a questionnaire (BD8) by the registrar. It is important that you complete this, as it acts as a trigger to help speed up payment of your benefits.

Widows who were already in receipt of the Widow's Pension before it was replaced by Bereavement Allowance in April 2001 are not affected by the change and will continue to receive their pension as normal.

Bereavement Payment

This is a tax-free, lump-sum payment to help you when your husband, wife or civil partner has died. To get Bereavement Payment you must usually be under state pension age (currently 65 for men and 60 for women). Even if you are over state pension age, you may be able to get one, if your husband, wife or civil partner was not getting a state pension. The time limit for claiming a Bereavement Payment is 12 months after the person's death. You can fill in a claim form, obtainable from The Pension Service: **www.gov.uk**.

Bereavement Allowance

This has replaced the Widow's Pension. As stated earlier, women already in receipt of Widow's Pension before 6 April 2001 are not affected and will continue to receive their pension as normal. Bereavement Allowance is for those aged between 45 and state pension age who do not receive Widowed Parent's Allowance. It is payable for 52 weeks; receipt in all cases is dependent on sufficient NIC having been paid. See website: **www.gov.uk**.

Bereavement Allowance is paid to widows and widowers between the ages of 55 and 59 inclusive. The standard weekly amount (2012/13) is £105.95. It is normally paid automatically once you have sent off your completed form BB1, so if for any reason you do not receive it you should enquire at your social security or Jobcentre Plus office. In the event of your being ineligible, owing to insufficient NIC having been paid, you may still be entitled to receive Income Support, housing benefit or a grant or loan from the social fund. Your social security or Jobcentre Plus office will advise you. As applies to Widow's Pension, widows who remarry or live with a man as his wife cease to receive Bereavement Allowance. See website: **www.direct.gov.uk/benefits**.

Widowed Parent's Allowance

This is a taxable benefit for widows or widowers who are under state pension age and who have at least one child for whom they are entitled, or treated as entitled, to Child Benefit. The current value (2012/13) is £105.95 a week plus a share of any additional state pension you have built up. The share of additional pension payable will be between 50 and 100 per cent depending on your date of birth. The allowance is usually paid automatically. If for some reason, although eligible, you do not receive the money, you should inform your social security or Jobcentre Plus office. See website: **www.direct.gov.uk**.

Retirement pension

Once a widow reaches 60, she will normally receive a state pension based on her own and/or her late husband's contributions. If at the time of death the couple were already receiving the state retirement pension, the widow will continue to receive her share. An important point to remember is that a widow may be able to use her late husband's NIC to boost the amount she receives.

Separate from the basic pension, a widow may also receive money from her late husband's occupational pension, whether contracted in or out of the state scheme. She may also get half of any of his graduated pension.

War widows and widowers

War Widow's or Widower's Pension is a tax-free pension for surviving widows, widowers or civil partners of veterans who died as a result of serving in HM armed forces before 6 April 2005. You may also be able to get extra money or help with funeral costs.

If your husband, wife or civil partner died as a result of serving in the forces before 6 April 2005, you may be able to get a War Widow's or Widower's Pension under the War Pensions Scheme. The Service Personnel and Veterans Agency will pay War Widow's or Widower's Pension if any of the following applied before 6 April 2005:

Your husband, wife or partner died as a result of a war injury, or because of a war-risk injury as a merchant seaman.

Your husband, wife or partner was getting a War Disablement Pension at the 80 per cent rate or higher and was getting Unemployability Supplement.

Your husband's, wife's or partner's death was due to, or happened sooner because of, their service with the Polish Forces under British command in the Second World War, or their service with the Polish Resettlement Forces.

Your husband, wife or partner received, or was entitled to, Constant Attendance Allowance under the War Pension Scheme at the time they died.

Your husband, wife or partner was a civil defence volunteer or a civilian and their death was due to, or happened sooner because of, a war injury or war service injury they suffered while serving in the Second World War.

If you are a widow, widower or surviving civil partner whose husband, wife or partner left service before 31 March 1973, you can keep your pension if you remarry, form a civil partnership or live with a new partner after 6 April 2005. Otherwise this pension may stop.

If you think you may be entitled to claim a War Widow's or Widower's Pension visit the **Service Personnel and Veterans Agency** website: **www.veterans-uk.info**.

Part-timers

Thanks in large part to the sex discrimination legislation being extended to include access to pension schemes, many part-timers who were previously excluded can now join their employer's occupational pension scheme as of right – or may even be able to claim retrospective membership for the years they were 'unlawfully excluded'. Their claim can be backdated only to 1976 or, if later, to the start date of their employment and must be made (at the absolute latest) within six months of their leaving the job.

Part-timers who wish to claim must apply to an employment tribunal and, as a condition of receiving any backdated benefits due, must pay contributions in respect of those years. Although it is perhaps stating the obvious, successful appeals are not automatic, as the issue will be judged solely on grounds of sex discrimination and not on exclusion for other reasons.

Chapter Four
Tax

I'm spending a year dead, for tax reasons. **DOUGLAS ADAMS**

The Chancellor of the Exchequer's closing words in his March 2012 Budget Speech were: 'This country borrowed its way into trouble. Now we're going to earn our way out.' For millions of UK pensioners, one of the changes George Osborne made ended a century-old tax break (introduced by Winston Churchill in 1925) and launched a £3 billion 'granny tax' raid on their finances. The news made national headlines for weeks afterwards, and is still the subject of fierce debate. So is this the worst time ever to be a pensioner? The media seem to think so. Abolishing age-related tax allowances completely from April 2013 may be intended to simplify the system, but it has been slammed by critics and labelled 'unfair'. This year's pensioners will find their tax allowance the same as the rest of the population, a move that will affect around 5 million people by 2015.

But 'bad news' is something the majority of older people tend to be better at dealing with than younger generations. By the time we reach 60, most of us have had to cope with a number of life's challenges, and have survived. It is possible that we manage better in tough times than others who are used to demanding, and getting, 'instant gratification'. While the dust settles on last year's changes, a financial spring clean might be sensible. Because the 2012 budget was so tough and hard hitting, with many alterations to the level of benefits, taxes and pensions, it is vital that everyone reaching retirement age should invest some time working out ways of reducing the amount of tax they pay before and during retirement. If you are new to retirement, now is a perfect time to consider a money makeover and check up on what the current taxation rules mean for you.

The most common types of tax (and we are familiar with most of them) are income tax, National Insurance Contributions, capital gains tax and inheritance tax. While you were employed you may have been contributing many thousands of pounds to HM Revenue & Customs (HMRC), but in practice you may have had very little direct contact with the tax system. The accounts department would have automatically deducted – and accounted for – the PAYE on your earnings as a salaried employee. If you were self-employed, or had other money unconnected with your job, you may have had more dealings with your tax office. On reaching retirement you should be able to calculate how much money (after deduction of tax) you will have available to spend: the equivalent, if you like, of your take-home pay. Understanding the broad principles could help you save money, by not paying more in taxation than you need.

The purpose of this chapter is not to criticize the Chancellor for the changes he has made, or to give tax planning advice. Censuring the Chancellor is best left to the Opposition; tax planning is a job for a specialist. Your tax adviser should be fully conversant with your financial affairs so that he or she can advise in the light of your own circumstances. The aim here is simply to remind you of the basics and to draw your attention to some of the latest variations that could have a bearing on your immediate or longer-term plans. The following information is based on our understanding, as at October 2012, of current taxation, legislation and HMRC practice, all of which are liable to change without notice. The impact of taxation (and any tax relief) depends on individual circumstances.

Income tax

This is calculated on all (or nearly all) of your income, after deduction of your personal allowance and, in the case of older married people, of the Married Couple's Allowance. The reason for saying 'nearly all' is that some income you may receive is tax free; types of income on which you do not have to pay tax are listed a little further on.

Most income counts, however. You will be assessed for income tax on your pension, interest you receive from most types of savings, dividends from investments, any earnings (even if these are only from casual work), plus rent from any lodgers, should the amount you receive exceed £4,250 a year. Many social security benefits are also taxable. The tax year runs from 6 April to the following 5 April, so the amount of tax you pay in any one year is calculated on the income you receive (or are deemed to have received) between these two dates. The four different rates of income tax for 2012/13 are:

1 The 10 per cent starting rate for savings, which applies to the first £2,710 of any savings income. If an individual's taxable non-savings income exceeds the starting rate limit, then the 10 per cent starting rate for savings will not be available for savings income.

2 The 20 per cent basic-rate tax for income up to £34,370.

3 The 40 per cent higher-rate tax, which is levied on all taxable income from £34,371 up to £150,000.

4 The top rate of 50 per cent on incomes in excess of £150,000. From April 2013, the 50 per cent top rate of tax will be cut to 45 per cent.

NB: 300,000 more people will be drawn into the higher rate (40 per cent) tax band from 2013/14 as the threshold is reduced from £42,475 to £41,450.

(The rates available for dividends for 2012/13 tax year are the 10 per cent dividend ordinary rate, 32.5 per cent dividend upper rate and the 42.5 per cent dividend additional rate. There rates are the same as the previous year, 2011/12.)

Tax allowances

Personal allowance

You don't pay tax on every single penny of your money. You are allowed to retain a certain amount before income tax becomes applicable. This is known as your personal allowance. When calculating how much tax you will have to pay in any one year, first deduct from your total income the amount represented by your personal allowance. You should add any other tax allowance to which you may be entitled – see further on. You will not have to pay any income tax if your income does not exceed your personal allowance (or total of your allowances), and you may be able to claim a refund for any tax you have paid, or that has been deducted from payments made to you, during the year.

Calculating your personal allowance since the introduction of independent taxation has become easier. Everyone receives the same basic personal allowance regardless of whether they are male, female, married or single. It does not matter where the income comes from, whether from earnings, an investment, a pension or another source.

The figures for the tax year 2012/13 are as follows:

The basic personal allowance for those aged under 65 is £8,105.

For people age 65–74, their tax-free personal allowance has been set at £10,500.

For those aged 75 and over, their personal allowance is £10,660.

But the biggest change is effective from April 2013. From this date, those reaching 65 will no longer receive a larger personal allowance than people of working age. This extra allowance gradually reduces for pensioners whose taxable income is between £24,000 and about £29,000. It disappears for any pensioner earning more than £29,000. There is also a gradual withdrawal of the basic personal allowance for everyone with income above £100,000, regardless of age.

From April 2013, the income tax personal allowances will change in the following way:

The under-65s personal allowance will increase by £1,100 to £9,205 from 6 April 2013. That relates to people born after 5 April 1948. A personal allowance of £10,500 will be restricted to most people born after 4 April 1938 but before 6 April 1948. The personal allowance of most people born before 6 April 1938 will be £10,660. The change means that as people turn 65, they will not be entitled to the higher personal allowance set aside for most pensioners. Instead they will receive the same as everyone else. As time goes on, more and more people will fall into this group.

HMRC is quoted as saying 'This measure will support the goal of a single personal allowance for all taxpayers, regardless of age, and spread tax relief fairly across working-age people and pensioners.'

Married Couple's Allowance

Married Couple's Allowance (for those aged under 75) is no longer applicable. Age-related Married Couple's Allowance (aged 75 and over) for 2012/ 13 is £7,705. The minimum amount of Married Couple's Allowance is £2,960.

Some important points you should know:

Married Couple's Allowance is available to people born before 6 April 1935. Tax relief for this allowance is restricted to 10 per cent.

A widowed partner, where the couple at the time of death were entitled to Married Couple's Allowance, can claim any unused portion of the allowance in the year he or she became widowed.

Registered blind people can claim an allowance of £2,100 a year. If both husband and wife are registered as blind, they can each claim the allowance. It is called the Blind Person's Allowance. If you think you would be eligible, you should contact your local tax office with relevant details of your situation. If you were entitled to receive the allowance earlier but for some reason missed out on doing so, you may be able to obtain a tax rebate.

Useful reading

For more detailed information about tax allowances, see HMRC website: **www.hmrc.gov.uk**. The Inland Revenue booklet, IR 121, *Approaching Retirement (A Guide to Tax and National Insurance Contributions)* is useful.

Same-sex partners

Same-sex couples are treated the same as married couples for tax purposes. As a result, they gain all the same tax advantages but also the same disadvantages. The most important is that only one property can qualify as their principal home for exemption from capital gains tax (CGT). Against this, there is no CGT to pay on transfer of assets between the couple, and similarly any assets left in a will to each other are free of inheritance tax. Other major areas affected are pension rights (other than the state scheme) and, though not specifically a tax issue, settlements between the couple in the event of a divorce.

Tax relief

Separate from any personal allowances, you can obtain tax relief on the following:

- a covenant for the benefit of a charity, or a donation under the Gift Aid scheme;

- contributions to occupational pensions, self-employed pension plans and other personal pensions;

- some maintenance payments, if you are divorced or separated and were aged 65 or older at 5 April 2000.

Mortgage interest relief

Mortgage interest relief was abolished on 6 April 2000. The only purpose for which relief is still available is in respect of loans secured on an older person's home to purchase a life annuity. However, to qualify, the loan must have been taken out (or at least processed and confirmed in writing) by 9 March 1999. Borrowers in this situation can continue to benefit from the relief for the duration of their loan. As before, the relief remains at 10 per cent on the first £30,000 of the loan.

Maintenance payments

Tax relief for maintenance payments was also withdrawn on 6 April 2000. Individuals in receipt of maintenance payments are not affected and will continue to receive their money free of income tax. Those who had to pay tax under the pre-March 1988 rules now also receive their payments free of tax. Most individuals paying maintenance, however, face higher tax bills. This applies especially to those who set up arrangements before the March 1988 Budget. While previously they got tax relief at their highest rate, from 6 April 2000 when maintenance relief was withdrawn they no longer get any relief at all. An exception has been made in cases where one (or both) of the divorced or separated spouses was aged 65 or over at 5 April 2000. Those paying maintenance are still able to claim tax relief – but only at the 1999/2000 standard rate of 10 per cent.

Pension contributions

HMRC sets limits on the contributions that individuals can invest in their pension plan and on the pension benefits they can receive. All company and personal pensions are now set under a single tax regime and new rules have been implemented.

Your annual contribution allowance is now £50,000 or 100 per cent of your income, whichever is less. You still have access to the same generous tax rebates and everyone gets back at least 25 per cent of what they pay in. It could be as much as 50 per cent depending on your circumstances. If you have contributed less than £50,000 in any of the last three tax years, you can use your leftover allowances to make additional pension contributions (up to 100 per cent of your income). Once you are 55 (and if you have a pension income of £20,000 per annum), you can withdraw lump sums. But if your withdrawal is above the 25 per cent tax-free lump-sum limit, it will be subject to income tax (see Chapter 3, Pensions, for more information).

For the tax year 2012/13, the Lifetime Allowance was reduced to £1.5 million (formerly it was £1.8 million). Funds in excess of the lifetime limit are subject to a 25 per cent recovery charge (ie tax) if taken as income, or 55 per cent if taken as a lump sum.

Fund protection

An individual whose pension fund was already over the lifetime limit before 6 April 2006 – or anticipated to become so before they draw their pension – was able to protect their fund from the recovery charge, provided the fund was formally registered with HMRC within three years of 6 April 2006 (A-day), ie 5 April 2009. It is now too late to apply for protection.

Tax-free lump sum

Everyone (provided the scheme rules permit) is entitled to take up to 25 per cent of the value of their fund or 25 per cent of their lifetime limit, whichever is lower. Additional Voluntary Contributions (AVCs) and the opted-out benefits from the State Second Pension can count towards the lump sum instead of, as before, having to remain in the fund to provide pension income.

There is no longer any requirement for members of company schemes to wait until they retire before accessing their lump sum. Should they wish to do so, they can now take the money at any time from the age of 55. Members of final salary schemes cannot take their lump sum in isolation. There is now also greater flexibility for employees nearing retirement, who as well as taking their tax-free lump sum can also (provided their scheme rules allow) start drawing some pension income while still remaining at work part time.

Scheme rules

The fact that HMRC has changed the rules is unfortunately no guarantee that individuals will be able to take full advantage of all the new options that have become available. Their employer's pension scheme rules will need to have been altered accordingly, which may not always be the case. Before making any definite plans, it is advisable to check first with whoever is responsible for the company pension scheme.

Pension Credit

Pension Credit is a means-tested state benefit for those over 60, giving certain pensioners extra money each week. It's made up of two elements –

the 'Guarantee Credit' element and the 'Savings Credit' element. Pension Credit guarantees everyone aged 60 and over an income of at least £142.70 a week if you are single and £217.90 a week if you have a partner. Also, if you or your partner is 65 or over, you may be rewarded for saving for your retirement: up to £18.54 a week if you are single or £23.73 a week if you have a partner. You should get more Pension Credit if you have caring responsibilities, are severely disabled or have certain housing costs.

If you apply over the phone for Pension Credit and, at the same time, for housing and council tax benefits, the Pension Service will automatically send its claim information to the appropriate local authority. This does away with the need for another claim form to be completed and signed. Also claimants are now able to spend up to 13 weeks abroad (increased from four weeks) and still retain entitlement to Pension Credit. This brings the benefit into line with housing and council tax benefits. The backdating of Pension Credit claims is now limited to three months, to bring it into line with other benefits.

For further information, see Chapter 3, Pensions, or look under 'Pension Credit' on the website: **www.gov.uk**.

Tax-free income

Some income you may receive is entirely free of tax. It is important to know what income is non-taxable and what can be ignored for tax purposes. If you receive any of the following, you can forget about the tax aspect altogether (for a full list see Citizens Advice Bureau website: **www.adviceguide.org.uk** – taxable and non-taxable income):

Attendance Allowances;

Back to Work Bonus;

Bereavement Payment;

Child Benefit; NB: Child Benefit cuts to be phased in for families with at least one parent earning £50,000, and axed for those on £60,000;

Child dependency additions;

Council Tax Benefit;

Disability Living Allowance;

Housing Benefit;

Industrial Injuries disablement pension;

Income-related Employment and Support Allowance;

Income Support (in some circumstances, such as when the recipient is also getting Jobseeker's Allowance, Income Support benefit will be taxable);

Social Fund payments;

Pension Credit;

all pensions paid to war widows (plus any additions for children);

pensions paid to victims of Nazism;

certain disablement pensions from the armed forces, police, fire brigade and merchant navy;

annuities paid to the holders of certain gallantry awards;

the £10 Christmas bonus (paid to pensioners);

the Winter Fuel Payment (paid to pensioners);

the extra £400 Winter Fuel Payment paid to households with a resident aged 80 and over;

National Savings Premium Bond prizes;

winnings on the National Lottery and other forms of betting;

rental income of up to £4,250 a year from letting out rooms in your home;

income received from certain insurance policies (mortgage payment protection, permanent health insurance, creditor insurance for loans and utility bills, various approved long-term care policies) if the recipient is sick, disabled or unemployed at the time the benefits become payable;

SAYE bonuses;

all income and dividends received from savings in an Individual Savings Account (ISA);

all dividend income from investments in venture capital trusts (VCTs).

The following are not income, in the sense that they are more likely to be one-off rather than regular payments. However, as with the above list they are tax free:

virtually all gifts (in certain circumstances you could have to pay tax if the gift is above £3,000 or if, as may occasionally be the case, the money from the donor has not been previously taxed);

a redundancy payment, or a golden handshake in lieu of notice, up to the value of £30,000;

a lump sum commuted from a pension;

a matured endowment policy;

accumulated interest from a Tax Exempt Special Savings Account (TESSA) held for five years;

dividends on investments held in a Personal Equity Plan (PEP);

compensation money paid to people who were mis-sold personal pensions;

compensation paid to those who were mis-sold free-standing AVCs (FSAVCs). To qualify for exemption from tax, the money must be paid as a lump sum as opposed to annual payments.

Income tax on savings and investments

Savings

For the tax year 2012/13 the 10 per cent starting rate applies to savings income up to £2,710.

Investments

For most investments on which you are likely to receive dividends, basic-rate tax will have been deducted before the money is paid to you. If you are a basic-rate taxpayer, the money you receive will be yours in its entirety. If you pay tax at the higher rate, you will have to pay some additional tax and should allow for this in your budgeting.

Exceptionally, there are one or two types of investment where the money is paid to you gross – without the basic-rate tax deducted. These include NS&I income bonds, capital bonds, the NS&I Investment Account and all gilt interest. (People who prefer to receive gilt interest net can opt to do so.) As with higher-rate taxpayers, you will need to save sufficient money to pay the tax on the due date.

Avoiding paying excess tax on savings income

Banks and building societies automatically deduct the normal 20 per cent rate of tax from interest before it is paid to savers. As a result, most working people, except higher-rate taxpayers, can keep all their savings without having to worry about paying additional tax. While convenient for the majority, a problem is that some 4 million people on low incomes – including in particular many women and pensioners – are unwittingly paying more tax than they need. Those most affected are non-taxpayers (anyone whose taxable income is less than their allowances) who, although not liable for tax, are having it taken from their income before they receive the money.

Non-taxpayers can stop this happening quite simply by requesting their bank and/or building society to pay any interest owing to them gross, without deduction of tax at source. If applicable, all you need do is request form R85 from the institution in question or HMRC Enquiry Centre, which you will then need to complete. If you have more than one bank or building society account, you will need a separate form for each account. People who have filled in an R85 should automatically receive their interest gross. If your form was not completed in time for this to happen, you can reclaim the tax from your tax office after the end of the tax year in April.

Reclaiming tax overpaid

If you are a non-taxpayer and have not yet completed an R85 form (or forms), you are very likely to be eligible to claim a tax rebate. To obtain a claim form and, if relevant, copies of form R85 for you to complete and give to your bank or building society, see website: **www.hmrc.gov.uk**.

Mistakes by HMRC

HMRC does sometimes make mistakes. Normally, if it has charged you insufficient tax and later discovers the error, it will send you a supplementary demand requesting the balance owing. However, under a provision known as the 'Official Error Concession', if the mistake was due to HMRC's failure 'to make proper and timely use' of information it received, it is possible that you may be excused the arrears. For this to be likely, you will need to convince HMRC that you could reasonably have believed that your tax affairs were in order. Additionally, HMRC itself will need to have been tardy in notifying you of the arrears: this will normally mean more than 12 months after the end of the tax year in which HMRC received the information indicating that more tax was due.

Undercharging is not the only type of error. It is equally possible that you may have been overcharged and either do not owe as much as has been stated or, not having spotted the mistake, have paid more than you needed to previously. In time HMRC may notice the error and send you a refund, but equally it may not. So if you have reason to think your tax bill looks wrong, check it carefully. Then, if you think there has been a mistake, write to your tax office explaining why you think the amount is too high. If a large sum is involved it could well be worth asking an accountant to help you.

As part of the Citizen's Charter, HMRC has appointed an independent Adjudicator to examine taxpayers' complaints about their dealings with HMRC and, if considered valid, to determine what action would be fair. Complaints appropriate to the Adjudicator are mainly limited to the way HMRC has handled someone's tax affairs, for example excessive delay, errors, discourtesy or how discretion has been exercised. In deciding fair treatment, the Adjudicator has power to recommend the waiving of a payment or even the award of compensation if, as a result of error by HMRC, the complainant had incurred professional fees or other expenses. Before approaching the Adjudicator, taxpayers are expected to have tried to resolve the matter either with their local tax office or, should that fail, with the regional office.

Genuine mistakes are excused by HMRC but individuals may need to convince officials that they had not been careless in completing their returns, otherwise they could be at risk of incurring a penalty of 30 to 100 per cent of the tax involved, plus the tax owed itself and interest, and potentially HMRC widening its focus on you and your tax affairs.

Important dates to remember: The deadline for filing paper self-assessment forms for the 2012/13 tax year is 31 October 2013. Those filing online will have until 31 January 2014.

Further information

For further information, see HMRC booklet *Code of Practice 1, Putting Things Right: How to complain*, available from tax offices. Contact the Adjudicator's Office for information about referring a complaint. The Adjudicator acts as a fair and unbiased referee looking into complaints about HMRC, including the Tax Credit Office, the Valuation Office and the Office of the Public Guardian and the Insolvency Service. See website: **www.adjudicatorsoffice.gov.uk**.

The **TaxPayers' Alliance** has a campaign team of energetic volunteers committed to achieving a low-tax society. It has over 18,000 supporters and is regularly mentioned in the media. See website: **www.taxpayersalliance.com**.

TaxHelp for Older People (TOP) is an independent, free tax advice service for over-60s whose household income is less than £17,000 a year. This organization offers the service originally provided through the Low Incomes Tax Reform Group (associated with the Chartered Institute of Taxation) but is now provided by Tax Volunteers, an independent organization. See website: **www.taxvol.org.uk**.

Here are some useful tax forms that can help you:

R40 – If you want to claim back tax paid on savings and investments, you need to complete this form. Remember that you need one for each year you are claiming for.

R85 – Getting your interest paid without tax being taken off. Not a taxpayer? This form will save you having to claim tax back each year. You can use this if your total taxable income (before tax is taken) is below your personal allowance. Ask for one at your bank or building society, sign it and hand it back.

P161 – Are you going to be 65 (60 for a woman) in this tax year? Or is your income changing, for example, state pension and private pensions are due to start? If yes, this is a very important form. It will help you inform HMRC of your age and income, allowing it to give you your age allowance and your new tax codes.

R27 – This form helps you to settle the tax affairs of someone who has died. If you have recently been bereaved and have informed HMRC, it should send you one. It is worth completing because it often creates a repayment and helps to sort out any final transfer of Married Couples' Allowance. Your solicitor, if you have one, will usually deal with it for you.

P53 – If you have recently taken a lump sum rather than buying an annuity (pension), you will have noticed that an enormous amount of tax was deducted before you received it. If you want to claim this back immediately rather than waiting until the end of the tax year, you should complete a P53.

P45 – You should receive one of these when you finish work with an employer. If you start a new job in the same tax year it is important that you give it to your new employer. It will ensure you are given the correct tax code and the right tax is deducted.

P46 – As important as the P45. If you start a new job and you do not have a P45 you must complete a P46. Your employer should prompt you to do this. If not, ask for one. This form also sorts out your tax codes.

Forms 575 and 18 – If you are thinking of transferring some of your Married Couples' Allowance, Form 575 allows you to transfer the excess at the end of the tax year. Form 18 allows you to transfer the minimum amount.

Most forms can be obtained via the HMRC website: **www.hmrc.gov.uk**.

Tax Credits

Since the Budget in 2012 there are a whole host of changes to the tax credits system. In part these are the result of the government's austerity drive. There are two tax credits that could be of interest: the Working Tax Credit (WTC) and the Child Tax Credit (CTC). The amount of tax credits you get depends on how many children you have living with you, whether you work and how many hours you work, if you pay for childcare, if you or any child living with you has a disability, or if you are coming off benefits. A recent budget change is that from April 2012 the 50-plus element will no longer be available for those claiming Working Tax Credit.

Working Tax Credit

This is an earnings top-up given to low-income workers, including the self-employed. Eligibility is normally restricted to couples and single parents with a low income. In certain circumstances, including in particular households with three or more dependent children or where a member of the family has a disability, those with slightly higher incomes could still be eligible to apply. HMRC advises that the easiest way to check is to complete the form listed under 'Tax credits' on its website: **www.hmrc.gov.uk**.

To qualify, claimants (other than a few exceptions) have to work for 24 hours a week between them, not 16, to qualify for Working Tax Credit. One member of the couple will have to work for at least 16 hours per week. Working parents can receive up to 80 per cent of eligible childcare costs. All recipients receive the payment direct from HMRC into their bank, building society, Post Office or National Savings account either weekly or four-weekly.

Child Tax Credit

This is a cash payment given to all families with a low household income that have at least one child under 16, or under 20 if in full-time education, and is paid in addition to a basic tax credit payment. The money, which is on top of Child Benefit, is paid direct to the main carer. The amount of credit varies according to parental income but since 6 April 2011 families with an income of more than £40,000 have seen their eligibility for CTC reduced. The couple and lone parent elements of working tax credit stay the same as in the last financial year.

Need to claim

Payment is not automatic. In both cases – Working Tax Credit and Child Tax Credit – you need to complete an application form, obtainable from any Tax Enquiry Centre or via website: **www.gov.uk** – Tax Credits.

NB: Child Tax Credit is one area where independent taxation could be said not to apply, as eligibility is based on the combined income of the parents.

Post-war credits

Post-war credits are extra tax that people had to pay in addition to their income tax between April 1941 and April 1946. The extra tax was treated as a credit to be repaid after the war. People who paid credits were given certificates showing the amount actually paid. Repayment started in 1946, initially only to men aged 65 or over and to women aged 60 or over, but the conditions for claiming varied over the years until 1972, when it was announced that there would be a 'general release' and that all credits were to be repaid without any further restrictions. In 1972 people who could produce at least one of their post-war credit certificates were invited to claim. In cases where the original credit holder has died without claiming repayment and the post-war credit certificate is still available, repayment can be made to the next of kin or personal representative of the estate. Interest is payable on all claims at a composite rate of 38 per cent. The interest is exempt from income tax. All claims should be sent to the **Special Post-War Credit Claim Centre** at HM Revenue & Customs, HM Inspector of Taxes, PWC Centre V, Ty Glas, Llanishen, Cardiff CF4 5TX.

Tax rebates

When you retire, you may be due for a tax rebate. If you are, this would normally be paid automatically, especially if you are getting a pension from your last employer. The matter could conceivably be overlooked, either if you are due to get a pension from an earlier employer (instead of from your last employer) or if you will be receiving only a state pension and not a company pension in addition.

In either case, you should ask your employer for a P45 form. Then either send it – care of your earlier employer – to the pension fund trustees or, in the event of your receiving only a state pension, to the tax office together with details of your age and the date you retired. Ask your employer for the address of the tax office to which you should write. If the repayment is made to you more than a year after the end of the year for which the repayment is due – and is more than £25 – HMRC will automatically pay you (tax-free) interest. HMRC calls this a 'repayment supplement'.

NB: of course everyone likes a tax rebate and HMRC processes tens of thousands per year after checking self-assessment returns. But however welcome a cash payment may seem, don't believe any e-mail promising a refund. These are 'phishing' scams, designed to get your financial details. HMRC says it never sends notifications of a tax rebate by e-mail, or asks you to disclose personal or payment information by e-mail. For more advice see website: **www.hmrc.gov.uk/security**.

Mis-sold PPI

Millions of borrowers have been receiving refunds after being mis-sold payment protection insurance (PPI) with credit cards and personal loans. This is good news as many are receiving cheques for thousands of pounds. Even better, they are being paid 8 per cent interest on the refunds, to compensate for being without their money all that time. *But* while there is no tax to pay on the refund element, which simply returns their own money to them, they have to pay tax on the interest, just as they do on earned interest in a savings account, depending on their tax situation in the year they receive the money.

Some lenders are deducting basic tax at 20 per cent, which non-taxpayers can reclaim, and higher-rate payers must report to the Revenue. The longer someone has been without their money, the higher the interest proportion of it will be.

Capital gains tax (CGT)

You may have to pay capital gains tax if you make a profit (or, to use the proper term, 'gain') on the sale of a capital asset, for example stocks and shares, jewellery, any property that is not your main home, and other items of value. CGT applies only to the actual gain you make, so if you buy shares to the value of £100,000 and sell them later for £125,000, the tax office will be interested only in the £25,000 profit you have made.

Not all your gains are taxable. There is an exemption limit of £10,600 a year. (This limit remains unchanged for the year 2012/13). A very important point for married couples to know is that as a result of independent taxation each partner now enjoys his or her own annual exemption of £10,600 instead of, as before, their gains being aggregated (ie added together) for tax purposes. This means in effect that, provided both partners are taking advantage of their full exemption limit, a couple can make gains of £21,200 a year free of CGT. However, it is not possible to use the losses of one spouse to cover the gains of the other. Transfers between husband and wife remain tax free, although any income arising from such a gift will of course be taxed. Income will normally be treated as the recipient's for tax purposes.

Currently, any gains you make are taxed at 18 per cent for basic-rate taxpayers and 28 per cent for higher-rate and additional-rate taxpayers. (This rate is also unchanged from the previous year). Entrepreneurs and small business investors have been boosted in recent budgets by wide-ranging changes to flagship tax incentive schemes. Company owners will benefit from a doubling of the lifetime limit on 'entrepreneurs' relief' to £10 million from 6 April 2011. The relief limits CGT to 10 per cent on the sale of business assets under certain conditions.

Free of capital gains tax

The following assets are not subject to CGT and do not count towards the gains you are allowed to make:

> your main home (but see the note below);
>
> your car;
>
> personal belongings up to the value of £6,000 each;
>
> proceeds of a life assurance policy (in most circumstances);
>
> profits on UK government stocks;

National Savings certificates;

SAYE contracts;

building society mortgage cashbacks;

futures and options in gilts and qualifying corporate bonds;

Personal Equity Plan (PEP) schemes (now automatically ISAs);

gains from assets held in an Individual Savings Account (ISA);

Premium Bond winnings;

betting and lottery winnings and life insurance policies if you are the original owner;

gifts to registered charities;

small part-disposals of land (limited to 5 per cent of the total holding, with a maximum value of £20,000);

gains on the disposal of qualifying shares in a Venture Capital Trust (VCT) or within the Enterprise Investment Scheme (EIS), provided these have been held for the necessary holding period (see below).

Enterprise Investment Scheme (EIS)

Changes to investment limits and qualifying criteria will allow more companies to attract up to £10 million a year of equity investment through the Enterprise Investment Scheme (EIS) and Venture Capital Trusts (VCTs) – both tax-efficient investment schemes – since April 2012.

The rate of Income Tax relief available under EIS rose from 20 to 30 per cent in April 2011, while the personal annual investment allowance doubled in 2012 to £1 million. Companies with as many as 250 employees and gross assets of up to £15 million qualify – up from the current level of 50 staff and gross assets of £7 million.

This is a complex area and it is recommended that you seek advice from your tax adviser. See HMRC website: **www.hmrc.gov.uk**.

Your home

Your main home is usually exempt from CGT. However, there are certain 'ifs and buts' that could be important. If you convert part of your home into an office or into self-contained accommodation on which you charge rent, the part of your home that is deemed to be a 'business' may be separately assessed – and CGT may be payable when you come to sell it. (CGT would not apply if you simply take in a lodger who is treated as family, in the sense of sharing your kitchen or bathroom.)

If you leave your home to someone else who later decides to sell it, then he or she may be liable for CGT when the property is sold (although only on the gain since the date of death). There may also be inheritance tax implications, so if you are thinking of leaving or giving your home to someone you are strongly advised to consult a solicitor or accountant. If you own two homes, only one of them is exempt from CGT, namely the one you designate as your 'main residence'.

Selling a family business

With taper relief having been abolished in April 2008, the CGT now payable if you are selling a family business is 28 per cent for higher-rate and additional-rate taxpayers, but the reduced level of 18 per cent for basic-rate taxpayers. One possible option is the CGT deferral relief allowable to investors in an EIS.

Investors – including entrepreneur owners or directors with gains arising from the sale of shares in their own companies – can defer paying CGT and in many cases can also obtain income tax relief at 20 per cent on investments of up to £500,000 a year, provided gains are reinvested in qualifying unquoted companies (including AIM and Ofex companies) within three years. In recent years, some of the rules have been altered to create a more unified system of venture capital reliefs. The key changes that potential investors should note are:

the amount that can be invested is now £500,000 (previously £400,000);

the amount an individual may invest in shares issued in the first half of the tax year and qualifying for income tax relief for the previous year is now £50,000 (previously £25,000);

qualifying companies are limited to £7 million of gross assets before an investment (£8 million after an investment); and

companies with property-backed assets, such as farming and nursing homes, no longer qualify as eligible trading companies.

This is a complex area, so before either retiring or selling shares you should seek professional advice.

Useful reading

For further information about capital gains tax, see booklet CGT1, *Capital Gains Tax: An Introduction*, available from any tax office. There are also a number of useful Helpsheets downloadable from the HMRC website: **www.hmrc.gov.uk**.

Inheritance tax (IHT)

Inheritance tax (IHT) is the tax that is paid on your 'estate'. Broadly speaking, this is everything you own at the time of your death, less any debts you have. It's sometimes payable on assets you may have given away during your lifetime. Assets include property, possessions, money and investments.

The Chancellor has frozen the inheritance tax threshold (the level at which you'll need to pay tax) at £325,000 until 2014/15. The threshold amount for married couples and civil partners is £650,000. The value of estates over and above the allowance is taxed at 40 per cent.

Before any tax is calculated, there are a number of exemptions and other concessions that may be relevant. There is no immediate tax on lifetime gifts between individuals. The gifts become wholly exempt if the donor survives for seven years. When the donor dies, any gifts made within the previous seven years become chargeable and their value is added to that of the estate. The total is then taxed on the excess over £325,000. Chargeable gifts benefit first towards the £325,000 exemption, starting with the earliest gifts and continuing in the order in which they were given. Any unused balance of the £325,000 threshold goes towards the remaining estate.

Under the new rules, the £325,000 threshold allows married couples or civil partners to transfer the unused element of their IHT-free allowance to their spouse or civil partner when they die. For many couples this effectively doubles the tax-free amount they can bequeath to their children. IHT will, however, still be levied at 40 per cent above £325,000 on the estate of anyone who is single or divorced when they die.

To encourage donating to charity, the government has changed the tax law, starting in April 2012, and reduced the inheritance tax payable on estates that give at least 10 per cent to charity. It's called Legacy 10 and anyone who leaves at least one tenth of their estate to charity will have the remainder taxed at 36 per cent against the usual 40 per cent inheritance tax rate. (There is, however, no advantage to people with estates below the inheritance tax threshold.) Existing wills can be amended by codicil to include this 10 per cent provision.

Gifts or money up to the value of £3,000 can also be given annually free of tax, regardless of the particular date they were given. Additionally, it is possible to make small gifts to any number of individuals free of tax, provided the amount to each does not exceed £250.

A previous loophole, whereby it was possible for an owner to dispose of assets such as houses, paintings or boats but continue to enjoy the benefit of them, no longer exists. Under the current rules, designed to tighten up on avoidance of IHT, people who continue to have some usage of the property they formerly owned but do not pay the market rent will be charged yearly income tax on the retained benefit. As an alternative to the income tax charge, taxpayers can elect for IHT treatment on the relevant property in due course. The time limit for electing is the same as the self-assessment deadline for making a return for the tax year in which an individual is first liable for the pre-owned asset (POA) charge. For assistance see website: **www.gov.uk** – Probate and Inheritance Tax Helpline.

While most ex-owners or their heirs will end up paying one way or another, the Chancellor has built in certain exclusions and exemptions, including preserving the important principle that transfers of property between spouses remain exempt from any tax. Tax will equally not be charged if the asset is sold for full market value or if, owing to a change in circumstance, an owner who had previously given away a property needs to reoccupy his or her former home.

Quite apart from IHT, capital gains tax may have to be paid on any asset you left to a beneficiary, or as part of your estate, that is subsequently sold. HMRC treats such assets as having been acquired at the date of death and at their prevailing market value at the time. By the same token, CGT will have to be paid on any gain that has built up on an asset you gave away during your lifetime and that is subsequently sold.

Another important consideration that should not be overlooked is the need to make a will. The rules of intestacy are very rigid, and neglecting to make a proper will can have serious consequences for those whom you wish to benefit. (For further information, see 'Wills', in Chapter 16.) Likewise, if you have already written a will, it is strongly recommended that you have this checked by a professional adviser to ensure that you do not give money unnecessarily to HMRC. In view of the recent changes to IHT, check with your professional adviser or HMRC.

Tax treatment of trusts

There may be inheritance tax to pay when assets – such as money, land or buildings – are transferred into or out of trusts when they reach a 10-year anniversary. There are complex rules that determine whether a trust needs to pay IHT in such situations. Under the new rules for aligning the IHT treatment for trusts, those who have set up or have an interest in 'accumulation & maintenance' trusts (A&Ms) and/or 'interest in possession' trusts (IIPs) that do not meet new IHT rules about their terms and the circumstances in which they were created are most affected. The new rules came into effect on 22 March 2006 for new trusts, additions of new assets to existing trusts, and other IHT-relevant events in relation to existing trusts. Transitional rules provided for a period of adjustment for certain existing trusts to 6 April 2008.

Discretionary trusts are assessed for IHT on their 10th anniversary and every 10 years thereafter. Distributions from the trust may also trigger an IHT charge. These rules apply to trusts created during the settler's lifetime and those created within the settler's will. Since 2008, the same treatment applies to funds gifted on or after 22 March 2006 into most IIP and A&M trusts.

This is a particularly complex area, and professional advice is recommended. Further information is available on website: **www.hmrc.gov.uk** – Inheritance tax and trusts.

Independent taxation

Both husband and wife are taxed independently on their own income. Each has his or her own personal allowance and rate band, and both independently pay their own tax and receive their own tax rebates. Moreover, independent taxation applies equally to the age-related additions, and both husband and wife are now eligible for their own higher tax allowance from the age of 75.

A further important point for many couples is that independent taxation does not apply simply to income tax but equally to both capital gains tax and inheritance tax. As a result, both husband and wife enjoy their own CGT exemption (£10,600 in the 2012/13 tax year) and their own exemption from IHT (£325,000 – this limit frozen until 2014/15). Property left to a surviving spouse is, as before, free of inheritance tax.

Self-assessment

If you are one of the 9 million people who need to complete a tax return, you will probably be all too familiar with self-assessment. The tax return forms are sent out in April, and the details you need to enter on the form you receive in April 2013 are those relating to the 2012/13 tax year.

Even if a taxpayer has never had a tax return, and so is unlikely to be directly affected by self-assessment unless his or her circumstances change, all taxpayers now have a legal obligation to keep records of all their different sources of income and capital gains. These include:

details of earnings plus any bonus, expenses and benefits in kind received;

bank and building society interest;

dividend vouchers and/or other documentation showing gains from investments;

pension payments, eg both state and occupational or private pensions;

miscellaneous income, such as freelance earnings, maintenance payments and taxable social security benefits;

payments against which tax relief can be claimed (eg charitable donations or contributions to a personal pension).

HMRC advises that taxpayers are obliged to keep these records for 22 months after the end of the tax year to which they relate. If you are self-employed or a partner in a business, as well as the above list you also need to keep records of all your business earnings and expenses, together with sales invoices and receipts. All records (both personal and business) need to be kept for five years after the fixed filing date.

Those most likely to be affected by the self-assessment system include anyone who normally receives a tax return, higher-rate taxpayers, company directors, the self-employed and partners in a business. If your only income is your salary from which tax is deducted at source, you will not have to worry about self-assessment. If, however, you have other income that is not fully taxed under PAYE (eg possibly benefits in kind or expenses payments) or that is not fully taxed at source, you need to notify HMRC within six months of the end of the tax year, and you may need to fill in a tax return.

The same may be true when you retire. Even though you may not think of yourself as wealthy, if your financial affairs change, as they sometimes do on retirement (eg if you become self-employed or receive income that has not already been fully taxed), it is your responsibility to inform HMRC and, depending on the amount of money involved, you may need to complete a tax return. The government has recently revised the guidelines, and higher-rate taxpayers will no longer automatically receive a self-assessment form if their affairs can be handled through the PAYE system.

A very important point to know for anyone who might be feeling worried is that *self-calculation is optional*. If you think the calculations are too complicated or that you might be at risk of making a mistake, HMRC will continue as before to do the sums for you. Until recently, taxpayers who wanted HMRC to calculate their tax liability for them had to file their return by an earlier date. Today, this is no longer an issue. Instead, what matters is whether you file online or submit a paper return. Paper returns must be filed by 31 October each year; the deadline for online filing is 31 January the following year.

Further information

See booklets SA/BK4, *Self-Assessment – A General Guide to Keeping Records*; SA/BK6, *Self-Assessment – Penalties for Late Tax Returns*; SA/ BK7, *Self-Assessment – Surcharges for Late Payment of Tax* and SA/BK8, *Self-Assessment – Your Guide*, all obtainable free from any tax office. See website: **www.gov.uk** or HMRC website: **www.hmrc.gov.uk**.

Retiring abroad

There are many examples of people who retired abroad in the expectation of being able to afford a higher standard of living and who returned home a few years later, thoroughly disillusioned. As with other important decisions, this is where it is essential to research your options thoroughly. It is crucial to investigate property prices, as well as the cost of health care. As anyone who has ever needed a doctor or dentist abroad knows, the term 'free health service' does not always mean what it says. While these and similar points are perhaps obvious, a vital question that is often overlooked is the taxation effects of living overseas. If you are thinking of retiring abroad, do look into the effect this will have on your finances before you go.

Taxation abroad

Tax rates vary from one country to another: a prime example is VAT, which varies considerably in Europe. Additionally, many countries levy taxes that don't apply in the UK. Wealth tax exists in quite a few parts of the world. Estate duty on property left by one spouse to another is also fairly widespread. There are all sorts of property taxes, different from those in the UK, which – however described – are variously assessable as income or capital. Sometimes a special tax is imposed on foreign residents. Some countries charge income tax on an individual's worldwide income, without the exemptions that apply in the UK.

Apart from the essential of getting first-class legal advice when buying property overseas, if you are thinking of retiring abroad the golden rule must be to investigate the situation thoroughly before you take an irrevocable step, such as selling your home in the UK. A common mistake is for people to misunderstand their UK tax liabilities after their departure.

Your UK tax position if you retire overseas

Many intending emigrants cheerfully imagine that, once they have settled themselves in a dream villa overseas, they are safely out of the clutches of the UK tax office. This is not so. You first have to acquire non-resident status. If you have severed all your ties, including selling your home, to take up a permanent job overseas, this is normally granted fairly quickly. But for most retirees, acquiring unconditional non-resident status can take up to three years. The purpose is to check that you are not just having a prolonged holiday but are actually living as a resident abroad. During the check period, HMRC may allow you conditional non-resident status and, if it is satisfied, full status will be granted retrospectively.

Rules

The rules for non-residency are pretty stringent. You are not allowed to spend more than 182 days in the UK in any one tax year, or to spend more than an average of 90 days per year in the UK over a maximum of four tax years. Even if you are not resident in the UK, some of your income may still be liable for UK taxation.

UK income tax

All overseas income (provided it is not remitted to the UK) is exempt from UK tax liability. Income deriving from a UK source is, however, normally liable for UK tax. This includes any director's or consultant's fees you may still be receiving, as well as more obvious income such as rent from a property you still own.

An exception may be made if the country in which you have taken up residency has a double tax agreement with the United Kingdom (see below). If this is the case, you may be taxed on the income in your new residence – and not in the UK.

Additionally, interest paid on certain British government securities is not subject to tax. Non-residents may be able to arrange for their interest on a British bank deposit or building society account to be paid gross. Some former colonial pensions are also exempt.

Double tax agreement

A person who is a resident of a country with which the UK has a double taxation agreement may be entitled to exemption or partial relief from UK income tax on certain kinds of income from UK sources and may also be exempt from UK tax on the disposal of assets. The conditions of exemption or relief vary from agreement to agreement. It may be a condition of the relief that the income is subject to tax in the other country.

NB: if, as sometimes happens, the foreign tax authority later makes an adjustment and the income ceases to be taxed in that country, you have an obligation under the self-assessment rules to notify HMRC.

Capital gains tax

This is only charged if you are resident or ordinarily resident in the UK; so if you are in the position of being able to realize a gain, it is advisable to wait until you acquire non-resident status. However, to escape CGT you must wait to dispose of any assets until after the tax year of your departure and must remain non-resident (and not ordinarily resident) in the UK for five full tax years after your departure. Different rules apply to gains made from the disposal of assets in a UK company; these are subject to normal CGT.

Inheritance tax

You escape IHT only if:

you were domiciled overseas for all of the immediate three years prior to death;

you were resident overseas for more than three tax years in your final 20 years of life; and all your assets were overseas.

Even if you have been resident overseas for many years, if you do not have an overseas domicile you will have to pay IHT at the same rates as if you lived in the UK.

Domicile

Broadly speaking, you are domiciled in the country in which you have your permanent home. Domicile is distinct from nationality or residence. A person may be resident in more than one country, but at any given time he or she can be domiciled in only one. If you are resident in a country and intend to spend the rest of your days there, it could be sensible to decide to change your domicile. If, however, you are resident but there is a chance that you might move, the country where you are living would not qualify as your domicile. This is a complicated area, where professional advice is recommended if you are contemplating a change.

UK pensions paid abroad

Any queries about your pension should be addressed to the International Payments Office, **International Pensions Centre**. For contact details see website: **www.gov.uk** – International Pensions Centre.

Technically your state pension could be subject to income tax, as it derives from the UK. In practice, if this is your only source of UK income, tax is unlikely to be charged. If you have an occupational pension, UK tax will normally be charged on the total of the two amounts. Both state and occupational pensions may be paid to you in any country. If you are planning to retire to Australia, Canada, New Zealand or South Africa, it would be advisable to check on the up-to-date position regarding any annual increases you would expect to receive to your pension. Some people have found the level of their pension frozen at the date they left the UK, while others have been liable for unexpected tax overseas.

If the country where you are living has a double tax agreement with the UK, as previously explained, your income may be taxed there and not in the UK. The UK now has a double tax agreement with most countries. For further information, check the position with your local tax office. If your pension is taxed in the UK, you will be able to claim your personal allowance as an offset.

Health care overseas

People retiring to another EU country before state retirement age can apply for a form E106, which will entitle them to state health care in that country on the same basis as for local people. An E106 is valid only for a maximum of two and a half years, after which it is usually necessary to take out private insurance cover until state retirement age is reached. More information and advice can be obtained from the website: **www.gov.uk** – Britons living abroad. Thereafter, UK pensioners can request the International Pensions Centre at Newcastle (see under 'UK pensions paid abroad' above) for a form E121, entitling them and their dependants to state health care as provided by the country in which they are living.

Useful reading

The Tax Guide 2012 by David Genders, published by Kogan Page (new edition due May 2013); see website: **www.koganpage.com**. *Residents and Non Residents – Liability to Tax in the UK*, (IR20) is available from any tax office. Leaflet SA29, *Your Social Security Insurance, Benefits and Health Care Rights in the European Community*, contains essential information about what to do if you retire to another EU country. It is available from any social security or Jobcentre Plus office or website: **www.jobcentreplus.gov.uk**.

Chapter Five
Investment

Money frees you from doing things you dislike. Since I dislike doing nearly everything, money is handy. **GROUCHO MARX**

Most people would agree that money is always useful. But over the past few years it has been hard to get a decent return on any savings or investments due to rock-bottom interest rates and rising inflation. Some experts predict that interest rates will remain low for another year at least, and no one really expects them to rise significantly for some years. This is not good news for people relying on their savings to provide an income in retirement.

Last year, while we celebrated HM The Queen's Diamond Jubilee, we might have tried to remember what £100 would have purchased in 1952, compared to 2012. There is a remarkable difference. According to This is Money (the financial website of the year) £100 at the time of the Coronation could have purchased a decent second-hand car, or paid quite a good pro-portion of the deposit on a new home. By contrast, in today's money, it would probably cover only the cost of a week's groceries, a tank of petrol or a decent meal out with the family.

So what do you think might have represented the best investment over the past 60 years: shares, gold, property or savings? A house 60 years ago would have cost just under £2,000, according to Nationwide. Today it would be worth £165,000, representing a handsome return on your invest-ment. Whereas a £100 investment in shares would have returned just under £108,000, the same investment in gilts would have returned £6,850 and £100 deposited in a building society account would be worth around £6,000. So investing in a broad basket of shares appears to have been a shrewd way of saving for the long term. But of course none of these figures includes the effect of inflation, so real returns would have been far less impressive. Also, the impact of dividend reinvestment was huge so far as equities are concerned. So if you excluded dividends, the return would have been a fraction of the original figure quoted. The halcyon era for stock market investing certainly was from the early 1950s to the late 1980s.

Forgetting bonds and shares, gold has enjoyed a decent run recently. Six decades ago £100 would have bought you just over eight ounces of gold, which would be worth £8,167 today. This is based on an historical bullion price of £12.36 at 1952 exchange rates, so a good investment – but not the best. What about diamonds? The primary source of diamond prices only goes back to 1978. A one carat, top quality diamond has risen 52 per cent in value in that 34-year period. So if you were very lucky, you might have seen the price of top diamonds double in 60 years.

What came out top? Fine wine ... investors who bottled £100 in time for the Queen's coronation would have seen it rise to £478,000 in today's money (**www.thisismoney.co.uk/money/investing/article-2153637/What-best-investment-past-60-years.html**).

However, for those of us who need to make our money work hard for us while we enjoy our retirement, the best thing is to research ways of investing our money where yields beat the cost of living. The slight fall in inflation last year meant that prudent pensioners can now find savings accounts that beat inflation, and some fixed-rate bonds and cash ISAs which keep pace with the cost of living after tax. (This information was found on the comparison website: **www.moneysupermarket.com**.)

In addition to this, if you have modest amounts to save, there are still ways to build a nest egg and get a worthwhile return on your money. According to AgeUK's personal finance expert, here are some tips on making the most of saving and investing:

1 Save regularly, by setting up a monthly payment. If you get a pension increase, use part of it to increase the amount you save.

2 Be prepared – the first priority must be to build up a 'rainy day' fund. Ideally you should aim for three months' income in accounts you can access immediately.

3 Have a goal. Saving is easier if you know what you want to save for – a holiday, Christmas or a new car.

4 Don't let the taxman take 20p out of every £1 interest you earn. Use tax-free havens such as ISAs or National Savings Certificates or Premium Bonds.

5 Study the 'best buy' tables in your paper or on money comparison websites. Exclude those where the bonus lasts for less than a year.

Also check what access the account offers. Fixed-notice and fixed-term accounts pay more.

6   No investment is worth sleepless nights, so don't put your money anywhere you are uncertain of. If a deal looks too good to be true it probably is.

7   Disloyalty pays. Shop around regularly to be sure you still have the best-paying account.

8   Few accounts pay rates that match, let alone beat, inflation. Some new Index-Linked National Savings Certificates are being relaunched, so watch out and grab them – the last ones offered tax-free bonuses that matched inflation plus a percentage point or so on top.

9   Balancing risk and reward is key. Unfortunately life isn't risk free. Each individual has a different attitude to risk and there is a wide range of investments to choose from. Try to work out how risk averse you are.

10   Finally, don't forget the old adage about not putting all your eggs in one basket. Diversify and only take risks which you can afford.

Since everyone has different financial aims, there is no one-size-fits-all approach to investing. In very simple terms, there are four different types of investment you could consider:

1   *Cash investments* can be made into a bank account or cash ISA. These are generally short term and offer easy access to your money. They are lower risk and so the potential returns are much less than other types of investment. Your money is secure, but there is a real risk it will lose value due to tax and inflation.

2   *Bonds and gilts* are, effectively, an IOU from the government or big companies. When you buy one you are lending money that earns an agreed fixed rate of interest. Government bonds (called gilts) are backed by the state and are as good as guaranteed. Corporate bonds carry greater risk but offer the possibility of improved returns.

3   *Investing in property* directly as a buy-to-let investor or indirectly through certain investment funds carries more risk. Property prices go down as well as up, and it can take longer to sell property. So if you are thinking of investing in property, be sure to seek advice beforehand.

4   *Shares* are sometimes referred to as 'equities'. Investing in shares basically means putting money on the stock market. You can do this

by buying shares in individual companies or by investing through a professionally managed investment fund, such as a unit trust. There are a variety of unit trusts available, each with different objectives and each carrying different levels of risk and reward.

But whatever stage of life you've reached, your first priority for savings should usually be an emergency fund. This is money you can draw on to meet unexpected expenses, without having to borrow. While you are working many experts recommend that you have a fund equal to at least three months' take-home pay. This helps to protect your finances if you are off work due to illness or made redundant. As you get older you may not need such a big fund. Think about what emergencies you might face, how much they might cost and what you need to have put away for a rainy day.

Before we move on, just a word about inflation. This is any pensioner's worst enemy. As inflation rises, savings income is at risk. Between May 1990 and May 2010 inflation reduced the spending power of £1,000 to £564, a reduction of almost 50 per cent. Cash on deposit is relatively secure, offers immediate access and your capital is guaranteed up to the sterling equivalent of £100,000 (currently £85,000) under the Financial Services Compensation Scheme. However, once you have enough saved for a rainy day, it could pay to consider assets that offer higher potential returns.

Sources of investable funds

If you are looking at your investment options, you will need to work out where your investable funds are likely to be found. Possible sources of quite significant capital include:

Commuted lump sum from your pension. There is now one set of rules for all types of pension scheme, with members allowed a maximum of 25 per cent of their pension fund or 25 per cent of their lifetime limit, whichever is lower. There is no tax to pay when you receive the money.

Insurance policies designed to mature on or near your date of retirement. These are normally tax free.

Profits on your home, if you sell it and move to smaller, less expensive accommodation. Provided this is your main home, there is no capital gains tax to pay.

Redundancy money, golden handshake or other farewell gift from your employer. You are allowed £30,000 redundancy money free of tax. The same is usually true of other severance pay up to £30,000. But there can be tax to pay if, however worded, your employment contract indicates that these are deferred earnings.

Sale of SAYE and other share option schemes. The tax rules vary according to the type of scheme, the date the options were acquired and how long the shares were held before disposal. Since the rules are liable to change with each Budget statement, for further information see HMRC website: **www.hmrc.gov.uk**.

General investment strategy

Investments differ in their aims, their tax treatment and the amount of risk involved. One or two categories are best suited to the wealthy who can afford to take significant risks. Others, such as certain types of National Savings, would be more appropriate for the less affluent. If you are taking the idea of investing seriously, the aim for most people is to acquire a balanced portfolio. This could comprise a mix of investments variously designed to provide some income to supplement your pension and also some capital appreciation to maintain your standard of living in the long term.

Except for annuities and National Savings & Investments, which have sections to themselves, the different types of investment are listed by groups, as follows: variable interest accounts, fixed interest securities, equities and long-term lock-ups. As a general strategy and particularly in the current economic climate, it is a good idea to mix and match so your investments are spread across several groups. Here are some websites that are well worth checking out and have information on savings and investments:

Citizens Advice Bureau: **www.adviceguide.org.uk**;

Ethical Money: **www.ethicalmoney.org**;

Money Advice Service: **www.moneyadviceservice.org.uk**;

Money Facts: **www.moneyfacts.co.uk**;

Money Supermarket: **www.moneysupermarket.com**;

This is Money: **www.thisismoney.co.uk**;

Which?: **www.which.co.uk**.

Annuities

Those who have saved for retirement, by investing in a personal or company money-purchase plan, may be worried by the thought that their hard-saved money may not buy them as much pension income as they should get. The most popular way to convert the money saved up in a pension pot into income is to invest in an annuity. These are policies set up by insurance companies that promise to pay a guaranteed income for life, no matter how long the policyholder lives – in return for you handing over your pension savings. (An annuity is simply a pension but not everyone realizes that.) The money is paid to you by the annuity provider (insurer) and can be paid monthly, quarterly or annually. You can choose from a range of annuities: make sure it is the right type to suit your own needs. You do not need to use all your pension fund for an annuity. You can take 25 per cent of your fund as a tax-free lump sum. Annuity income is taxed, just like any other form of income, so if you are over the basic-rate threshold you'll pay 20 per cent on it. To find out how much you'll pay, use **www.incometaxchecker.com.**

You can use your pension pot to buy one, two or several different types of annuity that can help generate the income required. The income you receive will remain the same year in, year out. Once you've chosen your annuity provider, you cannot change your mind. That is why it is so important to think carefully before deciding which provider and product to choose. Payments are calculated according to life expectancy tables, and for this reason annuities are not such an attractive investment for those under 70. Other than your age, the key factor affecting the amount you will receive in payments is the level of interest rates at the time you buy: the higher these are, the more you will receive.

Unless you've picked a special type of annuity, payments usually stop when you die, even if you've only just taken it. While you live your annuity payout is safe because UK regulated insurers are covered by the Financial Services Compensation Scheme. That usually guarantees the annuity if the insurance company goes bust; currently you'd get at least 90 per cent of the payout due.

Savers are no longer forced to use most of their pension to buy a guaranteed income for life. Rules requiring most people to spend three-quarters of their pension savings on annuities have been scrapped. Since April 2011 pensioners are allowed to delay the purchase for as long as they wish or not buy one at all. This means they could pass their pension savings on to their heirs.

However, should you wish to purchase an annuity it would probably give you more immediate income than any other form of investment. But whether you actually get good value depends on how long you live. When you die, your capital will be gone and there will be no more payments, so if you die a short while after signing the contract, it will represent very bad value indeed. On the other hand, if you live a very long time, you may more than recoup your original capital. As a precaution against early death, it is possible to take out a capital-protected annuity, an annuity that includes a guaranteed payment period, or an annuity that transfers to your partner for the duration of his or her life. Any of these options will reduce the annuity income you receive but could be worth considering if your primary concern is to give your partner (or other beneficiaries) added security.

Factors that affect the income you receive from an annuity include: the size of your pension fund; whether you want the income to remain the same or increase each year; if you want to pass it to your spouse or dependants after death; your health. From the end of 2012 insurers are no longer allowed to take gender into account when fixing annuity rates. Rates for men will get worse – but might not improve much for women either.

One risk if you delay taking an annuity is that you will miss out on the income you would have received had you bought one earlier. Unless you are tactically delaying or looking to use a special type of delaying product, it is usually best to sort it out sooner. If you are tempted to delay because it seems such a big task choosing an annuity, you can ease the pain if you make the decision in stages.

The rate you get depends on the market. If you choose to delay because you hope annuity rates will rise, you could be in for a shock. Since we are all living longer, this means providers are having to pay out for longer, so rates are dropping.

Types of annuities

There is a whole range of annuities you can buy. Once you've bought an annuity, you usually can't change your mind so it is important to find the right one for you. Think carefully about any special needs you may have: are you anxious to make sure your retirement income is paid to your spouse on your death; do you want your income to rise with inflation?

Four months before you retire, you will receive information from your pension company about your options. Laziness is the only reason to opt for a provider's default rate. The annuity sector is growing, and with it the choices you can have when selecting your annuity. Don't forget annuity income is just like any other and therefore it will be taxed. You have a personal allowance (which is the amount of money you can earn tax free) and above that you pay 20 per cent tax; the next band is 40 per cent. Personal tax allowances increase at age 65, and then again at 75.

Check you are getting the correct allowance and that you have the right tax code. This tells the pension company how much tax to deduct and there is no guarantee that it will be right. For more information see **www.incometaxcalculator.com**. Specialist help for older people is available from **www.taxvol.org.uk**.

Most annuities fall into one of two main categories: conventional/level and investment-linked.

Conventional/level annuities

You will receive a fixed income for life – either at one level or varying (linked to inflation). This is the simplest and most straightforward annuity available. Approximately 85 per cent of people choose this type because they have the benefit of certainty. You know what your income will be for the rest of your life, no matter how long you live. But you will no longer gain from the investment of your pension fund. They are not flexible, so if you die (even if this is after only one payment) the fund is lost. Also, if the annuity rates are low at the time you lock into the scheme, your retirement income will be smaller than it possibly could be.

Investment-linked annuities

The amount you get for your annuity is dependent on the performance of one or more stock market-type investments. These annuities expose your pension funds to the ups and downs of the stock market. There is the possibility of rising retirement income: you are taking the risk that you may get less in the hope you will get more. Income levels will fluctuate and reduce in poor investment conditions, although there is a minimum limit below which your annuity income cannot fall. This type of annuity should be considered only after taking independent financial advice, and by those who have other assets on which they can live should the income level drop.

Remember: it is your choice whether you go down the conventional annuity route or choose the investment-linked product. Whichever route you choose, there's no going back on your decision, so take your time.

There are a few variations on each type: some additions can be made to whichever option you choose.

Guaranteed annuity

These pay out for a set number of years, even if you die. Such guarantees reduce the income, but not dramatically if you're younger. If you die within the guarantee period, your nominee will receive the balance of the guarantee as gradual income.

Joint-life annuities

These annuities continue to pay out after one partner dies. They are particularly suitable if you are married or in a civil partnership, and more especially if one partner has no pension. But they come at a cost: you will receive a lower income level. Joint-life annuities pay out as long as one of a couple is living and you have a choice of percentages for the survivor's pension, such as 100 per cent, 50 per cent and two-thirds, which are commonly offered.

Escalating annuities

This is where income grows with inflation. Inflation can have a detrimental effect on your income after you retire. Even at 3 per cent, inflation would mean a pension being halved in real terms in 23 years from when you retire. So if you want your annuity to increase with the cost of living, this is the type to choose. It is a conventional annuity that allows income to grow with inflation. It is linked to a measure of inflation (like CPI) or set to rise by a certain percentage each year. These are known as inflation-linked annuities. Annuities can also be linked to the stock market through an investment annuity.

Don't automatically opt for an inflation-linked annuity because you think it is protection against inflation. These are expensive and how well they perform compared to conventional annuities depends on what happens to inflation and how long you live. By choosing one of the inflation-linked annuities you could get an income 30 per cent to 40 per cent lower initially. The big question is, do you want relatively less money today and more later on in life, or vice versa?

Enhanced/impaired annuities

This type of annuity means more cash for smokers or those with poor health. They offer extra cash if your life is likely to be shorter than average. Poor health can mean a richer annuity because the insurance company calculates the length of time you are likely to live. You might like to opt for this type even if you feel fit and don't smoke. Some 40 per cent of people should consider buying an enhanced annuity as it could make a huge difference to their income. You can qualify on grounds such as blood pressure, high cholesterol or being overweight.

Remember that you can combine annuities. You do not have to use your pension pot for just one product. There are a number of imponderables, however – factors about which you cannot ever be certain. These include how long you will live, whether inflation will increase or decrease, and whether your personal situation will change. If you have a large pension pot, having a combination of products may be the solution. The normal rules of financial planning apply: spread your risk.

Variable annuities

These products are also known as 'third-way' products and guaranteed drawdown plans. They are sort of halfway between standard and invest-ment annuities. They provide a guaranteed lifetime income that is payable regardless of investment returns, but with the potential of a boost on top due to the investment. So you benefit from a guaranteed income for life without actually buying an annuity.

Also included are regular investment lock-ins, so if the fund increases in value so does the level of income. However, if the fund value falls, the income remains at the level of the last lock-in. Funds can be paid to bene-ficiaries on death. The guarantee depends on the financial strength and solvency of the insurance company. So the question is: how strong are the guarantees likely to be if the firm gets into difficulties? Flexibility is achieved through the rules for drawdown, which allow for income flexibility, control over investments and choice of death benefits.

There are some caveats with these products, however. The main ones are commission being paid to financial advisers who sell them and the fact that they are expensive and in many cases people would be better off with an annuity or an unsecured pension.

Alternatives to annuities

An unsecured pension (USP), formerly known as income drawdown, allows you to take the 25 per cent tax-free lump sum and keep hold of your pension fund rather than trading it in for an annuity. You can then also take an annual income of up to 1.2 times the amount you'd get with a conventional annuity, plus the money can be passed on to your family.

By doing this you can keep the bulk of your pension fund invested, until age 75, at which point you must buy an annuity. You do need to have other cash available to live on into retirement. USPs are relatively high risk and are generally not recommended for those with pension funds worth less than £200,000.

An alternatively secured pension (ASP) is a new type of limited drawdown plan that you can use after the age of 75. An ASP works in much the same way as a USP; the difference is that the maximum income you can draw is 90 per cent of what you'd get with a level single lifetime annuity, and the minimum is 55 per cent. You might consider ASPs to maximize the death benefits for your family, if you do not need to use your pension pot to fund retirement and are against buying an annuity. When you die, the remaining fund must be used to provide benefits for any surviving dependants, although there are potentially very large tax charges associated with this. You can pass on any funds at death to charity, without incurring tax, provided there are no dependants remaining.

Fixed-term annuities are similar. With these you invest in a plan that provides guaranteed income payments for a set number of years or until you reach 75. At the end of the period you get a guaranteed maturity sum and are free to go back into the market to buy another type of annuity. These are a useful way to postpone your final annuity purchase, if you think your circumstances will change. They allow you to choose from a range of income and death benefit options now, as well as deciding what maturity amount you wish to have returned at the end of the term.

Tax

It is important in all the above plans to carefully consider the tax implications. Income tax on optional annuities is relatively low, as part of the income is allowed as a return on capital that is not taxable. Pension-linked annuities are fully taxable.

How to obtain an annuity

The annuity market is expanding rapidly and there is a vast choice of products. Specialists in annuity advice are:

Annuity Direct: **www.annuitydirect.co.uk**;

Annuity Advisor: **www.annuity-advisor.co.uk**;

Annuity Bureau: **www.annuity-bureau.co.uk**;

Hargreaves Lansdown: **www.H-L.co.uk**;

Origen Annuities: **www.origenfsannuities.co.uk**;

William Burrows: **www.williamburrows.com**.

You can also buy an annuity either direct from an insurance company or via an intermediary, such as an Independent Financial Adviser (IFA). It is wise to research this thoroughly and shop around, since (as mentioned above) the payments vary considerably. With many advisers you can choose how you pay. If you already have an IFA, he or she will talk you through the various options. Otherwise, to find an IFA, see Chapter 6, Financial advisers, or consult the professional advice websites:

Unbiased.co.uk: **www.unbiased.co.uk**;

The Institute of Financial Planning: **www.financialplanning.org.uk**;

Personal Finance Society (PFS) **www.findanadviser.org**.

National Savings & Investments (NS&I)

NS&I is one of the biggest savings institutions in the country, guaranteed by the government, and all investments are backed by HM Treasury. For many people it is attractive because it is extremely easy to invest in NS&I products. All you need do is go to the post office for information or check the **NS&I** website: **www.nsandi.com**. Most types of investment offered by NS&I are broadly similar to those provided by banks and other financial bodies. Full details of all their products are listed on the website, so only brief details appear here.

NS&I Savings Certificates, of which there are two types (fixed interest and index linked), are free of tax. Although in most cases they do not pay a particularly high rate of interest, any investment that is tax free is worth considering. For non-taxpayers who invest in NS&I products there is no need to complete an HM Revenue & Customs (HMRC) form to receive their money in full, as this is automatic.

The main investments offered by National Savings & Investments are:

Easy Access Savings Accounts. This is an easy way to build up your savings, with instant access to your money and the option to save regularly by standing order. The account offers variable, tiered rates of interest and allows instant access through the post office or cash machines.

Income Bonds. A safe and simple way of earning additional income every month. They pay fairly attractive, variable, tiered rates of interest, increasing with larger investments. Interest is taxable, but paid in full without deduction of tax at source. There is no set term for the investment.

Fixed Interest Savings Certificates are lump-sum investments that earn guaranteed rates of interest over set terms. There are two terms: two years and five years. For maximum benefit, you must hold the certificates for five years.

Index-linked Savings Certificates. Inflation-beating tax-free returns guarantee that your investment will grow in spending power each year whatever happens to the cost of living. Certificates must be retained for either three or five years. Interest is tax free.

Children's Bonus Bonds allow you to invest for a child's future in their own name – and there's no tax to pay on the interest or bonuses. Interest rates are fixed for five years at a time plus a guaranteed bonus. These are tax free for parents and children and need not be declared to HMRC.

Complaints

If you have a complaint about any NS&I product, you should raise this with the Director of Savings. Should the matter not be resolved to your satisfaction it can be referred to the **Financial Ombudsman Service**; see website: **www.financial-ombudsman.org.uk**.

Variable interest accounts

You can save in a wide range of savings accounts with banks, building societies, credit unions and National Savings & Investments (NS&I) – already mentioned. Most banks and building societies offer interest-bearing current accounts but they have different interest rates and access conditions. Because there are around 54 million current accounts in the UK, there is a lot of competition among banks to get business and persuade people to switch their accounts.

The difference between in-credit and overdraft rates vary considerably so check very carefully what charges apply before you move. Another point to investigate is whether there is a fixed monthly or other charge. This can sometimes change at fairly short notice. You should check your monthly statement carefully and consider moving your account if you are dissatisfied. Banks and building societies frequently introduce new accounts with introductory bonuses, which are then slashed in value after a few months. Although this could equally apply to internet accounts, they could still be worth investigating as, generally speaking, they tend to offer more competitive rates.

Although keeping track may be fairly time consuming, at least comparing the rates offered by different savings institutions has become very much easier, as all advertisements for savings products must now quote the annual equivalent rate (AER). Unlike the former variety of ways of expressing interest rates, the AER provides a true comparison taking into account the frequency of interest payments and whether or not interest is compounded.

But a word of caution: Silver Savers should beware of being ripped off by banks that tempt them into opening an age-tailored account. Millions of over-50s sign up for a specialist savings account on the assumption they will receive a premium interest rate because of their age. But recent research by investment advice firm Governor Money has found mature customers are losing out significantly compared to normal all-round products. The over-50s are being advised to show added caution when signing up to a savings account, particularly if it is tailored to their age. By looking only at over-50s products, savers would be ignoring over 93 per cent of the market. There are around 43 different variable-rate bank accounts available for the over-50s in the UK, offered by 22 different providers (The Mature Times – **www.maturetimes.co.uk**).

Definition

Other than the interest-bearing current accounts described above, these are all 'deposit'-based savings accounts of one form or another, arranged with banks, building societies, the National Savings & Investments Bank, and some financial institutions that operate such accounts jointly with banks. The accounts include, among others, instant-access accounts, high-interest accounts and fixed-term savings accounts.

Your money collects interest while it is in the account, which may be automatically credited to your account or for which you may receive a regular cheque. Some institutions pay interest annually; others – on some or all of their accounts – will pay it monthly. If you have a preference, this is a point to check.

Although you may get a poor return on your money when interest rates drop, your savings will nearly always be safe, as you are not taking any kind of investment risk. You'll usually get back the money you put in plus interest, unless the bank or building society gets into serious financial difficulty. For your protection, provided you deal with an authorized bank, up to £85,000 of your money will be 100 per cent protected under the **Financial Services Compensation Scheme**. See website: **www.fscs.org.uk**.

Access

Access to your money depends on the type of account you choose: you may have an ATM card and/or chequebook and withdraw your money when you want; you may have to give a week's notice or slightly longer; or, if you enter into a term account, you will have to leave your money deposited for the agreed specified period. In general, accounts where a slightly longer period of notice is required earn a better rate of interest.

Sum deposited

You can open a savings account with as little as £1. For certain types of account, the minimum investment could be anything from £500 to about £5,000. The terms tend to vary according to how keen the institutions are, at a given time, to attract small investors.

Tax

With the exception of cash ISAs which are tax free, and of the National Savings & Investments Bank, where interest is paid gross, tax is deducted at source – so you can spend the money without worrying about the tax implications. However, you must enter the interest on your tax return and, if you are a higher-rate taxpayer, you will have additional liability.

Basic-rate taxpayers pay 20 per cent on their bank and building society interest. Higher-rate taxpayers pay 40 per cent. Non-taxpayers can arrange to have their interest paid in full by completing a certificate (R85, available from HMRC or the bank) that enables the financial institution to pay the interest gross. If you largely rely on your savings income and believe you are or have been paying excess tax, you can reclaim this from HMRC. For further information, see 'Income tax on savings and investments' in Chapter 4.

Choosing a savings account

There are two main areas of choice: the type of savings account and where to invest your money. The relative attractions of the different types of account and of the institutions themselves can vary according to the terms being offered at the time. Generally speaking, however, the basic points are as follows.

Instant-access savings account

This attracts a relatively low rate of interest, but it is both easy to set up and very flexible, as you can add small or large savings when you like and can usually withdraw your money without any notice. It is an excellent temporary home for your cash if you are saving short term for, say, a holiday. However, it is not recommended as a long-term savings plan.

High-interest savings account

Your money earns a higher rate of interest than it would in an ordinary savings account. However, to open a high-interest account you will need to deposit a minimum sum, which could be £500 to £1,000. Although you can always add to this amount, if your balance drops below the required minimum your money will immediately stop earning the higher interest rate. Terms vary between providers. There may be a minimum and/or maximum monthly sum you can pay into the account. Also, some accounts have a fixed term, at the end of which your money will no longer earn the more favourable rate of interest. Usually interest is only paid yearly, and you can only withdraw yearly.

Fixed-term savings account

You deposit your money for an agreed period of time, which can vary from a few months to over a year. In return for this commitment, you will normally be paid a superior rate of interest. As with high-interest accounts, there is a minimum investment: roughly £1,500 to £10,000. If you need to withdraw your money before the end of the agreed term, there are usually hefty penalties. Before entering into a term account, you need to be sure that you can afford to leave the money in the account. Additionally, you will need to take a view about interest rates: if they are generally low, your money may be better invested elsewhere.

Equity-linked savings account

This offers a potentially better rate of return, as the interest is calculated in line with the growth in the stock market. Should the market fall, you may lose the interest, but your capital should normally remain protected. The minimum investment varies from about £500 to £5,000 and, depending on the institution; the money may need to remain deposited for perhaps as much as five years. Do ensure you fully understand all the terms and conditions, as rules vary.

ISA savings

See later in this chapter, page 115.

Information

For banks, enquire direct at your nearest high street branch. There will be leaflets available describing the different accounts in detail, or if you have any questions you can ask to see your bank manager. You can also investigate the other banks to see whether they offer better terms. For building societies, enquire at any branch. There is such a wide range of these that it is advisable to look at a number of them, as the terms and conditions may vary quite widely.

The **Building Societies Association** offers information and advice on savings and types of accounts and much more. See its website: **www.bsa.org.uk**.

The safety of your investment

Investors are protected by the legislative framework in which societies operate and, in common with bank customers, their money (up to a stated maximum) is protected under the **Financial Services Compensation Scheme**. See website: **www.fscs.org.uk**.

Complaints

If you have a complaint against a bank or building society, you can appeal to the **Financial Ombudsman Service** (FOS) to investigate the matter, provided the complaint has already been taken through the particular institution's own internal disputes procedure – or after eight weeks if the problem has not been resolved – and provided the matter is within the scope of the Ombudsman Scheme. Generally speaking, the FOS can investigate complaints about the way a bank or building society has handled some matter relating to its services to customers. See website: **www.financial-ombudsman.org.uk**.

Fixed interest securities

In contrast to variable interest accounts, fixed interest securities pay interest at a rate that does not change with any external variable. The coupon payments are known in advance. Coupons are almost always all for the same amount and paid at regular intervals, regardless of what happens to interest rates generally. There are two risks with fixed income securities: credit risk and interest rate risk.

Credit risk is one of the main determinants of the price of a bond. The price of a debt security can be explained as the present value of the payments (of interest and repayment of principal) that will be made. Credit risk is an issue for lenders such as banks. In this context, the key is the risk of losses to the bank, so correlation with the bank's other lending is what matters, not correlation with debt available in the market.

Interest rate risk is simply the risk to which a portfolio or institution is exposed because future interest rates are uncertain. Bond prices are interest rate sensitive so if rates rise, the present value of a bond will fall sharply. This can also be thought of in terms of market rates: if interest rates rise, then the price of a bond will have to fall for the yield to match the new market rates. The longer the duration of a bond, the more sensitive it will be to movements in interest rates. Banks can have significant interest rate risk: they may have depositors locked into fixed rates and borrowers on floating rates or vice versa. Interest rate risk can be hedged using swaps and interest rate-based derivatives.

If you buy when the fixed rate is high and interest rates fall, you will nevertheless continue to be paid interest at the high rate specified in the contract note. However, if interest rates rise above the level when you bought, you will not benefit from the increase. Generally these securities give high income but only modest, if any, capital appreciation. The securities include high interest gilts, permanent interest-bearing shares, local authority bonds and stock exchange loans, debentures and preference shares.

Gilt-edged securities

Definition

Gilts, or gilt-edged securities, are bonds issued by the UK government that offer the investor a fixed interest rate for a predetermined, set time, rather than one that goes up or down with inflation. While their value, like shares, is prone to fluctuation, gilts are well known for their security and are viewed as the safest of investments, hence their original name, 'gilt-edged securities'. While stock has a redemption date, typically between five and 25 years, it can be sold at any time for the present market price. Investors are not tied down and there are no penalties for selling the stock. By the time the redemption date is reached, the government will pay the investor the face value of the stock, which could be more or less than the original price, providing a capital gain or loss.

You can buy and sell gilts on the stock market or use the Bank of England's dealing service. Gilt value is influenced by many factors, including inflation, other competing forms of investment and the time left till maturity. Buying gilts is best done when interest rates are high and look likely to fall. When general interest rates fall, the value of the stock will rise and can be sold profitably. When buying or selling, consideration must be given to the accrued interest that will have to be added to or subtracted from the price quoted. Gilts are complicated by the fact that you can either retain them until their maturity date, in which case the government will return the capital in full, or sell them on the London Stock Exchange at market value.

Investors have continued to invest in them as a safe haven, and so have pushed up their prices. The result has been that the available return, or yield, on buying them has fallen. The yields are now approaching 2 per cent and there are some predictions that they may even fall below this level. This is a real possibility if bank interest rates remain at current levels.

Index-linked gilts

Index-linked gilts are government-issued bonds – glorified IOUs – that you can buy to obtain a guaranteed rate of return over inflation. They performed impressively in 2011, with some funds that invest in them providing returns of well over 10 per cent. If you are buying them now you will be doing so at a premium and it is likely you will suffer capital losses as their value falls back, even while your income remains above inflation. However, if you are less worried about preserving your capital and require inflation-linked income, then these can still be useful in a balanced portfolio.

Tax

Gilt interest from whatever source is paid gross. Gross payment does not mean that you avoid paying tax, rather that you must allow for a future tax bill before spending the money. Recipients who prefer to receive the money net of tax can ask for this to be arranged. A particular attraction of gilts is that no capital gains tax is charged on any profit you may have made, but equally no relief is allowed for any loss.

How to buy

You can buy gilts through banks, building societies, a stockbroker or a financial intermediary, or you can purchase them through **Computershare Investor Services**; see website: **www.computershare.com**. In all cases, you will be charged commission.

Assessment

Gilts normally pay reasonably good interest and offer excellent security, in that they are backed by the government. You can sell at very short notice, and the stock is normally accepted by banks as security for loans, if you want to run an overdraft. However, gilts are not a game for amateurs as, if you buy or sell at the wrong time you could lose money; and, if you hold your stock to redemption, inflation could take its toll on your original investment. Index-linked gilts, which overcome the inflation problem, are generally speaking a better investment for higher-rate taxpayers – not least because the interest paid is very low.

Gilt plans

This is a technique for linking the purchase of gilt-edged securities and with-profit life insurance policies to provide security of capital and income over a 10- to 20-year period. It is a popular investment for the commuted lump sum taken on retirement. These plans are normally obtainable from financial intermediaries, who should be authorized by the Financial Services Authority (FSA).

Permanent interest-bearing shares (PIBS)

These are a form of investment offered by some building societies to financial institutions and private investors as a means of raising share capital. They have several features in common with gilts, as follows. They pay a fixed rate of interest that is set at the date of issue; this is likely to be on the high side when interest rates generally are low and on the low side when interest rates are high. The interest is usually paid twice yearly and – again, similarly to gilts – there is no stamp duty to pay or capital gains tax on profits. Despite the fact that PIBS are issued by building societies, they are very different from normal building society investments and have generally been rated as being in the medium-to-high risk category. Anyone thinking of investing their money should seek professional advice.

Equities

These are all stocks and shares, purchased in different ways and involving varying degrees of risk. They are designed to achieve capital appreciation as well as give you some regular income. Most allow you to get your money out within a week. Millions of people in the UK invest in shares. Equity securities usually provide steady income as dividends but there is always some risk. They may fluctuate significantly in their market value with the ups and downs in the economic cycle and the fortunes of the issuing firm. Investing has become very much easier, largely as a result of the increase in the number of internet-based trading facilities.

For those who believe in caution, the gamble can be substantially reduced by avoiding obviously speculative investments and by choosing a spread of investments, rather than putting all your eggs in one basket. Equities include ordinary shares, unit trusts, OEICs (see below), investment trusts and REITs.

Equities probably provide the greatest potential for income that can beat inflation over the medium to long term. Dividend yields on many equity funds are currently in excess of 3–4 per cent per annum, due to the corporate world's finances being in a healthier state than those of governments. Most businesses are well placed to continue to pay decent levels of dividends unless there is a protracted period of economic recession.

Unit trusts and OEICs

Definition

Unit trusts and OEICs (Open-Ended Investment Companies, a modern equivalent of unit trusts) are forms of shared investments, or funds, which allow you to pool your money with thousands of other people and invest in world stock markets. Your money is pooled in a fund run by professional managers, who invest the capital in a wide range of assets including equities, bonds and cash. The advantages are that it is usually less risky than buying individual shares, it is simple to understand, you get professional management and there are no day-to-day decisions to make. Additionally, every fund is required by law to have a trustee (called a 'depository' in the case of OEICs) to protect investors' interests.

Unit trusts have proved incredibly popular because your money is invested in a broad spread of shares and your risk is reduced, but they are rapidly being replaced by the OEIC (pronounced 'oik'). The FSA's rules governing which types of fund can convert to OEICs were relaxed in 2001 and since then the majority of fund management groups have converted their unit trusts to OEICs or launched such funds.

The minimum investment in some of the more popular funds can be as little as £25 a month or a £500 lump sum; both are relatively painless and a good way to get on the first rung of investing in the stock market. You could, however, invest a much higher amount. Investors' contributions to the fund are divided into units (shares in OEICs) in proportion to the amount they have invested. Unit trusts and OEICs are both open-ended investments. As with ordinary shares, you can sell all or some of your investment by telling the fund manager that you wish to do so. The value of the shares you own in an OEIC, or units in a unit trust, always reflects the value of the fund's assets. The key differences between the two are:

Pricing: when investing in unit trusts, you buy units at the offer price and sell at the lower bid price. The difference in the two prices is known as the spread. To make a return the bid price must rise above the offer before you sell the units. An OEIC fund contrastingly has a single price, directly linked to the value of the fund's underlying investments. All shares are bought and sold at this single price. An OEIC is sometimes described as a 'what you see is what you get' product.

Flexibility: an OEIC fund offers different types of share or sub-fund to suit different types of investor. The expertise of different fund management teams can be combined to benefit both large and small investors. There is less paperwork as each OEIC will produce one report and accounts for all sub-funds.

Complexity: unit trusts are, legally, much more complex, which is one of the reasons for their rapid conversion to OEICs. Unit trusts allow an investor to participate in the assets of the trust without actually owning any. Investors in an OEIC buy shares in that investment company.

Management: with unit trusts, the fund's assets are protected by an independent trustee and managed by a fund manager. OEICs are protected by an independent depository and managed by an authorized corporate director.

Charges: unit trusts and OEICs usually have an upfront buying charge, typically 3–5 per cent, and an annual management fee of between 0.5 and 1.5 per cent. It is possible to reduce these charges by investing through a discount broker or fund supermarket, but bear in mind that this means acting without financial advice. Charges on OEICs are relatively transparent, shown as a separate item on your transaction statement.

Investment trusts

Over the past decade investment trusts beat unit trusts in eight of nine key sectors. There are four major advantages an investment trust has over a unit trust:

1 *Cost*. The initial charges on unit trusts typically range from 4 to 6 per cent but there is also the annual fee costing in the region of 1.5 to 2 per cent. An investment trust also levies annual fees, but on average they are lower. The main reason is that most investment trusts don't pay commission to financial advisers.

2 *Gearing*. Like other companies, investment trusts are fairly free to borrow for investment purposes. Unit trusts, however, are usually restricted by regulation. But when markets are rising and the trust is run well, gearing will deliver superior returns.

3 *Size*. Investment trusts tend to be smaller than unit trusts on average, and so are less unwieldy and more focused on their investment objectives. To grow beyond their initial remit, they need permission from shareholders. Many also have a fixed life expectancy. Conversely, unit trusts are called 'open ended' because they can expand and contract to meet demand. (Big is not always beautiful.)

4 *Discounts*. Because their shares are listed and traded freely (unlike a unit trust, where all deals go via the fund manager and a unit price is only available at prescribed times), investment trusts can end up with a market capitalization that is greater than (at a 'premium'), or lower than (at a 'discount') its assets under management (the 'net asset value', or NAV). If the discount narrows after you buy you'll make a small gain on top of any increase in the trust's NAV.

How to obtain

Units and shares can be purchased from banks, building societies, insurance companies, stockbrokers, specialist investment fund providers and Independent

Financial Advisers, directly from the management group and via the internet. Many of the larger firms may use all these methods. For a list of unit trusts, investment trusts and OEICs the **Investment Management Association** (IMA) website gives information: **www.investmentfunds.org.uk**. Other useful websites include:

> **www.thisismoney.co.uk/investing;**
>
> **www.moneyweek.com;**
>
> **www.moneysupermarket.com;**
>
> **www.investment-advice.org.uk;**
>
> **www.investorschronicle.co.uk.**

For further information on investment advice, see Chapter 6, Financial advisers.

Tax

Units and shares invested through an ISA have special advantages (see 'Individual Savings Account', below). Otherwise, the tax treatment is identical to that of ordinary shares.

Assessment

Unit trusts and OEICs are an ideal method for smaller investors to buy stocks and shares: both less risky and easier. This applies especially to tracker funds, which have the added advantage that charges are normally very low. Some of the more specialist funds are also suitable for those with a significant investment portfolio.

Complaints

Complaints about unit trusts and OEICs are handled by the **Financial Ombudsman Service** (FOS). It has the power to order awards of up to £100,000. Before approaching the FOS, you must first try to resolve the problem with the management company direct via its internal complaints procedure. If you remain dissatisfied, the company should advise you of your right to refer the matter to the FOS; see website: **www.financial-ombudsman.org.uk.**

The safety of your investment

Investors are protected by the legislative framework and, in common with bank customers, their money (up to a stated maximum) is protected under the **Financial Services Compensation Scheme** (FSCS); see website: **www.fscs.org.uk**.

Ordinary shares listed on the London Stock Exchange

Definition

Public companies issue shares as a way of raising money. When you buy shares and become a shareholder in a company, you own a small part of the business and are entitled to participate in its profits through a dividend, which is normally paid six monthly. Dividends go up and down according to how well the company is doing, and it is possible that in a bad year no dividends at all will be paid. However, in good years, dividends can increase very substantially.

The money you invest is unsecured. This means that, quite apart from any dividends, your capital could be reduced in value – or if the company goes bankrupt you could lose the lot. Against this, if the company performs well you could substantially increase your wealth. The value of a company's shares is decided by the stock market. Thousands of large and small investors are taking a view on each company's prospects, and this creates the market price. The price of a share can fluctuate daily, and this will affect both how much you have to pay if you want to buy and how much you will make (or lose) if you want to sell. See the **London Stock Exchange** website: **www.londonstockexchange.com**, to find a list of brokers in your area that would be willing to deal for you. Alternatively, you can go to the securities department of your bank or to one of the authorized share shops, which will place the order for you.

Whether you use a stockbroker, a share shop, a telephone share-dealing service or the internet, you will be charged both commission and stamp duty, which is currently 0.5 per cent. Unless you use a nominee account (see below), you will be issued with a share certificate that you or your financial adviser must keep, as you will have to produce it when you wish to sell all or part of your holding. It is likely, when approaching a stockbroker or other share-dealing service, that you will be asked to deposit money for your investment upfront or advised that you should use a nominee account. This is because of the introduction of several new systems, designed to speed up and streamline the share-dealing process.

There are three types of share, all quoted on the London Stock Exchange, that are potentially suitable for small investors. These are investment companies, REITs and convertible loan stocks. Other possibilities, but only for those who can afford more risky investments, are zero coupon loan stocks and warrants.

Investment companies are companies that invest in the shares of other companies. They pool investors' money and so enable those with quite small amounts to spread the risk by gaining exposure to a wide portfolio of shares, run by a professional fund manager. There are hundreds of different companies to choose from; see the **Association of Investment Companies** website: **www.theaic.co.uk**.

Real estate investment trusts (REITs). This type of fund operates similarly to investment trusts. They pool investors' money and invests it for them collectively in commercial and residential property. They offer individuals a cheap, simple and potentially less risky way of buying shares in a spread of properties, with the added attraction that the funds themselves are more tax efficient, as both rental income and profits from sales are tax free within the fund. Also, if wanted, REITs can be held within an ISA or Self-Invested Personal Pension (SIPP). There are numerous UK companies that have converted to REIT status. Stockbrokers and Independent Financial Advisers are able to provide information and it is recommended that professional advice is taken before investing.

Convertible loan stocks give you a fixed guaranteed income for a certain length of time and offer you the opportunity to convert them into ordinary shares. While capital appreciation prospects are lower, the advantage of convertible loans is that they usually provide significantly higher income than ordinary dividends. They are also allowable for ISAs.

Zero coupon loan stocks provide no income during their life but pay an enhanced capital sum on maturity. They would normally only be regarded as suitable for higher-rate taxpayers, and professional advice is strongly recommended.

Warrants are issued by companies or investment trusts to existing shareholders either at launch or by way of an additional bonus. Each warrant carries the right of the shareholder to purchase additional shares at a predetermined price on specific dates in the future. Warrants command their own price on the stock market. They are a high-risk investment, and professional advice is essential.

Tax

All UK shares pay dividends net of 10 per cent corporation tax. Basic-rate and non-taxpayers have no further liability to income tax. Higher-rate taxpayers must pay further income tax at 22 per cent. Quite apart from income tax, if during the year you make profits by selling shares that in total exceed £10,600 (the annual exempt amount for an individual in 2012/13) you will be liable for capital gains tax, which is now calculated at a flat rate of 28 per cent.

Assessment

Although dividend payments generally start low, in good companies they are likely to increase over the years and so provide a first-class hedge against inflation. The best equities are an excellent investment. In others, you can lose all your money. Good advice is critical, as this is a high-risk, high-reward market.

Individual Savings Account (ISA)

Definition

ISAs are savings accounts launched in April 1999 as a replacement for PEPs and TESSAs. They contain many of the same advantages in that all income and gains generated in the account are tax free. They are simply a tax-free savings account. There is a subscription limit. There are two types of ISA: cash ISAs and stocks and shares ISAs. Since 6 April 2012 it has been possible to invest £5,640 per year in a cash ISA and up to £11,280 in a stocks and shares ISA without paying any income tax on the interest.

From 6 April 2012 the ISA limits increased in line with the RPI on an annual basis. In the event that the RPI is negative, the ISA limits will remain unchanged. The cash ISA limit remains half the value of the stocks and shares ISA limit.

New junior ISAs have an annual contribution allowance of £3,600 (2012/13) and are available to all children born on or after 3 January 2011, or born before September 2002, or are under 18 and do not have a Child Trust Fund (see below).

Tax

ISAs are completely free of all income tax and capital gains tax. You should be aware that a 20 per cent charge is levied on all interest accruing from non-invested money held in an ISA that is not specifically a cash ISA.

Assessment

ISAs offer a simple, flexible way of starting, or improving, a savings plan, although sadly they are no longer as attractive as they once were, and some readers may now find better homes for investing their money. While cash ISAs remain useful, as all interest is tax free, stocks and shares ISAs – while still potentially worthwhile for higher-rate taxpayers – offer fewer advantages to basic-rate taxpayers as a result of the charges and the removal of the dividend tax credit.

For further information on the various forms of ISAs, see these websites:

www.thisismoney.co.uk/investing;

www.moneyweek.com;

www.moneysupermarket.com;

www.investment-advice.org.uk;

www.investorschronicle.co.uk;

www.investmentfunds.org.uk.

NB: Be warned, however, that two years after a promise to improve their service, cutting the number of days allowed for a transfer from 30 to 15, banks continue to lose transfer money, causing delays and short-changing their ISA customers. Complaints have poured in from ISA savers who have been tempted with tax-free offers – who have tried, and failed – to have their savings transferred from one cash ISA to another. The over-60s, who rely on their savings to bolster their pensions, are being hardest hit because they must move their money regularly to earn decent interest rates. The best way of dealing with this situation is to know the rules:

1 Go to your new ISA provider and ask it to arrange the transfer. Industry guidelines give banks and building societies 15 working days to carry out the transfer.

2 Complain to the bank or building society immediately the 15 days are up.

3 Your old ISA provider must inform you and your new ISA provider if it thinks there will be a delay of five days or more.

4 You earn your new interest rate from the date of the cheque sent from your old provider or day 16 of the transfer process, whichever is the sooner.

5 Some providers pay the higher rate from the day they receive your application form (source: **www.thisismoney.co.uk**).

Child Trust Funds

Children born after December 2010 are not eligible for a Child Trust Fund. However, accounts set up for eligible children will continue to benefit from tax-free investment growth. Withdrawals will not be possible until the child reaches 18. The child, friends and family will be able to contribute £1,200 per year and it will still be possible to change the type of account and move it to another provider. See website: **www.childtrustfund.gov.uk**.

Useful Reading

How the Stock Market Works by Michael Becket of the *Daily Telegraph*, published by Kogan Page; see website: **www.koganpage.com**.

Long-term lock-ups

Certain types of investment, mostly offered by insurance companies, provide fairly high guaranteed growth in exchange for your undertaking to leave a lump sum with them or to pay regular premiums for a fixed period, usually five years or longer. The list includes life assurance policies, investment bonds and some types of National Savings Certificates.

Life assurance policies

Definition

Life assurance can provide you with one of two main benefits: it can either provide your successors with money when you die or it can be used as a savings plan to provide you with a lump sum (or income) on a fixed date. In the past, it was very much an 'either/or' situation: you chose whichever type of policy suited you and the insurance company paid out accordingly. In recent years, however, both types of scheme have become more flexible, and many policies allow you to incorporate features of the other. This can have great advantages from the point of view of enabling you to 'have your cake and eat it', but the result is that some of the definitions appear a bit contradictory. There are three basic types of life assurance: whole-life policies, term policies and endowment policies.

Whole-life policies are designed to pay out on your death. In its most straightforward form, the scheme works as follows: you pay a premium every year and, when you die, your beneficiaries receive the money. As with an ordinary household policy, the insurance holds good only if you continue the payments. If one year you did not pay and were to die, the policy could be void and your successors would receive nothing.

Term policies involve a definite commitment. As opposed to paying premiums every year, you elect to make regular payments for an agreed period, for example until such time as your children have completed their education, say eight years. If you die during this period, your family will be paid the agreed sum in full. If you die after the end of the term (when you have stopped making payments), your family will normally receive nothing.

Endowment policies are essentially savings plans. You sign a contract to pay regular premiums over a number of years and in exchange receive a lump sum on a specific date. Most endowment policies are written for periods varying from 10 to 25 years. Once you have committed yourself, you have to go on paying every year (as with term assurance). There are heavy penalties if, having paid for a number of years, you decide that you no longer wish to continue.

An important feature of endowment policies is that they are linked to death cover. If you die before the policy matures, the remaining payments are excused and your successors will be paid a lump sum on your death. Endowment policies have long been a popular way of making extra financial provision for retirement. They combine the advantages of guaranteeing you a lump sum with a built-in life assurance provision. The amount of money you stand to receive, however, can vary hugely, depending on the charges and how generous a bonus the insurance company feels it can afford on the policy's maturity. Over the past few years, pay-outs have been considerably lower than their earlier projections might have suggested. Aim to compare at least three policies before choosing.

Both whole-life policies and endowment policies offer two basic options: with profits or without profits. Very briefly the difference is as follows:

Without profits. This is sometimes known as 'guaranteed sum assured'. What it means is that the insurance company guarantees you a specific fixed sum (provided of course you meet the various terms and conditions). You know the amount in advance and this is the sum you – or your successors – will be paid.

With profits. You are paid a guaranteed fixed sum plus an addition, based on the profits that the insurance company has made by investing your annual or monthly payments. The basic premiums are higher and, by definition, the profits element is not known in advance. If the insurance company has invested your money wisely, a 'with profits' policy provides a useful hedge against inflation. If its investment policy is mediocre, you could have paid higher premiums for very little extra return.

Unit linked. This is a refinement of the 'with profits' policy, in that the investment element of the policy is linked in with a unit trust.

Premiums can normally be paid monthly or annually, as you prefer. The size of premium varies enormously, depending on the type of policy you choose and the amount of cover you want. Also, of course, some insurance companies are more competitive than others. As a generalization, higher premiums tend to give better value, as relatively less of your contribution is swallowed up in administrative costs.

As a condition of insuring you, some policies require that you have a medical check. This is more likely to apply if very large sums are involved. More usually, all that is required is that you fill in and sign a declaration of health. It is very important that this should be completed honestly: if you make a claim on your policy and it is subsequently discovered that you gave misleading information, your policy could be declared void and the insurance company could refuse to pay.

Many insurance companies offer a better deal if you are a non-smoker. Some also offer more generous terms if you are teetotal. Women generally pay less than men of the same age because of their longer life expectancy.

How to obtain

Policies are usually available through banks, insurance companies, Independent Financial Advisers and building societies. The biggest problem for most people is the sheer volume of choice. Another difficulty is often understanding the small print: terms and conditions that sound very similar may obscure important differences that could affect your benefit. An accountant could advise you, in general terms, whether you are being offered a good deal or otherwise. However, if it is a question of choosing a specific policy best suited to your requirements, it is usually advisable to consult an IFA. For help in finding an IFA in your area, see website **www.unbiased.co.uk**; **www.financialplanning.org.uk**; **www.findanadviser.org**. See also Chapter 6, Financial advisers.

Disclosure rules

Advisers selling financial products have to abide by a set of disclosure rules, requiring them to give clients certain essential information before a contract is signed. Although for a number of years the requirements have included the provision of both a 'key features' document (explaining the product, the risk factors, charges, benefits, surrender value if the policy is terminated early, tax treatment and salesperson's commission or remuneration) and a 'suitability letter' (explaining why a particular product or policy was recommended), the FSA recently decided to revamp the rules to provide consumers with clearer and more comprehensive information.

As a result, advisers must now give potential clients two 'key facts' documents: one entitled 'About our services', describing the range of services and the type of advice on offer; and a second entitled 'About the cost of our services', including among other information details of the advisers' own commission charges and – for comparison purposes – the average market rate. Importantly too, IFAs must offer clients the choice of paying fees or paying by commission.

For further information consult the **Association of British Insurers** (ABI) website: **www.abi.org.uk**.

Tax

Under current legislation, the proceeds of a qualifying policy – whether taken as a lump sum or in regular income payments (as in the case of family income benefit) – are free of all tax. If, as applies to many people, you have a life insurance policy written into a trust, there is a possibility that it could be hit by the new inheritance tax rules affecting trusts if the sum it is expected to pay out is above the (2012/13) £325,000 IHT threshold. The best advice is to check with a solicitor.

Assessment

Life assurance is normally a sensible investment, whether the aim is to provide death cover or the benefits of a lump sum to boost your retirement income. It has the merit of being very attractive from a tax angle, and additionally certain policies provide good capital appreciation – although a point to be aware of is that recent bonuses have tended to be considerably lower than their projected amount. However, you are locked into a long-term commitment. So, even more than in most areas, choosing the right policy is very important. Shop around, take advice and, above all, do not sign anything unless you are absolutely certain that you understand every last dot and comma.

Complaints

Complaints about life assurance products, including alleged mis-selling, are handled by the **Financial Ombudsman Service** (FOS). Before approaching the FOS, you first need to try to resolve a dispute with the company direct. See website: **www.financial-ombudsman.org.uk**.

The **Financial Services Compensation Scheme** (FSCS) is the compensation fund of last resort for customers of authorized financial services firms. If a firm becomes insolvent or ceases trading, the FSCS may be able to pay compensation to its customers. See website: **www.fscs.org.uk**.

Alternatives to surrendering a policy

There are heavy penalties if you surrender an endowment policy before its maturity. Some people, however, may wish to terminate the agreement regardless of any losses they may make or investment gains they may sacrifice. Instead of simply surrendering the policy to the insurance company, people in this situation may be able to sell the policy for a sum that is higher than its surrender value. See the **Association of Policy Market Makers** website: **www.apmm.org**.

For those looking for investment possibilities, second-hand policies could be worth investigating. Known as traded endowment policies (TEPs), they offer the combination of a low-risk investment with a good potential return. Owing to increased supply, there is currently a wide range of individual policies and a number of specialist funds managed by financial institutions. A full list of appropriate financial institutions and authorized dealers that buy and sell mid-term policies is obtainable from the Association of Policy Market Makers. It can also arrange for suitable policies to be valued by member firms, free of charge.

Bonds

Bonds generally offer less opportunity for capital growth; they tend to be lower risk as they are less exposed to stock market volatility; and they have the advantage of producing a regular guaranteed income. There are many different types of bonds, with varying degrees of risk. The three main types are government bonds (called gilt-edged securities or 'gilts'), corporate bonds and investment bonds:

1 *Gilts*, which are explained earlier in this chapter, are the least risky. They are secured by the government, which guarantees both the interest payable and the return of your capital in full if you hold the stocks until their maturity.

2 *Corporate bonds* are fairly similar except that, as opposed to lending your money to the government, you are lending it to a large

company, rather than owning a piece of it, as you do with an equity. This means that there are some key differences between the two (bonds and equities). First, the company has to repay the loan at some point. This is known as the bond's redemption date, which is when it will pay out the 'face value' of the bond (often £100 for a standard bond). The company also has to pay interest on the loan – this is known as the 'coupon'. After they are issued, bonds trade in the secondary market, just like shares. This means they won't always be priced at their 'face value'. Bond prices are driven by two main factors: interest rates and credit risk. Most bonds have a fixed income; the longer the time to maturity, the more sensitive the bond is to changes in interest rates.

One reason to hold bonds is for income. Should corporate profits stall, companies might have to cut dividends. But unlike dividends, bond coupons can't be suspended, so your income is more predictable.

The main risks to bonds are rising interest rates and credit risk. To hedge against these you should diversify: buy a portfolio of different maturity date bonds and spread your corporate bond companies across different industry sectors.

The risk is higher because the company could fail and might not be able to make the payments promised. In general, the higher the guaranteed interest payments, the less totally secure the company in question.

3 *Investment bonds* are different in that they offer potentially much higher rewards but also carry a much higher degree of risk. Because even gilts can be influenced by timing and other factors, if you are thinking of buying bonds, expert advice is very strongly recommended. They are discussed in more detail below.

Investment bonds

Definition

This is the method of investing a lump sum with an insurance company, in the hope of receiving a much larger sum back at a specific date – normally a few years later. All bonds offer life assurance cover as part of the deal. A particular feature of some bonds is that the managers have wide discretion to invest your money in almost any type of security. The risk/reward ratio is, therefore, very high. They can produce long-term capital growth but can also be used to generate income.

While bonds can achieve significant capital appreciation, you can also lose a high percentage of your investment. An exception is guaranteed equity bonds, which, while linked to the performance of the FTSE 100 or other stock market index, will protect your capital if shares fall. However, while your capital should be returned in full at the end of the fixed term (usually five years), a point not always appreciated is that, should markets fall, far from making any return on your investment you will have lost money in real terms: first, because your capital will have fallen in value, once inflation is taken into account; second, because you will have lost out on any interest that your money could have earned had it been on deposit.

All bond proceeds are free of basic rate tax, but higher rate tax is payable. However, higher-rate taxpayers can withdraw up to 5 per cent of their initial investment each year and defer the higher-rate tax liability for 20 years or until the bond is cashed in full, whichever is earlier. Although there is no capital gains tax on redemption of a bond (or on switching between funds), some corporation tax may be payable by the fund itself, which could affect its investment performance. Companies normally charge a front-end fee of around 5 per cent plus a small annual management fee, usually not related to performance.

Tax

Tax treatment is very complicated, as it is influenced by your marginal income tax rate in the year of encashment. For this reason, it is generally best to buy a bond when you are working and plan to cash it after retirement.

Offshore bonds

As tax reliefs vanish, some investors are looking for alternatives and it has been suggested that offshore bonds are the new pensions. There has been a recent surge of interest in offshore bonds from high earners looking for an alternative to pensions for their retirement savings. Offshore bonds provide significant tax savings for investors because up to 5 per cent of capital can be withdrawn while deferring higher-rate tax for up to 20 years with no immediate tax to pay.

Offshore bonds are an insurance 'wrapper' round a portfolio of investments, which receive tax advantages by allowing you to defer the tax on the growth of the investments. Capital growth in an onshore bond is taxed at 20 per cent, whereas offshore bond capital grows tax free. While basic-rate taxpayers have no more tax to pay when they cash in an onshore investment bond, higher-rate taxpayers must pay a further 20 per cent and top-rate taxpayers must pay 30 per cent. With offshore bonds there is no tax to pay until you encash the bond, when higher-rate taxpayers will pay the entire 40 per cent and the top-rate payers will be liable for 50 per cent.

Charges for offshore bonds are high: typically 0.3 to 1 per cent upfront plus £400 to 0.25 per cent a year, depending on how much is invested. Adviser commission on top means the bonds are generally best for investments greater than £100,000 and held for more than five years. In comparison with pensions, these schemes are being increasingly recommended for retirement savings for higher-rate taxpayers who use their ISA and capital gains allowance, and no longer benefit from higher-rate tax relief.

Investor protection

There are now stringent rules on businesses offering investment services, and a powerful regulatory body, the Financial Services Authority (FSA). This is charged by Parliament with responsibility for ensuring that firms are 'fit and proper' to operate in the investment field and for monitoring their activities on an ongoing basis. The main effects of these safeguards are as follows.

Investment businesses (including accountants or solicitors giving investment advice) are not at liberty to operate without authorization or exemption from the FSA. Operating without such authorization or exemption is a criminal offence.

Previously, under what was known as 'polarization', businesses providing advice on investment products either could operate as 'tied agents', limited to selling their own in-house products (or those of a single provider), or had to be Independent Financial Advisers, advising on products across the whole market. The FSA recently took the view that this was too restrictive and, with the aim of providing consumers with greater choice, has now authorized a new category of adviser known as a 'multi-tied agent', able to offer the products from a chosen panel of providers.

Whether tied, multi-tied or independent, advisers must give customers certain information before a contract is signed. Under the disclosure rules, this includes two 'key facts' documents – 'About our services' and 'About the cost of our services' – plus a 'suitability letter' explaining the rationale on which recommendations are based.

Among other important details, the information must provide a breakdown of the charges (expressed in cash terms), describe the payment options (commission and/or fee) and, in the case of commission, must quote both the adviser's own commission and the average market rate.

Investment businesses must adhere to a proper complaints procedure, with provision for customers to receive fair redress, where appropriate. Unsolicited visits and telephone calls to sell investments are for the most part banned. Where these are allowed for packaged products (such as unit trusts and life assurance), should a sale result the customer will have a 14-day cooling-off period (or a seven-day 'right to withdraw' period if the packaged product is held within an ISA and the sale follows advice from the firm). The cooling-off period is to give the customer time to explore other options before deciding whether to cancel the contract or not.

A single regulatory authority

Finding out whether investment businesses are authorized or not and checking up on what information they are required to disclose is now much easier. All former self-regulating organizations (including the PIA, IMRO and SFA) have now been merged under the Financial Services Authority, with the purpose of improving investor protection and of providing a single contact point for enquiries. See website: **www.moneyadviceservice.org.uk**.

A single Ombudsman scheme

The single statutory Financial Ombudsman Service (FOS) was set up in December 2001. It replaced the various former schemes that used to deal with complaints about financial services. It provides a 'one-stop shop' for dissatisfied consumers. The schemes concerned are: Banking Ombudsman, Building Societies Ombudsman, Insurance Ombudsman, Personal Insurance Arbitration Service, PIA Ombudsman, Investment Ombudsman, SFA Complaints Bureau (and Arbitration Schemes) and FSA Complaints Unit.

A welcome result of there being a single Ombudsman scheme is that the FOS covers complaints across almost the entire range of financial services and products – from banking services, endowment mortgages and personal pensions to household insurance and stocks and shares. The list equally includes unit trusts and OEICs, life assurance, FSAVCs and equity release schemes. A further advantage is that the FOS applies a single set of rules to all complaints. Since April 2007 the Financial Ombudsman Service has also covered – for the first time – the consumer-credit activities of businesses with a consumer-credit licence issued by the Office of Fair Trading. Consumer-credit activities now covered by the Ombudsman range from debt consolidation and consumer hire to debt collecting and pawnbrokers.

Complaints

If you have a complaint against an authorized firm, in the first instance you should take it up with the firm concerned. You may be able to resolve the matter at this level, since all authorized firms are obliged to have a proper complaints-handling procedure.

The Financial Ombudsman Service advises that the best approach is to start by contacting the person you originally dealt with and, if you phone, to keep a written note of all telephone calls. If complaining by letter, it helps to set out the facts in logical order, to stick to what is relevant and to include important details such as your policy or account numbers. You should also keep a copy of all letters, both for your own record purposes and as useful evidence should you need to take the matter further.

If you have gone through the firm's complaints procedure, or if after eight weeks you are still dissatisfied, you can approach the FOS, which will investigate the matter on your behalf and, if it finds your complaint is justified, may require the firm to pay compensation; depending on your losses, this could be up to £100,000. If you disagree with the Ombudsman's decision, this does not affect your right to go to court should you wish to do so. See the **Financial Ombudsman Service** (FOS) website: **www.financial-ombudsman.org.uk**.

The **Financial Services Compensation Scheme** (FSCS) is the compensation fund of last resort for customers of authorized financial services firms. If a firm becomes insolvent or ceases trading the FSCS may be able to pay compensation to its customers. See website: **www.facs.org.uk**.

Warning

The existence of the FSA enables you to check on the credentials of anyone purporting to be a financial adviser or trying to persuade you to invest your money in an insurance policy, bond, unit or investment trust, equity, futures contract or similar. If either they or the organization they represent is not authorized by the FSA, you are very strongly recommended to leave well alone.

Scams

Last year a record £126 per second was lost to fraud. Half of all victims were aged between 41 and 60. With billions being wiped off pensions and investments, those despairing about getting a decent return on their savings are particularly at risk. No wonder they are the perfect target for sophisticated conmen. Current scams involve investments in fine wine, land, green energy and gold.

Boiler room scams

Major scams to watch out for include boiler rooms.

Boiler rooms are businesses that use high-pressure sales techniques to sell 'sure-thing' investments with the promise of massive returns. What in fact they are selling is worthless stock in often unquoted companies that are either overvalued or simply don't exist at all. Boiler room operatives generally cold call their targets, using phone numbers from publicly available shareholder lists. A slick salesman rings and tries to sell you investments which he claims will make an amazing profit. Because it's against the law for investors to cold call in the UK, they tend to be based abroad (often Spain, Switzerland or the United States), where they're beyond the jurisdiction of the Financial Services Authority (FSA). They can approach anyone, anywhere.

A boiler room can look and sound legitimate. It may mention companies you've heard of, give itself a UK address or phone number, and have a professional-looking website. Callers are notoriously persistent, and can hound a victim for months in the hope of a sale, catching out even seasoned investors. The FSA watchdog reports that around 700 people each year lose more than £20,000 to these. Remember, as a general rule, if an opportunity sounds too good to be true, then it almost certainly is.

If you think you are being targeted by a boiler room, you can protect yourself by never buying anything from a so-called investment salesman. The FSA's advice is not to worry about being polite, just hang up. If someone tries to sell you some land without planning permission, claiming it will increase in value, it is likely to be a land-banking scam. All too often the plots sold never receive planning permission. You could add to the £200 million lost on this scam over the past five years.

Ignore all e-mails from your bank asking you to click on a link. Also do not respond to anyone who claims to be calling from a bank and asking you to hand over your account details. It is prudent to keep your computer's anti-virus software updated to cut the risk of being caught out in phishing scams.

Steer clear of other frauds such as prizes for draws or lotteries you have never entered. Equally you may receive a letter from a law firm advising that you have been left millions of pounds in a distant relative's will. To take your share of the cash, all you have to do is to hand over your bank account details.

The FSA is so worried by the growth of these scams that it recently contacted 76,000 people to tell them they are on a so-called 'suckers' list, and are at even greater risk of being targeted.

If you are in any doubt about any company, make sure you search through an internet search engine, which should reveal reviews of the firm. If the majority of comments or reviews about a company are negative, this should set the alarm bells ringing.

Always check the FSA Register to ensure a firm is authorized. If the firm is not authorized, and things go wrong, you will not have any access to the Financial Ombudsman or to the Financial Services Compensation Scheme. Last year the FSA took over 5,000 calls from worried investors who believed they had fallen prey to fake financial investments. Some were left penniless because they were not covered by the government-backed compensation schemes that protect savers and investors. See the FSA website for more information on what to do: **www.fsa.gov.uk**.

Chapter Six
Financial advisers

A judge said that all his experience, both as counsel and judge, had been spent sorting out the difficulties of people who, upon the recommendation of people they did not know, signed documents which they did not read, to buy goods and services they did not need, with money they had not got.

GILBERT HARDING

Do you habitually read the small print? Have you understood all the terms and conditions written in that minute-sized font, printed on the back of the form you are about to sign? Let's hope you have. Financial decisions are so important, and should you make a bad one, it can be both serious and costly. In essence, where financial advice is concerned, it is quality not quantity that counts. If you have confidence in your professional adviser, you should be able to sleep soundly at night, knowing that you have made prudent and appropriate financial plans.

The best sort of financial adviser is someone who can explain something complicated that you don't understand in a simple uncluttered way that you can understand. It is easy to simplify and explain things if you know your subject. Today we are bombarded with freely available information from all directions but how do we know what quality it is, or even if it is genuine? Ideally what every client requires from his or her financial adviser is key information, presented simply, and in plain English. Good financial advisers are top-notch communicators and do not assume that their clients understand what they are talking about. They know that a nod of their client's head does not guarantee comprehension of the subject. They make sure it is impossible for their client to misunderstand them. That is how to judge the quality of a financial adviser.

The skilled financial adviser knows his or her client's needs, their level of wealth, personal circumstances, and, armed with all that knowledge, recommends financial products that are most suitable for them. The adviser can give his or her recommendations in writing or face to face. Subjects covered include everything from investment advice to pension planning, life assurance and other insurances. Although most professional advisers are sound, not everyone who proffers advice is qualified to do so. Before parting with your money, it is essential to ensure that you are dealing with a registered member of a recognized institution. Checking credentials has become much easier under the Financial Services Act.

Before making contact with a financial adviser it is generally a good idea to try to sort out your priorities. To help advisers give you quality advice, you will have to provide them with some detailed information about your personal financial situation. You should also be willing to answer some questions about your financial goals and attitude to risk. What are you looking for? Is it capital growth or is your main objective to increase your income? If you have special plans, such as helping your grandchildren, or if you need several thousand pounds to improve your home, these should be thought through in advance. They could have a bearing on the advice you receive. A further reason for doing some pre-planning is that certain types of advisers – for example, insurance brokers – do not specifically charge you for their time. Other professional advisers, such as accountants and solicitors, charge their fees by the hour.

Choosing an adviser

When choosing an adviser, there are usually four main considerations: respectability, suitability, price and convenience. Where your money is concerned, you cannot afford to take unnecessary risks. Establishing that an individual is a member of a recognized institution is a basic safeguard. But it is insufficient recommendation if you want to be assured of dealing with someone who will personally suit you. The principle applies as much with friends as with complete strangers. If you are thinking of using a particular adviser, do you already know him or her in a professional capacity? If not, you should certainly check on the adviser's reputation, ideally talking to some of his or her existing clients. Do not be afraid to ask for references. Most reputable professionals will be delighted to assist, as it means that the relationship will be founded on a basis of greater trust and confidence.

Firms giving financial advice must be regulated by the Financial Services Authority (FSA) or be agents of regulated firms. You can check particular firms on the FSA Register at **www.fsa.gov.uk**. (If they aren't regulated by the FSA, you won't have access to complaints and compensation procedures if things go wrong.) They have to meet certain standards which the FSA sets, regarding how they give you advice on types of insurance, mortgages and investments (such as personal pensions, life insurance and annuities). Some firms may give advice on all three product types, while others may only give advice on one or two of them. For example, mortgage advisers and insurance brokers can advise on mortgages and/or insurance, but can't give advice on investments such as pensions. You will usually have to pay for this advice, either in the form of a fee, commission or a combination of both. The firm will explain this.

Finally, a definition of financial advice. General product information you can gather yourself isn't financial advice. It does not matter whether this is from banks, building societies, insurance or investment companies. It is only financial advice if it takes into account your particular circumstances. If you buy a financial product without professional advice, you will have fewer grounds for complaint if the product turns out to be unsuitable. But if you do take advice and then find that the product wasn't suitable, you may have grounds to make a complaint and receive compensation for any loss. You can help prepare yourself for a meeting with a financial adviser by thinking about your needs and priorities.

For your protection

The **Financial Services Compensation Scheme** (FSCS) is the compensation fund of last resort for customers of authorized financial services firms. If a firm becomes insolvent or ceases trading the FSCS may be able to pay compensation to its customers. See website: **www.fscs.org.uk**.

Despite the safeguards of the Financial Services Act, when it comes to investment – or to financial advisers – there are no cast-iron guarantees. Under the investor protection legislation, all practitioners and/or the businesses they represent offering investment or similar services must be authorized by the FSA or, in certain cases, by a small number of designated professional bodies that themselves are answerable to the FSA. A basic question, therefore, to ask anyone offering investment advice or products is: are you registered and by whom? Information is easily checked via the **Financial Services Authority** website: **www.fsa.gov.uk**.

Accountants

Accountants are specialists in matters concerning taxation. If there is scope to do so, they can advise on ways of reducing your tax liability and can assess the various tax effects of the different types of investment you may be considering. They can also help you with the preparation of tax returns. Should you be considering becoming self-employed or starting your own business, they can assist you with some of the practicalities. These could range from registering for VAT to establishing a system of business accounts. Many accountants can also help with raising finance and offer support with the preparation of business plans. Additionally, they may be able to advise in a general way about pensions and your proposed investment strategy. Most accountants, however, do not claim to be experts in these fields. They may refer their clients to stockbrokers or other financial advisers for such specialized services. If you need help in locating a suitable accountant, any of the following should be able to advise:

> **Association of Chartered Certified Accountants** (ACCA):
> website: **www.accaglobal.com;**

> **Institute of Chartered Accountants in England and Wales** (ICAEW):
> website: **www.icaew.com;**

> **Institute of Chartered Accountants of Scotland** (ICAS):
> website: **www.icaew.com.**

Complaints

Anyone with a complaint against an accountancy firm should contact the company's relevant professional body for advice and assistance – see ACCA, ICAEW or ICAS, above.

Banks

Most people have a bank account, so there is no need to explain about clearing banks since they regularly bombard their clients with information on the latest products, services and rule changes. Since the recent banking crisis and the subsequent mergers and takeovers there are now fewer banks to choose from as well as fewer building societies visible on the high street. Banks provide comprehensive services, in addition to the normal account facilities. These include investment, insurance and tax-planning services, as well as how to draw up a will. Other more specialized banks such as Hoare's, Coutts and overseas banks are all part of the UK clearing system and can offer a very good service.

The main banks are listed below with their websites. If you prefer to call into your local branch, a specialist adviser should be able to assist you.

Barclays Bank plc offers customers a range of accounts to suit a variety of personal savings requirements. Additionally, a number of financial planning services are available through Barclays Bank subsidiary companies. These include personal investment advice, investment management, stockbroking, unit trusts, personal taxation, wills and trusts. Website: **www.barclays.co.uk**.

Co-operative Bank has a comprehensive range of products including current accounts, savings accounts, mortgages, credit cards, loans, insurance and investment services. It offers assistance with financial planning. Website: **www.co-operativebank.co.uk**.

HSBC offers financial products ranging from OEICs and ISAs to life assurance, which are selected according to a customer's requirements by a financial planning manager. HSBC Premier IFA offers investment management and estate planning services to clients who prefer to have a local specialist to look after their affairs on a regular basis. Website: **www.hsbc.co.uk**.

Lloyds TSB has a wide range of financial services, including current and savings accounts, home insurance, investment management and life assurance through Scottish Widows. As well as the classic account, which offers all the normal current account facilities, and the Gold Service, which among other facilities includes free travel insurance, there is Private Banking, which is a comprehensive wealth-management service tailored to individual requirements of individual customers. Website: **www.lloydstsb.com**.

NatWest (part of the RBS Group) has financial planning managers who can advise on a wide range of banking and financial planning services for retirement, including investment funds and ISAs. Website: **www.natwest.com**.

RBS (Royal Bank of Scotland) offers a comprehensive range of current accounts and savings products. The bank's Private Trust and Taxation Department offers free advice on making a will, although the usual legal fees are applicable if you proceed. Royal Scottish Assurance, the Royal Bank of Scotland's life assurance, pensions and investment company, offers a full financial planning service free of charge. Financial planning consultants can also recommend ISAs and unit trusts provided by the Royal Bank of Scotland unit trust managers. Website: **www.rbs.co.uk**.

Santander Group (formerly Abbey and now including Alliance & Leicester) offers a range of savings, mortgage, pension, current account, medical and other insurance products plus loans for such items as home improvements, a car or to finance a holiday. A broad range of savings accounts is available that includes branch-based, postal and internet instant-access accounts, and fixed and variable rate savings bonds, including a retirement income bond for the over-55s. Website: **www.santander.co.uk**.

Complaints

The FSA regulates the way banks and building societies do business with you. If you have a complaint about a banking matter, you must first try to resolve the issue with the bank or building society concerned. If you remain dissatisfied, you can contact the **Financial Ombudsman Service**; see website: **www.financial-ombudsman.org.uk**.

Independent Financial Advisers (IFAs)

The role of IFAs has become more important since the number of investment, mortgage, pension protection and insurance products has multiplied and financial decision making has become increasingly complicated. An Independent Financial Adviser is able to help guide you through the maze of products now available.

An IFA is the only type of adviser who is able to select from all the investment policies and products on offer in the marketplace. These include endowment policies, personal pensions, life assurance, permanent health insurance, critical illness cover, unit trusts, ISAs and other forms of personal investment such as, for example, mortgages. It is his or her responsibility to make sure you get the right product for your individual needs. In other words, he or she acts as your personal adviser and handles all the arrangements for you.

IFAs must assess whether customers are at risk of over-committing themselves or taking some other risk that might jeopardize their security. This means they have to gain a full understanding of your circumstances and requirements before helping to choose any financial products. They will record your information so you can double-check that they have understood. In turn, you should also ask your adviser a number of questions including – most important – by whom they are regulated. IFAs are bound to the Financial Services Authority rules, which oblige them to provide advice most suited to your personal requirements and your risk outlook. When recommending financial products they must take into account the benefits provided, charges, flexibility, service and financial strength.

All IFAs must be authorized and regulated by the Financial Services Authority and are obliged to offer what is termed 'suitable advice'. To check whether your IFA is registered, see the **FSA's Central Register** website: **www.fsa.gov.uk.**

Your adviser should provide you with two 'key facts' documents entitled 'About our services' and 'About the cost of our services', plus a 'suitability letter' explaining all these points. If for some reason you do not receive these or if there is anything you do not understand you should not hesitate to ask. Under rules brought in by the FSA, advisers who want to call themselves 'independent' have to offer clients the option of paying by fee. This means of course that clients incur an upfront charge.

To find an IFA, the following organizations provide advice:

Ethical Investment Research Service (EIRIS): **www.yourethicalmoney.org.** Information about product providers and other sources that provide ethical investments.

Institute of Financial Planning: www.financialplanning.org.uk. For help planning your finances.

MyLocalAdviser: www.mylocaladviser.co.uk. For financial advisers in your area.

The Personal Finance Society (PFS): **www.thepfs.org.** For financial advisers in your area.

Unbiased.co.uk: www.unbiased.co.uk. To find an independent financial adviser or mortgage broker in your area.

Insurance brokers

The insurance business covers a very wide range, from straightforward policies – such as motor or household insurance – to rather more complex areas, including life assurance and pensions.

Although many people think of brokers and IFAs as doing much the same job, IFAs specialize in advising on products and policies with some investment content, whereas brokers primarily deal with the more straightforward type of insurance, such as motor, medical, household and holiday insurance. Some brokers are also authorized to give investment advice. A broker will help you choose the policies best suited to you, determine how much cover you require and explain any technical terms contained in the documents. He or she can also assist with any claims, remind you when renewals are due and advise you on keeping your cover up to date. An essential point to check before proceeding is that the firm the broker represents is regulated by the FSA.

A condition of registration is that a broker must deal with a multiplicity of insurers and therefore be in a position to offer a comprehensive choice of policies. The FSA disclosure rules require brokers to provide potential customers with a 'key facts' document. This should include the cost of the policy (but not commission), as well as a 'suitability' statement explaining the reasons for the recommendation. The information must also draw attention to any significant or unusual exemptions. Generally speaking, you are safer using a larger brokerage with an established reputation. Also, before you take out a policy, it is advisable to consult several brokers in order to get a better feel for the market.

The British Insurance Brokers' Association represents nearly 2,200 insurance broking businesses and will help you find an insurance broker: see website: **www.biba.org.uk**.

Complaints

The Association of British Insurers (ABI) represents some 400 companies (as opposed to Lloyd's syndicates or brokers), providing all types of insurance from life assurance and pensions to household, motor and other forms of general insurance. About 90 per cent of the worldwide business done by British insurance companies is handled by members of the ABI. For information on insurance products see website: **www.abi.org.uk**.

Occupational pension advice

If you are (or have been) in salaried employment and are a member of an occupational pension scheme, the normal person to ask is your company's personnel manager or pensions adviser or, via him or her, the pension fund trustees. Alternatively, if you have a problem with your pension you could approach your trade union, since this is an area where most unions are particularly active and well informed.

If you are in need of specific help, a source to try could be **The Pensions Advisory Service.** For information on state, company, personal and stakeholder pensions, and for help with problems or complaints about pensions, see website: **www.pensionsadvisoryservice.org.uk.**

As with most other financial sectors, there is also a **Pensions Ombudsman.** You would normally approach the Ombudsman if neither the pension scheme trustees nor the Pensions Advisory Service are able to solve your problem. Also, as with all Ombudsmen, the Pensions Ombudsman can only investigate matters that come within his orbit. These are: complaints of maladministration by the trustees, managers or administrators of a pension scheme or by an employer; and disputes of fact or law with the trustees, managers or an employer. The Pension Ombudsman is also the Pension Protection Fund Ombudsman. See website: **www.pensions-ombudsman.org.uk.**

Another source of help is the **Pension Tracing Service,** which can provide individuals with contact details for a pension scheme with which they have lost touch. There is no charge for the service. See website: **www.direct.gov.uk/ pensions.**

Two other organizations that, although they do not advise on individual cases, are interested in matters of principle and broader issues affecting pensions, are the **National Association of Pension Funds,** which is committed to ensuring that there is a sustainable environment for workplace pensions, website: **www.napf.co.uk;** and **The Pensions Regulator,** for information about work-based pensions, website: **www.thepensionsregulator.gov.uk.**

Solicitors

Solicitors are professional advisers on subjects to do with the law or on matters that could have legal implications. They can assist with the purchase or rental of property, with drawing up a will, or if you are charged with a criminal offence or are sued in a civil matter. Additionally, their advice can be invaluable in vetting any important document before you sign it. If you do not have a solicitor (or if your solicitor does not have the knowledge to advise on, say, a business matter), often the best way of finding a suitable lawyer is through the recommendation of a friend or other professional adviser, such as an accountant.

If you need a solicitor specifically for a business or professional matter, organizations such as local Chambers of Commerce, small business associations, your professional institute or trade union may be able to put you in touch with someone in your area who has relevant experience.

Two organizations to contact for help are **The Law Society**, website: **www.lawsociety.org.uk**; and **Solicitors for Independent Financial Advice** (SIFA), which is the trade body for solicitor financial advisers. Its membership now also includes accountancy IFAs as members; see website: **www.sifa.co.uk**.

Community Legal Advice (CLA) is a free and confidential advice service paid for by Legal Aid. The Legal Services Commission runs the legal aid scheme and the CLA service in England and Wales. People living on a low income or benefits may be eligible for legal aid to get free specialist advice from qualified legal advisers. See website: **www.legalservices.gov.uk**.

Complaints

All solicitors are required by the Law Society to have their own in-house complaints procedure. If you are unhappy about the service you have received, you should first try to resolve the matter with the firm through its complaints-handling partner. If you still feel aggrieved you can approach the Law Society's Legal Complaints Service (LCS), which is an independent arm of the Law Society responsible for handling complaints against solicitors.

Should you feel you have been treated negligently, the LCS will help you either by putting you in touch with a solicitor specializing in negligence claims or by referring you to the solicitor's insurers. If it arranges an appointment for you with a negligence panellist, the panel solicitor will see you free of charge for up to an hour and advise you as to your best course of action.

The LCS can also help with matters such as overcharging. There is a procedure for getting your bill checked, the various time limits involved and the circumstances in which you might be successful in getting the fee reduced.

For practical assistance if you are having problems with your solicitor, you can approach the Legal Services Ombudsman. This must be done within three months or your complaint will risk being out of time and the Ombudsman will not be able to help you. See the **Legal Services Ombudsman** website: **www.legalombudsman.org.uk**.

General queries

For queries of a more general nature, you should approach the **Law Society**: see website: **www.lawsociety.org.uk**. For those living in Scotland or Northern Ireland, see **The Law Society of Scotland**: website: **www.lawscot.org.uk** or **The Law Society of Northern Ireland**: website: **www.lawsoc-ni.org**, respectively.

Stockbrokers

A stockbroker is a regulated professional broker who buys and sells shares and other securities through market makers or agency-only firms on behalf of investors. A broker may be employed by a brokerage firm. A transaction on the stock exchange must be made between two members of the exchange.

There are three types of stockbroking service:

Execution only which means the broker will carry out only the client's instructions to buy or sell.

Advisory dealing where the broker advises the client on which shares to buy and sell, but leaves the financial decision to the investor.

Discretionary dealing where the stockbroker ascertains the client's investment objectives and then makes all the dealing decisions on the client's behalf.

Roles similar to that of stockbroker include investment adviser and financial adviser. A stockbroker may or may not be an investment adviser.

It is difficult to be specific about the cost of using a stockbroker. While some now charge fees in the same way as, say, a solicitor, generally stockbrokers make their living by charging commission on every transaction. You will need to establish what the terms and conditions are before committing yourself, as these can vary quite considerably between one firm and another. A growing number of provincial stockbrokers are happy to deal for private investors with sums from about £5,000. Additionally, nearly all major stockbrokers now run unit trusts. Because through these they are investing collectively for their clients, they welcome quite modest investors with around £2,000.

To find a stockbroker: you can approach an individual through recommendation or visit the **London Stock Exchange** website: **www.londonstock-exchange.com,** or the **Association of Private Client Investment Managers and Stockbrokers** (APCIMS) website: **www.apcims.co.uk**.

Complaints

With money matters being on many people's minds at the moment, the following suggestions may be helpful if you have a financial problem you cannot resolve. If you need to make a complaint about a financial product or service, these tips are worth noting:

1 **What are you unhappy about?** Be clear in your own mind what the problem is, and how you would like it to be settled.

2 **Try to stay calm.** No matter how upset you might be, try to be calm and polite. This can help you get your points across more clearly and effectively.

3 **Get in touch.** First, contact the business you think is responsible and explain what has gone wrong. Try to have any relevant information to hand, for example statements or policy documents.

4 **Write or phone?** It can be a good idea to put your complaint in writing – and keep a copy of your letter. If you prefer to call, make a note of the time and date of the call, the details of what was said and the name and telephone number of the person you spoke to.

5 **Taking things further.** The business will have a complaints procedure – if the person you are dealing with isn't able to take the necessary action to resolve your complaint, say you want to take things further. If the business doesn't settle the matter to your satisfaction, the Financial Ombudsman Service may be able to help (see below).

If you have a complaint about a stockbroker or other member of the former Securities and Futures Authority (SFA), you should write to the compliance officer of the stockbroking firm involved.

Should the company not resolve the matter to your satisfaction, and you wish to take things further, you can contact the **Financial Ombudsman Service** (FOS).

Financial Ombudsman Service (FOS)

This is a free service, set up by law with the power to sort out problems between consumers and financial businesses. Follow the steps outlined above, then contact the FOS, who will investigate your complaint. If the Ombudsman considers the complaint justified, it can award compensation. See **Financial Ombudsman Service** website: **www.financial-ombudsman.org.uk**.

The FOS is the single contact point for dissatisfied customers, as it covers complaints across almost the entire range of financial services, including consumer credit activities (such as store cards, credit cards and hire purchase transactions). The service is free, and the FOS is empowered to award compensation of up to £150,000, an increase from last year's maximum of £100,000. However, before contacting the FOS you must first try to resolve your complaint with the organization concerned (see above). Also, the Ombudsman is powerless to act if legal proceedings have been started. See the **Financial Ombudsman Service** website: **www.financial-ombudsman.org.uk**.

Other useful websites are:

www.ukinvestmentadvice.co.uk;

www.thisismoney.co.uk;

www.moneyweek.com;

www.wwfp.net;

www.best-advice.co.uk;

www.investment-advice.org.uk.

Chapter Seven
Budget planner

I'm living so far beyond my income that we may almost be said to be living apart. **E E CUMMINGS**

Budgeting and planning ahead will help you make the most of your money in retirement. Not everyone relishes the prospect of budgeting, but unless you want to be living a long way apart from your income, it is essential to do it.

Spending only a few minutes a week reviewing and planning your budget can make a real difference.

The impact of retirement: monthly savings and costs

In this chapter it's not possible to cover everything, but the main things are listed. Once you've an idea of what you will need money for, the next thing is to make what you've got go as far as possible. The best way to do this is to track your everyday income and expenditure and then plan well ahead for future events. Drawing up a budget – a record of where your income comes from and how you spend it – will help you keep track of your money and manage your finances. Ask yourself the question: how is my budget likely to change in the years ahead? Some of your income (such as state pension) increases each year to keep pace with inflation, but if any of your income is fixed, its buying power will fall as prices rise. You may want to think about taking steps to protect your financial security, for example by saving extra now to help you cope with higher prices later on.

If retirement is imminent, then doing the arithmetic in as much detail as possible will not only reassure you but also help you plan your future life with greater confidence. You'll feel better knowing how you stand financially. Don't forget that there are probably a number of options open to you. Examining the figures written down will highlight the areas of greatest flexibility. One tip, offered by one of the retirement magazines, is to start living on your retirement income some six months before you retire. Not only will you see if your budget estimates are broadly correct, but since most people err on the cautious side when they first retire you will have the bonus of all the extra money you will have saved.

If retirement is still some years ahead, there will be more unknowns and more opportunities. When assessing the figures, you should take account of your future earnings. Perhaps you should also consider what steps you might be able to take under the pension rules to maximize your pension fund. You could also consider whether you should be putting money aside now in a savings plan and/or making other investments. Imprecise as they will be, the budget planner estimates you make in the various income and expenditure columns should indicate whether, unless you take action now, you could be at risk of having to make serious adjustments in your standard of living later on. To be on the safe side, assume an increase in inflation. Everyone should, if they possibly can, budget for a nest egg to help cover the cost of any emergencies or special events that may come along.

See Tables 7.1 and 7.2.

TABLE 7.1

Items	Estimated monthly *savings*
National Insurance Contributions	....
Pension payments	....
Travel expenses to work	....
Bought lunches	....
Incidentals at work, eg drinks with colleagues, collections for presents	....
Special work clothes	....
Concessionary travel	....
NHS prescriptions	....
Eye tests	....
Mature drivers insurance policy	....
Retired householders insurance policy	....
Life assurance payments and/or possible endowment policy premiums	....
Other	....
TOTAL	....

NB: You should also take into account reduced running costs if you move to a smaller home; any expenses for dependent children that may cease; other costs such as mortgage payments that may end around the time you retire; and the fact that you may be in a lower tax bracket and may not be liable for National Insurance Contributions.

TABLE 7.2

Items	Estimated monthly *costs*
Extra heating and lighting bills	....
Extra spending on hobbies and other entertainment	....
Replacement of company car	....
Private health care insurance	....
Longer or more frequent holidays	....
Life and permanent health insurance	....
Cost of substituting other perks, eg expense account lunches	....
Out-of-pocket expenses for voluntary work activity	....
Other	....
TOTAL	....

NB: Looking ahead, you will need to make provision for any extra home comforts you might want and also, at some point, for having to pay other people to do some of the jobs that you normally manage yourself. If you intend to make regular donations to a charity or perhaps help with your grandchildren's education, these too should be included in the list. The same applies to any new private pension or savings plan that you might want to invest in to boost your long-term retirement income.

Tax

Many people have difficulty understanding the tax system, and you should certainly take professional advice if you are in any doubt at all. However, if you carefully fill in your expected sources of income and likely tax implications in Tables 7.3 and 7.4, it should give you a pretty good idea of your net income after retirement and enable you to make at least provisional plans. Remember too that you may have one or two capital sums to invest, such as:

the commuted lump sum from your pension;

money from an endowment policy;

gains from the sale of company shares (SAYE or other share option scheme);

profits from the sale of your home or other asset;

money from an inheritance.

TABLE 7.3

A. Income received *before* tax	
Basic state pension	....
State graduated pension	....
SERPS/State Second Pension	....
Occupational pension(s)	....
Stakeholder or personal pension	....
State benefits	....
Investments and savings plans paid gross, eg gilts, National Savings	....
Other incomes (eg rental income)	....
Casual or other pre-tax earnings	....
TOTAL	....
Less: Personal tax allowance and possibly also Married Couple's Allowance	....
Basic-rate tax	....
TOTAL A	....
B. Income received *after* tax	
Dividends (unit trusts, shares, etc)	....
Bank deposit account	....
Building society interest	....
Annuity income	....
Other (including earnings subject to PAYE)	....
TOTAL B	....
Total A + Total B	....
Less: higher-rate tax (if any)	....
Plus: Other tax-free receipts, eg some state benefits, income from an ISA	....
Investment bond withdrawals, etc	....
Other	....
TOTAL NET INCOME	....

TABLE 7.4

Normal regular expenditure	
Items	Estimated monthly cost
Food	....
Rent or mortgage repayments	....
Council tax	....
Repair and maintenance costs	....
Heating	....
Lighting and other energy	....
Telephone/mobile/internet	....
Postage (including Christmas cards)	....
TV licence/Sky/digital subscription	....
Household insurance	....
Clothes	....
Laundry, cleaner's bills, shoe repair	....
Domestic cleaning products	....
Miscellaneous services, eg plumber and window cleaner	....
Car (including licence, petrol, etc)	....
Other transport	....
Regular savings and life assurance	....
HP and other loan repayments	....
Outgoings on health	....
Other	....
TOTAL	....

NB: Before adding up the total, you should look at the 'Normal additional expenditure' list, as you may well want to juggle some of the items between the two.

TABLE 7.5

Normal regular expenditure	
Items	Estimated monthly cost
Gifts	....
Holidays	....
Newspapers/books/CDs/DVDs	....
Computer (including broadband)	....
Drink	....
Cigarettes/tobacco	....
Hairdressing	....
Toiletries/cosmetics	....
Entertainment (hobbies, outings, home entertaining, etc)	....
Miscellaneous subscriptions/ membership fees	....
Gifts, charitable donations	....
Expenditure on pets	....
Garden purchases	....
Other	....
TOTAL	....

NB: For some items, such as holidays and gifts, you may tend to think in annual expenditure terms. However, for the purpose of comparing monthly income versus outgoings, it is probably easier if you itemize all the expenditure in the same fashion. Also, if you need to save for a special event such as your holiday, it helps if you get into the habit of putting so much aside every month (or even weekly).

Chapter Eight
Your home

If you have a garden and a library, you have everything you need. CICERO

Home Sweet Home. As we get older our home becomes increasingly precious to us. After all, we've worked for years to pay for it and have coped with increasing living costs over that period. Retirement offers us the chance to reflect for a moment, and perhaps ask ourselves whether our current home is still the place we really want to be. Recent statistics reveal that 79 per cent of British pensioners now own their homes, up from 62 per cent in 1991. But several recent news and media reports have used the rather unpleasant term 'hoarding' to describe the living arrangements of older people whose children have grown and left home. It has been suggested by The Intergenerational Foundation that these people, many of them pensioners, should give up the homes they have worked a lifetime for in favour of the younger generations who 'need' them. The Foundation suggests that working families do not have enough living space, while older people are 'selfishly' holding on to homes and space they no longer need. This is an interesting new form of ageism: the divide between the housing 'haves' and 'have nots' moving from one being dominated by wealth or class to one being dominated by age. Although many of us over-60s do decide to exchange our family homes for smaller establishments, the choice should remain firmly with us and nowhere else.

www.seniorsdiscounts.co.uk

To put things in perspective, did you know that last year (Diamond Jubilee year), the average house price was 105 times higher than it was in 1952 when HM The Queen came to the throne? Climbing onto the property ladder that year required a mere £1,500. By the time of the Silver Jubilee in 1977, the average price was just under £10,000. In 2012 Britain's average house price was £160,000 – 16 times higher than in 1977. Since we in the UK are well known for our love of bricks and mortar, these figures go some way to prove what a reliable investment property has been over the long term.

There is no question that people still see their house as a good investment. However, it is important to make the distinction between people appreciating the value of their house and those actually planning to use that asset to help fund their retirement. Only 11 per cent of a total sample surveyed (for the *Visions of Britain 2020 – Ageing and Retirement Report* by the Futures' Foundation/Friends' Provident) plan on selling or downsizing their property to fund retirement and an even smaller proportion (6 per cent) plan on releasing the equity in their property. Age UK's research shows people who have bought equity release are positive, which was unexpected since some equity release schemes had a tarnished reputation. But the majority of the over-65s say they want to stay in their own home when they retire.

Some baby boomers (the generation reaching retirement age now), however, do decide to downsize. In fact, exchanging a large-sized family house for a smaller one was the biggest reason for moving home in nine out of 10 regions in England and Wales last year. These people may be rich on paper – in terms of property wealth – but short of cash because of the high cost of living coupled with rock-bottom interest rates on savings and poor returns on pension investments. So whether you wish to have less space or release cash, either for yourself or to help adult children cover debts or pay for the deposit on a property of their own, the decision to sell must be yours. It is also one which should not be taken without a lot of consideration.

In retirement, of course, our needs change and not just in terms of space required. Perhaps the neighbourhood in which you've lived for years and brought up the family has altered considerably? Maybe old friends have moved away and the quiet road has become a busy thoroughfare, or you may no longer know any of your neighbours. One of the most important decisions to be taken as you approach retirement is whether you should move house or stay put. If the latter is your choice, you might want to consider making changes to where you live.

To many people, one of the biggest attractions once they've finished work is the pleasure of being able to move home. Not being tied to an area within easy commuting distance, at last they can indulge their long-held plans of living in a new area (possibly a new country). Although this could turn out to be everything they desire, without any real assessment of the pros and cons, some do regret having made a hasty decision. It is sensible at least to examine the various options. An obvious possibility is to stay where you are and perhaps adapt your present home to make it more suitable for your requirements. If it's getting harder to look after a house and garden that are now much too big for you, remember that striving to maintain the status quo is no longer necessary.

You might decide to move nearer to family or friends; or possibly consider moving into accommodation that is smaller, easier and more economic to maintain. Perhaps you might look at a new location where you can enjoy all the activities that you have been looking forward to in your retirement. Purpose-designed retirement housing is another option that suits increasing numbers of people, and there is such a wide choice available.

Lots of people are conditioned to think of retirement as being a time for selling up and relocating. An all-too-common mistake is for people to retire to a place where they once spent an idyllic holiday, perhaps 15 or 20 years previously, without further investigation. Resorts that are glorious in midsummer can be bleak and damp in winter. They can also be pretty dull when the tourist season is over. Equally, many people sell their house and move somewhere smaller without sufficient thought. It may be that once you're spending more time at home you will want more space, rather than less.

Although moving may be the right solution for some, especially if you want to realize some capital to boost your retirement income, there are plenty of ways of adapting a house to make it more convenient and labour saving. Likewise, you may be able to cut running costs, for example with better insulation. Before you come to any definite decision, ask yourself a few down-to-earth questions:

What are your main priorities? Do you want to be closer to your family? Would a smaller, more manageable home be easier for you to run? Would a reduction in running costs be helpful? What about realizing some capital to provide you with extra money for your retirement? Have you thought about living in a particular town or village that you know and like and where you have plenty of friends? Or does the security of being in accommodation that offers some of the facilities you may want as you become older sound attractive? Would, say, a resident caretaker and the option of having some of your meals catered for, appeal to you?

Whatever you decide is bound to have advantages and drawbacks; life is full of compromises. But it is important that you weigh up the pros and cons carefully, so that you don't end up making a choice that – while attractive in the short term – you regret later on.

Staying put

Since moving house is said to be one of the most stressful things in life, if you're a home owner who needs more space, it makes sound common sense in the current climate to extend rather than sell up. With house prices seeming unlikely to rise much over the next few years, many people's instinct is to sit tight. If this idea appeals to you, spend a bit of time working out whether there are ways of adapting your home to provide what you want. If your house is too big, you might think about reusing the space in a better way. Would it be possible, for example, to turn a bedroom into an upstairs study? Or perhaps you could convert a spare room into a separate workroom for hobbies and get rid of the clutter from the main living area? Have you thought about letting one or two rooms? As well as solving the problem of wasted space, it would also bring in some extra income.

Ways of increasing the size of your property

There are all kinds of ways to improve your property and maximize its potential: from relatively simple cosmetic updates (such as redecorating) to more complicated work including adding a new kitchen or bathroom. Before embarking on any improvements, it is sensible to work out which ones will be most suitable and add value to your property. Large-scale projects such as loft conversions and extensions inevitably involve some financial investment. But the total cost of improving your home may be lower than the cost of moving, once fees and stamp duty are taken into account. A loft conversion is popular as it can add an extra bedroom and possibly even a bathroom. Building an extra room as an extension is the next favourite, followed by adding a conservatory, a new kitchen, central heating, bathrooms and new windows. But there are some exciting options available to those ready for a challenge. Whatever you decide, stick to the rules. Any new work must comply with building regulations. Most important, under the Party Wall Act, where appropriate you must also notify your neighbours.

Adding an extension to the back of your property is one of the most popular ways to add space – because this is where most people have their garden. It is also the most practical option. Costs vary depending on the quality of the fixtures and fittings, as well as local labour rates. Smaller extensions to the rear or side of a property can often be built without having to make a planning application, provided that the design complies with the rules for permitted development (see **www.planningportal.gov.uk**). It is wise always to check with your local authority first before committing to any work.

The most ambitious scheme, of course, would be to become your own neighbour, by purchasing the next-door property and knocking through. This solution to requiring more space (whatever the reason might be – such as moving relatives close to you while retaining some independence) works for some people. Knocking through allows more space than an extension without incurring moving costs or leaving the neighbourhood. This option is neither cheap nor simple. However, it is possible to knock through almost any age or style of property so long as it is adjoining. Professional advice from an architect is essential so that the required planning permissions can be sought. Also it is sensible to take a holistic approach so that the finished conjoined house looks right. This makes selling the property much easier in the future and it is vital to bear this point in mind however you plan to extend your property.

Alternatively, if you live in an apartment you might be able to buy the adjoining unit or the one above or below then knock through or install a staircase to achieve double living space. Any construction work being undertaken must, of course, adhere strictly to planning and building regulations and you must ensure the project is completed properly. Although it may be tempting to cut corners, it is never advisable. Things can come back to haunt you at a later date should you want to sell. With regard to any home extension or 'knock-through' option, provided you can remain living in the property while the building work is being carried out, the disruption is less dramatic. Owners living onsite often make for a smoother and swifter conclusion to the project.

Despite being pricier than a conventional extension, if there is no scope to go outwards or upwards, extending below ground level is proving increasingly popular. This is particularly so in higher-value areas such as central London. Planning permission is normally required but is not usually an obstacle, even within a conservation area, because the new space has no visual impact on the street-scape. Some local authorities don't even require a planning application. Converting an existing cellar is less expensive and does not usually require planning permission (however, do check first with your local authority). For further information see **www.basements.org.uk**.

Another popular way to increase space in your home is to build above a garage. A conversion of this kind is reasonably simple and increases the size of your home easily and quickly. Remember to do your sums before you start. You will want to compare building costs with how much value the extra rooms are likely to add to your home. Any scheme would be subject to appropriate planning permission being granted. This is needed because of the extra height and alteration to the roof line. Whether your garage is single size or double, attached or detached, this type of extension is one of the quickest 'wins' because you are working with what you've got and you are spared the necessity of digging new foundations. However, existing foundations will need to be checked to prove they can sustain the extra load. Also, there are few implications for disruption to the rest of the house, particularly if the garage is detached. You could of course extend into the garage itself as well as building above, if it's not being used to house the car. Rooms above a detached garage make an ideal guest suite, office, study, granny or nanny flat (or somewhere to carry on a noisy hobby). Should this idea appeal, there are some specialist companies dealing solely with garage conversions.

Some possible changes

A few judicious home improvements carried out now could make the world of difference in terms of comfort and practicality. Many of us carry on for years with inefficient heating systems that could be improved relatively easily and cheaply. Stairs need not necessarily be a problem, even when you are very much older, thanks to the many types of stair lifts now available. Even so, a few basic facilities installed on the ground floor could save your legs in years to come. Similarly, gardens can be redesigned to suit changing requirements. Areas that now take hours to weed could be turned into extra lawn or a patio.

Many people now have the collective right to buy the freehold of their building and the individual right to extend their leases at a market price. This came about as a result of the Leasehold Reform, Housing and Urban Development Act 1993, which extended the right of enfranchisement to thousands of flat leaseholders. Among other requirements to enfranchise, your flat must be held under a lease that was originally granted for more than 21 years, and the eligible tenants of at least half of the flats in the block must also wish to buy the freehold. Before proceeding, you would be advised to obtain a professional valuation as a first step to establishing a fair price to which the landlord will be entitled. 'Fair price' is made up of the open market value of the building, half of any mortgage value that may be payable, plus possible compensation to the landlord for any severance or other losses. If you have a dwindling lease but do not wish to enfranchise, the more straightforward purchase of a 90-year lease extension might be a better option.

Many people actually want protection from a landlord but do not necessarily want to buy the freehold or extend the lease. If this is important to you, leaseholders' rights are much stronger than they were. Among other rights, where leaseholders believe that their service charges are unreasonable they can ask a leasehold valuation tribunal, rather than a court, to determine what charge is reasonable. This includes work that has been proposed but not yet started. Also, where there are serious problems with the management of a building, tenants can ask the tribunal to appoint a new manager. Importantly, leasehold valuation tribunals are less formal than a court and avoid the risk of potentially unknown costs being awarded. Further information is available from your local **Citizens Advice Bureau** or see their website: **www.citizensadvice.org.uk**.

Additionally, the Common-hold and Leasehold Reform Act 2002 introduced a new right to take over the management of flats without having to prove fault on the part of the landlord. It made buying the freehold or an extended lease of a flat easier, strengthened leaseholders' rights against unreasonable service charges, prevented landlords from taking any action for unpaid ground rent unless this has first been demanded in writing, made lease variations easier to obtain and provided further protection for the holding of leaseholders' monies. Furthermore, landlords are not able to commence forfeiture proceedings to obtain possession of the property unless they have first proved an alleged breach of the lease before a leasehold valuation tribunal. Where the breach relates to arrears, they must also have proved that the sum demanded is reasonable.

Information

Further information obtainable from **The Leasehold Advisory Service**; see website: **www.lease-advice.org**.

Landmark Leasehold Advisory Services specializes in providing legal services to residential leaseholders of England and Wales; see website: **www.landmarklease.com**.

For advice on leasehold legislation and policy, see the **Department for Communities and Local Government** website: **www.communities.gov.uk**.

Moving to a new home

Some people say that moving to a new home is one of the most stressful things in life. If you do decide to move, it makes sense that the sooner you start looking for your new home the better. There is no point in delaying the search until you retire unless you have to. With time to spare, you will have a far greater choice of properties and are less likely to indulge in any panic buying. While a smaller house will almost certainly be easier and cheaper to run, make sure that it is not so small that you are going to feel cramped. Remember that, when you and your partner are both at home, you may need more room to avoid getting on top of each other. Also, if your family lives in another part of the country, you may wish to have them and your grandchildren to stay. Conversely, beware of taking on commitments such as a huge garden. While this might be a great source of enjoyment when you are in your 60s, it could prove a burden as you become older.

If you are thinking of moving out of the neighbourhood, there are other factors to be taken into account such as access to shops and social activities, proximity to friends and relatives, availability of public transport and even health and social support services. While these may not seem particularly important now, they could become so in the future. Couples who retire to a seemingly 'idyllic' spot often return quite quickly. New friends are not always easy to make.

The question of downsizing is something that affects many over-60s. If you are considering moving to a smaller property, you will have to face the painful challenge of deciding what to keep and what to discard. The ideal way of solving such a problem is to enlist help from a professional organizer, a feng shui or decluttering expert. But if that sounds a bit dramatic, how about following some of these practical suggestions? Don't think of it as 'downsizing', rather look at is as 'rightsizing'. You are sensibly moving to a home that is the right size for you, at this time of your life. Rather than thinking 'What should I leave behind?' think 'What do I actually need?'

Top of the list should be things you love and will want to enjoy in your new home. Don't take possessions to keep a cherished memory alive; a framed photograph of the occasion takes up much less space. Check with family members to see if there are any items they want, and let them take them now. Be firm and explain to your young people that you can no longer act as free storage for all their old possessions. If they can't remove them, or don't want them, then it's off to the charity shops or the recycling centre. Finally don't keep something because it's still in good condition, even if you don't use it. Let it go to someone who could use it. For more information on how to downsize without pain, contact APDO UK (the Association of Professional Declutterers and Organisers, formed in 2004). Website: **www.apdo-uk.co.uk**.

Another thing to note when viewing your potential new home, reported in the *Daily Telegraph* recently, is the colour of the front door of the house. This apparently is a good indicator of what sort of person lives behind it. The study of 2,000 home owners, for paint and wallpaper specialist Farrow & Ball, found that people with green front doors are elegant and sophisticated, while those with black doors are focused on their careers. Red means residents are likely to be happy extroverts. But beware; those living behind grey doors are the least happy.

Something else to bear in mind when considering relocating is that some rural areas have hidden levels of deprivation. Research compiled in 2010 by Gloucestershire Rural Community Council (GRCC) found that around a third of that county's population – about 200,000 people – live in rural areas and some 16,000 are classified as income deprived. This comes as a shock to many people who believe that everyone who lives in the countryside has an idyllic existence. If you are elderly or infirm, living in the country can create massive challenges, particularly if you have a long-term illness. Lack of public transport is one of the main causes of rural deprivation, with the loss of village shops and post offices being another. Anyone considering a major lifestyle change, such as moving to a rural location in retirement, should take time and review all options before coming to a decision.

So-called 'retirement areas' can mean that you are cut off from a normal cross-section of society, and health services are likely to be overtaxed. While retiring to the country can be glorious, city dwellers should, however, bear in mind some of the less attractive sides of rural living. Noise, for example low-flying aircraft and church bells, can be an unexpected irritant. If you are not used to it, living near a silage pit or farm can also be an unpleasant experience. Another question: would a small village or seaside resort offer sufficient scope to pursue your interests once the initial flurry of activity is over?

Even if you think you know an area well, check it out properly before coming to a final decision. If possible, take a self-catering let for a couple of months, preferably out of season when rents are low and the weather is bad. A good idea is to limit your daily spending to your likely retirement income rather than splurge as most of us do on holiday. Do your research and visit **www.upmystreet.com** or **www.neighbourhoodstatistics.co.uk**.

This is even more pertinent if you are thinking of moving abroad, where additional difficulties can include learning the language, lower standards of health care and the danger of losing contact with your friends. Another problem for expatriates could be a change in the political climate of that country. This could result in your not being so welcome in your adopted country and a drop in the purchasing power of your pension. For more information on the financial implications of living overseas, see the section 'Retiring abroad', below.

Counting the cost

Moving house can be an expensive exercise but, if you can afford to move, some good bargains can be had. It is estimated that the cost is between 5 and 10 per cent of the value of a new home, once you have totted up extras such as search fees, removal charges, insurance, stamp duty, VAT, legal fees and estate agents' commission.

SDLT

The rate of Stamp Duty Land Tax (SDLT), or stamp duty for short, is currently 0 per cent on properties up to the value of £125,000. Properties purchased costing £125,001 to £250,000 will incur a rate of 1 per cent stamp duty. From £250,001 to £500,000 it is 3 per cent for all buyers, rising to 4 per cent for all purchasers on properties costing over £500,000 to £1 million. SDLT is 5 per cent on properties from over £1 million to £2 million. Over £2 million from 22 March 2012 the SDLT is 7 per cent. On properties over £2 million purchased by certain persons and corporate bodies, the SDLP is 15 per cent. To find out more about this, see HM Revenue & Customs website: **www.hmrc.gov.uk**.

When buying a new home, especially an older property, it is essential to have a full building (structural) survey done before committing yourself. This will cost in the region of £500 for a small terraced house but is worth every penny. In particular, it will provide you with a comeback in law should things go wrong. A valuation report, while cheaper, is more superficial and may fail to detect flaws that could give you trouble and expense in the future.

If you are buying a newly built house, there are now a number of safeguards against defects. Most mortgagors will lend on new homes only if they have a National House Building Council (NHBC) warranty or its equivalent. The NHBC operates a 10-year 'Buildmark' residential warranty and insurance scheme under which the builder is responsible for putting right defects during the first two years. It is designed to protect owners of newly built or newly converted residential housing if a problem does occur in a new home registered with NHBC. If the home owner and builder do not agree on what needs to be done, NHBC can carry out a free independent resolution investigation and, if judged necessary, will instruct the builder to carry out repair works. If a problem becomes apparent after more than two years, the home owner should contact NHBC, as the 'Buildmark' covers a range of structural aspects as well as double glazing, plastering and staircases. See **NHBC** website: **www.nhbc.co.uk**.

Also helpful to home buyers, the Land Registry allows members of the public to seek information directly about the 20 million or so properties held on its register via the **Land Registry** website: **www.landregistry.gov.uk**.

Home information packs (HIPs)

Home Information Packs (known as HIPs) were suspended from 21 May 2010. Homes marketed for sale since that date no longer require an HIP, but the requirement for the Energy Performance Certificate (EPC) has been retained, whether you are selling or renting out.

Energy Performance Certificates (EPCs)

An EPC rates the property's energy use and suggests ways to make energy-saving improvements. The EPC rating is on an A–G scale (like the EU energy label used on fridges and other white goods); the higher the rating, the more energy efficient the home is. The average UK home has a 'D' rating, and the Energy Saving Trust suggests you think carefully before choosing any home with an 'F' or 'G' rating. For its size it will be expensive to heat, and your carbon footprint will also be larger. Newer homes generally use less energy, so buyers or renters looking at a recently built home would expect to see an EPC rating of 'B' or above. EPCs are produced by accredited Domestic Energy Assessors and cost from £30 to £80, depending on the size of the property. Sellers are required to commission, but won't need to have received, an EPC before marketing their property.

Information

For details about local Domestic Energy Assessors see **EPC Register**; website: **www.epcregister.com**.

For a free and impartial home energy check visit **Energy Saving Trust;** website: **www.energysavingtrust.org.uk.**

For advice on leasehold legislation and policy, see the **Department for Communities and Local Government** website: **www.communities.gov.uk.**

Bridging loans

Tempting as it may be to buy before you sell, unless you have the money available to finance the cost of two homes – including possibly two mortgages – you need to do your sums very carefully indeed. Bridging loans are a way of getting over the problem, but can be a very expensive option. As an alternative to bridging loans, some of the major institutional estate agents operate chain-breaking schemes and may offer to buy your property at a discount (some 10 or 12 per cent less than the market price). Some companies that could help:

BridgingLoans.co.uk website: **www.bridgingloans.co.uk;**

Best Bridging Loans website: **www.bestbridgingloans.co.uk;**

BridgingLoansUK.co.uk website: **www.bridgingloansuk.co.uk.**

Estate agents

Finding your dream house may prove harder than you think. It can take months of exhaustive searching, yet some people catch sight of their perfect future home by casually searching on the internet or scanning the property pages of a local paper.

The National Association of Estate Agents (NAEA) runs a service called **Property Live,** a network of estate agents working with like-minded professionals committed to making the moving experience straightforward by providing access to a professional, friendly property service. See website: **www.propertylive.co.uk.**

For protection, there is a Property Ombudsman scheme to provide an independent review service for buyers or sellers of UK residential property in the event of a complaint. As with most Ombudsman schemes, action can be taken only against firms that are actually members of the scheme. See **The Property Ombudsman** website: **www.tpos.co.uk.**

The 1993 Property Misdescriptions Act prohibits estate agents and property developers from making misleading or inflated claims about a property, site or related matter. For further information see the **Royal Institution of Chartered Surveyors** (RICS) website: **www.rics.org.**

Retiring abroad

Do you dream of retiring to the sun? It could be a real option, but think carefully before making the leap. You will need to consider the cost and legal aspects of buying property in the country you are looking at. Local taxes, inheritance laws and many other aspects can be very different. A number of people contemplating an adventurous retirement raise funds on their family home in the UK and purchase a small property abroad, becoming what is known as 'residential tourists'. This means they travel to and from their other house without much luggage and spend several months at a time in their overseas home. Such a property abroad tends to fall into the category of 'lock up and leave' so that travelling to and from it is fairly easy. This bridges the gap between selling up and moving completely from the country you've lived in for years. It allows a certain amount of thinking time before you make a decision on whether or not the foreign property will at some point become your 'forever' home.

As a word of warning, you may have read reports on the thousands of expat British pensioners who retired to Spain some years ago. They are now attempting to flee that country's deepening economic gloom only for some to find their escape routes have been blocked due to their inability to sell up and return to the UK. Spanish property prices have dropped almost 50 per cent from their peak before the recession. Dreams of blissful retirement in the sun have been dashed by the decline in the value of the pound against the euro and dwindling interest rates on their savings. This situation is unlikely to improve quickly. More than half of the 800,000 Brits estimated to have moved to Spain during the good times are aged over 50. In recent surveys over 50 per cent of them expressed a wish to exchange their shattered sunshine dreams for the grey skies of Britain (source: *The Oldie* magazine – March 2012).

Should you be considering retiring abroad, this needs a lot of careful planning. If the country is English-speaking no new language skills will be needed. While a pleasure for some people, the thought of having to learn a new language could for others be quite a challenge. Also, there are a number of additional costs, besides purschasing the property, which can sometimes get overlooked: legal expenses, notary fees, stamp duty, registration fees and local taxes, costs of a solicitor and surveyor, to name a few. The purchase of another car, insuring the vehicle, new furniture, washing machine, dishwasher, fridge and freezer have to be taken into account, and there will be the costs of making a new will. Removal costs from the UK to the new country can be quite heavy too.

So if you decide to retire overseas, be careful. Some ways of protecting yourself when buying property abroad include:

- Get all documents translated.

- If you are given something to sign, make sure you have a 14-day cooling-off period.

- Take the documents home to the UK and speak to a lawyer and financial adviser over here rather than in the country overseas.

- Make sure the lawyer you use is independent and not involved in the sale in any way.

- Do not use a lawyer recommended by the seller.

- If you are buying a repossessed property, find out what happened.

- If you are borrowing money, go to a reputable bank. The bank manager will want to be sure the deal is sound – this adds another layer of checks and protection.

There are many websites offering advice and information on retiring abroad. (When checking out websites generally, do look for comments and reviews from people who have already used any you find interesting.) Look at:

www.gov.uk – Britons preparing to move or retire abroad;

www.propertyinretirement.co.uk – section on Retiring Abroad;

www.buyassociation.co.uk – section on Advice on Retiring Abroad and Homes Abroad;

www.retirementexpert.co.uk – popular locations when retiring abroad;

www.shelteroffshore.com – information on living abroad;

www.expatfocus.com – provides essential information and advice for a successful move abroad.

Removals

Professional help is essential for anyone contemplating a house move. Whether you are moving to the next street, or halfway across the world, using a reputable firm of removers and shippers will remove many of the headaches. A full packing service is something that should be considered, and saves much anxiety and a lot of your time. Costs vary depending on the type and size of furniture, the distance over which it is being moved and other factors, including insurance and seasonal troughs and peaks. Obviously, valuable antiques will cost more to pack and transport than standard modern furniture. It pays to shop around and get at least three quotes from different removal firms. Remember, however, that the cheapest quote is not necessarily the best. Find out exactly what you are paying for and whether the price includes packing and insurance.

The **British Association of Removers** (BAR) promotes excellence in the removals industry; for approved firms all of whom work to a rigorous code of practice, see website: **www.bar.co.uk**.

Retirement housing and sheltered accommodation

The terms 'retirement housing' and 'sheltered accommodation' cover a wide variety of housing but generally mean property with a resident manager/caretaker, an emergency alarm system, optional meals and some communal facilities such as living rooms, garden and laundry. Guest accommodation and visiting services such as hairdressers and chiropodists are sometimes also available. A number of companies offer extra care and nursing facilities in some of their developments. Designed to bridge the gap between the family home and residential care, such housing offers continued independence for the fit and active within a secure environment. Much of it is owned and run by local authorities, housing associations and charities. There are also a number of well designed, high-quality private developments of 'retirement homes' now on the market, for sale or rent, at prices to suit most pockets.

Many of the more attractive properties – and among the most expensive – are in converted country houses of architectural or historical merit, or in newly developed 'villages' and 'courtyard' schemes. As a general rule, you have to be over 55 when you buy property of this kind. While you may not wish to move into this type of accommodation just now, if the idea interests you in the long term it is worth planning ahead, as there are often very long waiting lists. For full details see Chapter 15, Caring for elderly parents.

Other options

Caravan or mobile home

Many retired people consider living in a caravan or mobile home. These can be kept either in a relative's garden or on an established site, possibly at the seaside or in the country. You may already own one as a holiday home that you are thinking of turning into more permanent accommodation. If you want to live in a caravan on land you own or other private land, you should contact your local authority for information about any planning permission or site licensing requirements that may apply.

If, on the other hand, you want to keep it on an established site, there is a varied choice. Make absolutely sure, whichever you choose, that the site owner has all the necessary permissions. You should check this with the planning and environmental health department of the local authority. It should be noted that many site owners will not accept prospective residents' own mobile homes but require them to buy one from the site or from an outgoing resident. The rights of owners of residential mobile home sites and of residents who own their mobile home but rent their pitch from a site owner are set out in the Mobile Homes Act 1983.

Find out what conditions both the local authority and the site owner attach to any agreement (by law the site owner must provide a written statement setting out terms such as the services provided, charges and maintenance of the site). You should also check your statutory rights (which should be included in the written statement), in particular regarding security of tenure and resale. Under the Act, residents have the right to sell their unit to a person approved by the site owner, who will be entitled to up to 10 per cent commission on the sale price. In the event of a dispute, since 30 April 2011 disputes under the Mobile Homes Act 1983 are being dealt with by Residential Property Tribunals in place of the County Court.

It should also be noted that ordinary caravans are not always suitable as long-term accommodation for the over-60s. Modern residential park homes, which are not all that different from bungalows, have the advantage of being more spacious and sturdier but, though usually cheaper than a house of equivalent size, are nevertheless a major expense. Moreover, the law regarding such purchases is complex, and legal advice is very strongly recommended before entering into a commitment to purchase a park home.

Visiting an exhibition dedicated to park homes will give you lots of useful information. The main national exhibitions held annually, relating to park and holiday homes, are: The National Park and Holiday Homes Show, The Park and Holiday Homes Show and The World of Park and Leisure Homes.

Park Home & Holiday Caravan magazine is the UK's biggest and best-selling park home magazine and is full of information for those interested in park homes. See website: **www.parkhomemagazine.co.uk**.

Companies that specialize in new homes for sale on residential parks, ready for immediate occupation, can be found on website: **www.parkhome-living.co.uk**, or are listed below:

Berkeley Parks, website: **www.berkeleyparks.co.uk**;

Britannia Parks, website: **www.britanniaparks.com**;

Pathfinder Park Homes, website: **www.pathfinderhomes.co.uk**;

Regency Park Homes, website: **www.regencyparkhomes.co.uk**;

Tingdene Residential Parks, website: **www.tingdene.net**;

Wessex Park Homes, website: **www.wessexparkhomes.co.uk**.

Mobile Homes – A guide for residents and site owners is a free booklet available from your housing department or from the **Department for Communities and Local Government**, website: **www.communities.gov.uk**.

Self-build

More than 25,000 people a year, including many in their 50s and over, are now building their own homes. With typical cost savings estimated at between 25 and 40 per cent, the number has been growing. New building methods have been developed that defy the assumption that you need to be fit or young to undertake such a project, and many older people have successfully become self-builders. No prior building experience is necessary, although this of course helps.

Some building societies offer self-build mortgages to enable borrowers to finance the purchase of land plus construction costs. However, as with any mortgage, it is essential to make sure that you are not in danger of over-committing yourself. It is also as well to be aware that obtaining planning permission from local councils can often be a protracted business and could add to the cost if you have to submit new plans. Most self-builders work in groups and/or employ subcontractors for some of the more specialized work, but individuals who wish to build on their own can make arrangements with an architect or company that sells standard plans and building kits.

Here are some useful websites for you to search:

www.homebuilding.co.uk: Home-building and renovating – self-build and house renovation website, featuring house plans, building costs, house design, land for sale, exhibitions and all the information you will need including a self-build cost calculator to help you calculate your self-build costs for building your own home.

www.buildstore.co.uk: Self-build, renovation, plots of land for sale, buying building materials and seeing how others build their own home, including UK map of land for sale, plot search and calculator for working out your self-build costs.

www.gov.uk: Raising the money to build your own home – about 25,000 people build their own homes in the UK each year and this number is rising.

www.builditthisway.co.uk: Self-build, building your own home, the ultimate DIY project, using practical examples showing the most cost-effective way to build a small house using time-honoured traditional methods.

www.selfbuildland.co.uk: Self-build land for sale in the UK. A portal for building plots for sale if you are looking to self-build your own home.

www.cat.org.uk: The Centre for Alternative Technology provides a free information and advice service on sustainable living and environmentally responsible building.

How green is your house?

With so much publicity about global warming, recycling, going green and reducing carbon footprints, becoming eco-friendly is something everyone should consider. You could set about such home improvements straight away with the specific aim of making your home as energy saving, economical and convenient as possible. Improvements are often easier to afford when you are still earning a regular salary. So if you are still working, you may find it easier to put up with the mess when you are not living among it 24 hours a day. The sooner you start the earlier you will reap the benefit.

Solar panels

Only a year or so ago pensioners were being urged to think seriously about installing solar panels, but time was of the essence regarding this. The money you could earn through the feed-in tariff was due to drop in 2012, but nobody envisaged the scale of the government's rate cuts. The money that could be earned from fixing up solar panels has been reduced by about half, though systems installed before 3rd March 2012 will continue to benefit from the old, much higher, tariff rates for the next 25 years. Even though the cost of solar panels is falling, the returns from installing them are nowhere near as good as they were a year ago. On the other hand it is still worth doing the sums. As energy costs rise, a solar panel on your roof may still be worth the investment.

The best place to find out more is the Energy Saving Trust at **www. energysavingtrust.org.uk.**

Insulation

When you retire, you may be at home more during the day so are likely to be using your heating more intensively. One of the best ways of reducing those now alarmingly increasing utility bills is to get your house properly insulated. Heat escapes from a building in four main ways: through the roof, walls, floor and loose-fitting doors and windows. Insulation not only can cut the heat loss dramatically but will usually more than pay for itself within four or five years.

Loft insulation

As much as 25 per cent of heat in a house escapes through the loft. The answer is to put a layer of insulating material, ideally 220 to 270 millimetres thick according to the material used, between and across the roof joists. You may be able to lay this yourself. The materials are readily available from builders' merchants. If you prefer to employ a specialist contractor, you can find one through the **National Insulation Association** website: **www.nationalinsulationassociation.org.uk.**

Doors and windows

A further 25 per cent of heat escapes through single-glazed windows, half of which could be saved through double glazing. There are two main types: sealed units and secondary sashes (which can be removed in the summer). Compared with other forms of insulation, double glazing is expensive; however, it does have the additional advantage of reducing noise levels. Since April 2002, any replacement doors and windows installed have to comply with strict thermal performance standards. The work will need to be done by an installer who is registered under the FENSA scheme; see the **Glass and Glazing Federation** website: **www.ggf.co.uk.**

Effective draught proofing saves heat loss as well as keeping out cold blasts of air. It is also relatively cheap and easy to install. Compression seals are the simplest and most cost-effective way to fill the gap between the fixed and moving edges of doors and windows. They are mounted by a variety of methods and supplied in strip form. For draught proofing older sliding-sash windows and doors, wiper seals, fixed with rustproof pins and screws, need to be used. For very loose-fitting frames, gap fillers that can be squeezed from a tube provide a more efficient seal between frame and surround, but this is normally work for a specialist. If you do fit draught seals, make sure you leave a space for a small amount of air to get through, or you may get problems with condensation. If the house is not well ventilated, you should put in a vapour check to slow down the leakage of moisture into the walls and ceiling. For advice on durable products and contractors, see the **Draught Proofing Advisory Association** website: **www.dpaa-association.org.uk**.

Heat loss can also be considerably reduced through hanging heavy curtains (both lined and interlined) over windows and doors. If you make sure your curtains cover the windowsill or rest on the floor you will keep warmer. It is better to have curtains too long than too short.

Wall insulation

More heat is lost through the walls than perhaps anywhere else in the house: it can be as much as 50 per cent. If your house has cavity walls – and most houses built after 1930 do – then cavity wall insulation should be considered. This involves injecting mineral wool (rock wool or glass wool), polystyrene beads or foam into the cavity through holes drilled in the outside wall. It is work for a specialist and, depending on what grants are applicable, may be free or could cost upwards of £350. Against this, you could expect a typical saving of around 25 per cent off your heating bill each year. In most cases the initial outlay should be recovered in less than four years. Make sure that the firm you use is registered with a reputable organization, such as the British Standards Institution, or can show a current Agrément Certificate for the system and is approved by the British Board of Agrément (BBA). If a foam fill is used, the application should comply with British Standard BS 5617 and the material with BS 5618.

Solid wall insulation can be considerably more expensive, but well worthwhile, providing similar savings of around 25 per cent off your annual heating bill. Again, this is work for a specialist and involves applying an insulating material to the outside of the wall, plus rendering or cladding. Alternatively, an insulated thermal lining can be applied to the inside. Landlords who install wall insulation can offset up to £1,500 of the cost, per building, against income tax. This used only to apply to loft and cavity wall insulation but has now been extended to include solid wall insulation. The scope of the relief (officially known as the Landlord's Energy Saving Allowance) was further extended to include draught proofing and insulation for hot water systems. Floor insulation is included in the list of energy-saving items that qualify for the allowance. NB: the £1,500 cap, which previously applied to the building, now applies per property, so if there are two flats in the building, the £1,500 cap now applies to each one.

For further information and addresses of registered contractors, see:

British Board of Agrément, website: **www.bbacerts.co.uk**;

British Standards Institution, website: **www.bsigroup.co.uk**;

Cavity Insulation Guarantee Agency (CIGA), website: **www.ciga.co.uk**;

Eurisol UK Ltd, website: **www.eurisol.com**;

Insulated Render & Cladding Association Ltd, website:
www.inca-ltd.org.uk;

National Insulation Association, website:
www.nationalinsulationassociation.org.uk.

Floor insulation

Up to 15 per cent of heat loss can be saved through filling the cracks or gaps in the floorboards and skirting. If you can take up your floorboards, rock wool or glass wool rolls can be extremely effective when fixed underneath the joists. Filling spaces with papier mâché or plastic wool will also help, especially if a good felt or rubber underlay is then laid under the carpet. Be careful, however, that you do not block up the underfloor ventilation, which is necessary to protect floor timbers from dampness and rot. Solid concrete floors can be covered with cork tiles or carpet and felt or rubber underlay. See **Energy Saving Trust** website: **www.energysavingtrust.org.uk**.

Hot water cylinder insulation

If your hot water cylinder has no insulation, it could be costing you several pounds a week in wasted heat. A British Standard insulating jacket fitted around your hot water cylinder will cut wastage by three-quarters. Most hot water tanks now come ready supplied with insulation. If not, the jacket should be at least 75 millimetres thick. See **Energy Saving Trust** website: **www.energysavingtrust.org.uk**.

Grants

There are many schemes for helping pensioners with heating bills and insulation costs. The big six electricity companies give a £120 annual rebate to certain customers, especially anyone on a small pension. Those receiving the guaranteed credit element of Pension Credit automatically get the money. At their discretion, energy companies can also give the refund to other vulnerable customers, including people with a disability or long-term illness. For this broader group, each company can choose exactly who qualifies and how many refunds they give out. It is up to you to contact your energy supplier and consider switching to a more generous one if they turn you down.

For information about grants and deals for older people, including free insulation and money for heating improvements, contact the Energy Saving Trust: website **www.energysavingtrust.org.uk**.

Here are some other websites that give advice and information on this subject:

www.insulationgrants.info: Home insulation grants – government grants for insulation.

www.freeinsulation.co.uk: government-backed grants available for cavity wall and loft insulation.

www.getinsulation.co.uk: New cavity wall and loft insulation. Apply for 100 per cent grants.

www.which.co.uk: Pensioners urged to claim government grants to help meet the cost of insulating their homes.

www.lioninsulation.co.uk: Home insulation grants available for loft and cavity wall insulation and draughtproofing.

www.saga.co.uk/money: Home help, grants for home improvements.

www.homeheatingguide.co.uk: Elderly people on Pension Credit are eligible for grants for home insulation.

www.government-grants.co.uk: Grants for loft and cavity wall insulation available.

Further details can be obtained from **www.gov.uk** or from **www.warmfront.co.uk**.

Heating

It may be possible to save money by using different fuels or by heating parts of your house by means of different systems. This could apply especially if some rooms are only used occasionally. Your local gas and electricity offices can advise on heating systems, running costs and energy conservation, as well as heating and hot water appliances.

The **Solid Fuel Association** website gives advice and information on all aspects of solid fuel heating, including appliances and installation; website: **www.solidfuel.co.uk**. The **Building Centre** website has a wide range of information on building products with consumer guidance; website: **www.buildingcentre.co.uk**.

Buying and installing heating equipment

When buying equipment, check that it has been approved by the appropriate standards approvals board.

For *electrical equipment*, the letters to look for are BEAB (British Electrotechnical Approvals Board) or CCA (CENELEC Certification Agreement), which is the European Union equivalent.

For *gas appliances*, look for the CE mark, which denotes that appliances meet the requirements of the Gas Appliance (Safety) Regulations Act 1995. Domestic solid fuel appliances should be approved by the Solid Fuel Appliances Approval Scheme; check the sales literature.

Gas appliances should only be installed by a Gas Safe Register registered installer (Gas Safe Register replaced CORGI as the gas registration body on 1 April 2009). Registration is compulsory by law. As a further safeguard, all registered gas installers carry a Gas Safe Register ID card with their photo, types of gas work they are competent to do, their employer's trading title and the Gas Safe Register logo. After a gas appliance has been installed, you should receive a safety certificate from the Gas Safe Register, proving that it has been installed by a professional. You should keep this safe, as you may need it should you want to sell your home in the future. See the **Gas Safe Register** website: **www.gassaferegister.co.uk**.

Additionally, members of the Heating and Ventilating Contractors' Association can advise on all types of central heating. All domestic installation work done by member companies is covered by a free three-year guarantee. See the **Heating and Ventilating Contractors' Association** website: **www.hvca.org.uk**.

When looking for contractors to install your equipment, an important point to note is that new legislation places tighter controls on the standard of electrical and other installation work in households across England and Wales. It is now a legal requirement for electricians as well as kitchen, bathroom and gas installers to comply with Part P of the Building Regulations. You would therefore be well advised to check that any contractor you propose using is enrolled with the relevant inspection council or is a member of the relevant trade association.

Electricians should be approved by the **NICEIC**. All approved contractors are covered for technical work by the NICEIC Complaints Procedure and Guarantee of Standards Scheme and undertake to work to British Standard 7671. Any substandard work must be put right at no extra cost to the consumer. For local approved contractors see website: **www.niceic.org.uk**.

An alternative source for finding a reputable electrician is the **Electrical Contractors' Association**. Its members, all of whom have to be qualified, work to national wiring regulations and a published ECA Code of Fair Trading. There is also a work bond, which guarantees that, in the event of a contractor becoming insolvent, the work will be completed by another approved electrician: see website: **www.eca.co.uk**.

Tips for reducing your energy bills

Energy can be saved in lots of small ways. Taken together, they could amount to quite a large cut in your bills. Here are some suggestions from **www.energychoices.co.uk**:

Switch suppliers. This is one of the simplest ways of saving money. More than 4 million people switched their energy supplier last year, cutting their bills by around £150 each, according to Ofgem. However, according to research by the University of East Anglia, 47 per cent of households have never switched their supplier.

Look after your boiler. The current lifespan of a boiler is around 10 years, after which it will begin to lose efficiency, wasting both your gas and cash. When replacing your boiler ensure you opt for an 'A' rated one displaying the Energy Saving Recommended logo. Choosing a heating system with a condensing boiler and heating controls could make a huge difference over time.

Insulate your home. Insulating your home is probably the most cost-effective way of reducing your home's fuel consumption. If your home has cavity walls, installing cavity wall insulation could significantly reduce the amount of energy you use to heat your home. Solid walls lose even more heat than cavity walls, so if your home has solid walls, the only way to reduce this heat loss is to insulate them on the inside or the outside. By adding weatherproof insulating treatment to the outside of the walls, the average household could save about £380 a year. As a significant amount of heat loss is through the roof, installing loft insulation is a simple and cost-effective way to reduce your heating bills, and can be done without the need for professionals.

Turn down the temperature. According to the Energy Saving Trust, turning down your thermostat by one degree centigrade can save up to 10 per cent on your heating bill. Best of all you are unlikely to notice the change.

Energy-saving light bulbs. One of the quickest and easiest ways you can immediately start saving energy is by switching to energy-saving light bulbs. They typically last 12 times longer than ordinary bulbs and, priced from around £3 each, could potentially save you a staggering £7 per year per bulb.

Change your habits. If you're conscientious about saving energy it can have a significant impact on your energy bills. Electrical appliances still use around 70 per cent of their usual energy when left on standby, so turning them off will trim your energy use. Closing curtains at dusk will stop heat escaping through the windows. If you are going away during the winter, leave your thermostat on a low setting to provide protection from freezing at minimum cost.

Watch your water usage. Taking showers instead of baths uses a whopping 30 per cent less water. If you have more bedrooms than people in your home you could save over £200 by switching to a water meter, so you only pay for the water you actually use. If you're unsure, contact your water company and ask for a 'water meter calculator'. With an accurate comparison this will make it easy for you to work out if you would save.

Change your appliances. Domestic appliances account for 47 per cent of a household's total electricity consumption, according to the Energy Saving Trust. Fridges and freezers account for 18 per cent of the electricity bill in a typical house; washing machines, tumble-dryers and dishwashers for 14 per cent and cooking appliances for 15 per cent. Watch out for the AAA energy rating logo on any new appliances.

Insure your boiler. If you've ever had to pay for emergency heating repairs you'll know how expensive this can be. For peace of mind take out boiler insurance, such as British Gas's Home Care (**www.britishgas.co.uk**).

Separate thermostats. If you have separate thermostats for your heating system and hot water cylinder, you can set it at around 60 degrees Celsius to enable you to keep hot water for taps at a lower temperature than for the heating system.

If your heating or water bills are unusually high, if you need more heat or water because of a disability or medical condition, you could qualify for the Social Tariff from your energy suppliers. You will find their telephone number on your bill. If you are disabled or exceptionally vulnerable, you can ask your gas or electricity supplier to put you on the Priority Service Register.

British Gas offers an **Essentials Programme** with a range of products, services and advice for vulnerable customers (such as those with low incomes and disabilities). To find out more about this see website: **www.britishgas.co.uk**.

The **Energy Saving Trust** has information on grants and money-saving ideas. See website: **www.energysavingtrust.org.uk**. **Consumer Direct** is the government-funded consumer advice service; see website: **www.gov.uk** – government, citizens and rights. Two other useful websites are: **www. moneysavingexpert.com** and **www.seniorsdiscounts.co.uk**.

Improvement and repair

If your house needs structural repairs, a wise first step would be to contact the **Royal Institution of Chartered Surveyors** to help you find a reputable chartered surveyor. See website: **www.rics.org**.

Local authority assistance

The Regulatory Reform Order (RRO) gives local authorities greater discretionary powers to provide assistance – such as low-cost loans and grants – to help with renovations, repairs and adaptations to the home, or to help someone move to more suitable accommodation if that is a better solution. Any assistance given, however, must be in accordance with the authority's published policy. For further information contact the environmental health or housing department of your local authority.

Disabled facilities grant (DFG)

This helps towards the costs of adapting your home to enable you to live there, should you become disabled. A grant can be obtained from your local council. It can cover a wide range of improvements to enable someone with a disability to manage more independently, including, for example, adaptations to make the accommodation safe for a disabled occupant, work to facilitate access either to the property itself or to the main rooms, the provision of suitable bathroom or kitchen facilities, the adaptation of heating or lighting controls, or improvement of the heating system. Provided the applicant is eligible, a mandatory grant of up to £30,000 may be available in England for all the above (local authorities may use their discretionary powers to provide additional assistance), £25,000 in Northern Ireland and up to £36,000 in Wales.

As with most other grants, there is a means test. The local authority will want to check that the proposed work is reasonable and practicable according to the age and condition of the property, and the local social services department will need to be satisfied that the work is necessary and appropriate to meet the individual's needs. The grant can be applied for either by the disabled person or by a joint owner or joint tenant or landlord on his or her behalf. For further information, contact the environmental health or housing department of your local authority. See website: **www.gov.uk** – Disabled people.

Do not start work until approval has been given to your grant application, as you will not be eligible for a grant once work has started.

Community care grant

People on low incomes or the disabled may be eligible for help from the Social Fund: see website: **www.gov.uk** – Money, tax and benefits.

Other help for disabled people

Your local authority may be able to help with the provision of certain special facilities such as a stair lift, telephone installations or a ramp to replace steps. Apply to your local social services department and, if you encounter any difficulties, ask for further help from your local disability group or Age UK group.

Useful contacts:

APHC Ltd (Association of Plumbing and Heating Contractors Ltd) maintains a national register of licensed members and can put you in touch with a reputable local engineer. See website: **www.competentpersonsscheme.co.uk**.

Association of Building Engineers can supply names of qualified building engineers/surveyors. See website: **www.abe.org.uk**.

Association of Master Upholsterers & Soft Furnishers Ltd has a list of over 500 approved members; see website: **www.upholsterers.co.uk**.

The Building Centre has displays of building products, heating appliances, bathroom and kitchen equipment and other exhibits and can give guidance on building problems. See website: **www.buildingcentre.co.uk**.

Federation of Master Builders (FMB): lists of members are available from regional offices. See website: **www.fmb.org.uk**.

Guild of Master Craftsmen can supply names of all types of specialist craftspeople including, for example, carpenters, joiners, ceramic workers and restorers. See website: **www.guildmc.com**.

Institute of Plumbing and Heating Engineering can provide a list of professional plumbers. See website: **www.ciphe.org.uk**.

Royal Institute of British Architects (RIBA) has a free Clients Service which, however small your building project, will recommend up to three suitable architects. See website: **www.architecture.com**.

Royal Institution of Chartered Surveyors (RICS) will nominate qualified surveyors in your area, who can be recognized by the initials MRICS or FRICS after their name. See website: **www.rics.org**.

The Scottish and Northern Ireland Plumbing Employers' Federation (SNIPEF) is the national trade association for all types of firms involved in plumbing and domestic heating in Scotland and Northern Ireland. See website: **www.snipef.org**.

Home improvement agencies (HIAs)

Home improvement agencies (sometimes known as 'staying put' or 'care and repair' agencies) work with older or disabled people to help them remain in their own homes by providing advice and assistance on repairs, improvements and adaptations. They also advise on the availability of funding and welfare benefits, obtain prices, recommend reliable builders and inspect the completed job.

The British Legion and Age UK offer a handyman service to carry out small household repairs, and keep a list of Home Improvement Agencies:

Age UK website: **www.ageuk.org.uk**.

British Legion website: **www.britishlegion.org.uk/can-we-help**.

Foundations is the national body for Home Improvement Agencies in England, providing a range of services for agencies. See website: **www.foundations.uk.com**.

Information on Home Improvement Agencies and care and repair in the UK can be found by contacting **EAC** (Elderly Accommodation Counsel) which helps older and elderly people with their housing, support and care needs. See website: **www.housingcare.org**.

Another possibility is the **Anchor Trust**, which offers comprehensive home care for the elderly, including home maintenance services. See website: **www.anchor.org.uk**.

Safety in the home

Did you know that less than one per cent of older people become crime victims in any one year? Falls are a much bigger risk, affecting one in three people over 65 every year. Accidents in the home account for 40 per cent of all fatal accidents, resulting in nearly 5,000 deaths a year. Seventy per cent of these victims are over retirement age, and nearly 80 per cent of deaths are caused by falls. A further 3 million people need medical treatment. The vast majority of accidents are caused by carelessness or by obvious danger spots in the home that for the most part could very easily be made safer. Tragically, it is all too often the little things that we keep meaning to attend to but never quite get round to that prove fatal. Here are a few suggestions for you to make your home safer.

Steps and stairs should be well lit, with light switches at both the top and the bottom. Frayed carpet is notoriously easy to trip on. On staircases especially, defective carpet should be repaired or replaced as soon as possible. All stairs should have a handrail to provide extra support – on both sides if the stairs are very steep. It is also a good idea to have a white line painted on the edge of steps that are difficult to see – for instance in the garden or leading up to the front door.

It may be stating the obvious to say that climbing on chairs and tables is dangerous – and yet we all do it. You should keep proper steps, preferably with a handrail, to do high jobs in the house such as hanging curtains or reaching cupboards.

Floors can be another danger zone. Rugs and mats can slip on polished floors and should always be laid on some form of non-slip backing material. Stockinged feet are slippery on all but carpeted floors, and new shoes should always have the soles scratched before you wear them. Remember also that spilt water or talcum powder on tiled or linoleum floors is a major cause of accidents.

The *bathroom* is particularly hazardous for falls. Sensible precautionary measures include using a suction-type bath mat and putting handrails on the bath or alongside the shower. For older people who have difficulty getting in and out of the bath, a bath seat can be helpful. Soap on a rope is safer in a shower, as it is less likely to slither out of your hands and make the floor slippery. Regardless of age, you should make sure that all medicines are clearly labelled. Throw away any prescribed drugs left over from a previous illness.

The *kitchen* is another place where it is important to be careful. Spills should be wiped up immediately to avoid slips. Any items you use regularly should be kept easily within reach. If you are having trouble preparing meals or doing the cleaning, your local social services can assist you with advice on helpful equipment. The Disability Living Foundation can provide equipment such as handrails, automatic lights and kettle tippers.

Falls are a great risk for older people. For every two people who fracture a hip in later life, one never regains the same level of mobility. So it pays to try to prevent such accidents. If you have a fall:

Stay calm. If you're unhurt, look for something firm to hold on to and get slowly to your feet again.

Then sit down and rest.

If you are injured, try to get comfortable, stay warm, and shift position every half hour or so until help arrives.

Should you have had several falls or fear falling, ask your GP to refer you to an NHS Falls Clinic.

A falls prevention nurse can test your balance, recommend foot care and make sure you stay as fit as possible.

Fires can all too easily start in the home. If you have an open fire, you should always use a fireguard and sparkguard at night. The chimney should be regularly swept at least once a year, maybe more if you have a wood-burning stove. Never place a clothes horse near an open fire or heater, and be careful of flammable objects that could fall from the mantelpiece. Upholstered furniture is a particular fire hazard, especially when polyurethane foam has been used in its manufacture. If buying new furniture, make sure that it carries a red triangle label, indicating that it is resistant to smouldering cigarettes. Furniture that also passes the match ignition test carries a green label. 'Combustion modified foam' that has passed the BS 5852 test now has to be used.

Portable heaters should be kept away from furniture and curtains and positioned where you cannot trip over them. Paraffin heaters should be handled particularly carefully and should never be filled while alight. Avoid leaving paraffin where it will be exposed to heat, including sunlight. If possible, it should be kept in a metal container outside the house. Never dry clothes near a portable heater or open fire.

Gas appliances should be serviced regularly by British Gas or other Gas Safe Register registered installers. You should also ensure that there is adequate ventilation when using heaters. Never block up air vents: carbon monoxide fumes can kill.

If you smell gas or notice anything you suspect could be dangerous, stop using the appliance immediately, open the doors and windows and call the National Grid 24-hour emergency line free: 0800 111 999.

More than one in three fires in the home are caused by accidents with *cookers*. Chip pans are a particular hazard: only fill the pan one-third full with oil and always dry the chips before putting them in the fat or, better still, use oven-ready chips that you just pop into the oven to cook. Pan handles should be turned away from the heat and positioned so you cannot knock them off the stove. If you are called to the door or telephone, always take the pan off the ring and turn off the heat before you leave the kitchen.

Cigarettes left smouldering in an ashtray could be dangerous if the ashtray is full. Smoking in bed is a potential killer.

Faulty electric wiring is another frequent cause of fires, as are overloaded power points. The wiring in your home should be checked every five years and you should avoid using too many appliances off a single plug. Ask an electrician's advice about what is the maximum safe number. Use only plugs that conform to the British Standard 1363. It is a good idea to get into the habit of pulling the plug out of the wall socket when you have finished using an appliance, whether TV or toaster.

All electrical equipment should be regularly checked for wear and tear, and frayed or damaged flexes immediately replaced. Wherever possible, have electric sockets moved to waist height to avoid unnecessary bending whenever you want to turn on the switch. In particular, *electric blankets* should be routinely overhauled and checked in accordance with the manufacturer's instructions. It is dangerous to use both a hot water bottle and electric blanket – and never use an under blanket as an over blanket.

Electrical appliances are an increasing feature of labour-saving *gardening* but can be dangerous unless treated with respect. They should never be used when it is raining. Moreover, gardeners should always wear rubber-soled shoes or boots, and avoid floppy clothing that could get caught in the equipment.

As a general precaution, keep *fire extinguishers* readily accessible. Make sure they are regularly maintained and in good working order. Portable extinguishers should conform to BS EN 3 or BS 6165. Any extinguishers made before 1996 should conform to BS 5423, which preceded BS EN 3. Many insurance companies now recommend that you install a smoke alarm, which should conform to BS 5446-1:2000 or BS EN 14604:2005, as an effective and cheap early-warning device.

Here are some useful websites:

www.dlf.org.uk;

www.info.co.uk/HomeSafetyForSeniors;

www.home-security-action.co.uk/home-safety-for-the-elderly;

www.saferhouses.co.uk/HomeSafetyElderly;

www.ageuk.org/home-and-care;

www.indobase.com/home/age-lifestyle/home-for-elderly;

www.independentliving.co.uk.

Home security

According to the Home Office, the elderly are not more at risk from crime than any other section of society. Should you feel nervous or vulnerable, the crime prevention officer at your local police station will advise you on how to improve your security arrangements. He or she will also tell you whether there is a Neighbourhood Watch scheme and how you join it. This is a free service that the police are happy to provide. Most burglaries are opportunist crimes. Don't be an easy target.

The most vulnerable access points are doors and windows. Simple pre-cautions such as fitting adequate locks and bolts can do much to deter the average burglar. Prices for a good door lock are about £60 to £80 plus VAT, and prices for window locks are about £15 to £20 plus VAT per window. Doors should have secure bolts or a five-lever mortise lock strengthened by metal plates on both sides, a door chain and a spy hole in the front door. Additionally, you might consider outside lights (ideally with an infrared sensor) to illuminate night-time visitors and an entry-phone system requiring callers to identify themselves before you open the door.

Windows should also be properly secured with key-operated locks. The best advice is to fit locks that secure them when partially open. Install rack bolts or surface-mounted security press bolts on French windows, and draw your curtains at night so potential intruders cannot see in. Louvre windows are especially vulnerable because the slats can easily be removed. A solution is to glue them in place with an epoxy resin and to fit a special louvre lock. An agile thief can get through any space larger than a human head, so even small windows such as skylights need properly fitted locks. Both double glazing and Venetian blinds act as a further deterrent. If you are particularly worried, you could also have bars fitted to the windows or install old-fashioned internal shutters that can be closed at night. Alternatively, many DIY shops sell decorative wrought-iron security grilles.

An obvious point is to ensure that the house is securely locked, both front and back doors, whenever you go out, even for five minutes. If you lose your keys, you should change the locks without delay. Insist that official callers such as meter readers show their identity cards before you allow them inside. If in doubt about unexpected callers, keep them out. Gas, electric and water companies can give meter readers and engineers a password so you know they are genuine. You could fit a locking chain and spy hole on your front door for peace of mind.

If you are going away, even for only a couple of days, remember to cancel the milk and the newspapers. You might also like to take advantage of the **Royal Mail's Keepsafe** service. It will store your mail while you are away and so avoid it piling up and alerting potential burglars to your absence. There is a charge for the service, which starts at £8.95 for up to 17 days. See website: **www.royalmail.com/redirections**.

If your home will be unoccupied for any length of time, it is sensible to ask the local police to put it on their unattended premises register. Finally, consider a time switch (cost around £15) that will turn the lights on and off when you are away and can be used to switch on the heating before your return.

If you want to know of a reputable locksmith, you should contact the **Master Locksmiths Association**; website: **www.locksmiths.co.uk**.

The BBC Crimewatch Roadshow (**www.bbc.co.uk/crimewatchroadshow**) offers the following tips to stay safe:

1 Keep your possessions safe by securing your home. You may be entitled to help towards paying for security improvements from your local council. Check with the housing department about these payments.

2 Don't keep large amounts of money in your home. Keep it in a bank or building society where it is much safer.

3 Get to know your neighbours, as it will be helpful to both of you if you are aware of each other's routines.

4 Make sure you have good exterior lighting on your home. Call the council and let them know if street lights have burned out on your road.

5 It is especially important not to let strangers into your home. Fit a door chain and viewer.

6 Never give out personal details, such as credit card information, to strangers who call to see you.

7 Never let a maintenance or service man who has just turned up at your door into your home.

8 Always check the ID of maintenance men that you are expecting. You can check these details with their employer before you let them in. If in doubt, ask them to come back when someone else is with you.

9 If you're out after dark, leave a light and radio on in the sitting room.

10 Get advice from the Crime Prevention Officer at your local police station. Some areas have schemes to help older people.

Further useful information is supplied by:

Victim Support, a support and witness service for those affected by crime; see website: **www.victimsupport.com**.

Trustmark Scheme, which finds reliable, trustworthy tradesmen; see website: **www.trustmark.org.uk**.

Trading Standards, where you can search for trusted traders in your area: see website **www.tradingstandards.gov.uk**.

Age UK Advice, provide a booklet *Staying Safe*. See website: **www.ageuk.org.uk**.

Safe Partnership runs local schemes providing free home security to vulnerable people: **www.safepartnership.org**.

Consumer Direct can be contacted if you have problems or disagreements with suppliers of goods or services; from overcharging to faulty goods, from dodgy workmanship to reporting unscrupulous traders or 'cowboys' or scams. See **www.gov.uk** – Consumer rights.

Burglar alarms and safes

More elaborate precautions such as a burglar alarm are among the best ways of protecting your home. Although alarms are expensive – they cost from about £450 to well in excess of £1,000 for sophisticated systems – they could be worth every penny. In the event of a break-in, you can summon help or ask the police to do what they can if you are away.

Many insurance companies will recommend suitable contractors to install burglar alarm equipment. The **National Security Inspectorate** website lists approved contractors in your locality that install burglar alarm systems to, among others, British and European standards. There are 700 recognized firms and some 1,000 branches. The National Security Inspectorate will also investigate technical complaints. See website: **www.nsi.org.uk**.

If you keep valuables or money in the house, you should think about buying a concealed wall or floor safe. If you are going away, it is a good idea to inform your neighbours so that if your alarm goes off they will know something is wrong. Burglar alarms have an unfortunate habit of ringing for no good reason (a mouse or cat can trigger the mechanism), and many people ignore them as a result. It is advisable to give your neighbours a key so that they can turn off and reset the alarm should the need arise.

Insurance discounts

According to recent research, seven out of 10 householders are underinsured, some of them unknowingly but some intentionally to keep premiums lower. This could be dangerous because in the event of a mishap they could end up seriously out of pocket. With recent increases in premiums, many readers may feel that this is hardly the moment to be discussing any reassessment of their policy. However, there are two good reasons why this could be sensible. First is because the number of burglaries has risen, so the risks are greater. But, more particularly, you may be able to obtain better value than you are getting at present. A number of insurance companies now give discounts on house contents premiums if proper security precautions have been installed.

Some insurance companies approach the problem differently and arrange discounts for their policyholders with manufacturers of security devices. If you would welcome independent advice on choosing a policy, you could contact the **Institute of Insurance Brokers** (IIB) for details of local IIB brokers; website: **www.iib-uk.com**. See also the 'Insurance' section, below.

Personal safety

Older people who live on their own can be particularly at risk. A number of personal alarms are now available that are highly effective and can generally give you peace of mind. A sensible precaution is to carry a 'screamer alarm', sometimes known as a 'personal attack button'. These are readily available in department stores, electrical shops and alarm companies.

A telephone can also increase your sense of security. Some families come to an arrangement whereby they ring their older relatives at regular times to check that all is well. Older people feel particularly vulnerable to mugging. While the dangers are often exaggerated, it must be sensible to take all normal precautions. The police are of the view that many muggings could be avoided if you are alert, think ahead and try to radiate confidence.

Many councils run community alarm schemes. For a small fee you get a panic button, usually on a pendant or wristband, so you can contact an emergency operator if you have a fall, are taken ill, or suspect a break-in. The operator phones a friend, relative or the emergency services. Age UK has been running its alarm scheme for 30 years but try your council first.

Insurance

As you near retirement, it is sensible to reassess your building and home contents policy. If the insurance was originally arranged through your building society, it may cease when your mortgage is paid off. In this case it will be essential for you to arrange new cover directly. Similarly, when buying for cash rather than with a mortgage – for instance when moving to a smaller house – it will be up to you to organize the insurance and to calculate the rebuilding value of your home. It is advisable to get a qualified assessor to do this for you.

The value of your home may have increased considerably since you purchased it. The cost of replacing the fabric of your house, were it to burn down, could possibly be significantly greater than the amount for which it is currently insured. Remember, you must insure for the full rebuilding cost: the market value may be inappropriate. Your policy should also provide money to meet architects' or surveyors' fees, as well as alternative accommodation for you and your family if your home were completely destroyed by fire.

If you are planning to move into accommodation that has been converted from one large house into several flats or maisonettes, check with the landlord or managing agent that the insurance on the structure of the total building is adequate. All too often people have found themselves homeless because each tenant insured only his or her own flat and the collective policies were not sufficient to replace the common parts.

If, when buying a new property, you decide to take out a new mortgage, contrary to what many people believe, you are under no obligation to insure your home with the particular company suggested by your building society. It is not being recommended here that you should necessarily go elsewhere: the point is that, as with all insurance, policies vary and some are more competitive than others.

About 2 million people live under threat of flooding in the UK – about one in 10 homes – and over 270,000 are at risk. Worrying about floods while suffering from the drought restrictions we have experienced recently seems perverse, but the owners of some 200,000 properties in flood-prone areas in the UK could soon have difficulty getting insurance. Even if they manage to find a policy that will cover them for flood damage, the premiums might well be unaffordable or impose excesses as high as £20,000.

In July 2008, insurance companies entered a five-year agreement with the government to continue insuring existing customers in flood-prone areas, predicated on the government improving flood defences. However, they believe there is little sign of this happening. The agreement runs out in July 2013, but home owners living in high-risk areas whose annual policies expired after July 2012 could face problems finding affordable insurance much sooner. If there is no new agreement, insurers can refuse to insure high-risk properties, or charge what they like.

The Association of British Insurers (ABI) has been putting pressure on the government to act to ensure that everyone living in a flood-risk area can continue to buy affordable insurance. Insurance companies want the government to improve flood defences or subsidize premiums. Some specialist insurance brokers may be able to find policies for flood-prone property but these will be expensive. It is advisable to check whether you live in a high-risk area and, if so, take steps to protect your property. This could cut your insurance premium by 10 per cent. According to the Association of British Insurers it can cost up to £40,000 to protect your home fully from flood damage. Information on flood-risk areas can be obtained from **Flood-line**, a flood warning and advice service run by the Environment Agency. See website: **www.environment-agency.gov.uk**.

It is unwise to skimp on protecting your home and possessions. While you might be able to pay for minor losses and repairs out of your own pocket, without insurance a major loss could be a financial disaster. Another important extra feature of home insurance is 'public liability cover'. This is designed to meet claims against you as a home owner, tenant or landlord – for example if a visitor tripped and was injured in your home (contents insurance) or if a tile fell from your roof and damaged a neighbour's car (buildings insurance) – and you are found liable for the damage or injury.

Buildings insurance

If you rent your home, it's up to your landlord to arrange buildings insurance. If you own your own home, it's up to you. Even if you no longer have a mortgage, make sure your home is insured. BCIS, the **RICS's Building Cost Information Service**, provides cost information on all aspects of construction. It has an online calculator at **www.bcis.co.uk** to estimate how much cover you need.

Contents insurance

Make sure you have the right level of cover. If you insure for more than your belongings are worth you are wasting money. However, if you insure for less (underinsure) you risk having any claim scaled back proportionately. Once you stop work, you may need to review the value of your home contents. You may have new items you have bought with a retirement lump sum.

With older possessions, you should assess the replacement cost and make sure you have a 'new for old' or 'replacement as new' policy. Most insurance companies offer an automatic inflation-proofing option for both building and contents policies. You should not forget to cancel items on your contents policy that you no longer possess. You must also add new valuables that have been bought or received as presents. In particular, do check that you are adequately covered for any home improvements you may have added, such as a new kitchen or garage, conservatory, extra bathroom, swimming pool or other luxury.

Where antiques and jewellery are concerned, simple inflation-proofing may not be enough. Values can rise and fall disproportionately to inflation and depend on current market trends. For a professional valuation, contact the **British Antique Dealers' Association** (BADA), website: **www.bada.org** or **LAPADA** (Association of Art & Antiques Dealers), website: **www.lapada.org**. Either of these organizations can advise on the name of a specialist. Photographs of particularly valuable items can help in the assessment of premiums and settlement of claims, as well as give the police a greater chance of recovering them in the case of theft. Property marking, for example with an ultraviolet marker, is another useful ploy, as it will help the police trace your possessions should any be stolen.

The **Association of British Insurers** has information on various aspects of household insurance and loss prevention; see website: **www.abi.org.uk**.

The **British Insurance Brokers' Association** can provide information on registered insurance brokers in your area; see website: **www.biba.org.uk**.

Some insurance companies offer home and contents policies for older people (age 50 and over) at substantially reduced rates. The rationale behind such schemes is that older people are less likely to leave their homes empty on a regular basis (ie 9 to 5) and are therefore less liable to be burgled. In some cases, policies are geared to the fact that many retired people have either sold or given away many of their more valuable possessions and therefore need to insure their homes only up to a relatively low sum. See the following websites for more information on such policies:

www.rias.co.uk;

www.castlecover.co.uk;

www.ageuk.org.uk;

www.staysure.co.uk;

www.50plusinsurance.co.uk;

www.over50insurance.org;

www.saga.co.uk.

An increasing number of insurance companies offer generous no-claims discounts. Another type of discount-linked policy that is becoming more popular is one that carries an excess, whereby the householder pays the first chunk of any claim, say the first £100 or £250. Savings on premiums can be quite appreciable, if you check what terms they offer.

Warning: Beware misplaced loyalty to an insurance provider. If you automatically renew your policy every year with the same company, you may find that your premiums have increased each year. Look at one of the comparison websites to see what other providers might quote for an identical amount of cover. If it is substantially less, it would pay you to switch to being a 'new' customer elsewhere.

Financial institutions are keen on 'loyalty marketing' but if they fail to understand that loyalty should work both ways, they deserve it when customers walk away to sign up to their competitors. Don't be fooled into staying with a provider just because you feel that your loyalty will be rewarded. Nowadays *disloyalty* pays because the winners are those customers who constantly switch from one provider to another.

Raising money on your home – equity release

Many home owners find that when they reach later life they have wealth tied up in their home but fewer savings or less income than they would like. If you are in this situation you could consider using your home as a source of extra cash. The most obvious way to raise money from your home would be to sell it and buy somewhere cheaper (often referred to as 'downsizing'). If you don't want to move, or can't move, another option is equity release. It is important to check before taking such a step that it is the right choice for you, both now and in the future.

Taking money out of your home through an equity release scheme is a monumental – and one-way – decision. *Which?* magazine recently tested the quality of advice given by some specialist equity release advisers and found worrying shortcomings. Four advisers failed its mystery shopping test completely and only two gave excellent advice. A good adviser will tell you about themselves and what they charge, analyse your financial situation and explain the various equity release schemes, other ways in which you can improve your income, and the penalty charges you would incur if you wanted to get out of the scheme without leaving your house. (The Consumer Credit Counselling Service (CCCS) – a debt charity that gives free advice including impartial guidance on equity release – was the only adviser to pass on all the *Which?* best-practice tests. Elsewhere advice can cost up to £1,000. Website: **www.cccs.co.uk**.)

An equity release plan allows you to use some of the capital you have tied up in your home while keeping the right to carry on living there for as long as you need. Homes are often people's greatest asset, yet the value remains untapped. It is an agreement between a home owner (aged 55 or over) and a provider, which enables the home owner to receive cash from the money tied up in their home. The money is free of tax and enables home owners to benefit from the value of their home.

Since April 2007, reversion schemes have come under the regulation of the FSA. Releasing equity from your home could reduce your entitlement to some state benefits. It could also make a difference to your tax position, and it will reduce the value of your estate when you die. The important thing with equity release is to make sure your family knows all about your plans. Since the loan, plus any interest, is paid off when you die, not letting your family know about the equity release scheme could mean they have a shock at a time when they are least able to cope with it.

There are two main types of plan: a lifetime mortgage and a home reversion plan. With a *lifetime mortgage* you raise money by taking out a mortgage against your property. The loan is repaid when the home is eventually sold. With a *home reversion plan* you sell part, or all, of your home now in return for a cash sum. You have the right to stay in your home as a tenant, paying little or no rent.

Equity release plans are designed to run until you die or move out, for example if you move permanently into a care home. You can have a plan just for yourself, or for you and your partner. In the latter case, the plan runs until you both no longer need the home.

How a lifetime mortgage works

Lifetime mortgages are the most commonly used type of equity release. Like an ordinary mortgage, a lifetime mortgage is a loan secured against your home, but a lifetime mortgage is normally repaid only when you no longer need to live there.

When taking out a lifetime mortgage you usually choose between borrowing a single lump sum or using a flexible or drawdown facility to provide a series of regular or ad hoc payments. This facility can be useful if you need extra income, because you pay interest only on the money you have drawn so far.

Most lifetime mortgages are 'roll-up loans'. This means you normally don't make any monthly repayments. Instead, interest is added to the loan and repaid only when your home is eventually sold. Usually interest is charged at a fixed rate. This means you can predict with certainty how the amount you owe will grow. Be wary of taking out a variable-rate plan where you do not have this certainty.

With a roll-up loan, the amount you owe can increase quickly. This may mean that, when your home is eventually sold, there may be little or nothing left from the proceeds after the loan is repaid. Most roll-up lifetime mortgages have a 'negative-equity guarantee' that promises the maximum you owe will not exceed the value of your home when it is sold.

How a home reversion plan works

With a home reversion plan you sell some, or all, of your home to a company (or in some cases, an individual investor) for less than the market value. In return you get a lump sum (which could be paid as a single sum or in instalments), a monthly income or both. You get the proceeds of the sale now. You no longer own your home, or the part you sold, but you have the right to stay there until you die or move out.

When your home is eventually sold, the reversion company gets all of the proceeds if you sold the whole of your home to them. If you sold part of your home, the reversion company gets its share – for example, if you sold half your home, the reversion company would take half the proceeds.

When you take out a home reversion plan, you don't get the full market value of your property on the part you sell. For example, if you sold part of your home with a market value of £100,000, you might get, say, £50,000. The difference between what you give up and what you get reflects the cost to the reversion company of waiting to gets its money back while letting you live in the property for little or no rent. The size of the difference depends on how long the company thinks it must wait, which in turn depends on your:

- age – the older you are when you take out the plan, the shorter the period you are expected to live, so the larger the sum you can get;

- sex – women tend to live longer than men, but from the end of 2012 insurers have not been allowed to take gender into account when fixing annuity rates. Rates for men will get worse – but might not improve much for women;

- health – if your life expectancy is reduced because of poor health, some providers may offer a higher amount.

Tips for choosing the right equity release scheme:

- Explore all other options first to make sure you find out how equity release would affect your entitlement to state benefits.

- Borrow just the minimum amount you need to or choose a drawdown scheme that will give you the option to borrow money as and when you need it.

Consider taking out a scheme that lets you make interest payments each month if you can afford to.

Choose a scheme with no early-repayment charges, or ones that apply only for a limited period.

'Sale and Rent Back' schemes are not the same as, nor similar to, equity release. This is a sector to steer clear of. Companies typically offer to buy your home at a discounted price and there are serious pitfalls.

How much equity release might cost

Arrangement and administration fees: the plan provider will normally charge an arrangement fee (say £750). With a drawdown mortgage or instalment reversion plan, there may be a separate administration fee for each withdrawal.

Valuation and legal fees: you will have to pay for a surveyor to value your property (say around £200 for a medium-sized property) and a solicitor to handle the paperwork and check the legal aspects of the agreement (from, say, £300 to £700). You must pay the valuation fee in advance but the provider might reimburse this if the plan goes ahead. Some deals refund your legal costs too. Costs that are not reimbursed can usually be deducted from the sum you raise.

Insurance and maintenance: in addition to the direct costs of the scheme, the provider will require you to have buildings insurance and to maintain the property to a reasonable standard.

NB: equity release plans are complex. Taking out an equity release plan is a major financial decision. You are strongly recommended to get advice from an independent financial adviser specializing in equity release and a solicitor who is familiar with this type of plan. The adviser will check whether a scheme is suitable for you and, if so, which type and provider to choose. The adviser must also check the impact a scheme might have on any state benefits you could claim, or refer you to another organization to check this. You should get legal advice – and use your own solicitor (not one appointed by the equity release firm). You should also ensure that the property is independently valued by a qualified surveyor. The adviser may charge a fee, be paid by commission, or a combination of both. For further information see the Money Advice Service website: **www.moneyadviceservice.org.uk**.

Finally, make sure you check with the **Equity Release Council**. This is the industry body for the equity release sector. Born from the expansion of the remit of SHIP (formerly Safe Home Equity plans), the Equity Release Council represents the providers, qualified financial advisors, lawyers, intermediaries and surveyors who work in the equity release sector. For further information see website: **www.equityreleasecouncil.com**.

Alternatively, the **Equity Release Information Centre** publishes a free 32-page guide to equity release. Visit **www.askeric.tv**

The following websites offer further information:

www.homereversionschemes.co.uk;

www.sixtyplusonline.co.uk;

www.societyoflaterlifeadvisers.co.uk;

www.learnmoney.co.uk;

www.which.co.uk/equityrelease.

Using your home to earn money

Rather than move, many people whose home has become too large are tempted by the idea of taking in tenants. For some it is an ideal plan, for others a disaster. At best, it could provide you with extra income and the possibility of pleasant company. At worst, you could be involved in a lengthy legal battle to regain possession of your property.

There are three broad choices: taking in paying guests or lodgers, letting part of your home as self-contained accommodation, or renting the whole house for a specified period of time. In all cases for your own protection it is essential to have a written agreement and to take up bank references, unless the let is a strictly temporary one where the money is paid in advance. Otherwise, rent should be collected quarterly and you should arrange a hefty deposit to cover any damage. An important point to be aware of is that there is now a set of strict rules concerning the treatment of deposits, with the risk of large fines for landlords and agents who fail to abide by them.

Lodgers: In a move to encourage more people to let out rooms in their home, the government allows you to earn up to £4,250 (£2,150 if letting jointly) a year free of tax. Any excess rental income you receive over £4,250 will be assessed for tax in the normal way. For further information see **HMRC** website: **www.hmrc.gov.uk** and Gov.uk website: **www.gov.uk**. If you have a mortgage or are a tenant yourself (even with a very long lease), check with your building society or landlord that you are entitled to sublet.

Paying guests or lodgers

This is the most informal arrangement, and will normally be either a casual holiday-type bed-and-breakfast let or a lodger who might be with you for a couple of years. In either case, the visitor will be sharing part of your home, the accommodation will be fully furnished, and you will be providing at least one full meal a day and possibly also basic cleaning services.

You do not have to commit to having a lodger around the house full-time; you can start with a short-term arrangement to see how you find it. Some employees and lecturers need a room only between Monday and Friday, keeping your weekends clear. Foreign students are around all term time but not in the holidays. Foreign language students might need a room only for one six-week term. You can stipulate whether to take younger or older people.

There are few legal formalities involved in these types of lettings, and rent is entirely a matter for friendly agreement. As a resident owner you are also in a very strong position if you want your lodger to leave. Lodging arrangements can easily be ended, as your lodger has no legal rights to stay after the agreed period. A wise precaution is to check with your insurance company that your home contents policy will not be affected, since some insurers restrict cover to households with lodgers. Also, unless you make arrangements to the contrary, you should inform your lodger that his or her possessions are not covered by your policy.

If, as opposed to a lodger or the occasional summer paying guest, you offer regular B&B accommodation, you could be liable to pay business rates. Although this is not new, it appears that in recent years the Valuation Office Agency has been enforcing the regulation more strictly against people running B&B establishments.

Holiday lets

It is a good idea to register with your tourist information centre and to contact the environmental health office at your local council for any help and advice.

Letting rooms in your home

You could convert a basement or part of your house into a self-contained flat and let this either furnished or unfurnished. Alternatively, you could let a single room or rooms. As a general rule, provided you continue to live in the house your tenant(s) have little security of tenure and equally do not have the right to appeal against the rent. Whether you are letting part of the house as a flat or simply a room to a lodger, you would be advised to check your home contents policy with your insurance company. For more information see the **Communities and Local Government** website: **www.communities.gov.uk.**

As a resident landlord, you have a guaranteed right to repossession of your property. If the letting is for a fixed term (eg six months or a year), the let will automatically cease at the end of that fixed period. If the arrangement is on a more ad hoc basis with no specified leaving date, it may be legally necessary to give at least four weeks' notice in writing. The position over notices to quit will vary according to circumstances. Should you encounter any difficulties, it is possible that you may need to apply to the courts for an eviction order.

Tax note

If you subsequently sell your home, you may not be able to claim exemption from capital gains tax on the increase in value of a flat if it is entirely self-contained. It is therefore a good idea to retain some means of access to the main house or flat, but take legal advice as to what will qualify.

Renting out your home on a temporary basis

If you are thinking of spending the winter in the sun or are considering buying a retirement home that you will not occupy for a year or two, you might be tempted by the idea of letting the whole house. In spite of the changes in the Housing Act 1996, there are plenty of horror stories of owners who could not regain possession of their own property when they wished to return. For your protection, you need to understand the assured short-hold tenancy rules. Unless notified in advance that you need the property back sooner (there are very few grounds on which you can make this notification) or unless earlier possession is sought because of the tenant's behaviour, your tenant has the right to stay for at least six months and must be given two months' notice before you want the tenancy to end.

It is strongly advisable to ask a solicitor or letting agent to help you draw up the agreement. Although this provides for greater protection, you will probably still require a court possession order if your tenant will not leave after you have given the required amount of notice. The accelerated possession procedure may help in some cases to speed up the process.

In most circumstances by far the safest solution if possible is to let your property to a company rather than to private individuals, since company tenants do not have the same security of tenure. However, it is important that the contract should make clear that your let is for residential, not business, purposes. Before entering into any agreement, you should seek professional advice. Further information is available from your local housing department, or the **Communities and Local Government** website: **www.communities.gov.uk**.

And some other ideas...

If you think a little extra cash might be useful, depending on where you live (such as near a festival site or theme park), you could turn your garden into a 'micro campsite' and earn up to £40 per night. A newly launched website **www.campinmygarden.com** aims to create a community of like-minded garden hosts and campers who will offer and use the temporary micro campsites in preference to overcrowded and underplumbed festival ones. The only proviso is that fresh water should be available. Whether you want a queue of muddy festival goers outside your bathroom in the morning is a matter for you to decide.

Should you have extra space in your house and don't mind renting out a room, by signing up to certain websites you can reach potential guests from all round the world. Try: **gumtree.com; airbnb.co.uk; wimdu.co.uk; spareroom.co.uk; crashpadder.com; uk.easyroommate.com**.

If you'd rather not have people, you can make extra money out of the empty space in your house by renting out your cellar or loft as storage space to people who have too much stuff (**storemates.co.uk**). If parking is difficult or expensive in your area, drivers will pay to use your parking space or garage (**yourparkingspace.co.uk; parkatmthouse.com; parklet.co.uk**).

You can offer your home for film and advertisement locations if you can cope with a lot of disruption. But it pays good money and film producers need other types of homes besides stately ones. Look at **film-locations.co.uk**.

Holiday lets

Buying a future retirement home in the country and renting it out as a holiday home in the summer months is another option worth considering. As well as providing you with a weekend cottage at other times of the year and the chance to establish yourself and make friends in the area, it can prove a useful and profitable investment.

As long as certain conditions are met, income from furnished holiday lettings enjoys most – but not all – of the benefits that there would be if it were taxed as trading income rather than as investment income. In practical terms, this means that you can claim 10 per cent writing-down capital allowances on such items as carpets, curtains and furniture as well as fixtures and fittings, thereby reducing the initial cost of equipping the house. Alternatively, you can claim an annual 10 per cent wear-and-tear allowance. The running expenses of a holiday home, including maintenance, advertising, insurance cover and council tax (or business rates – see below), are all largely allowable for tax, excluding that element that relates to your own occupation of the property. Married couples should consider whether the property is to be held in the husband's or the wife's name, or owned jointly. A solicitor or accountant will be able to advise you.

To qualify as furnished holiday accommodation, the property must be situated in the UK, be let on a commercial basis, be available for holiday letting for at least 140 days during the tax year and be actually let for at least 70 days. Moreover, for at least seven months a year, not necessarily continuous, the property must not normally be occupied by the same tenant for more than 31 consecutive days. This still leaves you with plenty of time to enjoy the property yourself.

There is always the danger that you might create an assured tenancy, so do take professional advice on drawing up the letting agreement. Similarly, if you decide to use one of the holiday rental agents to market your property, get a solicitor to check any contract you enter into with the company. For more information see the **RICS** (Royal Institution of Chartered Surveyors) website: **www.rics.org**.

A further point to note is that tax inspectors are taking a tougher line as to what is 'commercial', and loss-making ventures are being threatened with withdrawal of their tax advantages. To safeguard yourself, it is important to draw up a broad business plan before you start and to make a real effort to satisfy the minimum letting requirements. In particular, you should be aware that HMRC has been targeting landlords in the belief that many have been failing to declare their rental income or have overcalculated the amount of tax relief to which they are entitled.

Tenants' deposits

The Tenancy Deposit Scheme came into force in April 2007 and affects all landlords who let out property under an assured short-hold tenancy. Its purpose is variously to ensure tenants get back the amount owing to them, to make any disputes about the deposit easier to resolve and to encourage tenants to look after the property during the agreed term of their let. The big difference as a result of this new law is that, instead of simply holding the deposit until all or part of it is due to be returned, landlords or agents must now protect it under an approved scheme. Failure to do so within 14 days of receiving the money could result in the landlord being forced to pay the tenant three times the deposit amount.

The two types of tenancy deposit protection schemes available for landlords and letting agents are insurance-based schemes and custodial schemes. All schemes provide a free dispute resolution service. The schemes allow tenants to get all or part of their deposit back when they are entitled to it and encourage tenants and landlords to make a clear agreement from the start on the condition of the property. The schemes make any disputes easier to resolve.

With *insurance-based schemes* the tenant pays the deposit to the landlord. The landlord retains the deposit and pays a premium to the insurer – the key difference from the custodial scheme. Within 14 days of receiving a deposit, the landlord or agent must give the tenant the details about how his or her deposit is protected including the contact details of the tenancy deposit scheme selected, the landlord or agent's contact details, how to apply for the release of the deposit, information explaining the purpose of the deposit, and what to do if there is a dispute about the deposit.

At the end of the tenancy, if an agreement is reached about how the deposit should be divided, the landlord or agent returns all or some of the deposit. If there is a dispute, the landlord must hand over the disputed amount to the scheme for safekeeping until the dispute is resolved. If for any reason the landlord fails to comply, the insurance arrangements will ensure the return of the deposit to the tenant if he or she is entitled to it.

Custodial schemes are where the tenant pays the deposit to the landlord or agent. The landlord or agent then pays the deposit into the scheme. Within 14 days of receiving a deposit, the landlord or agent must give the tenant details about how his or her deposit is protected, including the contact details of the tenancy deposit scheme selected, the landlord or agent's contact details, how to apply for the release of the deposit, information explaining the purpose of the deposit, and what to do if there is a dispute about the deposit.

At the end of the tenancy, if an agreement is reached about how the deposit should be divided, the scheme will return the deposit, divided in the way agreed by both parties. If there is a dispute, the scheme will hold the deposit until the dispute resolution service or courts decide what is fair. The interest accrued by deposits in the scheme will be used to pay for the running of the scheme and any surplus will be used to offer interest to the tenant, or to the landlord if the tenant isn't entitled to it. For further information see **www.gov.uk** – Tenancy Deposit Schemes.

Finally, property that is rented 'commercially' (ie for 140 days or more a year) is normally liable for business rates, instead of the council tax you would otherwise pay. This could be more expensive, even though partially allowable against tax.

Useful reading

The Complete Guide to Letting Property by Liz Hodgkinson, published by Kogan Page, £10.99 (website: **www.koganpage.com**).

Benefits and taxes

Housing Benefit

Provided you have no more than £16,000 in savings, you may be able to get help with your rent from your local council. You may qualify for Housing Benefit whether you are a council or private tenant or live in a hotel or hostel. Housing Benefit is fairly complicated and the following outline is intended only as a very general guide. For more detailed advice about your own particular circumstances, contact your local authority or your Citizens Advice Bureau.

The amount of benefit you get depends on five factors: the number of people in your household; your eligible rent (up to a prescribed maximum); your capital or savings; your income; and your 'applicable amount', which is the amount of money the government considers you need for basic living expenses. These are defined roughly as follows.

Eligible rent

This includes rent and some service charges related to the accommodation but excludes meals, water rates and, as a rule, fuel costs. An amount will generally also be deducted for any adult 'non-dependant' (including an elderly relative) living in your household, based on a reasonable contribution on their part towards housing costs. This does not apply to commercial boarders or subtenants – but any income from a boarder or subtenant will be taken into account.

Capital

Any capital or savings up to £6,000 will be disregarded and will not affect your entitlement to benefit. People with savings or capital between £6,000 and £16,000 will receive some benefit, but this will be on a sliding scale, with every £500 (or part of £500) over £6,000 assessed as being equivalent to an extra £1 a week of their income. (See the paragraph below starting 'If your income is less than your applicable amount…'.) This is called 'tariff income'. If you have savings of more than £16,000, you will not be eligible for Housing Benefit at all. 'Capital' generally includes all savings, bonds, stocks and shares and property other than your own home and personal possessions. The capital limits are the same for a couple as for a single person.

Income

Income includes earnings, social security benefits, pension income and any other money you have coming in after tax and National Insurance Contributions have been paid. While most income counts when calculating your entitlement to Housing Benefit (NB: a couple's income is added together), some income may be ignored, for example all Disability Living Allowance and Attendance Allowance; the first £5 of earnings (single person), £10 of earnings (couple) or £20 of earnings if your 'applicable amount' includes a disability premium or carer's premium; and a £25 disregard for lone parents. War pensions are also ignored in part.

Applicable amount

Your 'applicable amount' will generally be the same as any benefit to cover weekly living expenses you would be eligible for and consists of your personal allowance and personal allowances for any younger children (normally those for whom you are receiving Child Benefit), plus any premiums (ie additional amounts for pensioners, the disabled and so on) to which you might be entitled. Details of allowances and premium rates can be found on website: **www.gov.uk**.

If your income is less than your applicable amount you will receive maximum Housing Benefit towards your eligible rent (less any non-dependant deduction). You may be eligible for Income Support if your capital is less than £8,000, or less than £16,000 if you are aged 60 or over. If your income is equal to your applicable amount, you will also receive maximum Housing Benefit. If your income is higher than your applicable amount, a taper adjustment will be made and maximum Housing Benefit will be reduced by 65 per cent of the difference between your income and your applicable amount. If this leaves you with Housing Benefit of less than 50p a week, it is not paid.

How to claim

If you think you are eligible for benefit you can apply online or ask your council for an application form. It should let you know within 14 days of receiving your completed application whether you are entitled to benefit, and will inform you of the amount. See website: **www.gov.uk** – Benefits.

Special accommodation

If you live in a mobile home or houseboat, you may be able to claim benefit for site fees or mooring charges. If you live in a private nursing or residential care home you will not normally be able to get Housing Benefit to help with the cost. However, you may be able to get help towards both the accommodation part of your fees and your living expenses through Income Support or possibly under the Community Care arrangements. If you make a claim for Income Support you can claim Housing Benefit and Council Tax Benefit at the same time.

Council tax

Council tax is based on the value of the dwelling in which you live (the property element) and also consists of a personal element – with discounts and exemptions applying to certain groups of people.

The property element

Most domestic properties are liable for council tax, including rented property, mobile homes and houseboats. The value of the property is assessed according to a banding system, with eight different bands (A to H). The banding of each property is determined by the government's Valuation Office Agency. Small extensions or other improvements made after this date do not affect the valuation until the property changes hands. The planned council tax revaluation in England, due to take place in 2007, was postponed.

Notification of the band is shown on the bill when it is sent out in April. If you think there has been a misunderstanding about the valuation (or your liability to pay the full amount) you may have the right of appeal.

Liability

Not everyone pays council tax. The bill is normally sent to the resident owner or joint owners of the property or, in the case of rented accommodation, to the tenant or joint tenants. Married couples and people with a shared legal interest in the property are jointly liable for the bill, unless they are students or severely mentally impaired. In some cases, for example in hostels or multi-occupied property, a non-resident landlord or owner will be liable but may pass on a share of the bill to the tenants or residents, which would probably be included as part of the rental charge.

The personal element

The valuation of each dwelling assumes that two adults will be resident. The charge does not increase if there are more adults. However if, as in many homes, there is a single adult, your council tax bill will be reduced by 25 per cent. Certain people are disregarded when determining the number of residents in a household. There are also a number of other special discounts or exemptions, as follows:

People who are severely mentally impaired are disregarded or, if they are the sole occupant of the dwelling, qualify for an exemption.

Disabled people whose homes require adaptation may have their bill reduced to a lower band.

People on Income Support should normally have nothing to pay, as their bill will be met in full by Council Tax Benefit.

Disabled people on higher-rate Attendance Allowance need not count a full-time carer as an additional resident and therefore may continue to qualify for the 25 per cent single (adult) householder discount. Exceptions are spouses or partners and parents of a disabled child under 18 who would normally be living with the disabled person and whose presence therefore would not be adding to the council tax.

Young people over 18 but still at school are not counted when assessing the number of adults in a house.

Students living in halls of residence, student hostels or similar are exempted; those living with a parent or other non-student adult are eligible for the 25 per cent personal discount.

Service personnel living in barracks or married quarters will not receive any bill for council tax.

Discounts and exemptions applying to property

Certain property is exempt from council tax, including:

Property that has been unoccupied and unfurnished for less than six months.

The home of a deceased person; the exemption lasts until six months after the grant of probate.

A home that is empty because the occupier is absent in order to care for someone else.

The home of a person who is or would be exempted from council tax because of moving to a residential home, hospital care or similar.

Empty properties in need of major repairs or undergoing structural alteration can be exempt from council tax for an initial period of six months, but this can be extended for a further six months. After 12 months, the standard 50 (or possibly full 100) per cent charge for empty properties will apply.

Granny flats that are part of another private domestic dwelling may be exempt, but this depends on access and other conditions. To check, contact your local Valuation Office.

Business-cum-domestic property

Business-cum-domestic property is rated according to usage, with the business section assessed for business rates and the domestic section for council tax. For example, where there is a flat over a shop, the value of the shop will not be included in the valuation for council tax. Likewise, a room in a house used for business purposes will be subject to business rates and not to council tax.

Appeals

If you become the new person responsible for paying the council tax (eg because you have recently moved or because someone else paid the tax before) on a property that you feel has been wrongly banded, you have six months to appeal and can request that the valuation be reconsidered. Otherwise, there are only three other circumstances in which you can appeal:

if there has been a material increase or reduction in the property's value;

if you start, or stop, using part of the property for business or the balance between domestic and business use changes;

if either of the latter two apply and the listing officer has altered the council tax list without giving you a chance to put your side.

If you have grounds for appeal, you should take up the matter with the Valuation Office (see local telephone directory). If the matter is not resolved, you can then appeal to an independent valuation tribunal. For advice and further information, contact your local Citizens Advice Bureau.

Council Tax Benefit

If you cannot afford your council tax because you have a low income, you may be able to obtain Council Tax Benefit. The help is more generous than many people realize. For example, people on Pension Credit (Guarantee Credit) are entitled to rebates of up to 100 per cent. Even if you are not receiving any other social security benefit, you may still qualify for some Council Tax Benefit. The amount you get depends on your income, savings, personal circumstances, who else lives in your home (in particular whether they would be counted as 'non-dependants') and your net council tax bill (ie after any deductions that apply to your home). If you are not sure whether your income is low enough to entitle you to Council Tax Benefit, it is worth claiming, as you could be pleasantly surprised.

If you disagree with your council's decision, you can ask for this to be looked at again (a revision) or you can appeal to an independent appeal tribunal, administered by the Appeals Service. If you are still dissatisfied, you may apply for leave to appeal to the Social Security Commissioners, but only on a point of law. If you want a revision, you should get on with the matter as soon as possible, as if you delay your request may be out of time.

Apart from Council Tax Benefit for yourself, you may also be able to get help with your council tax if you share your home with someone who is on a low income. This is known as 'Second Adult Rebate' or 'Alternative Maximum Council Tax Benefit'. See website: **www.direct.gov.uk**.

Useful organizations include:

Citizens Advice Bureau, website: **www.citizensadvice.org.uk**;

Federation of Private Residents' Associations Ltd (FPRA), which is the national not-for-profit organization for private residents and residents' associations; website: **www.fpra.org.uk**;

Shelter, the housing and homelessness charity; website: **www.shelter.org.uk**.

Chapter Nine
Leisure activities

Every time I see an adult on a bicycle, I no longer despair for the future of the human race. **H G WELLS**

The fiercest desire in middle age is to do nothing at all. I wonder about this. On the one hand, giving in to idleness feels like the first step on the leafy back-road to retirement, a long slow death of the mind and of the spirit, before the body finally conks out. On the other hand, the prospect of a quick lie-down right now seems rather enticing. Why fight it?

For now that ambition has left us, flying out of the window to latch itself on to some unsuspecting young person, we need something to fill the void. An afternoon nap will fill the next hour or so, but it isn't a long-term solution. Inactivity only works when it is framed by bursts of activity. Otherwise it becomes hard to distinguish from coma...

Marcus Berkmann, *A Shed of One's Own –*
Midlife without the Crisis

Do you have time for an afternoon nap? Or are you worried about how you'll fill hour upon hour of emptiness in your retirement? Somehow the older generation generally don't seem to have all that much trouble in handling their leisure time, mostly because they are so busy there's hardly enough of it to worry about. They have plenty of activity in their lives, and some say they are lucky to get to sit down after lunch, let alone drift off to sleep for a few precious moments. But it would be well worth finding time to dip into Marcus Berkmann's book if you can fit in a bit of reading in between your other activities, because it's highly entertaining and insightful.

Whatever amount of leisure time you have available in retirement, there is almost certainly something you will be looking forward to doing. Maybe during the years spent working you promised yourself that when retirement came along, you would dust off your tennis racquet, improve your golf handicap, learn a language, take up a new hobby, or simply spend a lot more time in your garden. Whether you tend towards studying, sports or crafts there are loads of suitable activities for everyone's tastes on offer locally or nationally. You may need to do a bit of research, but that is easy on the internet. Most clubs and societies have websites, giving information for potential members. Many organizations have concessionary rates for people of retirement age, as do a number of theatres and other places of entertainment. Given the immense variety of tantalizing options available, it's not surprising that many retired people find they have never been so busy.

But did you know that two-thirds of people over 65 are still 'digitally excluded' – missing out on all the many benefits of being online? It's a stubbornly high figure into which a whole series of initiatives has failed to make inroads. Campaigners now hope to use qualified Digital Champions developed within organizations and communities to bridge that gap. Digital Unite, one of the UK's main providers of digital skills learning, launched its online academy in March 2012 through which those who already know their way around a computer can acquire the skills – and qualifications – to become effective Digital Champions. A new section has been added in this chapter on computing and IT, listing a number of websites to help those who wish to become more computer literate in retirement.

So what hobbies do you have? When you are not working, what do you enjoy as a leisure activity? Are you looking forward to challenging your brain with studying for a degree or trying your hand at an entirely new pastime? You can do anything from basket weaving to bridge, archery to amateur dramatics. You can join a music-making group, a Scrabble club or a film society, or become a beekeeper. If you are interested in heritage, there are any number of historic homes and beautiful gardens to visit, as well as museums, art galleries, abbeys and castles. Additionally, almost every locality now has excellent sports facilities and there is scope for complete novices to take up bowls, golf, badminton, croquet and many other activities. Similarly, there are dancing and keep fit classes, railway enthusiasts' clubs and groups devoted to researching local history.

This chapter is best read in conjunction with Chapter 14, Holidays, as many of the organizations listed there – such as the Field Studies Council – would be equally relevant here. However, to avoid repetition, most are described only once. Those that appear in Chapter 14 either tend in the main to offer residential courses or would probably involve most people in spending a few days away from home to take advantage of the facilities. Website addresses are shown, but prices are not included, since they can change at any time before or after going to press. The latest information is always available on the relevant website, so it is recommended that you check there for further details.

Adult education

Have you ever longed to take a degree, learn about computing, study philosophy or do a course in archaeology? Opportunities for education abound, and there are scores of other subjects easily available to everyone, regardless of age or previous qualifications.

Not all educational courses are free, and this fact can deter a number of people from taking the opportunity to learn. However, there are a number of different funding options available for those over 50. Adult financial learning awards, bursaries and grants may be available to help with fees and course materials, depending on the course and learning institute. Those who have never taken any form of educational course through a university or college may also be able to obtain financial assistance.

Where to find help. Retired people and those over 50 have a number of different resources when it comes to finding information on education and funding. Agencies such as Saga, AgeUK and LaterLife will all supply information on free and subsidized educational courses. Local libraries are one of the best places to obtain information on educational matters.

The great thing about learning is there is no knowing where it will take you. Learning new skills will always be beneficial and can lead on to new opportunities. Many retired people have gone on to obtain degree qualifications and have actually found new careers in later life. Retirement can open up a whole new world when it comes to learning and professional development.

Here are some of the leading websites for available courses throughout the UK:

Adult Education Finder provides information about all adult education centres, education services and online adult educational courses in the UK. Website: **www.adulteducationfinder.co.uk**.

BBC Learning: learn with the BBC through online courses and study. Website: **www.bbc.co.uk/learning/adults**.

Home Learning College, the UK's leading home study provider, offers a huge range of home study courses. See website: **www.homelearningcollege.com**.

National Extension College (NEC) offers over 150 home study courses and 200 resource titles and has been providing distance learning courses for over 40 years. See website: **www.nec.ac.uk**.

National Institute of Adult Continuing Education (NIACE) aims to encourage all adults to engage in learning of all kinds. See website: **www.niace.org.uk**.

Open and Distance Learning Quality Council (ODLQC) is the UK guardian of quality in open and distance learning. Set up originally by the government in 1968, it is now an independent organization. See website: **www.odlqc.org.uk**.

Open University (OU) is a world leader in modern distance learning, the pioneer of teaching and learning methods that enable people to achieve their career and life goals studying at times and in places to suit them. For those aged 50 and over there are a huge number of courses that are entirely free. See website: **www.open.ac.uk**.

University extra-mural departments – non-degree and short courses

Many universities have a department of extra-mural studies that arranges courses for adults, sometimes in the evening or during vacation periods; here are a few:

Birkbeck, University of London is a world-class research and teaching institution, and London's only specialist provider of evening higher education. See website: **www.bbk.ac.uk**.

U3A (The University of the Third Age) is the national representative body for the Universities of the Third Age in the UK. U3As are self-help, self-managed, lifelong learning cooperatives for older people. The U3A website has a diverse list of courses available online, which have been specifically designed for those in later life who are looking to learn some new skills. See website: **www.u3a.org.uk**.

Workers' Educational Association (WEA) is the UK's largest voluntary sector provider of adult learning with part-time adult education courses for everyone. See website: **www.wea.org.uk**.

Animals

If you are an animal lover, it is likely that you already have connections with charities and organizations that relate to your favourite animals, but here are some suggestions, which include online publications:

Birdlife International Community, the site full of information for those interested in bird life across the globe. See website: **www.birdlie.org**.

British Beekeepers Association aims to promote the craft of beekeeping and advance the education of the public in the importance of bees in the environment. See website: **www.bbka.org.uk**.

Your Cat **magazine** contains articles of interest to cat lovers. See website: **www.yourcat.co.uk**.

Dogs Monthly **magazine** has loads of information for all dog lovers. See website: **www.dogsmonthly.co.uk**.

Horse and Hound **magazine** for latest equestrian news. See website: **www.horseandhound.co.uk**.

RSPCA is the UK's leading animal welfare charity. Its website is all about animals: pets, horses, wildlife and farm animals. See **www.rspca.org.uk**

Wildfowl & Wetlands Trust (WWT) is a leading conservation organization saving wetlands for wildlife and people across the world. See website: **www.wwt.org.uk**.

Arts

Wherever you live you can enjoy the arts. Whether you are interested in active participation or just appreciating the performance of others, there is an exhilarating choice of events, including theatre, music, exhibitions, film making and so on. Many entertainments offer concessionary prices to retired people.

Regional Arts Council offices

The Arts Council England works to get great art to everyone by champion-ing, developing and investing in artistic experiences that enrich everyone's lives. For information and details of each regional office, see website: **www.artscouncil.org.uk**. The area each regional office covers is:

Arts Council England, East: Bedfordshire, Cambridgeshire, Essex, Hertfordshire, Norfolk, Suffolk, and the unitary authorities of Luton, Peterborough, Southend-on-Sea and Thurrock.

Arts Council England, East Midlands: Derbyshire, Leicestershire, Lincolnshire (excluding North and North East Lincolnshire), Northamptonshire, Nottinghamshire, and the unitary authorities of Derby, Leicester, Nottingham and Rutland.

Arts Council England, London: Greater London.

Arts Council England, North East: Durham, Northumberland, the metropolitan authorities of Gateshead, Newcastle upon Tyne, North Tyneside, South Tyneside and Sunderland, and the unitary authorities of Darlington, Hartlepool, Middlesbrough, Redcar and Cleveland, and Stockton-on-Tees.

Arts Council England, North West: Cheshire, Cumbria, Lancashire, the metropolitan authorities of Bolton, Bury, Knowsley, Liverpool, Manchester, Oldham, Rochdale, St Helens, Salford, Sefton, Stockport, Tameside, Trafford, Wigan and Wirral, and the unitary authorities of Blackburn with Darwen, Blackpool, Halton and Warrington.

Arts Council England, South East: Buckinghamshire, East Sussex, Hampshire, Isle of Wight, Kent, Oxfordshire, Surrey, West Sussex, and the unitary authorities of Bracknell Forest, Brighton and Hove, Medway Towns, Milton Keynes, Portsmouth, Reading, Slough, Southampton, West Berkshire, Windsor and Maidenhead, and Wokingham.

Arts Council England, South West: Cornwall, Devon, Dorset, Gloucestershire, Somerset, Wiltshire, and the unitary authorities of Bath and North East Somerset, Bournemouth, Bristol, North Somerset, Plymouth, Poole, South Gloucestershire, Swindon and Torbay.

Arts Council England, West Midlands: Shropshire, Staffordshire, Warwickshire, Worcestershire, the metropolitan authorities of Birmingham, Coventry, Dudley, Sandwell, Solihull, Walsall and Wolverhampton, and the unitary authorities of Herefordshire, Stoke-on-Trent, Telford and Wrekin.

Arts Council England, Yorkshire: North Yorkshire, the metropolitan authorities of Barnsley, Bradford, Calderdale, Doncaster, Kirklees, Leeds, Rotherham, Sheffield and Wakefield, and the unitary authorities of East Riding of Yorkshire, Kingston upon Hull, North East Lincolnshire, North Lincolnshire and York.

For those who wish to join in with amateur arts activities, public libraries keep lists of choirs, drama clubs, painting clubs and similar in their locality.

Films

Cinema is a hugely popular art form. Should you enjoy film, you might think of joining a film society or visiting the National Film Theatre. Here are some other ideas:

British Federation of Film Societies (BFFS) is the national organization for the development and support of the film society and community cinema movement in the UK. It offers a wide range of services and resources dedicated to the needs of community cinemas. See website: **www.bffs.org.uk**.

British Film Institute (BFI) has a world-renowned archive, cinemas, festival, films, publications and learning resources to inspire you. See website: **www.bfi.org.uk**.

Music and ballet

From becoming a Friend and supporting one of the famous 'Houses' such as Covent Garden to music making in your own right, here are some suggestions:

Friends of Covent Garden. Becoming a Friend of Covent Garden is the best way to keep up with events at The Royal Opera House, attend talks, recitals, study days, master classes and some 'open' rehearsals of ballet and opera. See website: **www.roh.org.uk**.

Friends of English National Opera (ENO). As a Friend of ENO, you support the work of the Company and enjoy privileges such as priority booking, dress rehearsals and many other events. See website: **www.eno.org**.

Friends of Sadler's Wells receive 2-for-1 ticket offers, up to 25 per cent off tickets and discounts on programmes and merchandise. See website: **www.sadlerswells.com**.

Music making

Whatever style of music you enjoy, there are associations to suit your taste. Here are some contacts:

Handbell Ringers of Great Britain promotes the art of handbell tune ringing in all its forms. For more information see website: **www.hrgb.org.uk**.

Making Music supports and champions over 3,000 voluntary and amateur music groups throughout the UK. For more information see website: **www.makingmusic.org.uk**.

National Association of Choirs represents and supports over 500 choirs and 26,000 voices, all of them amateur and voluntary, throughout the UK. For more information see website: **www.nationalassociationofchoirs.org.uk**.

Society of Recorder Players brings together recorder players of all ages from all over the UK. For further information see website: **www.srp.org.uk**.

Poetry

There is an increasing enthusiasm for poetry and poetry readings in clubs, pubs and other places of entertainment. Special local events may be advertised in your neighbourhood.

The Poetry Society is a charitable organization providing support and information and aims to create a central position for poetry in the arts. For further information see website: **www.poetrysociety.org.uk**.

Television and radio audiences

People of all ages, backgrounds and abilities enjoy participating as members of studio audiences and contributors to programmes. For those wishing to take part there are a couple of websites that can help:

Applause Store is the one-stop shop for literally thousands of free television and radio audience tickets to the very best entertainment, music, comedy, chat, sitcom, reality and award shows produced at many different studios and locations around the world. See website: **www.applausestore.com**.

BBC Shows: Be in the audience – free tickets for shows. See website: **www.bbc.co.uk/showsandtours/tickets**.

Theatre

Details of current and forthcoming productions for national and regional theatres, as well as theatre reviews, are well advertised in the press and on the internet. Preview performances are usually cheaper, and there are often concessionary tickets for matinees.

Ambassador Tickets sells tickets from the UK's largest theatre group. See website: **www.ambassadortickets.com**.

Barbican is the largest multi-arts and conference centre in Europe, presenting a diverse range of art, film, music, theatre, dance and education events. See website: **www.barbican.org.uk**.

National Theatre stages over 20 theatre productions each year in three auditoriums – the Lyttleton, Cottesloe and Olivier theatres. See website: **www.nationaltheatre.org.uk**.

Official London Theatre is the capital's only official theatre website. It has the latest news on listings, what's on, how to buy tickets, and events. See website: **www.officiallondontheatre.co.uk**.

Scottish Community Drama Association (SCDA) is a community-based organization and operates through 24 district committees throughout Scotland. For further information see website: **www.scda.org.uk**.

Theatre Network is a social network and online magazine for the performing arts industry with news and features, as well as national and regional theatre listings and review guides. See website: **www.uktheatre.net**.

TKTS is the one-stop shop for buying half-price and discount live theatre tickets in the West End. Located in the Clocktower Building on the south side of Leicester Square, it is open to personal callers only on the day of the performance; see website: **www.tkts.co.uk**.

Visual arts

If you enjoy attending exhibitions and lectures, membership of some of the arts societies offers a good choice:

Art Fund exists to secure great art for museums and galleries all over the UK for everyone to enjoy. All funding is privately raised and the Art Fund has over 80,000 members. There are art tours at home and abroad led by experts. See website: **www.artfund.org**.

Contemporary Art Society exists to support and develop public collections of contemporary art in the UK. Members' events include visits to artists' studios and private collections, previews and parties at special exhibitions, and trips outside London and overseas. See website: **www.contemporaryartsociety.org**.

National Association of Decorative & Fine Arts Societies (NADFAS) is an arts-based charity with over 340 local decorative and fine arts societies in the UK and mainland Europe. It promotes the advancement of arts education and appreciation and the preservation of our artistic heritage with day events and tours organized both in the UK and abroad. See website: **www.nadfas.org.uk**.

Royal Academy of Arts. Friends of the Royal Academy receive many benefits including unlimited access to the world-renowned exhibition programme with guests, and the award-winning *RM* quarterly magazine. See website: **www.royalacademy.org.uk**.

Tate is a public institution, owned by and existing for the public. Tate's mission is to increase public knowledge, understanding and enjoyment of British modern and contemporary art through its collection and programmes in and beyond its galleries. See website: **www.tate.org.uk**.

Painting as a hobby

If you are interested in improving your own painting technique, art courses are available at your local adult education institute. Your library may have details of painting groups and societies in your area.

The **Society for All Artists** (SAA), which exists to inform, encourage and inspire all who want to paint, whatever their ability, provides all that you need to enjoy this hobby. Find out more on its website: **www.saa.co.uk**.

Computing and IT

As mentioned at the beginning of the chapter, there are still a large number of over-65s who are 'digitally excluded' – not using computers or the internet. As we all know, education and learning need not stop when retirement starts.

One of the many bonuses of retirement is having extra time to try out new activities. Learning new skills is a great way to keep the mind active and to socialize. Computing is one of the most popular classes for retired people. In most cases, learning these skills is completely free.

Local libraries have set times throughout the week for retired people to either learn computing skills or update skills they already have. Library staff will teach retired people on a one-to-one basis, and this service is entirely free of charge. The plus point of learning skills such as the internet is that it can lead on to other free learning applications. There is a huge range of free learning resources available on the internet, if you know where to look.

Learning how to use a computer is not difficult – in many cases you can learn online at your own speed, in the comfort of your own home. If you prefer to enrol in a course with other people, that is also possible. (You will find many opportunities to enrol in classes in the earlier section 'Adult education'.) Or you could find a tutor to teach you how to use a computer on a one-to-one basis. Here are a few possibilities:

Digital Unite, one of the UK's main providers of digital skills learning, has launched an online academy.
See **www.aboutacademy.digitalunite.com**.

Pearson's Love to Learn Internet Basics course See website:
www.lovetolearn.co.uk.

Which? Guides have four *Made Easy* titles to help you understand computers and the internet; step-by-step guides you can trust: *Internet Made Easy for the Over-50s*; *Using your PC Made Easy*; *Laptops and Mobile Devices Made Easy*; *PC Problem Solving Made Easy*. See website: **www.which.co.uk/books**.

Crafts

The majority of suggestions are contained in Chapter 14, Holidays, variously under 'Arts and crafts' and 'Special interest holidays', since many organizations offer residential courses and painting holidays. If you are interested in a particular form of craft work many of the societies and others listed in Chapter 14 should be able to help you. Here are a few additional possibilities:

Basketmakers' Association promotes classes, courses, exhibitions, lectures and discussions on all aspects of basket making, chair seating and allied crafts. See website: **www.basketassoc.org**.

The **Crafts Council**'s aim is to make the UK the best place to make, see, collect and learn about contemporary craft, visit markets, fairs, galleries, shops and outlets for craft work. See website: **www.craftscouncil.org.uk**.

Open College of the Arts (OCA) is an educational charity established to widen participation in arts education, to acquire or improve skills or gain a higher education qualification. See website: **www.oca-uk.com**.

Creative writing

It is said that there is a book in everyone, and many retired people have a yen to write. As this is a solitary occupation you may find that joining a writing group is a worthwhile and pleasurable thing to do. The National Association of Writing Groups – **www.nawg.co.uk** – is one place to find a local one; though please note that not all creative writing groups are linked to that site. For example, some operate as an adjunct to other organizations, such as U3A (the University of the Third Age). In a group such as this, people take turns to read what they write, if the group is small enough. Other groups may be organized so that they are prompted by set exercises or chosen topics. Whatever the style, creative writing groups provide company, support and a degree of critique too. Some specialize, but many take fiction, non-fiction and poetry in their stride, so you can write anything from an essay to an article, from a rant to a novel – and, who knows, you might even get published and earn some money.

If any of this interests you, something else to check is *Writing Magazine*. This is a monthly journal designed to help aspiring and actual writers. Patrick Forsyth (a many-times-published Kogan Page author) writes regularly for that magazine, and is a great fan of writing groups. 'They are,' he says, 'if not essential, a very great help to those who love to write, but lack confidence, want a bit of advice, support or motivation. I certainly recommend you give attendance a go. Getting published in not easy, and it is said that the single word that best describes a writer with no persistence is *unpublished*. But it *is* possible and seeing a book or article with your name on, and having it followed by a cheque, is very satisfying.' Patrick knows; the latest of his many books, a hilarious critique of inappropriate public writing, is called *Empty when Half Full*.

Dance/keep fit

Clubs, classes and groups exist in all parts of the country offering ballroom, old-time, Scottish, folk, ballet, disco dancing and others. Additionally, there are music and relaxation classes, aerobics and more gentle keep fit sessions. Many of the relaxation and keep fit classes are particularly appropriate for older people. Find out what is available in your area from your library, or see the list below (there are further suggestions in Chapter 13, Health, 'Keep fit'):

British Dance Council is the governing body of all competition dancing in the UK. It can put you in touch with recognized dance schools in your area. See website: **www.british-dance-council.org**.

English Folk Dance and Song Society is one of the leading folk development organizations in the UK. It aims to place the indigenous folk arts of England at the heart of our cultural life. See website: **www.efdss.org**.

Imperial Society of Teachers of Dancing is a registered educational charity providing education and training for dance teachers, from ballet to ballroom. See website: **www.istd.org**.

Keep Fit Association (KFA) offers 'Fitness through movement, exercise and dance' classes. There are hundreds of classes throughout the UK for all ages and abilities. See website: **www.keepfit.org.uk**.

Royal Scottish Country Dance Society aims to preserve and further the practice of traditional Scottish country dancing. It has 170 branches worldwide which offer instruction at all levels. See website: **www.rscds.org**.

Sport and Recreation Alliance is the new name for CCPR, or the Central Council for Physical Recreation. It is the umbrella organization for the governing and representative bodies for all sport in the UK. See website: **www.sportandrecreation.org.uk**.

Games

Many local areas have their own backgammon, bridge, chess, whist, dominos, Scrabble and other groups that meet together regularly in a club, hall, pub or other social venue to enjoy friendly board games. Information on any local clubs should be available from your library. Here are some national organizations which will put you in touch with local groups:

English Bridge Union is a membership organization committed to promoting the game of duplicate bridge. Members receive a wide range of services including details of tournaments and bridge holidays at home and abroad. See website: **www.ebu.co.uk**.

English Chess Federation aims to promote the game of chess as an attractive means of cultural and personal advancement, providing information about chess clubs and tournaments throughout England. See website: **www.englishchess.org.uk**.

Scrabble Clubs UK is the association that promotes interest in the game and coordinates all the Scrabble tournaments in the UK. See website: **www.absp.org.uk**.

Gardens and gardening

Courses, gardens to visit, special help for people with disabilities, and how to run a gardening association; these and other interests are all catered for by the following organizations:

English Gardening School teaches all aspects of gardening; courses range from one day to an academic year, at Chelsea Wharf. See website: **www.englishgardeningschool.co.uk**.

Garden Organic is the national charity for organic gardening and has been at the forefront of organic gardening for over half a century. Based at Ryton in Warwickshire. See website: **www.gardenorganic.org.uk**.

Gardening for Disabled Trust provides practical and financial help to disabled people who want to continue to garden actively despite advancing age or disability. See website: **www.gardeningfordisabledtrust.org.uk**.

National Gardens Scheme has over 3,700 gardens to choose from in England and Wales, mostly privately owned. Over half a million visitors enjoy visiting gardens that open to the public just a few days each year. See website: **www.ngs.org.uk**.

National Society of Allotment & Leisure Gardeners Ltd aims to
protect, promote and preserve allotments for future generations.
It acts as a national voice for allotment and leisure gardeners.
See website: **www.nsalg.org.uk**.

Royal Horticultural Society is the UK's leading gardening charity
dedicated to advancing horticulture, promoting gardening
and inspiring all those with an interest in gardening.
See website: **www.rhs.org.uk**.

Scotland's Gardens Scheme facilitates the opening of large and small
gardens throughout Scotland that are of interest to the public.
See website: **www.gardensofscotland.org**.

Thrive is a small national charity that uses gardening to change the
lives of disabled people. See website: **www.thrive.org.uk**.

History

People with an interest in the past have so many activities to choose from –
visit historic monuments, including ancient castles and stately homes, in
all parts of the country; explore the City of London; study genealogy or
research the history of your local area. Here are some organizations to
consider:

Age Exchange is the UK's leading charity working in the field of
reminiscence and works to improve the quality of life for older
people through reminiscence-based creative workshops. See website:
www.age-exchange.org.uk.

Architectural Heritage Society of Scotland is concerned with the
protection, preservation, study and appreciation of Scotland's
buildings. Six regional groups organize local activities and carry
out casework. See website: **www.ahss.org.uk**.

Bekonscot Model Village is the world's oldest model village, with
1.5 acres of model railways, towns and landscapes. See website:
www.bekonscot.co.uk.

British Association for Local History aims to encourage and promote
the study of local history as an academic discipline as well as
a rewarding leisure pursuit. See website: **www.balh.co.uk**.

City of London Information Centre acts as a tourist office for the area, located in St Paul's Churchyard. Among the many attractions are: St Paul's Cathedral, the Guildhall, Dr Johnson's House, the Monument, Barbican, the Central Criminal Court and several museums. See website: **www.visitthecity.co.uk**.

English Heritage champions our historic places and advises the government and others to help today's generation get the best out of our heritage and ensure it is protected for future generations. See website: **www.english-heritage.org.uk**.

Federation of Family History Societies is an educational charity that exists to represent the interests of family historians generally and especially the preservation and availability of archival documents. See website: **www.ffhs.org.uk**.

Garden History Society is dedicated to the conservation and study of historic designed gardens and landscapes. It has helped save or conserve scores of important gardens. See website: **www.gardenhistorysociety.org**.

Georgian Group exists to preserve Georgian buildings and to stimulate public knowledge and appreciation of Georgian architecture and town planning. Members enjoy day visits and long weekends to buildings and gardens, private views of exhibitions and a programme of evening lectures in London. See website: **www.georgiangroup.org.uk**.

Historic Houses Association (HHA) represents 1,500 privately owned historic houses, castles and gardens throughout the UK. Around 300 HHA houses are open to the public for day visitors. See website: **www.hha.org.uk**.

Historical Association supports the study and promotes the enjoyment of history. It believes that historical awareness is essential for the 21st-century citizen. See website: **www.history.org.uk**.

Monumental Brass Society is for all those interested in any aspect of monumental brasses and incised slabs of all dates and in all countries. See website: **www.mbs-brasses.co.uk**.

National Trust exists to protect historic buildings and areas of great natural beauty in England, Wales and Northern Ireland.

Membership gives you free entry to the Trust's many properties and to those of the National Trust for Scotland. See website: **www.nationaltrust.org.uk**.

National Trust for Scotland cares for over 100 properties and 183,000 acres of countryside. Members also enjoy free admission to any of the National Trust properties in England, Wales and Northern Ireland. See website: **www.nts.org.uk**.

Northern Ireland Tourist Board has a free information bulletin, *Visitor Attractions*, listing historic sites and other places of interest. See website: **www.discovernorthernireland.com**.

Oral History Society promotes the collection, preservation and use of recorded memories of the past for projects in community history, schools, reminiscence groups and historical research. See website: **www.ohs.org.uk**.

Society of Genealogists promotes the study of family history and the lives of earlier generations. Its library houses a huge collection of family histories, civil registration and census material. See website: **www.sog.org.uk**.

Victorian Society campaigns to preserve fine Victorian and Edwardian buildings in England and Wales for future generations. See website: **www.victorian-society.org.uk**.

Magazines

There are a number of magazines dedicated to the over-50s with articles and features on topics that include health, finance and lifestyle. Here are some:

Healthylife has articles and information on a wealth of lifestyle essentials, from health and nutrition to money, retirement and relationships. See website: **www.healthylife-mag.co.uk**.

50 Plus Magazine – the local magazine for the over-50s. See website: **www.50plusmagazine.co.uk**.

Over 65 Magazine is an online publication aimed at mature readers who are young at heart. See website: **www.over65magazine.co.uk**.

Retirement Today is a lifestyle magazine aimed at the active retired or those contemplating retirement. See website: **www.retirement-today.co.uk**.

Third Age the lifestyle magazine with interesting, entertaining and inspirational information for the over-50s. See website: **www.thirdage.co.uk**.

YOURS Magazine, Britain's leading magazine for the over-50s. See website: **www.greatmagazines.co.uk/women/yours-magazine**.

Museums

Most museums organize free lectures, guided tours and sometimes slide shows on aspects of their collections or special exhibitions. If you join as a Friend, you can enjoy certain advantages, such as access to private views, visits to places of interest, receptions and other social activities. Here are some suggestions:

British Association of Friends of Museums (BAFM) is an umbrella organization that acts as a national forum for Friends and volunteers who support museums around the UK. See website: **www.bafm.org.uk**.

Ashmolean Museum of Art and Archaeology is a university museum and a department of the University of Oxford. Its mission is to make its collections available to the widest possible audience both now and in the future. See website: **www.ashmolean.org**.

British Museum Friends enjoy free entry to exhibitions and evening openings as well as information about lectures, study days and 'visits behind the scenes'. See website: **www.britishmuseum.org**.

Friends of the Fitzwilliam Museum receive regular mailings with information about museum events, including exhibitions, concerts, lectures and parties in the Cambridge area and throughout the UK. See website: **www.fitzmuseum.cam.ac.uk**.

Friends of the National Maritime Museum enjoy the museum complex, housed in Greenwich Park, which comprises the largest maritime museum in the world, Wren's Royal Observatory and Inigo Jones's Queen's House. See website: **www.nmm.ac.uk**.

Friends of the V&A (Victoria and Albert Museum) have free admission to V&A exhibitions, members' previews, a programme of events and a free subscription to *V&A Magazine*. See website: **www.vam.ac.uk**.

Membership of the National Museums of Scotland gives regular
mailings and the *Explorer* magazine, invitations to lectures and
other events, and free admission to exhibitions and some sites.
See website: **www.nms.ac.uk**.

Nature and conservation

Many conservation organizations are very keen to recruit volunteers; the
majority are therefore listed in Chapter 12, Voluntary work. Also, many
of those concerned with field studies arrange courses and other special
activity interests where there is usually a residential content, so more are
listed in Chapter 14, Holidays. Here are a few that don't appear elsewhere
in this book:

Field Studies Council is an environmental educational charity committed
to helping people understand and be inspired by the natural world.
Fieldwork and cross-curricular courses inspire thousands of students
each year through its countrywide network of 17 centres across the
UK. See website: **www.field-studies-council.org**.

Forestry Commission's mission is to protect and expand Britain's
forests and woodlands and increase their value to society and the
environment. See website: **www.forestry.gov.uk**.

Inland Waterways Association is a national charity run by over
17,500 volunteers, which campaigns for the use, maintenance
and restoration of Britain's inland waterways. See website:
www.waterways.org.uk.

Wildlife Trust is the largest UK voluntary organization dedicated
to conserving the full range of the UK's habitats and species.
There are 47 local Wildlife Trusts caring for 2,500 nature reserves
and campaigning for the future of our threatened wildlife.
See website: **www.wildlifetrusts.org**.

Public library service

The public library in the UK is an endangered species and needs your support.
Britain's public library service has been under tremendous threat recently
due to local authority spending cuts. Although a number have been closed,

many local support groups have sprung into action to save their local libraries, with – in some cases – volunteers taking over the running of the entire premises. The UK library service is a huge resource, which not only lends millions of books free each year, but also CDs and DVDs. Most are now equipped with the internet, so visitors can browse websites and do research. One of its traditional main attractions is as a source of masses of information about both local and national activities. Additionally, there are reference sections containing newspapers and periodicals as well as a wide selection of reference books covering any subject.

Among the many other facilities on offer, large-print books are available at most libraries, as are musical scores, leaflets on state benefits, consumer information and details of local community activities. Major libraries also have computer databases and can provide specialized information from Europe and North America. If the information you require is not available in the library itself, the trained staff will normally do their best to tell you where you might find it.

The UK's public library service is excellent – please help to keep it going by using your local facilities.

Sciences and other related subjects

If astronomy, meteorology or geology fascinate you, there are several societies and associations that may be of interest:

British Astronomical Association is open to all people interested in astronomy. See website: **www.britastro.org**.

Geologists' Association organizes lectures, field excursions and monthly meetings at Burlington House. See website: **www.geologistsassociation.org.uk**.

Royal Meteorological Society, which includes among its membership both amateurs and professionals, exists to advance meteorological science. See website: **www.rmets.org**.

Special interests

Whether your special enthusiasm is stamp collecting or model flying, most of the associations listed organize events, answer queries and can put you in contact with kindred spirits:

British Association of Numismatic Societies (BANS) helps to coordinate the activities of some 65 local societies, whose members are interested in the study or collection of coins and medals. See website: **www.coinclubs.freeserve.co.uk**.

British Model Flying Association (BMFA) is responsible nationally for all types of model flying, organizing competitions and fun-fly meetings and advice and guidelines on model flying. See website: **www.bmfa.org**.

Miniature Armoured Fighting Vehicle Association (MAFVA) is an international society providing advice and information on tanks and other military vehicles and equipment. See website: **www.mafva.net**.

National Association of Flower Arrangement Societies (NAFAS) has over 70,000 members who attend NAFAS events, the National Show, and take part in courses in floral art and design. See website: **www.nafas.org.uk**.

National Philatelic Society for those interested in stamp collecting, buying and selling stamps through the society's auctions or postal packet scheme. See website: **www.ukphilately.org.uk**.

Railway Correspondence and Travel Society is Britain's leading railway enthusiast group for those interested in railways past, present and future. See website: **www.rcts.org.uk**.

Sport

Retirement is an ideal time to get fit and take up a sporting hobby. To find out about opportunities in your area, contact your local authority recreational department or your local sports or leisure centre.

Angling

Angling Trades Association promotes the interests of anglers and angling, including educational and environmental concerns, where to find qualified tuition, local tackle dealers and similar information. See website: **www.anglingtradesassociation.com**.

Badminton

Badminton England is the sport's governing body in England. Many categories of membership are available. Most sports and leisure centres have badminton courts and give instruction. See website: **www.badmintonengland.co.uk**.

Bowling

Bowls Development Alliance is the united body of Bowls England, English Indoor Bowling Association, English Short Mat Bowling Association and British Crown Green Bowling Association. It is a game that is available to everyone from 8 to 80. See websites: **www.esmba.co.uk**, **www.bowlsengland.com**, **www.eiba.co.uk** and **www.crowngreenbowls.org**.

English Bowling Association has 2,600 local clubs, many of which provide instruction for beginners by qualified coaches. A national competition for 55-plus singles and pairs is organized through clubs each year. See website: **www.bowlsengland.com**.

Clay pigeon shooting

Clay Pigeon Shooting Association (CPSA) is an association of individual shooters and a federation of clubs. As a member you have public liability insurance of £5 million, your scores are recorded in the national averages and you can compete in national events. See website: **www.cpsa.co.uk**.

Cricket

England and Wales Cricket Board (ECB) To play, watch or help at cricket matches, contact your local club or contact the ECB to get in touch with your county cricket board. See website: **www.ecb.co.uk**.

Kia Oval is home to the Surrey County Cricket Club and one of the main venues for international and county cricket. Club membership entitles you to free or reduced price tickets for the Members' Pavilion to watch international matches as well as county events. See website: **www.kiaoval.com**.

Lord's Cricket Ground offers a conducted tour of Lord's that includes the Long Room, the futuristic Media Centre and the MCC Museum, where the Ashes urn is on display. Senior citizens can attend County Championship matches and the National League matches for half price. See website: **www.lords.org**.

Croquet

Croquet Association – a number of local authorities as well as clubs now offer facilities for croquet enthusiasts, and this association runs coaching courses and can advise about clubs, events, purchase of equipment and other information. See website: **www.croquet.org.uk**.

Cycling

CTC (Cyclists' Touring Club) protects and promotes the rights of cyclists. There is also a veterans' section. See website: **www.ctc.org.uk**.

Darts

British Darts Organisation – this organization organizes over 800 darts events throughout the country each year. See website: **www.bdodarts.com**.

Golf

English Golf Union is one of the largest sports governing bodies in England, looking after the interests of over 1,900 golf clubs and 740,000 members. See website: **www.englishgolfunion.org**.

Golfing Union of Ireland: website: **www.gui.ie**.

Scottish Golf Union: website: **www.scottishgolfunion.org**.

Welsh Golfing Union: website: **www.golfunionwales.org**.

National Golf Unions can provide information about municipal courses and private clubs, of which there are some 1,700 in England alone. Additionally, many adult education institutes and sports centres run classes for beginners.

Running

ARC – The Association of Running Clubs is the governing body for running clubs. Their website gives information on road-running clubs and their activities throughout the UK. See website: **www.runningclubs.org.uk**.

Swimming

British Swimming is the new name for the Amateur Swimming Federation of Great Britain Ltd. See website: **www.swimming.org**.

Table tennis

English Table Tennis Association – ETTA is the association for this sport, enjoyed by people of all ages and all levels of competence. See website: **www.englishtabletennis.org.uk**.

Veterans English Table Tennis Society – VETTS holds regional and national championships including singles and doubles events for various ages over 40. See website: **www.vetts.org.uk**.

Tennis

Lawn Tennis Association – for information about anything to do with tennis, from advice on choosing a racquet to obtaining tickets for major tournaments. See website: **www.lta.org.uk**.

Vets Tennis GB promotes competitions for older players in various age groups from 35 to 80 years, with information on club, county and international events. See website: **www.lta.org.uk**.

Veteran rowing

British Rowing has enthusiasts aged from 31 to well past 80, and for those who enjoy a competitive edge there are special races and regattas, with types of boat including eights, fours and pairs, as well as single, double and quadruple sculling. See website: **www.britishrowing.org**.

Walking

Ramblers' Association – provides a comprehensive information service on all aspects of walking and can advise on where to walk, clothing and equipment and organized walking holidays, as well as details of the 450 local groups throughout the country. See website: **www.ramblers.org.uk**.

Windsurfing

Seavets, affiliated to the Royal Yachting Association, aims to encourage the not-so-young of all abilities to enjoy the challenge of windsurfing. See website: **www.seavets.co.uk**.

Yachting

Royal Yachting Association – RYA has 2,200 affiliated clubs and more than 1,500 recognized training centres. It provides a comprehensive information service for boat owners, with advice on everything from moorings to foreign cruising procedure. See website: **www.rya.org.uk**.

Women's organizations

Women today participate in almost any activity on equal terms with men. But there are women's clubs and organizations that continue to enjoy enormous popularity:

Association of Inner Wheel Clubs UK (the Inner Wheel was originally for the wives of Rotarians) – for more information see website: **www.associationofinnerwheelclubs**.

Mothers' Union (MU) promotes Christian care for families internationally in 81 countries with over 4 million members. See website: **www.themothersunion.org**.

National Association of Women's Clubs has over 150 clubs with nearly 6,000 members nationally, open to women of all ages, faiths and interests. See website: **www.nawc.org.uk**.

National Women's Register (NWR) is an organization of 400 groups of 'lively minded women' who meet informally in members' homes to enjoy challenging discussions. The groups choose their own topics and many also arrange a varied programme of social activities. See website: **www.nwr.org.uk**.

Scottish Women's Rural Institutes (SWRI) is one of the largest women's organizations in Scotland and has around 22,000 members of all ages who enjoy social, recreational and educational activities. See website: **www.swri.org.uk**.

Townswomen's Guilds is one of the UK's leading women's organizations, providing fun, friendship and a forum for social change since 1929. Over 34,000 women nationwide have joined Townswomen. See website: **www.townswomen.org.uk**.

The **Women's Institute** (WI) is the largest national organization for women, with nearly 205,000 members in 6,500 WIs. It plays a unique role in providing women with educational opportunities and the chance to take part in a wide variety of activities and campaigns. See website: **www.thewi.org.uk**. If you live in Northern Ireland, there is the **Federation of Women's Institutes of Northern Ireland** website: **www.wini.org.uk**.

For people with disabilities

Facilities for the disabled have improved dramatically in recent years, so there are fewer activities from which disabled people are now excluded. Fencing is one which is fun and exciting, and a good way to keep in shape. It involves panache, style and grace, and can be done in a wheelchair. While wheelchair fencing is very different from the sport of ambulant fencers, the weapons and their usage remain the same. To find out more about wheelchair fencing, a good starting point is the **British Disabled Fencing Association** (BDFA). The BDFA's website offers a huge amount of information including how and where you can find a local fencing club. See website: **www.bdfa.org.uk**.

For many blind or partially sighted people the following websites may be of interest, as they feature talking books.

AudioGo (formerly BBC Audiobooks) publish an extensive range of comedy, drama and factual programmes from BBC Radio in addition to recordings of novels, history and biography titles. Most titles are available in both CD and download format. To browse through the collection, visit the website: **www.audiogo.co.uk**.

Calibre Audio Library has audio books that bring the pleasure of reading to people who have sight problems, dyslexia or other disabilities that prevent them from reading a print book; this service is entirely free. See website: **www.calibre.org.uk**.

Listening Books is a UK charity providing a large collection of audio books to over 15,000 people nationwide who find it difficult or impossible to read due to illness or disability. Audio books are sent through the post on CD or downloaded online and streamed from this website: **www.listening-books.org.uk**.

RNIB's **Talking Book Service** offers over 18,000 audio books, paid for by annual subscription, and delivered direct to your door. Talking books are recorded in DAISY CD, which makes them easy to navigate. See website: **www.rnib.org.uk**.

Public transport

One of the big gains of reaching retirement age is the availability of cheap travel. Local authorities are now required to offer men, as well as women, concessionary bus fares from the age of 60 instead of men having to wait till 65 before being able to benefit. Bus travel, for the moment, is free out of peak hours, anywhere in the country; coaches very often have special rates for older people. Senior Railcards, available to men and women over 60, offer wonderful savings. Details of all these are given in Chapter 14, Holidays.

Chapter Ten
Starting your own business

ALLAN ESLER SMITH

Allan is a fellow of the Institute of Chartered Accountants and specializes in helping people start up in business. He has helped thousands of mature people do this, and shares his hints and tips in this chapter.

You can find Allan at **www.allaneslersmith.com** and can follow him on Twitter at @allaneslersmith.

Perfect freedom is reserved for the man who lives by his own work and in that work does what he wants to do.

R G COLLINGWOOD (1889–1943) *SPECULUM MENTIS*

A record 450,000 people set up their own business in 2011/12 and became their own boss. So whether it is earning £5,000 to supplement a pension or building a business that can keep you earning and occupied for years to come, this is the chapter for you. While financially rewarding, this is not the only reason people want to start a business as social and emotional benefits also feature. This chapter will show you how easy it is to start a small business and it is packed with hints and tips to grow an existing small business. Indeed you could start tomorrow and it could cost you less than £100. Importantly, in starting a small business you will not be alone and this chapter will also signpost you to plenty of help and support and most of it is free (it is just a matter of knowing where to look!). You are also in good company as 91 per cent of businesses in the UK have fewer than four staff and the enterprise culture in the UK is gathering momentum again.

This chapter will give you the confidence to get started and has plenty of straightforward simple advice. The key issues covered are:

Understanding the differences between starting a small business and employment, especially if both options are still open to you.

Failing to plan usually means you're planning to fail. So what's the plan?

Getting off to a good start – practical and emotional tips and buying your first equipment.

Administration, finance and tax – keep on top of the paperwork or it will keep on top of you!

Filling the diary with work and some clever tips for marketing that will make a difference.

The trading format – should you set up your own limited liability company or work as a sole trader or maybe go into partnership?

Other ways of getting started and operational issues.

Where you can go for further help – remember you are not alone and these are enterprising times in the UK.

Additionally, in the six real-life case studies featured at the end, you will see how Bob, Karin, Phil, Gill, and David fared when they set up their own businesses and how Paul is coping after his first business venture failed. What did or did not work for them? Finally a useful summary checklist has been included to help you tick off the key issues once you decide to get started in business.

Yes, you can!

Broadcaster Liz Barclay and Maree Atkinson of the Federation of Small Business share their insights into starting a business and share some tips and reveal that 'Yes, you can!'

Liz Barclay is one of the most recognized voices on British radio today with her common-sense approach to money and finance on *You and Yours*. Liz also writes for several monthly personal finance and small business magazines and shares her experience and tips below.

First, forget about the salary spiral where you will only consider taking a job that offers you as much as or more than you have earned in the past. Do your calculations carefully and work out how much you need to make to pay your bills and enjoy life. That shift in thinking alone opens up all sorts of possibilities. You can do work that pays less but that you enjoy more, choose your own working hours and when to take breaks and mix work with rest, play, retraining, learning and even unpaid voluntary work. The world is your oyster.

Many of the people I talk to, who are moving out of full-time employment, are thinking of retraining or brushing up long-disused skills at a further education college, or about how they can turn a hobby into an income-generating venture. Self-employment or starting a small business after a lifetime of being an employee can be daunting but it can be done and Allan's chapter will help you on the way. The people I know who are most successful are those who are doing something they love. Judith is writing verses for greetings cards and taking photos for postcards – using her creative side after retiring from social work. Dawn is going back to her artistic roots and Diane is teaching older people Pilates and complementary therapies. They're passionate about their businesses and willing to give them the time and TLC they need to make them flourish. Hard work doesn't seem like a chore so they're less likely to give up when the going gets tough, as it will.

The section within this chapter on 'Marketing tips to fill your diary' will assist you with your marketing and research. The case studies at the end of this chapter show how new start-up businesses have secured their very first few clients. On generating business ideas and marketing, Liz adds:

There are ideas everywhere. You don't have to come up with something new. You might do what you did before as an employee but on a consultancy basis with new customers. The more important thing is research. Be sure there are enough people who will pay you for what you do and that they have easy access to your products or services. Just because two tanning salons on the high street are buzzing doesn't mean there are enough customers to support a third. Many businesses that I saw fail had not done enough market research before spending money. Ask your customers what they like about your business and what they don't. Listen, act and add value – like the butcher in Glasgow who has long queues because he gives his customers recipes for the meat they buy. Talk to your employees who often know the business and customers better than you do. Keep building those relationships so that you spot the trends and stay ahead of the competition.

Liz's concluding advice is that 'success comes with having a positive and optimistic attitude to your business. This is a must – yes, you can. The glass is always half full! Be passionate about your business. Do not just turn up to work, but enjoy what you do. Put your life and soul into achieving a good day's work.'

Maree Atkinson runs her own business and sees hundreds of small businesses start up in her role as an award-winning membership adviser for the Federation of Small Business (FSB). The FSB has around 200,000 members and promotes and protects the interests of the self-employed and owners of small firms. For Maree the watchwords are 'Yes, you can,' but take special care over your marketing.

> Certainly starting a business later in life may be daunting – I can personally vouch for that. But one big advantage for mature entrepreneurs is the wealth of experience and contacts gathered in work and general life over many years. The more successful start-ups that I see have a real passion to succeed and normally a willingness to adapt. I would agree with Liz Barclay about the importance of market research and really getting to know your customers and the competition you face. This is also a key part of the business plan process that Allan details within this chapter. I definitely agree with Allan that the first draft of your business plan does not need to run on for pages and pages. Indeed some business plan 'templates' that I have seen put people off the whole planning process.
>
> I would encourage you to start the planning process by getting something down in writing to show you have researched and understood your target customers. Where are they? What is their profile and what might they need? What price are they prepared to pay? How will you get your product or service to them? These are all good starting questions and you can then build things from there by investigating the competition. With further help from your advice network your plan will start to take shape. Remember that there is a lot of help out there and you are definitely not alone. I see lots of idea sharing, hints and tips and introductions at the various members' networking and social events we run at the FSB.

Maree goes on to advise:

> There are also many courses, seminars and training events to help businesses start up and your accountant, FSB contact and Business Link (contact details are at the reference section of this chapter) should be able to point you in the right direction. As a bonus you may find that many are subsidized or free. I have some words of caution on this subject and then another tip. In my day-to-day work I find that new mature business owners might be shy or perhaps feel uncomfortable as it has been many years since they attended a course. Also, for various reasons some people think they have no need to take advice or go on training courses or perhaps they just feel out of their

comfort zone. In my experience these folk tend to struggle in the first year or two. I would strongly recommend that you take advantage of external support in the early years especially if it is free and of good quality. You'd be daft not to!

One other challenge that I see is new business owners becoming overwhelmed by the many hats they have to wear. People also underestimate the time it takes to do even the simplest of tasks. Perhaps this is because they came from larger organizations with in-house functions for marketing, legal, accounts and health and safety. Unless you bring in specialists to deal with these areas you are left with a choice: deal with the issues or they will simply get left behind. My top tip is therefore about managing your time and it is no shame to work with lists to make sure the must dos are tackled first and the other tasks scheduled in. If you find your precious family time is being spent on disliked jobs, think about hiring in help if you can afford it. I would also recommend checking out trade and professional associations (including the Federation of Small Business, which I represent) as these can provide a high level of support and contacts who can assist.

Maree's concluding advice is:

I must have seen over 2,000 people start up in business over the past seven years. Those that have taken time to research their product or service, sought input from others, understood the financial requirements and developed the plans needed to launch and continue have a much better prospect of success.

Some further marketing tips from Maree feature in the 'Marketing tips to fill your diary' section of this chapter.

Some of the differences between starting a small business and employment

In some cases where there is an opportunity to start a small business there could be a similar opportunity to take a full- or part-time employed position that might be quite similar in the actual work undertaken. Which route is right for you? Here are some of the many reasons for starting a small business:

focus on what you are best at or enjoy;

be your own boss;

provide a legacy for your children;

flexibility (around other interests/responsibilities);

freedom to organize things your way;

no commuting;

less direct involvement in internal politics and no more useless
meetings;

enjoy working on your own;

try something new/an experiment;

getting paid for overtime.

On the other hand here are some of the reasons for seeking a part- or full-time employed position:

a local employer;

security of income;

benefits of holiday pay, pension, paid sick leave, and perhaps private
health and life cover;

bonuses and perhaps a car;

team aspect and friendship of colleagues;

known travel requirements;

no personal liability if things go badly wrong;

staff discounts or other perks.

So what's the plan?

Assuming you still want to consider setting up a new business the next step is the plan. However, before getting into plans and 'Why bother?' it is probably useful to gain an overview of some common reasons why businesses fail and set this in context with the specifics of running a small business to help you succeed.

Firstly and importantly always remember that those thinking about setting up their own business in their 50s and 60s have a number of advantages: they probably have a specialist area of knowledge or expertise they have gained and they would rather continue to use it (than lose it). They may have been longing for an opportunity to do something different – possibly related to a lifelong interest that has been kept firmly on the back burner due to restrictions of time while they were employed. Perhaps they have a desire to do something 'useful' and regard working as a vocational thing rather than being profit driven, so are not motivated entirely for financial reasons. There are hundreds of success stories about those who took the plunge nearing or post-retirement to build a business that provided involvement, fun and income, plus a legacy for their children. However, for every two success stories there is a failure and your money could disappear fast if you set up in the wrong way or overstretch yourself. Worst of all you could lose your home if things go really badly wrong so the reasons below and tips throughout this chapter should help you understand and then deal with the risks.

Why businesses fail – learning the lessons

Businesses can fail for many reasons but if you can learn from the mistakes of others you will be doing yourself a favour.

The number-one reason why businesses fail is that *the market moves on and you are left behind*. Take time out to think and keep abreast of what your customers really want (have you tried asking them recently?); where are your competitors and what are they doing to keep on top of or ahead of the market and, overall, how is the market moving? Once you get left behind, you'll find the demand for your services declining and your income reducing – a rather toxic mix. Having said that you may be lucky enough to spot a niche that has been left behind and no one else is serving it!

A second reason (and one that may increase in 2013) is the *failure to deal with tax affairs properly*. The implications of penalties and interest levied by HMRC (HM Revenue & Customs) are often ignored and only hit home when it is too late. Keep your books properly and retain all records for six years after the year end – in brief, if you can't prove it, you may lose the tax benefit and pay additional tax, penalties and interest. If there is a problem, HMRC can go back and inspect previous years' accounts (for up to five years or even longer). If you fail to pay your tax fully when it is due, HMRC will pursue you vigorously and you are giving HMRC a reason to have a closer look at you and your business. On the other hand, if you have genuine cash flow difficulties and cannot pay your tax on the due date, talk to HMRC and you may find their attitude refreshing if it is the first time you have stumbled.

A third reason (and again one that may increase in 2013) is a *failure to manage your cash flow and this includes a lack of access to funding.* Vee Bharakda is a director of Business Recovery specialists Wilkins Kennedy and advises that 'access to funding is becoming a real issue! If you go to a bank they will want to know exactly why the business requires funding and will be vigilant in their lending criteria. They will require, in most cases, security over the business assets or the owners' residential homes.' Vee adds that 'in certain cases businesses have found alternative funding through invoice discounting and factoring which can be an effective way to fund an expanding business'. So for someone setting up in business in later life the scale of the anticipated business will be a key issue. On the one hand you may not need external finance if you fund the business from your own resources or if you start small and grow organically. On the other hand if external finance is needed you may have to 'get real' and recognize that banks and others are not in the habit of lending money to unviable propositions. It is often the case that the bank will be the largest stakeholder in a business. For this reason security is normally required, which may well include a charge on your home.

A *failure to plan and poor management* are a fourth reason for businesses failing. Vee Bharakda comments that the failure to plan and basic management deficiencies are often interlinked. 'Over the years we have seen various examples of inadequate management skills. The day-to-day running of the business sadly seems to take priority rather than planning for the future. Unfortunately the owners are so busy in immediate and minor issues that they fail to recognize the need to spend time on longer-term planning and strategic decisions and the business spirals downwards to failure.'

One common mistake by business owners is that they fall victim to the old excuse that 'my plan is in my head'. This is short-sighted as they usually take a triple hit because of:

- lack of clarity on objectives;
- lower-quality input from those that can help you;
- poor monitoring of how well you are actually doing.

Break the writer's block and set down your plan in writing for the year ahead. The starting point can be as simple as three handwritten pages defining a few well considered objectives, and a cash flow and profit-and-loss fore-cast for the year ahead linked to those objectives, plus a robust market-ing plan. More hints and tips on this basic, but effective, approach to a business plan are set out in the next section of this chapter. Don't expect perfection for the first draft, but do keep it under review; with focus and some decent effort it will start to pay off. Why not set yourself some stretch-ing objectives? You never know, you may be surprised at what you are capable of achieving!

A fifth reason for business failure is *bad debts* (where the customer goes bust and cannot pay your invoices), as this will come off your bottom-line profit and can really hurt. There are a few simple steps that you can take to reduce the potential of taking such a hit. What are your credit terms and have you encouraged all customers to pay electronically? Do you contact them as soon as your invoices become overdue? Do you require cash on delivery or prepayment. (PayPal and mobile credit card machines are transforming the payment services.) In some cases it is worth remembering that a bad customer is sometimes worse than no customer at all.

Vee Bharakda of Business Recovery specialists Wilkins Kennedy comments that 'Businesses tend to fail for the reasons Allan has mentioned and one additional reason that we have seen recently – trying to expand too quickly.' Vee goes on to explain: 'Some businesses start on the right track, but tend to expand far too quickly either by overtrading, selling more than their cash flow will allow, overproduction of stock or not researching the marketplace or competitors adequately.

'The most common mistake that we see in this area is businesses employ-ing the wrong staff and additional staff rather than first looking to motivate and incentivize the existing workforce. Extra staff increases overheads and decreases profit. Beware!'

So 'Why bother' when it comes to planning? The answer should now be evident from the above – you are improving your chances of succeeding and may even do rather better than you first thought. On that positive note Vee remembers many positive turnaround stories from her career in business recovery and believes that 'success comes from having a positive and op-timistic attitude to your business. Business owners need to be open-minded and realize that they do not need to know everything and must always be willing to learn and adapt with the business in mind. And with that in mind if a business owner is experiencing financial difficulties and is worried about the risk they could be facing it is always best to talk to a business recovery specialist sooner rather than later.'

What goes into a plan?

Assuming you still wish to consider starting a business it is now time to start preparing your plan. The starting point is to make a promise that you will put your plan down in writing. If you do not do this you will be like an ostrich with its head in the sand, not do yourself justice and will probably not achieve (or realize) your potential. Too many people run a mile when the subject of a plan comes up, especially the notion of a grand-sounding business plan. Perhaps armed with some confidence gained from a book on setting up a business, business banking literature, or even after attending a setting-up-in-business course, some new businesses start a plan but never get it finished.

The reason for this is twofold: first, fear of the planning process and, second, intimidation by some daunting plan templates and spreadsheets seen in books or banking literature. The prescription is a three-stage plan that will get you started and then, with experience, you can tweak it and make it that bit slicker. Please be assured that no one gets the first draft right but the important points are that it is down in writing, you've got started and you're not ignoring it.

Stage 1 of the plan: objectives

What, financially, do you need to set as objectives to bring you in that £5,000 or £20,000 or £60,000 that you want in your pocket? This takes a bit of thinking through and ties into the stage 3 section detailed below. Typically you should be able to come up with two or three simple objectives based on income, gross profit (if you sell stock) and overheads.

For a high-powered full-time management consultant who does not sell stock there could be just two objectives. *Objective 1*: I aim to invoice £40,000 in my first year of trading based on working at least 100 days at an average billing rate of £400 per day. I will review my billing rates quarterly and my performance monthly. *Objective 2*: I will aim to keep my overheads (after expenses recharged to clients) in my first year to £5,000.

For businesses that sell stock, *Objective 3* will be something like: I will aim to achieve the following gross profit percentages:

Product line A: 30 per cent;

Product line B: 40 per cent;

Product line C: 50 per cent.

Gross profit percentages are calculated using:

(Sales price less cost of materials/product sold ÷ sales price) × 100

The key point with objectives is that less gives more: you don't want a long list of objectives. Just isolate what is important, set them down and double-check that they are SMART (specific, measurable, achievable, realistic and timed).

Stage 2 of the plan: your market research

The next page of your plan should be all about your marketing effort, a topic often misunderstood and mistaken for advertising. Think about approaching this section under the following three headings.

Products

Start with your main product or service and think about the features and benefits of what you are selling. Understanding these and discussing them with your trusted advisers will allow you to start thinking about other related services or goods which you could offer. Can you now differentiate your product and have two or three products/services each with slightly different customers and competitors? For instance, the PC repair and installation business gave itself a new line of income by designing and offering 'easy as 123' computer training for late adopters of internet, e-mail and Skype.

Customers

For each main product area ask lots of questions to tease out your research. Who are my customers? Where are they based? When do they tend to buy? How and where do they tend to buy and at what price? How should I contact them? Keep asking those important questions of who, what, why, where, when and how and they will help you tease out all sorts of gems. This part of the plan is vital, as you will have read from the tips provided by Liz Barclay and Maree Atkinson in the 'Yes, you can!' section of this chapter.

Competitors

Again, ask yourself who, what, why, where, when and how?

Marketing plan: given your product(s), your potential customers and competitors, what marketing tools could you use to promote yourself to targeted customers? The output should be a series of activities that you can do to help get quality work and keep busy. Some further practical things that you can start doing straight away are set out in the marketing section later on in this chapter. The one problem, however, is that you usually end up with a jumble of unfocused ideas – the best way around that is to rank each idea on the basis of priority, impact and cost (free is good!).

Stage 3 of the plan: your income and expenditure forecast

This is your income and expenditure forecast for the year and this third page is the tricky one. The strong recommendation is that you map out the year ahead financially. This will then become your plan or 'map'. The beauty of it comes from then monitoring your actual performance against the plan and then doing something about it when you are off target. It is not a piece of mystic accounting mumbo-jumbo, it is just a map to help you get from where you start to where you want to be. Rather than reinventing the wheel, try searching the internet for a spreadsheet called a profit-and-loss forecast or income-and-expenditure forecast. You should be able to do this yourself but if it becomes a struggle, ask your accountant to help.

Is there more?

The above approach will give you a first draft and a start: more importantly it will give you potential go/no-go guidance and the steps towards starting your own business. It is surprising how many people forget about the total cost involved and tax; the reality of the end 'money to spend' can be quite sobering after you have got over the initial excitement of a potentially high sales figure. If you share a bank account with your partner remember to take your partner through the numbers and manage their expectations, as they may get even more excited when they see that attractive VAT-inclusive income land in the business account.

Once you have completed your first plan the secret is to keep it alive and keep reviewing how you are doing against it. Your plan can then be improved and extra sections or pages added to make it an even better tool, or you may find that the simple three-stage approach is all you need.

The *top tips* on your plan are:

Don't worry about calling it a business plan or such other high-powered term. Think of it only as a tool to help you get from where you are to where you want to be.

Commit your plan to writing – three or four pages initially is fine. If you don't write it down you will not be able to use it to tease out other opportunities, review it with your trusted advisers (a family member or friend that runs their own business, your accountant and perhaps a business adviser or mentor) and build on it.

Don't expect perfection as no one gets it right on the first, second or even third draft but do keep coming back to it and try to make it that little bit better each time.

Practical and emotional tips

If you are married or in a civil partnership your partner's attitude is crucial. Even if not directly involved, he or she will have to accept (at least) the loss of a room in the house being used as your office. There will be the added distractions of out-of-hours phone calls and, perhaps, suddenly cancelled social engagements. The checklist below will help you identify other issues that are either of a practical or emotional nature:

- First and foremost will you be doing something you really enjoy? If so the work itself is the motivator: you do it because you want to do it.

- Are you willing to turn your hand to support jobs (eg bookkeeping/ secretarial tasks such as invoicing)?

- Have you space available to work from home initially or would you need/prefer to rent accommodation?

- Can your family/partner cope with having you and your business in the house?

- Can you cope without the resources/back-up provided by an employer (IT/HR/training)? When you run your own business you have to do it yourself or buy it in.

- Have you the funds to manage any initial outlay (eg stock, equipment, new car or van, computer) or are the essential resources already to hand?

- Can you afford a period without income while you get yourself established?

- Are you self-reliant, self-motivated and self-disciplined?

- Can you remain positive and maintain a 'can do' aura in the face of difficulties?
- Can you divorce yourself from your domestic/social interests (eg the neighbour who drops in for a chat)?

This list is by no means exhaustive but the questions give an idea of the things that anyone contemplating starting their own business will face. The more you can answer 'yes' the more you are likely to be suited to starting your own small business.

The one *top tip* in this section relates to the nightmare scenario of your hard drive crashing without the content being backed up. Do invest in a facility to back up your business, bookkeeping and tax records. There are online software packages available that can run automatically every night for extra backup comfort.

On the subject of useful purchases you might want to consider:

- one or two lockable, fireproof filing cabinets;
- a desk;
- shelf space;
- a comfortable, adjustable office chair;
- minor stationery items (eg hole punch, paper guillotine, stapler, paper clips, plastic folders, dividers and files);
- headed notepaper, 'With compliments' slips and business cards (try to use professional association logos or other branding on your cards to help differentiate yourself when networking);
- a mobile phone in addition to your home and/or business telephone;
- a laptop or PC and printer;
- e-mail facility/broadband access to the internet;
- a photocopier and scanner.

Keep on top of the paperwork

Generally, this one topic causes the most groans! But simple bookkeeping, if done properly, is just a by-product of your business and flows naturally from raising sales invoices and paying for purchases. After all, you want to ensure that you are invoicing or charging the right amount to clients, that they pay the correct amount on the invoice (not all manage to do this) and identify any that do not pay at all. For a small business with only a few clients each month, the last issue will be picked up quickly. But if you have multiple clients you may miss an invoice that was never paid. You will never miss an unpaid invoice if you are on top of your bookkeeping.

An even more compelling reason for doing your own bookkeeping is that HMRC has a 'prove it or lose it' view if enquiring into an aspect of your tax return. Under the system of self-assessment, HMRC relies on you completing your tax returns. You sign the tax return (not your accountant or bookkeeper) and you are responsible for it. Paper or online tax returns are generally accepted as filed but HMRC always retains the ability to enquire into any aspect of a tax return; an enquiry may arise up to a year after you send it in.

In the case of an enquiry, HMRC tells you precisely what part of your tax return is under investigation; you are then expected to be able to validate every payment (excluding coin-operated vending machines that do not give a receipt) that you have made, with a supporting invoice or receipt (ie not a credit card payment slip with no substance detailing what was actually bought). HMRC will also track the invoice through to the payment on the bank or credit card statement to verify that it was valid expenditure. You can understand why HMRC does this, as the current biggest fraud found in small business accounts is false invoices drawn up with the help of cheap and widely available colour photocopiers, plus cutting and pasting from information on the web. The bank payment helps verify the expenditure as valid, and HMRC can also go to third parties directly for any further confirmation it needs. Understanding the approach that HMRC takes helps you to appreciate the need to retain all invoices and to record how and when they were paid. If you are unable to prove the expenditure, you lose it as far as HMRC is concerned, resulting in fewer purchases being accepted as a deduction from your profits and more tax to pay. There will also be penalties and interest to pay and the scope of its enquiries into your tax affairs will be widened.

Basic bookkeeping

All incoming and outgoing payments therefore need to be recorded throughout the year. These records must be retained for at least six years from the end of your accounting period. When recording income, you will need to differentiate between your fees and your expenses (or other 'recharged' items). You will also need to keep a record of income from other sources, such as bank/building society interest. Records of outgoings need to be categorized according to type. Examples of some categories you might need to consider are:

- stock;
- subscriptions/meeting fees;
- office equipment;
- office supplies;
- post and courier costs;
- travel fares, parking and subsistence;
- home office costs;
- telephone and internet;
- sundry;
- accountancy and professional fees;
- insurance.

Many small business owners opt to do their own bookkeeping, with or without the help of a computer software package. If you opt for a software package, choose one that fits your legal status (company or sole trader), uses English rather than accountancy-speak and easily produces reports. Sage and Intuit (which has the QuickBooks range of software) seem to be acceptable to most accountants, so check with yours. Generally speaking, accountancy fees will be less if your accountant is already familiar with the software; or it may turn out that the accountant has some Excel spreadsheets that will do the job. The accountant may also have a bookkeeping guide to help get you started. If not, maybe you have the wrong accountant. There are decent basic courses on bookkeeping and tax available from HMRC's business support team (**www.hmrc.gov/uk/bst**). These workshops are on a variety of subjects at locations throughout the country and are free of charge and are designed for everyone in business, especially new businesses or new employers.

If you are really averse to bookkeeping yourself, consider hiring a bookkeeper. Bookkeepers currently charge between about £15 and £23 per hour, depending on geographical location and experience and can be found in the local telephone directory. Fundamentally, bookkeepers are responsible for recording the transactions of your business and filing the paperwork and doing that all-important bank reconciliation (accounting-speak for ensuring that everything that has gone through your business bank account is recorded in the bookkeeping entries and vice versa).

Accountants

Depending on qualifications and experience, accountants and tax advisers assisting new small start-up businesses could charge from £35 to about £120 per hour to assist you in setting up in business and prepare your accounts and tax. The accountant and tax adviser should also spot issues that you may not have been aware of from a tax liability or claim perspective (income tax, corporation tax and VAT). More importantly, a good accountant who knows your industry area will be able to help with general guidance and input to your plan on marketing and pricing, drawing on experience beyond accounting and tax.

Some accountancy firms offer a combination of bookkeeping, accountancy and tax services and, if so, you can expect to pay a premium on the bookkeeping hourly rates quoted above. Always ask your trusted family members or friends if they can recommend an accountant. Remember to ask for confirmation of the accountant's qualifications (the type of qualification and whether their practising certificate has been issued by a recognized professional body) and check that they hold professional indemnity insurance. It is advisable to meet at least two accountants and see how you feel about rapport and the availability of proactive hints and tips. Will the person you meet be the person who does your accounts and tax and provides proactive advice? Always request written confirmation of hourly rates plus an estimate of fees for the year and obtain a proposed retainer specifying what you and the accountant will do and by when.

Finally, there is sometimes some confusion over the term 'audit of accounts'. Many years ago, smallish companies in the UK had to have an audit of their accounts. The turnover threshold (one of three thresholds) for being required to have an audit has been increased and currently stands at £6.5 million, so the vast majority of start-ups need not concern themselves with audited accounts.

Paying tax and national insurance

Sole traders

Self-employed individuals running their own businesses are usually called 'sole traders'. All new businesses that trade as sole traders need to register as self-employed with HMRC. While tax can be daunting, some sole traders with relatively straightforward billing and overheads have been able to undertake their own tax returns after researching the position. There are free help sheets available from Business Link and, as mentioned earlier in this section, there is also a lot of assistance available from HMRC. In the UK, sole traders pay income tax on their profits and HMRC tags this with the description 'Schedule D tax'. With income tax, you first have a personal allowance, which gives you a tax-free amount and then any excess income (including your profits) is taxed at 20 per cent, then 40 per cent and then 50 per cent. The precise yearly limits are available from the HMRC website or your accountant. In very broad terms, if you are under 65, you currently (summer 2012) have a tax-free allowance of £8,105 (this increases to £9,205 in April 2013). You are then taxed on the next £34,370 at 20 per cent and then 40 per cent tax applies to taxable income from £34,371 up to £150,000. Anything above £150,000 gets taxed at 50 per cent. The 50 per cent rate reduces to 45 per cent in April 2013. Many sole traders choose to run their bookkeeping for the year to 5 April to coincide with the tax year end (or 31 March, which HMRC effectively accepts as equivalent to 5 April).

If you are past the state retirement age or earn less than £5,595 from your business there will be no National Insurance Contributions (NICs) to pay. Subject to this, sole traders are liable for Class 2 NICs (currently a nominal amount of £2.65 per week), which are collected by direct debit either monthly or quarterly. The mandate is set up automatically when you register as self-employed. After starting, you have three months to register and if you forget there is an automatic £100 fine. You are also liable for the much more significant Class 4 NICs that are assessed and collected by HMRC at the same time as assessing your Schedule D tax. Currently these are at 9 per cent on profits between £7,605 and £42,475 and this reduces to just 2 per cent on profits over £42,475.

The payment of sole-trader income tax is reasonably straightforward but there is a twist in your first year of trading. Assuming that you have a year end of 5 April 2014, the first payment will be due by 31 January 2015 so you have a long period of (effectively) interest-free credit, as some of the profits on which the tax is due may have been earned as long ago as May 2013. With the first payment, however, you get a 'double whammy' as you also have to pay on 31 January 2015 a payment on account of your second year's trading. Then on 31 July 2015 you have to make a second on-account payment of the second year's trading. Both on-account payments are set by default on the basis of your Year 1 profits. You can 'claim' a reduction if year 2 is proving to have lower profits than year 1; your accountant will help you with this if it is appropriate.

After this initial tax famine, followed by double payment of tax, you will thereafter receive a tax demand twice a year. Payments need to be made by 31 January (during the tax year) and then by 31 July after the end of that tax year, with any over-/underpayment sorted out by the following 31 January. Many sole-trader businesses set up a reserve bank account in addition to their current account, and place a percentage of their income aside, which is earning interest each month (albeit not amounting to much in the current climate). This tactic should help you resist the temptation to raid money that is not for spending – and ensure you can pay your tax on time.

Additionally, as a self-employed person you are allowed certain other reliefs. Ask your accountant, but the following expenses and allowances are usually tax deductible:

Business expenses. These must be incurred 'wholly and exclusively' for the purposes of the trade. Office supplies that you buy will probably qualify; however, any business entertaining will not. Bad debts are usually allowable. Certain expenses incurred in advance of getting the business started are also permitted, for example necessary travelling, printing costs and telephoning.

Partially allowable expenses. These mainly apply if you are working from home. They include such items as the part of your rent, heating, lighting and telephone usage that you devote to business purposes, and also possibly some of the running expenses on your car, if you use your car for your business. Your business equipment and premises are capital items and cannot be counted as an expense. Instead they must be categorized under fixed assets and writing-down allowances are calculated at the year end, to reduce your profits (see capital allowances below).

Spouse's wages. If you employ your partner in the business, his or her pay (provided this is reasonable) qualifies as a legitimate expense, in the same way as any other employee's, but must of course be accounted for through the PAYE system.

Pension contributions. Tax relief is generally available for pension contributions at the higher of £3,600 (gross) or 100 per cent of relevant earnings up to a maximum of £50,000.

Capital allowances. These were overhauled in April 2012. There is an annual investment allowance (AIA) which provides tax relief on many types of expenditure on equipment up to £25,000 per annum of expenditure (except on certain items such as cars). This is then supplemented by writing-down allowances of between 8 and 20 per cent on any excess above the £25,000 AIA. This can be a complex area and if significant expenditure on plant and equipment is envisaged you should discuss this with an accountant.

Research and development. There are generous reliefs available if you can meet the stringent qualifying conditions. Best advice is to check with an accountant.

Interest on loans. Tax relief is given on money borrowed to invest in business expenses and equipment in most normal circumstances.

Partnerships

Partnership tax is broadly similar to the process described for a sole trader as above with the exception of some more paperwork. In addition to submitting each partner's individual personal self-assessment tax return a composite partnership tax return must also be submitted.

Limited company

As far as tax is concerned accountants love companies, as there is lots for them to do, lots of taxes and lots of accountancy fees. First and foremost, companies pay corporation tax on their income (currently 20 per cent). There is a higher rate of corporation tax of 24 per cent on profits above £300,000. Your company accounts need to be finalized and any corporation tax paid nine months after your year end.

The key point with a company is that the money coming in is not your money – it is the company's money – so how do you extract your money? The first option is salary and this means running a 'Pay As You Earn' (PAYE) system: another form of tax with a rigorous calculation regime and payments that have to be made to HMRC. PAYE carries the income tax rates as featured for the sole trader but the 'killer punch' is NICs unless you are past state retirement age and not required to pay them anymore. The term 'killer punch' is used because NICs on a company (even if it is just you alone as an employee) are the composite of employee *and* employer NICs (as the company is an employer). Currently these are 12 per cent employee NICs on £7,605 to £42,475 reducing to 2 per cent for amounts above £42,475 and then (make sure you are sitting down at this point), an additional 13.8 per cent employer NIC on everything above £7,488. The one saving grace is that the total salary (including employer NIC) is deductible when calculating the profits subject to corporation tax.

There is a daunting year-end routine involving a whole series of forms beginning with the letter P. Overall, the system is capable of being run by a business person with some oversight from an accountant and a decent piece of payroll software (and the free HMRC online service is also good). An alternative is to ask a bookkeeper, payroll bureau or your accountant to do it for you.

The second option for extracting funds is dividends (taking for granted that you have repaid expenses and any loan to get the company started). Dividends are not deductible when calculating your corporation tax. The big selling point for dividends is that, at face value, they are not subject to NIC. Depending on the level of dividends taken, there may be more tax to pay via your personal tax return if your income (ie salary, dividends and interest received from banks, etc) exceeds the higher-rate tax threshold. This is outside the scope of this chapter but your accountant will be able to assist you with this.

This leads us neatly into a possible 'tax trap' for the unwary freelancer who decides to set up as a company. As a director, you can decide whether or not to pay yourself a salary, dividends or both. The appeal of dividends is fairly obvious from the comment immediately above about the lack of NICs. However, this is before we have outlined HMRC regulation number 35 (IR35) that came into force in April 2000.

HMRC is particularly interested in ex-employees setting up service companies that work exclusively for their former employer and also 'personal service companies', to use an HMRC term. This is an extremely wide-ranging and difficult subject but, in very simplified terms, 'personal service companies' are basically one-person companies that provide services to one or a few clients. In very basic terms IR35 applies to those that could be seen to 'look like, act like and smell like an employee'. This situation is one of the subject matters of IR35 and is to be avoided if at all possible! Remember, IR35 only applies to companies (not sole traders).

There are many hints and tips and some urban myths about IR35 and you may encounter advice such as having substitution clauses in your contracts; having clauses in your contracts that mean you are not obliged to work certain days and the client is not obliged to give you work; having all the trappings of a 'genuine' business (business cards, headed paper, advertising, seeking to agree a 'price for the job', rather than an hourly rate, holding your own professional indemnity insurance and having your own website, etc).

The bottom line as we go into 2013 is that HMRC is strengthening its specialist compliance teams that investigate IR35. HMRC is also seeking to provide more information to assist businesses in understanding whether IR35 affects them. For instance, in the spring of 2012 HMRC specified 12 tests and depending on your answers you obtain a risk rating – the higher the score the lower your risk to IR35. You can quickly build up your score with some big hitting points, for instance operating from your own premises and actually substituting another person in the delivery of your services. As presently drafted (summer 2012) there are also some modest point earners (such as maintaining professional indemnity insurance and having a written business plan). On the other hand you can almost wipe out your points by going back to work for an employer that you were on PAYE with *'within the 12 months which ended on the last 31 March'*. HMRC provides some examples of freelancers and provides its view on the likely IR35 status. For some these tests will provide a quick fix to IR35 (own premises and a substitution 'arrangement') but for most freelancers it is now even more complex and seems to be a step backwards.

Tips and hints on IR35 are outside the scope of a guide like this. It is a big issue and one that you have first got to recognize and then do something about. One of the key players in helping freelancers guide themselves through the minefield of IR35 is the Professional Contractors Group (PCG) at **www.pcg.org.uk**. This organization, working in conjunction with a chartered accountant who understands IR35, is probably your next step if you are a freelancer and you trade as a company. Briefly, if you fall foul of IR35, the tax inspector will seek to set aside the dividends you have paid and treat the dividend payment as if it were subject to PAYE and NICs (including employer NICs). If you do find yourself subject to IR35 there is a complex eight-step calculation called a 'deemed payment' and there is a deemed payment calculator on HMRC's website: (**http://www.hmrc.gov.uk/leaflets/calc_deempyt.htm**).

Registering for VAT

Value Added Tax (VAT) was introduced back in 1973 and it seems that many people have lost sight of the name of this tax and especially the word 'added'. You are, in effect, adding a tax and are an unpaid tax collector.

If your taxable turnover is likely to be more than £77,000 in the first 12 months or less you must register for VAT unless your supplies/services are outside the scope of VAT. Remember that any expenses that you recharge to clients need to be included in the calculation of taxable turnover. Form VAT1 must be completed and sent to HMRC within 30 days of the end of the month in which the value of your taxable turnover exceeded £77,000 over a rolling 12 months.

UK business clients are invariably registered for VAT so are not concerned about having it added to your invoice. To avoid adding VAT to invoices for business clients in other EU countries it is essential to quote the client's VAT number on the invoice.

In addition, note that you can claim back VAT on pre-start/pre-registration expenditure involved in setting up the business. If you elect for 'Cash Accounting' status, this means that VAT only becomes payable or reclaimable when invoices are actually paid. It avoids having to pay the VAT on your own invoices before slow-paying clients pay you, which can add significantly to cash flow problems. On the other hand, if you have a client who pays you promptly, remember not to spend the cash before the quarter end when you have to submit your VAT return and payment. The VAT regime carries with it onerous fines and penalties for late payment and evasion, and is not to be taken lightly.

If your taxable turnover is below the limit, you may apply for voluntary VAT registration. Before applying, consider carefully whether registration will really be of benefit to you, that is, whether reclaiming the VAT paid on items needed for your business (such as office equipment) is worth the trouble of sending in mandatory, quarterly VAT returns and keeping separate VAT records for possible inspection by visiting VAT officers. One final positive if you do register for VAT is that it seems to give you added credibility with clients.

VAT flat rate scheme

HMRC introduced the flat rate scheme in 2004, with the aim of simplifying record keeping for small businesses. This allows you to charge VAT to your clients at the standard rate of 20 per cent and to pay VAT as a percentage of your VAT-inclusive turnover (instead of having to work out the VAT payable on your sales less purchases). You can apply to join the scheme if your taxable turnover (excluding VAT) will not be more than £150,000 in the next 12 months.

HMRC publishes a list of business categories from which you need to decide which best describes your business. A further bonus is that you can deduct 1 per cent from the flat rate that you use for your first year of VAT registration. As a tip, do not do anything without checking it out with your accountant as there are a few twists and turns that could make the VAT flat rate scheme unsuitable. But, at face value, it seems to have been beneficial to many small businesses. Further information can be gained from HMRC's website and inserting 'VAT flat rate scheme' into the internal search engine on that site.

Marketing tips to fill your diary

When you start a small business there are three marketing 'must haves'. The first is that you have something that people will want to buy. The second is you and your ability to present and be the face of a viable business. The third 'must have' does not come naturally to many people but it can be learnt and it can be improved. It is all about the ability to market the business.

It is a sad fact that many new owners/managers genuinely believe that marketing simply means placing an advert in some well known directory. Unfortunately this view of marketing means achieving only a fraction of the sales of any comparable business with a decent grasp of marketing.

The objective is to plan ahead, generate sales for your new business, anticipate when your sales will end or dip and start looking for ways you can promote your business before that happens. The pressure of meeting current deadlines and sales leaves little enthusiasm, energy or opportunity for chasing new work and sales. However, if you are to be a successful small business it is a basic necessity and one that you must address. The following eight tips should help you. Why not use these to assess your marketing to date and what more you can do?

Your own website and/or social media

Now that businesses rely so heavily on the internet have you thought about a website and/or harnessing social media to promote your business? Is there a vital domain name (website unique address) that you need to secure and register? This name, once registered, will require a web host. The web host is the 'nuts and bolts' of your website, because this is where you design and publish your web pages, add and improve them and operate your site. Reserving a domain name is easy and remarkably low cost. Search 'domain names and how to register them' and you will find millions of offers of advice. Instead, try asking friends who are already 'web savvy', or small business owners whom you know and who operate their business using a website. Don't ignore help that is right in front of your nose: young friends or relatives may know more than you do about this subject. They may even be keen to help you build and design your website.

Once your website is up and running, do not forget to promote it through any other advertising you do, printing your website address on your stationery and literature and social media profiles.

It is also worth checking out other websites including those run by trade or professional associations which may allow you to register and set up a profile. If you do not want to have your own website, you can set up profiles on various social media 'networking websites' such as LinkedIn and Facebook. Twitter with 500+ million accounts is growing rapidly and provides the benefits of building your online contacts (giving potential accessibility) and allowing you to showcase your expertise in a certain area. It can be linked to your LinkedIn and with some gentle early learning with a small group of 'safe' contacts you may soon be tweeting, following and retweeting (a world that may have been unheard of five years ago but is now vital to some businesses). Twitter can also be used for private communications if you wish. If you want to try it you can follow me on Twitter at allaneslersmith – I look forward to seeing you on Twitter.

Personal contacts and networking

Once you decide to set up your own business your personal contacts such as ex-colleagues or other small business owners will be a potential source of work. Too many small businesses forget that behind every contact there is another layer of potential contacts who are just one introduction away, so ignore this multiplier effect at your peril. In your first year you should be re-educating your contacts to think of you not as 'Jane who used to work at IBM' but Jane who now runs her own business advising small businesses on their IT needs. Do not be afraid to pick up the phone or send letters/flyers/business cards explaining your new business and what you can offer. Joining the best trade or professional association you can find will be a great way of networking with the added bonus of research facilities, information and other fringe benefits. Currently the Federation of Small Business and Professional Contractors Group receive very positive feedback and represent reasonable value for money. Contacts and other information are listed in the 'Further help, advice and training' section, below.

Discounts and offers

These can be used to great effect during seasonal dips, introducing a new service or clearing old stock. Whether it is 20 per cent off, a buy-one-get-one-free offer or the numerous variations of this basic approach there are three golden rules:

1 Always state the original or usual price (to show the value in the offer).

2 Always specify an expiry date.

3 Always explain that the offer is subject to availability.

Flyers and business cards

Generally speaking a response rate of 1 per cent to a flyer is considered fairly good. With some clever thinking you can increase the response rate. Have you targeted the flyer? A good example would be the wedding gown designer who neatly persuades the reception of a sought-after wedding location hotel to keep a flyer dispenser in their foyer.

Are you able to include your professional or trade association logo on your flyer and business cards. Have you asked if this is possible?

There are two sides to a flyer and business card – have you thought about putting information on the blank reverse side? Could this contain some useful tips or, perhaps, a special offer or discount? Anything that ensures the card or flyer is kept rather than dumped will help your business to edge ahead.

Testimonials

People generally buy on trust and never like to be made to look a fool. The intangible benefit of testimonials is simply that it shows prospective customers that you have done a good job and can be relied upon. Looked at in this way the benefit flowing from positive testimonials can be powerful and should never be underestimated.

Agencies

Agencies will be especially important for prospective consultants or contractors as most recruitment agencies also deal with full- and part-time contract positions. When marketing yourself to an agency the same rules apply as when marketing yourself to a potential employer. Good personal and written presentation will help the agency to sell you on to its clients, so take the time to get it right. Remember that it is in the agency's interest to find you work as it receives a fee for placing you.

Advertising

There are many options for advertising yourself and your business such as website banners, sponsored links on search engines such as Google, free and paid-for directory listings and sponsorships.

Another approach could be 'free' advertising through creating a press release that you forward to local or trade press with an interesting story (celebrities or hints and tips always go down well). Could you also publish it on your website or send it to your customers and ask them to refer to it with anyone that could be interested? You can also advertise yourself and your skills by writing articles in professional or trade journals – what do you have that is news or novel or leading edge?

Another subset of advertising is sponsorship. The driving instructor who sponsored the playing shirts on the local under-17 football team is a great example of cost-effective sponsorship.

Learn when to say no

This contradicts all the positive tips above but is generally the hardest lesson to learn and will probably only come with experience. The fear of losing a sale to a competitor or the uncertainty of where the next piece or work or sale will come from if you reject this one may induce you to overstretch or undercut yourself. If you continually face this dilemma it will only place unrelenting stress on you and you may not survive in business for long, so learn how to say no in a way that does not burn bridges.

Maree Atkinson of the Federation of Small Business (see the 'Yes, you can!' section of this chapter) has some additional tips to help you learn to say no.

Maree advises:

> **Be wary of the promises of business.** You will want to help customers and will want to secure those early sales. You may even find yourself bending over backwards to help. But have you given away your ideas and spent hours of your time with no prospect of the work? A very talented garden designer was asked

to redesign a large garden. Excited by the project he prepared some initial plans and the client made a number of changes which he incorporated. The client did go ahead with the work but used the plans with another contractor. I guess it is a balance between 'marketing time' and showing your wares but not going too far, which you will learn in time!

Marketing to the wrong people. In the early days of starting a small business you will receive invitations for a meeting from possible business partners or joint ventures who want to 'see if there's a way we could do some work together'. Networking is vital to many businesses but don't network with random people just because you think you're supposed to network. Do some research about the offer and listen to your 'gut feeling' before you say yes. In time work out what networking is best for you and what offers to explore further.

Maree's words remind me of Lord Alan Sugar's words on what makes an entrepreneur in his latest book *The Way I See It*. Lord Sugar's straightforward advice was that 'If you have partners, they have to bring something to the party.'

Trading formats

Sole trader

A self-employed person is someone who works for themselves instead of an employer and draws an income from their personally run business. If the profits from the work are accounted for on one person's tax return, that person is known as a sole trader. If the profits are shared between two or more people, it is a partnership (see below).

There is no clear definition of self-employment. Defining an employee, on the other hand, is slightly easier as it can generally be assumed that if income tax and NICs are deducted from an individual's salary before they are paid, then that individual is an employee.

Importantly, the business has no separate existence from the owner and, therefore, all debts of the business are debts of the owner who is personally liable for all amounts owed by the business. This strikes fear into the hearts of many business owners; you only need to think of the number of business owners who go bust every time a recession comes around and lose their house. Should this be a worry?

First and foremost, you must consider the risk to you in any work that you do. Could it go wrong and could you be sued? Is that a realistic prospect or so remote that it does not even warrant thinking about? Or is it somewhere in the middle? Can insurance help (see the section below)? Remember that such insurance is only as good as the disclosures you make and the levels of cover provided. At the end of the day you know your business, your customers and the work that you do, so the risk assessment can only be done by you.

How to start up as a sole trader

You can start trading immediately.

You can trade under virtually any name, subject to some restrictions that are mostly common sense, such as not suggesting something you are not (connection to government, royalty or international pre-eminence). A B Jones trading as Super Lawns is fine.

The full name and address of the owner and any trading name must be disclosed on letters, orders and invoices.

A phone call to HMRC's helpline for the newly self-employed (0845 915 4515) must be made within three months of starting up.

Partnership

Two or more self-employed people who work together on a business and share the profits are trading in partnership. The profits from the work are accounted for on a partnership tax return and extracts from that partnership tax return are then copied into the partner's individual tax returns.

The business has no separate existence from the partners and, therefore, all debts of the business are debts of the partners, so they are personally liable for all amounts owed by the business. In addition, partners are jointly and severally liable for the debts of the business or, put more simply, the last person standing pays the lot. There is a saying that you need to trust your business partner better than your husband/wife/civil partner.

As with sole traders, the first consideration is the potential for business risk since your personal wealth is backing the debts of the business. First and foremost you must consider the risk to you in any work that you do and, given the 'joint and several liability' point explained above, the trust and faith you have in your business partner. Could it go wrong and could you be sued? Is that a realistic prospect or so remote that it does not even warrant thinking about? Or is it somewhere in the middle? Can insurance help? Remember that such insurance is only as good as the disclosures you make and the levels of cover provided. At the end of the day you know your business, your business partner, your customers and the work that you do, so the risk assessment can only be done by you.

How to start up as a partnership

You can start trading immediately.

You can trade under virtually any name, subject to some restrictions that are mostly common sense, such as not suggesting something you are not (connection to government, royalty or international pre-eminence). A B Jones and A B Smith trading as J & S Super Lawns is fine.

You will need to consult a solicitor to assist with the preparation and signing of a partnership deed. The partnership deed is for your protection and is essential because it sets out the rules of the partnership including, for example, the profit or loss split between partners, what happens if one partner wishes to leave or you wish to admit a new partner.

The full name and address of the partners and any trading name must be disclosed on letters, orders and invoices.

A phone call to HMRC's helpline for the newly self-employed (0845 915 4515) explaining that you are starting a partnership must be made within three months of starting up.

Limited company

A limited liability company (often the shorthand of 'limited company' is used to describe this trading format) is a company whose liability is limited by shares and is the most common form of trading format. The company is owned by its shareholders. The company is run by directors who are appointed by the shareholders.

The shareholders are liable to contribute the amount remaining unpaid on the shares – usually zero as most shares are issued fully paid up. The shareholders therefore achieve limited liability.

How to start up a limited company

A company needs to be registered with Companies House and cannot trade until it is granted a Certificate of Incorporation. The registration process is a quick and inexpensive process using Companies House's web incorporation service (it currently costs £18 and is completed within 24 hours). Some people use a company formation agent (Google this term to find such an agent – there are plenty of them) and the process should cost less than £100.

The company name needs to be approved by Companies House and no two companies can have the same name. Names that suggest, for instance, an international aspect will require evidence to support the claim and certain names are prohibited unless there is a dispensation. An example of this latter category would be the word 'Royal'.

You must appoint a director and this 'officer' of the company carries responsibilities that can incur penalties and/or a fine. The appointment of directors should therefore not be done lightly. The full range of responsibilities is set out in The Companies Act; further guidance is available from the Companies House website (**http://www.companieshouse.co.uk**). Some examples of the responsibilities include the duty to maintain the financial records of the company, to prepare accounts, to retain the paperwork and to avoid conflicts of interest. Small businesses no longer have to have a separate company secretary but it can be useful to have another office-holder signatory and the risks associated with this position are relatively light.

In addition you will need to appoint a registered office, which is a designated address at which official notices and communications can be received. The company's main place of business is usually used as the registered office but you could also use the address of your accountant or solicitor (there may be a charge for this).

The advantages and disadvantages of the three formats are shown in Table 10.1.

TABLE 10.1

Advantages	Disadvantages
SOLE TRADER	
Simple to set up.	Personal liability.
Simple to run and you are in complete control of the business and make all the business decisions. You also enjoy the greatest freedom from regulation and paperwork.	Additional cost of the payment for insurance if considered appropriate.
Strictly speaking, you don't even need to maintain a separate bank account but it is advisable to do so.	

TABLE 10.1 *continued*

Advantages	Disadvantages
Much lower National Insurance Contributions (NICs) than a limited liability company.	Perceived lack of credibility.
Taxation is covered by a few extra pages on your income tax self-assessment and paid twice a year (January and July). Accountancy fees will be lower than if you run your own limited liability company.	
Only you, your accountant and HMRC need know your turnover, profits and income.	Employment agencies in certain sectors will not deal with sole traders. Instead they may ask you to take up a consulting or contracting position through a limited company which you set up, or through an umbrella company that they may introduce you to.
Tax breaks can be potentially more attractive than a company for a business with losses in the early years. Generally there are more attractive tax breaks for use of home office and use of a car for work.	
Simple to shut down. It is possible to start off as a sole trader and then convert to a company later on as the business grows or risks increase.	

PARTNERSHIP

Can be useful in husband-and-wife businesses and is simple to set up.	Personal liability and joint and several liability.
Simple to run but there are now at least two people making the decisions so not quite the same control as for a sole trader.	Cost of partnership deed.

TABLE 10.1 *continued*

Advantages	Disadvantages
Much lower NICs than a limited liability company.	Additional cost of insurance if considered appropriate.
Taxation is covered by a partnership tax return and extracts from this are copied on your income tax self-assessment and paid twice a year (January and July).	
Only you, your partners, your accountant and HMRC need know your turnover, profits and income.	
Tax breaks can be potentially more attractive than a company for a business with losses in the early years. Generally there are more attractive tax breaks for use of home office and use of a car for work.	

LIMITED COMPANY

Advantages	Disadvantages
Limited liability of shareholders.	In certain circumstances, directors may incur unlimited liability if they are found liable for fraudulent or wrongful trading.
Perceived credibility.	Formal accounts have to be prepared and filed at Companies House within nine months of the accounting year end. An annual return detailing the ownership of the company also has to be filed each year. Failure to deliver documents on time will result in a fine.
	An accountant will generally be required to prepare annual accounts but no audit is required for companies with a turnover of less than £6.5 million.

TABLE 10.1 *continued*

Advantages	Disadvantages
	Transparency of company name, accounts and directors at Companies House (if operating an especially sensitive business, consider obtaining a confidentiality order that helps mask personal information).
Employment agencies and recruitment consultants may require you to work through a limited company (or umbrella company).	More taxes to deal with.
	Every trading company must submit a corporation tax return.
	Directors who are also shareholders will usually receive their income via salary and/or dividends. Salaries are paid through PAYE and, therefore, a PAYE scheme will need to be set up and administered.
	HMRC requires all directors to submit self-assessment tax returns.
	NICs paid by a limited company may come as a surprise to new owner-directors. NICs are dependent on the salary drawn and are paid by both the company and the employee. This double NIC 'hit' means that a director taking profits as salary will pay more than double the NICs of a sole trader taking the same level of income. Income paid as dividends is not liable for NICs. Due to the significant savings derived, this has caused HMRC to review contracts and the level of dividends closely, under a regime known as IR35 which has been in place since 6 April 2000.
	IR35 and other tax 'pitfalls' (one of which is 'income shifting') will need to be understood and, if applicable, addressed.

This guide can only give an overview of how to set up and run a limited company and you are strongly advised to obtain a book on directors' duties and running a company. There are many on the market and a web search will identify several.

Alternative ways of getting started

Rather than start a new business, you could buy into one that is already established, or consider franchising.

Buying a business

Buying an established business can be an attractive route to becoming your own boss, as it eliminates many of the problems of start-up. The enterprise is likely to come equipped with stock, suppliers, an order book, premises and possibly employees. It is also likely to have debtors and creditors. Take professional advice before buying any business, even one from friends. In particular, you should consider why the business is being sold. It may be for perfectly respectable reasons – for instance, a change of circumstances such as retirement. But equally, it may be that the market is saturated, that the rent is about to go sky-high or that major competition has opened up nearby.

Before parting with your money, make sure that the assets are actually owned by the business and get the stock professionally valued. You should also ensure that the debts are collectable and that the same credit terms will apply from existing suppliers. Get an accountant to look at the figures for the last three years and have a chartered surveyor check the premises. It is also advisable to ask a solicitor to vet any legal documents, including staff contracts: you may automatically inherit existing employees.

The value of the company's assets will be reflected in its purchase price, as will the 'goodwill' (or reputation) that it has established. For more information, contact the agents specializing in small businesses, **Christie & Co**, see website: **www.christie.com**.

Franchising

Franchising has become an increasingly popular form of business, with attractions for both franchisor and franchisee. The franchisor gains as their 'brand' is able to expand quickly. The advantage to the franchisee is that there are normally fewer risks than starting a business from scratch.

A franchisee buys into an established business and builds up his or her own enterprise under its wing. In return for the investment plus regular royalty payments, he or she acquires the right to sell the franchisor's products or services within a specified geographic area and enjoys the benefits of its reputation, buying power and marketing expertise. As a franchisee you are effectively your own boss. You finance the business, employ the staff and retain the profits after the franchisor has had its cut. You are usually expected to maintain certain standards and conform to the broad corporate approach of the organization. In return, the franchisor should train you in the business, provide management support and give you access to a wide range of backup services.

The amount of capital needed to buy a franchise varies enormously according to the type of business, and can be anywhere between a few hundred pounds and £500,000 or more. The franchisee is normally liable to pay an initial fee, covering both the entry cost and the initial support services provided by the franchisor, such as advice about location and market research.

The length of the agreement will depend both on the type of business involved and on the front-end fee. Agreements can run from three to 20 years and many franchisors include an option to renew the agreement, which should be treated as a valuable asset.

Many franchises have built up a good track record and raising money to invest in good franchises may not be too difficult. Most of the leading high street banks operate specialist franchise loan sections. Franchisors may also be able to help in raising the money and can sometimes arrange more advantageous terms through their connections with financial institutions.

The **British Franchise Association** (BFA) represents 'the responsible face' of franchising, and its members have to conform to a code of practice. The BFA publishes a *Franchisee Guide*, which provides comprehensive advice on buying a franchise, together with a list of BFA member franchisors and affiliated advisers. It is well worth attending a franchise seminar to find out more and compare the various franchise options on offer.

A good franchisor will provide a great deal of invaluable help. However, some franchisors are very casual in their approach, lacking in competence, or even downright unethical. Make careful enquiries before committing any money: as basic information, you should ask for a bank reference together with a copy of the previous year's accounts. Also check with the BFA whether the franchisor in question is a member and visit some of the other franchisees to find out what their experience has been. Before signing, seek advice from an accountant or solicitor. For more information, see the British Franchise Association website: **www.thebfa.org**.

Operational and other issues

Inventions and intellectual property

If you have a clever idea that you would like to market, you should ensure that your intellectual property is protected. For information about patenting an invention and much more, look at the **UK Intellectual Property Office** website: **www.ipo.gov.uk**.

Licences

Certain types of business require a licence or permit to trade; these include pubs, off-licences, nursing agencies, pet shops, kennels, mini-cabs or buses, driving instructors, betting shops, auction sale rooms, cinemas, street traders and, in some cases, travel agents and tour operators. You will also require a licence to import certain goods. Your local authority planning office will advise you whether you require a licence, and in many cases your council will be the licensing authority.

Permissions

Depending on the nature of your business, other permissions may need to be obtained, including those of the police, the environmental health department, licensing authorities and the fire prevention officer. In particular, there are special requirements concerning the sale of food, and safety measures for hotels and guest houses. Your local authority will advise you on what is necessary.

Employing staff

Should you consider employing staff, you will immediately increase the complexity of your business. Sole traders who need to take on staff would be sensible to take advice before doing so on what roles and responsibilities this will involve. Many people starting a business wisely limit recruitment to the minimum in the early days, until they are sure that they can afford the cost of having permanent staff.

Once you become an employer, you take on responsibilities. As well as paying salaries, you will have to account for PAYE, keep National Insurance records and conform to the multiple requirements of employment legislation. While this may sound rather daunting, the government provides a service, staffed by new business advisers, to help small businesses employing staff for the first time get to grips with the tax and National Insurance systems. For further information see website: **www.hmrc.gov.uk**.

If you are still worried or don't want the bother of doing the paperwork yourself, your accountant is likely to be able to introduce you to a payroll service which will cost you money but will take the burden off your shoulders.

Personnel records

Many businesses find it useful to keep personnel records covering such information as National Insurance numbers, tax codes, merit appraisal reports and so on. For information on data protection see the **Information Commissioner** website: **www.ico.gov.uk**.

Employment legislation

As an employer, you have certain legal obligations in respect of your staff. The most important cover such issues as health and safety at work, terms and conditions of employment and the provision of employee rights including, for example, parental leave, trade union activity and protection against unfair dismissal. Very small firms are exempt from some of the more onerous requirements and the government is taking steps to reduce more of the red tape. However, it is important that you understand in general terms what legislation could affect you.

Minimum wage

There are now three main levels of minimum wage. For all workers aged 16–17 who are no longer of compulsory school age, the minimum hourly rate is £3.68; for those aged 18–20, the minimum is £4.98; and for those aged 21 and above, the minimum is £6.19 an hour. The apprentice rate for apprentices under 19 or 19 or over in the first year of their apprenticeship is £2.65.

Health and safety at work

The Health and Safety at Work Act applies to everyone in a business, whether employer, employee or self-employed. It also protects the general public who may be affected by your business activity. **The Health and Safety Executive** has a useful website: **www.hse.gov.uk**.

Discrimination

An employer, however small the business, may not discriminate against someone on the grounds of sex, race, disability, religion, marital status, sexual orientation or, since October 2006, age. This applies to all aspects of employment, including training, promotion, recruitment, company benefits and facilities. For further information see the **Equality and Human Rights Commission** website: **www.equalityhumanrights.com**.

Contract of employment

A contract of employment is an agreement entered into between an employer and an employee under which they have certain mutual obligations. It comes into being as soon as an employee starts work, when it is taken that he or she accepts the job on the terms offered. Within two months of the job starting, the employer must normally give the employee a written statement highlighting the key terms and conditions of the job, together with a general description of the duties.

Entitlement to a written statement applies to all staff, including part-timers and employees working on fixed-term contracts. By law, they are required to be treated no less favourably than comparable full-timers or permanent employees in respect of their terms and conditions of employment, including access to training, holiday entitlement and benefits. For further information and advice consult your local Citizens Advice Bureau or your solicitor, or see the ACAS website: **www.acas.org.uk**.

Disputes

If you find yourself with a potential dispute on your hands, it is sensible to approach **ACAS**, which operates an effective information and advisory service for employers and employees on a variety of workplace problems, including employment legislation and employment relations. It also has a wide range of useful publications, giving practical guidance on employment matters. See website: **www.acas.org.uk**.

Home office

Many people quietly 'set up shop' from home and there are no questions asked. There could, however, be trouble if in consequence of the business there is an increase in traffic, noise, smells or other inconvenience caused to neighbours. Even more likely, unless you own the freehold of your home, you could have problems with your landlord if the tenancy agreement states that the accommodation is for domestic use only. If you simply use your home as a telephone base, this will probably not be an issue, but if you have a stream of callers and a van parked outside, you could be accused of violating the lease. You may have to pay business rates (in addition to your council tax) on that part of your home you use as business premises.

Another possible downside of working from home is that this could have capital gains tax implications should you ever want to sell the property. As working out the various financial pros and cons has become rather a complex matter, before taking any decision you should take professional advice.

Insurance

Insurance is more than just a wise precaution. It is essential if you employ staff, have business premises or use your car regularly for commercial purposes. Many insurance companies now offer 'package insurance' for small businesses, which covers most of the main contingencies in a single policy. This usually works out cheaper than buying a collection of individual policies. If you buy a package, check that it contains whichever of the following are relevant to your needs. An insurance broker should be able to guide you through the risks and insurance products available:

Employers' liability. This is compulsory if you employ staff. It provides indemnity against liability for death or bodily injury to employees and subcontractors arising in connection with the business. Exceptionally, companies that employ only the owner of the business are not obliged to buy employers' liability insurance.

Product and public liability. This insures the business and its products against claims by customers or the public. It could also cover legal expenses and the cost of complying with enforcements or judgements.

Professional indemnity. This is now essential for all businesses offering investment advice in whatever form. It is also highly recommended for doctors, architects, consultants and other professionals who might be sued personally – or whose business might be sued – if a client suffered a mishap, loss or other damage in consequence of advice or services received. With the recent growth in litigation, many professional bodies are recommending that cover should continue after retirement in the event of an individual, or his or her estate, being sued for work done some years previously.

House insurance. If you operate your business from home, check that you have notified your house insurer of this fact and have implemented any conditions (if, for instance, you see clients at your home address you may find that your theft insurance has a condition placed upon it so that you are only covered for forced or violent entry).

Loss of profits or business interruption risk. This insures the business against loss of profits in the event of your having to cease or curtail trading for a time, owing to material damage. The two policies are normally linked. It should also cover the risk of breakdown of a key item of machinery.

Motor risks. This is compulsory for all motor vehicles. Check that you have notified your insurer if you use your motor vehicle for your business.

Life assurance. This is essential should you wish to provide for your own family or key employees' families or to ensure that funds are available to pay off any debts or to enable the business to continue in the event of your death.

Permanent health insurance. Otherwise known as 'income protection', it provides insurance against long-term loss of income as a result of severe illness or disability. Most income protection plans are pretty flexible and can be tailored to individual needs.

Key person insurance. This applies to the loss of a key person through prolonged illness as well as death. In small companies where the success or failure of the business is dependent upon the skills of two or three key executives, key person insurance is increasingly being written into investment deals as part of the necessary security demanded by banks, financial institutions and private investors. Remember, however, that whereas life insurance benefits your family, key person insurance benefits only the company.

Jury service insurance. Business people cannot seek automatic exemption from jury service even though prolonged absence from work could severely disrupt their business. Insuring against the risk of being called for jury service is therefore worth considering.

You should discuss these points with your insurance company or a broker. To find an insurance broker, see the **British Insurance Brokers' Association** website: **www.biba.org.uk**, or the **Association of British Insurers** website: **www.abi.org.uk**.

Property investment

A frequent avenue that some people explore when nearing retirement is property investment either in the UK or abroad. Since they may be armed with spare funds and perhaps have the advantage of more time available and perhaps even some maintenance skills, you can understand why this happens. Up until 2007 people thought they had it made in property investment with the magic mix of good capital growth and decent returns on their investment through rental income. The capital growth bubble burst in the summer of 2007 and some people have been nervous about this sector ever since. It is beyond the scope of this text to comment on whether or not the tide is turning but it can alert you to some of the key issues and potential sources of further help. Some of the issues are around minimizing your property tax bill, deciding whether to use a letting agent or not, complying with all the red tape and avoiding 'tenants from hell'.

Remember there are many players in this market including mortgage lenders, mortgage brokers, developers, property syndicates, letting agents, and most will know more than you and all will want some of your money. Some even pay for your flights and travel to visit property abroad and then play on this in a subsequent high-pressure sales environment. I strongly advise you never to give in and sign up. There will always, of course, be another day, another deal. The best advice I can give to anyone thinking about property investment is to invest £10 in David Lawrenson's best-selling property book *Successful Property Letting* and review his website, **www.lettingfocus.com**. This will open your eyes to some of the issues I have touched upon and will give you straightforward and clear advice and information on this market. For instance, one of David's candid tips is 'You must like property. So, if houses bore you stiff, you're probably better off doing something else.'

Another source of useful and free help is Hargreaves Lansdown's *Beginner's Guide to Buying Property Abroad*, which is available from their website at **www.hl.co.uk**.

Armed with this and advice from friends and relatives that have invested in property you might then be ready to put your toe in the water and start to explore this area.

Further help, advice and training

The very first paragraph of this chapter promised: '*Importantly, in starting a small business you will not be alone and this chapter will also signpost you to plenty of help and support and most of it is free (it is just a matter of knowing where to look!).*' This chapter alone will help you get started but you will need further help and information. Fortunately, small business is well served when it comes to general help and training. A number of organizations offer subsidized or free advice and training schemes. The best ones feature below.

Organizations providing free or subsidized help

Business Link

Business Link (**www.gov.uk**) is the government's online resource for businesses in England. It contains essential information, support and services for you and your business – whether you work for a large organization or are on your way to starting up. It also has a number of useful online tools, calculators, and best-practice case studies; and provides access to funding options, as well as wider support. My new business (at **www.businesslink. gov.uk/mynewbusiness**) is a comprehensive online resource which sets out, stage by stage, practical help for those interested in starting a business. It is packed with real-life examples and online tutorials that could make a difference to your plans.

Equivalent and more country-specific support is available at:

Northern Ireland – at **www.nibusinessinfo.co.uk**;

Scotland – at **www.business.scotland.gov.uk**;

Wales – at **www.business.wales.gov.uk**.

Start up Britain

Start up Britain has been set up by the government to help you find information about starting a business and contains offers and discounts available to new business start-ups. Further information is available from **www.startupbritain.org**.

Department of Business Innovation and Skills

The Department of Business Innovation and Skills has launched its free booklet 'Make business your business; a guide to starting and developing a new business'. The guide proclaims: 'No matter your age or standing, there is potential to turn a passion or skill from your professional or social life into a bright business idea' and is available from **www.bis.gov.uk**.

HMRC

Your local HMRC Business Education & Support Team provides free training events aimed at start-up businesses and on how to run a payroll. Further information is available at **www.hmrc.gov.uk/bst/index.htm**.

Adult education centres

Short courses in specific business skills are run by business schools and colleges of higher and further education. Various trade and professional associations also run courses. Further information is available from **www.learndirect.co.uk** and **www.gov.uk**, and the Workers Education Association on **www.wea.org.uk**.

PRIME

PRIME (The Prince's Initiative for Mature Enterprise) helps people over the age of 50 set up in business for themselves. PRIME offers free information, workshops and business networking events. It can refer people to accredited advisers for free business advice, and in some parts of the country can also offer free mentoring and other services. Should you be interested in self-employment, PRIME Business Club is full of practical ideas and helpful business information. See website: **www.primebusinessclub.co.uk**.

Tax Volunteers

Tax Volunteers is an independent free tax advice service for older people on low incomes who cannot afford to pay for professional advice. Website: **www.taxvol.org.uk**.

Other useful organizations

Lawyers for Your Business is a network of 1,000 solicitor firms in England and Wales offering specialist advice to small and medium-sized businesses. To help firms access business-related legal advice, Lawyers for Business offers a free half-hour initial consultation with a lawyer in your area who is a member of the scheme. Advice can be sought on a range of issues. To obtain a list of members see website: **www.lawsociety.org**.

Federation of Small Businesses (**www.fsb.org.uk**). The FSB represents great value for money. The networking opportunities and fringe benefits it provides makes it a 'must have' for most new small businesses.

Forum of Private Business, website: **www.fpb.org**.

Professional Contractors Group (PCG) The PCG's 'Guide to Freelancing' is free and can be downloaded from its website (**www.pcg.org.uk**). PCG's knowledge of and guidance on IR35 for consultants and contractors is second to none.

Business start-up websites. These are packed with free hints and tips and a useful one is **www.bstartup.com** and their exhibitions are free, well attended and have some excellent free workshops and guest speakers.

Useful reading

An extensive list of books for small and start-up businesses is published by Kogan Page, website: **www.koganpage.com**, including *Start Up and Run Your Own Business* and *Working for Yourself. An Entrepreneur's Guide*, both by Jonathan Reuvid, *Soul Trader*, by Rasheed Ogunlaru, *The Rebel Entrepreneur: Rewriting the Business Rulebook* by Jonathan Moules and *Successful Property Letting: How to Make Money in Buy-to-Let*, by David Lawrenson.

Case studies

Bob Owen – contemporary black-and-white photography; company

Bob is a former police officer and Royal Marine. He first became seriously interested in photography after a military surveillance photography course and, working in that capacity, developing and printing his own film. He carried on the interest in a similar vein during his police service, becoming a police photographer in tandem with other skills. He expanded his knowledge by working towards and becoming a Licentiate of the Royal Photographic Society and experimenting with a number of photography genres, notably black-and-white street photography. Prior to this year Bob had always anticipated a third career in the security industry following retirement from the police after 32 years' government service, but starting his own business has changed all his plans; 2012 saw Bob launching his new website **www.bobowen.co.uk**.

Why photography and wedding photography in particular?

I've always had a creative streak that never really was allowed full rein. I like working with people and I'm pretty confident around groups of folk. I retired in April 2012 and about a year before that and after some pretty stressful situations I wanted something that meant I was around people at a really positive time of their lives. That would allow me to be as creative as I wished. My photography passion was black-and-white documentary photography so it seemed logical to try and bring these threads together and start my own business in photography. I made sure I got the best possible training for that genre, including business advice, equipped myself suitably and spent a year assisting three of the best wedding photographers in the country. The practical advice, support and experience were invaluable but I think I also had a clear vision of what I wanted to do.

Why set up as a limited company?

I wanted the security of a company and the potential tax advantages if my income increased. Having some commercial photography interests I also realized that some companies preferred dealing with a limited company. It wasn't a straightforward decision and I did ponder on it. Only time will tell if it was the right one.

How did you get your first clients?

The first were by word of mouth and recommendation. I had to do some complimentary sessions, or for expenses only, but this enabled me to build a sufficiently diverse portfolio for a website and sample album. It was important to make the decision to start charging early enough and also to make sure I priced myself high enough. I think many photographers starting out try and compete on price, instead of differentiating themselves by their own style and 'eye'. I find that my clients identify more with the latter. Competing on price for a professional photographer is a downward spiral and a fundamental mistake as there will always be a good amateur who will work for less.

The best tip I was given was to work on developing your own style. It's a constant evolution and there is no end to the journey.

If you were starting again, what would you do differently?

Find a good accountant (one that specializes in small business and start-ups) that has a proven track record and learn more about the business side. It's sometimes difficult becoming a business person when you come from public service where, frankly, you're very sheltered from some hard realities. But I am getting there and so can others with decent help and support – and be prepared to listen to advice from your accountant and others that are in business but at the end of the day the decisions have to be yours.

Karin Whittaker – jewellery designer and maker; sole trader

Karin originally comes from Germany and lives with her husband and teenage daughter in the Forest of Dean. In 2005, after working in the arts, in both therapeutic teaching and designing/making, Karin decided to start her own silver jewellery design business. This was at first a bit of a hobby, but she soon realized she had a passion and aptitude for turning sterling silver sheet and wire into intricate shapes, making pendants, earrings and bracelets.

Karin is now concentrating on getting the jewellery business off the ground and has been selling her uniquely handcrafted products for over three years. Since the launch of a new selling website in 2011 (www.karosajewellery.co.uk), sales have increased. Karin's business profile has further increased with two awards in 2012 – the Rising Star and Business of the Year in the Forest Business Women's Network Awards. Karin is now developing her business by creating a range for a UK charity, teaching silversmithing and opening a workshop/studio in the Forest of Dean.

How have you found making and selling jewellery as a career?

It takes a few years to build up a name for yourself in this trade. There is a huge amount of competition, a lot of cheap imports, and in an age where people are being more careful with money, jewellery is not an easy business to be in. Jewellery is not the first thing people may want to buy! It is, after all, a luxury product or a treat and I found a niche which I could develop into a unique business.

As all those who work from home know, it is very important to have some sort of a routine in your work life. Otherwise you end up getting distracted and can find that you have problems with finishing jobs. I have certain days in the week when I only concentrate on jewellery work – it is very important as I currently have my jewellery bench in the kitchen!

Selling is a completely different subject; it doesn't come naturally to artists, and it's often at this point, when they struggle to sell their wares, that they give up. I found that craft fairs can be very disappointing. They might take place in areas where the footfall isn't great, or sometimes mass manufactured goods are sold a couple of tables away. I have a few shop outlets now, and, although the commission can be quite high (up to 100 per cent), a shop in a good location with regular clients can be a good place to sell.

Why did you set up as a sole trader?

For myself there was never actually a specific question of setting up a company or going as a sole trader. For me I was just going to work on my own and start off in a very small way and I wanted to keep things simple and personal. The complications of a limited company with its further tax implications just sounded too complicated to me. I like to be able to do everything myself as far as I can although I may have to rethink this in the near future.

What was the best tip you were given when you set up?

This tip came from the second meeting I attended as a member of the Forest of Dean Business Women's Network; and it is that 60 per cent of your business success comes from exposure. This is what I am trying to do this year and to get better known further afield. And it is the paradox of working on your own as an artist: you can do the work on your own and I absolutely love it but it is no good unless people know about you – an artist could create and create, but at some stage has to sell work.

If you were starting again, what would you do differently?

I should have started with a business plan. I should have also joined a business networking group straight away. Related to this it is the practical side of running a business, that is the part artists find hard – organizing the marketing, promotion, accounts, etc. Here I have realized that it is very rewarding to be part of a network of local enterprising women.

My next six months are now roughly planned out and I have joined a new networking group in Stroud and I have made valuable contacts there. I would also recommend joining an 'Action Learning Group' as it focuses you on business tasks and is especially helpful to creative types.

Phil Champ, FIMMM, MSLL, MFSB – product, industrial, mechanical designer; sole trader trading as Champ Industrial Design

Phil set up his own business in 2011 having worked as an employee in and around the design industry for over 30 years. In early 2011 Phil's then employer decided to restructure and ceased to offer product design as an activity. This left Phil wondering 'What now?' During the time spent creating a new CV and updating his portfolio and wondering if any of his interview suits would still fit, his phone started to ring. Past clients wondered whether he could carry out design projects for them as his former employer no longer offered this service. After some initial meetings and a consultation with his wife who is an AAT qualified bookkeeper, Phil decided to bite a big bullet and set up on his own business and Champ Industrial Design was born.

Why did you decide to set up as a sole trader rather than a limited company?

After consulting with my accountant (by the way, finding a good accountant was pretty much the first thing on my list of things to do before I even decided that I would try to set up on my own), I came to the conclusion that it would be the quickest and simplest way to get up and running quickly. There is, I believe, less paperwork involved in being a sole trader and I didn't want to overload my wife with too much paperwork.

How have you found your first year of trading?

A vertical line of learning – there has been no 'curve'! Business has been great but the new skills that you need to develop very quickly can be very distracting and time consuming. Writing non-disclosure agreements, terms and conditions, making sure that you have the right insurance policies in place. Making sure that your terms and conditions are legal and binding brings you into contact with the legal profession. What I found amusing here was that the first thing that the solicitor did was send me their eight-page terms and conditions document, all written in legalese which I had to try to understand and sign prior to them working for me on my terms and conditions!

How did you obtain your first few clients?

I was actually very lucky in that several of the clients from my previous job liked my work and approached me directly to see if I would like to work on certain projects for them. *Develop 3D*, a trade journal, interviewed me about setting up a design consultancy in the current economic climate as the government were encouraging people to consider self-employment. What came out of this was a three-page article with photographs of my work, which was a great free advert for my services – who says you have to pay for advertising? I see this done by more and more businesses now that I know what to look for. Articles seem to be a good win–win for all concerned.

What was the best tip you were given when you set up?

Get a good accountant who understands your industry, which I did. His first bit of advice was to join the Federation of Small Businesses, which again I did. This proved to be very useful in the first few months as the advice available was invaluable. They also help you realize that you are not alone and that there are other people out there in exactly the same boat as you are. Another good tip came from an unusual source. I had taken up the offer to meet with a 'business mentor' and had spent a whole morning with him. It was useful but I came away asking myself more questions than I had gone to see him with. On my way home, I popped into my local off-licence for a couple of bottles of wine for the weekend and there was an assistant there who I hadn't seen for a couple of years. He explained that he had now come back as manager. I asked him how it felt to be responsible, to which he replied, 'I have always been responsible; the difference is that I am now accountable.' I found this one small statement more useful than the whole three or so hours with the business mentor as it had totally highlighted my inner feeling of disquiet that I had felt since setting up. Once I realized that this was what the disquiet was about, I could set about dealing with it. I started to sleep a little better after this.

If you were starting again, what would you do differently?

I am not sure. I certainly didn't set out with any ambition of wanting to run a business, it was sort of thrust upon me by my previous employer's restructuring. I do constantly make an effort to be more organized but as a designer, your natural thought process is quite chaotic, lateral, and tangential. Thinking in logical straight lines sometimes takes a lot of a very different kind of concentration. It is easy to look back at the end of a project and understand the journey that you have been on but quite another to try and plot the journey at the beginning as each project and client is very different and has different needs of your service.

If it weren't for having a wife that does do the straight-line thinking and is very thorough and methodical and logical I would probably have given up and tried to find another 'normal' PAYE job, which makes me conclude that you need a good bookkeeper to keep you on the straight and narrow if your business exists in any 'creative' industry.

What are you looking to change in the year ahead?

I think self-discipline is important together with stricter allocation of time as there is a tendency to knee jerk every time a client asks something of you. This approach does not best serve their needs or allow you to fully concentrate on whatever the task at hand is. Another failing is not allocating enough time to create a decent website to profile the full range of my services. I just haven't been able to allocate the time to what is actually a pretty important advertising tool for a business these days. I have also become something of a workaholic and taking time out for other things is important. I guess that this is partly due to having my office at home. I need to learn how to shut the door and stay out sometimes! Have a look at my website at **www.champ-id.co.uk** and if I can be of help please just get in touch via the site.

Dr Gill Hannington – sole trader research consultant; part-time

Gill is a graduate in microbiology from a northern university with 10 years' academic research experience and 19 years' working for one major pharma company, rising from an assistant role to a senior line manager. Gill is a single parent with a teenage child. Two years ago Gill took a redundancy and retirement package without having any specific plans about what to do next. After a few months off, she was ready to work again but did not want to work full-time or go back to a line management role. Then a friend working for a recruitment agency specializing in clinical research roles let Gill know about an opportunity in a local pharmaceutical company to work part-time. Gill took the job, working freelance as a sole trader.

She also works voluntarily as a trustee for a community charity which organizes an annual music festival attended by 30,000 people over a two-day event and generates funds for community arts projects throughout the year.

How have you found freelancing?

I have the advantage that I have a small pension income in addition to what I earn. Without this I would feel more vulnerable to be without the relative security of being an employee. As it is, I like the independence of being freelance. After many years as a line manager I had to relearn project management but did not find that too difficult and I certainly don't miss line management. I find it liberating to just manage my projects and not get involved in office politics and business initiatives. I take pride in doing a good job and being freelance gives me scope to focus on just that.

Why did you set up as a sole trader?

I wanted to keep things as simple as possible. My aim was to supplement my other income so as to maintain my lifestyle and save for future big expenses such as university fees but I was not intending to maximize my earning potential. I am aware that some clients prefer to deal with a limited company so I would be prepared to do this in the future but so far it hasn't been necessary.

How did you obtain your first few clients?

I have never had to actively seek work and rely on networking and remember I only want to work part-time. Also, at this stage in my career I am not aiming to further develop my experience. I do know a lot of people in the pharmaceutical industry and I keep in contact with them for social reasons but I know these contacts would be useful if I was looking for work.

What was the best tip you were given when you set up?

I was very naive about how to manage my business finances but I got a lot of guidance from my accountant. Apparently some sole traders manage without an accountant but I wouldn't recommend it.

If you were starting again, what would you do differently?

I started working for my main client on an open-ended contract. In retrospect it would have been better to have an annually renewable contract as a prompt to review rates on a regular basis. Apart from that I wouldn't have done anything differently – working freelance has given me a good income and the opportunity to establish a healthy work–life balance including my voluntary work which I find extremely rewarding. An experience that I share with friends who also do voluntary work is that we find it more satisfying than the work we're paid to do, probably because our commitment and motivation have to be greater when there is no financial reward. It also has unique challenges such as how to manage people who are also not being paid. I would recommend anyone to get involved in the voluntary sector – it opens a whole new perspective on life!

David Truesdale – author

David retired from the Civil Service in 1998 on medical grounds and having amassed a large collection of military books and with a lifetime of interest in military history, decided to become a writer. His first book was published in 2000 and to date he has written nine books, six of which have been published. He writes for pleasure as opposed to profit, but manages to cover his expenses and fund a degree of travel and research. He works when the mood takes him, which can vary from 16-hour days to a leisurely five-day trip around a European battlefield.

Why did you start writing?

Over the years I have read many books on military history and frequently found shortcomings in maps, photographs or other illustrations. I felt the need to not only write about certain events that had been ignored or dealt with briefly, but to ensure that when a chapter was talking about a certain subject the relevant map or illustration was inserted. In terms of finances, being able to depend on a modicum of pension makes life feel more secure and covers basic living expenses. The ability to pick and choose my topics means I can concentrate on the lesser known subjects of history, as opposed to churning out another book on D-Day just because it's June!

How did you get your first book published?

My first book was written with a co-author and it was through his contacts that I became known to several publishers. Once you have produced your first work and it sells, the others follow on.

What was the best tip you were given when you started?

Put words on paper and initially footnote everything used as a source. When you have completed your manuscript it is so much easier to edit out a thousand words than to be searching for information to fill a chapter. Also, when dealing with controversial facts, footnotes help to protect you from future legal proceedings.

I have to add one more tip – join a trade or professional association and obtain an authoritative book. I joined the Society of Authors and I also found the *Writer's Handbook* a superb source of information and tips.

If you were starting again, what would you do differently?

Having done some work with both film and television, which is very profitable, I would be less antagonistic towards the media. I would also have created a 'study' sooner, as opposed to working on the kitchen table for the first few years.

Paul Riley – fire safety business; company

Paul served in the Battle of the Falklands with the Royal Navy, where he mastered a number of trades including serving as a fireman. Paul subsequently became the chief fire safety trainer for Kidde Thorn fire protection and later set up his own business in 1997.

Why did you set up as a company?

I set up as a limited company because I simply asked my potential customers what would they prefer and the majority said they would much rather deal with a company than a sole trader. It seems that companies can carry more credibility.

What services did you provide?

The core business was fire safety training and the style and method of delivery were well received and assisted my clients embedding important messages to their staff. Bolt-on services including fire extinguisher servicing, fireproofing and fire risk assessments were subsequently supplied. Basically if a client asked, 'Paul can you...?' and it was about fire safety the answer was always yes!

In 2004 a major bank asked me to provide my 'off the wall' training style electronically with something called e-Learning. To cut a long story very short it was successful and then another bank said they would like it and we ended up in three of the largest banks in the world as clients, without advertising. At the same time we won a group tender for three very large airports in the south-east to teach fire safety to potentially over 100,000 people every year. At this point I thought, 'Hang on – there's a real market out there,' so I took a large second mortgage on the house and I had eight people working for me and things where looking very rosy.

Where did it all go wrong?

The autumn 2008 banking crisis hit and soon banks cancelled orders and development of our software stalled. The airport training became incredibly wrapped up in internal politics and we ended up training fewer people that we predicted. I tried lots of different ways to maintain cash flow and looked at credit control and invoice factoring. The company became insolvent and in September 2009 I placed my company into administration.

What did you lose?

In the last three years I lost my house and cars (oh, and a wife) but now I've finished licking my wounds and decided it's time to start afresh. However, this time I and not my bank will be in control! I have a £1,000 loan from my sister and in the summer of 2012 I have started My Fire Safety Ltd with the tag line 'Because fire safety is all about you'. I am the sole employee, pulling in expertise as required and already have a few very nice clients.

What have you learnt?

Being on Working Tax Credits has humbled me and now I count every single penny. In purchasing I look for and find quality at a good price and use technology to talk with customers (Skype, etc) instead of visiting all customers. The recession has taught businesses to be selective and careful in their spending and I can see that clever businesses are embracing new communications technologies.

With hindsight I should not have been so loyal to all my staff when the company was not in a position to continue footing the wage bill after over-expanding.

Perhaps the most important message is that when the going gets tough the bank manager is *not* your friend as he is there to get as much money out of you as possible!! I had a great relationship with my bank manager – even on the day I placed my company into administration he said, 'Don't worry, Paul, there is no way they will take your house.' They did – the local manager has no influence at head office. I don't blame my manager, I just wish he had warned me 12 months earlier. I would also say never do debt factoring as the fees are so complex and so high once you actually get to grips with the reality of what you have signed up for. The better solution is to get your payment terms correct and then follow through with credit control and be prepared to have difficult but cordial conversations with your clients the day any payment is overdue.

My biggest message is put the past behind you. Constantly looking back with anger is damaging and eats you up. Things *do* get better. I have my youngest daughter back living with me and I am happy and looking forward to building my second business!

Starting and running a business – checklist

Starting or running a business can be fantastically rewarding. It might even be fun if your work is something you enjoy. It can also be daunting. There is a vast range of information available and this can sometimes lead to you feeling swamped. This checklist has been developed to help you along the path of starting and running a small business.

A suggested annotation for each item below follows:

N: Not applicable.

L: Come back to later (maybe insert a review date and High, Medium or Low priority).

W: Work on now.

C: Complete.

A: Talk to an accountant, business advisor and/or trusted friend that runs their own business.

Some items in the list below are for companies only (explained below where relevant).

1 You get yourself a map if you want to travel to somewhere new. In business it's just the same except you get yourself a **plan**. It is crucial to commit it to writing and don't expect to get it right first time (no one does!). A few pages are fine to start with. You will need to break the writer's block if you find yourself staring at a blank sheet of paper. The best way of doing this is just to start writing but make sure you include, at a very minimum, the following:

 – a few 'SMART' objectives (ie if each objective is not specific, measurable, achievable, realistic and timed then have another go). Also try to make your objectives a bit challenging – you might just surprise yourself; and:

– a profit-and-loss forecast for at least the year ahead (and the basic assumptions you have used as supporting notes); and:

– your marketing research (what the products are that you offer and who the customers are and the competitors for each); and finally:

– your marketing plan setting out, based on your market research, what you plan to do and when you plan to do it.

The plan can then develop with review, time and further research and grow as your business evolves. The above suggestions are just to help you get started. Importantly you should then review it with your accountant, a trusted friend that runs their own business and perhaps a business advisor or mentor – don't keep it to yourself. The plan will then start to develop and grow. There are some useful free templates available on the web but, right at the very start, don't feel you have to follow them slavishly if you find yourself bogged down and uninspired.

2 Choose your **trading format**, ie company (usually signified by 'limited') or sole trader or partnership or limited liability partnership. This is an important step and one to talk through with your accountant or a business adviser if you have one as they may have ideas on this that you have not considered.

Did you know that you can set up a company for as little as £18 with Companies House? See **www.companieshouse.gov.uk** and their 'web incorporation service'.

Understand your obligations and risks as a director (if trading as a company); see **www.companieshouse.co.uk** and their 'Life of a Company' guidance parts 1 and 2.

Understand the personal liability risks of sole trader/partnership and, indeed, joint and several liability if trading in partnership (sometimes referred to as 'last person standing pays the lot'!). If things go badly wrong your personal wealth and home could be placed on the line (but could insurance help?).

3 Choose your **accountant** – there are many accountancy organizations and the word accountant is not protected in the same way as, say, 'solicitor'. Chartered accountants are an example of a 'qualified' accountant and can be found at **www.icaew.co.uk** for the Institute of Chartered Accountants in England and Wales; **www.icas.org.uk** (Scotland) and **www.charteredaccountants.ie** (Ireland). Accountants

are usually prepared to see you for an initial 'no obligation' meeting. Be clear about who your regular contact will be and their qualifications, what they will do and you will do, an estimate of costs and ask for their hourly charging rates. All of this should be confirmed in writing to help avoid 'confusion'. Other points to consider are your rapport with your accountant and their knowledge of your industry.

4   Make sure you have a source of **legal help**. Could your local solicitor help? Alternatively your trade association may offer a free legal helpline which may get you by initially. Whether you need a solicitor or not depends very much on two things. First, the nature of your trade and the risks you are exposed to. Second, what crops up once you are in business (buying another business, litigation, claims etc; having a solicitor on standby can be useful and many solicitors will provide an initial free one-hour no-obligation consultation at the outset). An early legal question that will usually arise is about your terms and conditions of trade.

5   There is some **free government-funded help** out there and your starting point will be to register with your local organization which you will find at:

- England – **www.businesslink.co.uk**;
- Northern Ireland – at **www.nibusinessinfo.co.uk**;
- Scotland – at **www.business.scotland.gov.uk**;
- Wales – at **www.business.wales.gov.uk**.

Look out for the special 'starting up' sections in the above websites. Examples of the help and support that could be available would include: free guides, access to free or subsidized training, perhaps an introduction to a mentor and the signposting to grants and tax information. You should also check out the government-backed initiative **www.startupbritain.org** for inspiration and ideas. This really is a must do.

6   Consider taking help and advice from trusted friends or family that are in business already. Often this can yield great hints and tips. Can they help with your business plan? Remember you are not alone – there are about 4.7 million businesses in the UK and 91 per cent have fewer than four people.

7   Join the best **trade or professional association** that you can identify and consider the extra benefits each provides in the areas of research information, networking events, helplines, tax investigation help and insurance offerings. Consider joining the Federation of Small Business, **www.fsb.org.uk**. For consultants/interim managers also consider the Professional Contractors Group, **www.pcg.org.uk**, and the Management Consultants Association, **www.mca.org.uk**. If you are a consultant/contractor/interim manager I would strongly recommend downloading and keeping the PCG free 'Guide to Freelancing' – it really is one of the best written pieces I have come across and if you get no other document/help you must at least obtain this one if you are in that field.

8   Choose and if appropriate protect your **business name**. There is some useful free help available on **intellectual property** (patents, brands, etc) at the Intellectual Property Office at **www.ipo.gov.uk**.

9   Determine your ability to stay afloat during the first year by taking your profit-and-loss forecast from step 1 and then plan your **cash flow**. In addition, work out how much money you'll also need for equipment and other capital items when starting up.

    If you need financial help review your options for obtaining finance (personal loan, bank finance, bank overdraft, invoice discounting and grants).

    For the over-50s try **www.primeinitiative.co.uk**.

10 Choose a business **bank** account. Shop around for the best deal that suits your business (often a trade-off between the convenience of a local 'bricks and mortar' branch accompanied by internet banking versus free or reduced charges for internet-only accounts). Once the bank account is set up always remember that reconciling your bank account to your business accounts is one of the most important controls you can operate.

11 Assess your **pension** needs. See **www.unbiased.co.uk** for finding an Independent Financial Adviser or IFA.

12 Sort out your **tax and record keeping** (documents need to be kept for six years and you need to become a receipt/invoice hoarder with a logical 'system for filing), as the taxman might say 'prove it or lose it'. Check with your accountant that your proposed bookkeeping and record-keeping systems are acceptable before you buy them or start to build a system (whether manually written up or Excel or accounting software). Most accountants should be able to provide you with a free do-it-yourself Excel solution or point you to an online or software accounting solution.

13 Understand the implications of failing to deal with your **tax** affairs properly. This can be penalties ranging from 30 per cent to 100 per cent and interest. Indeed, failing to deal with tax affairs properly is one of the common reasons for a business failing. Some trade associations (for instance FSB and PCG mentioned above) include 'free' tax investigation cover – a very useful benefit but the best way to cover yourself is to maintain decent books and records and become a receipt hoarder.

14 Understand your **income tax obligations** and deadlines as a sole trader. Register with the newly self-employed helpline 0845 9154515 within three months of obtaining an income. This does not need to be done if you set up as a company.

15 For companies you need to understand your payment obligations (and timescales) on **PAYE and National Insurance** (this can also apply to sole traders who have employees) and corporation tax. Companies need to register for corporation tax within three months of securing an income, using form CT41G, and HMRC usually are proactive in sending this form are to you. If not, check and chase this up. Remember to sign up for and activate PAYE online – all reporting is done online and it takes about 10 days to activate the service first time round. HMRC run some useful free courses to help with payroll which you can find under 'Business Support Team' at **www.hmrc.gov.uk**. Alternatively you may want to outsource PAYE/payroll to a payroll agent where the costs are usually about £16 to £23 per hour.

   For companies you are obliged to file your annual accounts at Companies House and pay your corporation tax to HMRC nine months after your year end. When you start a business this may seem a long time away and your accountant would usually be expected to undertake these tasks. It is usually better to complete these tasks sooner rather than later after your year end so you can pick up learning points.

16 Understand your obligations regarding your company **Annual Return** (if trading as a company). This is a really straightforward routine and completed on the anniversary of setting up a company each year. Usually you can complete this form yourself. There is good-quality free help at Companies House, **www.companieshouse.gov.uk**.

17 Understand your obligations on **VAT**. The current registration threshold for compulsory registration is £77,000. If you do register for VAT consider VAT schemes especially the VAT flat rate scheme for small businesses. Once registered, diary your quarterly online VAT returns and payments and upon registering with HMRC they can also provide you with an alert/reminder service. The penalties for late filing of VAT returns increase with each late return.

18 Set up your **premises** so that you can work effectively. If you work from home manage your family's and neighbours' expectations – suddenly the phrase 'Time is money' takes on a new meaning.

19 Set up your **suppliers** (remember bills in the company or business name) and, if appropriate, stock control and delivery systems.

20 Consider **insurance** policies for identified business risks (professional indemnity, public liability, product liability, etc). An insurance broker can advise on this and you should also consider policies available via trade associations as these can provide increased cover at less cost.

21 Consider protecting the income you take from your business (especially if you have dependants) in the event of long-term **illness** or of **death** (**www.unbiased.co.uk** for finding an Independent Financial Adviser or IFA).

22 If running your **business at home** remember house insurance disclosure, ie you must tell your insurer that you run a business from home.

23 **Marketing and selling** will be massively important to your success. If you are not from a selling/marketing background talk to trusted friends who run their own business and your accountant/adviser or mentor about your market research and marketing plan. Understand your customers and what they need. Do not underestimate the importance of networking – it's usually more vital than vital.

24 Plan the **pricing** strategies for your product or service. A different package means a different price. How have you benchmarked your price and how have you differentiated your offering (features and benefits) to allow you to charge that little bit more? Conversely what features and benefits have you stripped out to allow you to offer a headline price that comes in beneath the competition (think budget airlines!)?

25 Plan your **marketing promotion strategy**. Remember that 'folk are different' and that it is a bit like fishing – you use different hooks depending on what you are trying to catch.

26 Get paid promptly for your sale. What are your **payment terms** (terms and conditions)? Follow up on outstanding debts. If you sell stock have you included a reservation of title clause to help you retrieve unpaid stock if your client goes bust?

27 Set up your **IT system** and support and have a system to back up your data securely. A stolen laptop or hard drive failure can be catastrophic on your business continuity if you have not backed up your data and systems.

28 Check whether you need to notify the Information Commissioner under the **data protection** laws (**www.ico.gov.uk**).

29 Consider other **red tape**, especially if your area is a specialized sector (food, health and safety, etc). Investigate and apply for the licences and permits that your business may need. To help understand any special needs of your business sector check with your trade association, which usually has a wealth of information and guidance available.

30 Review and update your business plan in the light of experience and keep it a living document.

Chapter Eleven
Looking for paid work

When a man tells you he got rich through hard work, ask him: Whose? **DON MARQUIS, QUOTED IN** *FORBES*

A new initiative was launched last year – 'Retirement in flux – changing perceptions of retirement and later life' by the International Longevity Centre UK, whose chief executive is Baroness Sally Greengross. In this study an argument is put forward for a 'retirement strategy' – that is, the introduction of gradual retirement, so as to remove the cliff edge which still separates work and retirement for many people in this country. With our increasing longevity, and the gradual rise in state pension age, people will be working for longer. Currently around 350,000 women aged over 65 are still working, while about 540,000 men of similar age are in employment. Two of the finest examples of people working beyond retirement in Britain are HM The Queen (86) and the Duke of Edinburgh, who will be 92 in 2013. They are outstanding as there are relatively few other over-85s actively working.

Would you be willing to work into your 80s and beyond? As mentioned at the beginning of the book, one octogenarian, reported in the press last year, explained the hazards of going to work having forgotten to put in his dentures. He is a hill farmer in the Highlands of Scotland. One morning he left home with his sheepdog and trekked for miles to find his sheep in order to move them to new grazing. He only realized his error when he found that without his teeth he couldn't whistle. The dog didn't understand his commands and the sheep took no notice. The poor chap had to trudge home, retrieve his dentures and get back up the hill to his flock in order to move them on. He claims still to be enthusiastic about his work, and continuing to run his farm, and regarded the whole episode with good humour.

Anyone in their 60s who is healthy and keen to play an active part in the labour market should be able to do so. After all, possessing years of experience, dedication and knowledge, the over-60s are a resource of great value to the economy and should not be overlooked. Prudential's 'Class of 2012' research showed that for this age group working part-time is the preferred option. Two in five (40 per cent) people planning to retire last year would be happy to work past 65 if they had the chance. The main motivation of retirees who want to stay in the workforce is driven not by a desire to maintain their standard of living, but rather to remain physically healthy, mentally active and retain their level of self-esteem. They would prefer to be doing something, not simply remaining at home; indeed the majority claim that they enjoy working.

Part-time work during retirement can bring health benefits and many people claim to be less stressed than those who give up work completely. But ideally this would be if you were working part-time in a job related to a previous career. Retirees who take on new jobs unrelated to previous careers are found to exhibit higher levels of stress, because they have to adapt to a new work environment and new work habits. Employment during retirement is known as bridge employment. Those who pick the right type of bridge should see positive health results. Another advantage is maintaining job status, which can affect positive well-being and result in good levels of self-esteem. It all depends, however, on choosing the right type of retirement work. Spending a number of retirement years in work which is not enjoyable will definitely be detrimental to physical and mental health.

Points to consider when choosing retirement employment should include:

- previous employers who might consider you for part-time jobs if you have enjoyed working for them;
- researching temporary job recruitment websites to find jobs that will be enjoyable;
- consider learning new skills that can lead to wider job options, if a fresh start is needed;
- when retirement is about to happen, ask present employers for part-time hours to help the transition;
- if money is not a factor, consider volunteer work or teaching and lecturing to pass on previous skills;
- don't jump at the first job offered, take time to weigh up options and don't be scared to hold off for the right job.

Many employers do welcome older workers, as they are viewed to be reliable and have years of experience. But birth dates can tend to blind potential employers to the range of skills and personal qualities exhibited by older workers from which their company could benefit. Ageism is something many people are faced with, despite the introduction of the Equality Act. It can affect someone's confidence, job prospects, financial situation and quality of life. Although seen as a workplace issue, it is not uncommon elsewhere. The new legislation passed over the last year or so has helped combat discriminatory practices based on age, and has opened up doors for people to carry on working past their usual retirement age. However, for those who have already retired, then find themselves either wanting or needing to go back to work, it is important to be able to break down the invisible barriers which many employers still put up.

One of the problems older workers tend to face when looking for another job after they retire is that of 'pigeonholing'. The fact is that over the course of your working life you will have inevitably picked up many skills – some of which may have been very specific to the nature of your job – but there are more skills and experience you possess which are transferable. In short, they could be utilized in a whole host of other jobs too. Be ready to show potential employers how keen you are to learn. Be able to demonstrate that taking on new training and learning new skills and working methods are not a problem to you. Another tip: older people should place less emphasis on their monetary value to an organization and focus on what skills and experience they can bring to it, and what they hope to gain from the experience too. Although the main reason most people go out to work is for the money, this is not always the overriding purpose for mature workers.

Because employers know that skills and experience often come at a price, they may look for a younger, less experienced person and train him or her up, thus saving money. You may have to be prepared to work for less money than you used to earn, and show your potential employer that you are more than willing to pass on some of your skills to other less experienced colleagues. One of the older workers' trump cards is reliability. You may want to work because you need the money, or you don't have to return to work but have chosen to do so anyway. Whichever is the case, they will be inclined to think you'll be reliable, and this can be reinforced by references from previous employers. Provided you come across well at interview, potential employers are likely to value your stability. You will probably remain in the job longer than a younger person who may regard it as a career stepping stone and wish to move on somewhere else within a year or so. Some companies might feel that a mature worker would not fit in with the rest of the employees, if, say, they are all under 30. Yet many employers do now have a policy of recruiting older workers.

If you want a quick guide to some of the best (and worst) paid jobs in Britain, you can view an article on This is Money (the financial website of the year – **www.thisismoney.co.uk**). It will tell you some things you might not know, such as that an RAF pilot and a pole dancer have certain things in common. Apart from the fact that they both fly through the air (each in their own special way), according to a survey of earnings across the nation, both take home roughly the same salary. TV presenters Peter and Dan Snow (father and son), divided the country's workers into 10 different pay brackets, starting at less than £10,000 and ending with more than £1 million. It showed that the fortunes of farmers have dropped so dramatically over the past 50 years that they now share the same bracket as sewer cleaners, mortuary assistants and checkout staff (£10,000–£20,000). The real-life James Bonds, in M15, earn the same as binmen, vicars, carpenters and NHS nurses (£20,000–£30,000). A bit higher up on £30,000–£40,000 are the pole dancers and the RAF pilots, along with bishops, police constables, sandwich shop managers, vets, London cab drivers, architects and paramedics. Nearly 6 million were in the lowest pay bracket of less than £10,000, including cleaners and hairdressers.

While the average British salary is just under £25,000, two-thirds of the population still earn under the national average, while fewer than 5,000 earn more than £1 million. To be in the top 10 per cent of earners, you need to be on a salary of just £46,000. Most of the country's spiritual leaders earn less than the national average, despite acting as public speakers, wedding planners, undertakers and fundraisers for more than 70 hours a week.

Although potential jobs in retirement may not include becoming an RAF pilot or a pole dancer, experts predict that the current 'grey army' of workers is set to expand further, as those of retirement age want to continue working. This could be for one of two reasons: improved standards of health or because they simply enjoy it. It could be that lower income in retirement, savings and pensions not being adequate, is the prevailing factor. Whatever your reason, enjoy your job hunting.

Financial considerations

Since the abolition of the earnings rule, no matter what age you are or how much you earn there is no longer any forfeit to your state pension, although of course you may have to pay tax on your additional income. If you are working close to a full-time week and/or have enough money to live on, there could be an advantage in asking the DWP to defer your pension, as this will entitle you to a bigger one in the future. Each year of deferral earns an increment of about 10.4 per cent of the pension. Another advantage is that, if you choose to defer your pension by at least a year, you will have the option of taking the money as a taxable lump sum instead of in higher weekly pension payments.

Decisions concerning your occupational pension

These could also arise, particularly if you are looking not so much for a retirement job as for a last big move before you retire. Most (though not all) pension schemes apply actuarial reductions for early retirement. Joining a new pension scheme in late middle age, though not impossible, can present difficulties or impose certain limitations. One of the reasons is that many employers are revising their pension schemes, with rather less generous benefits for new members.

National Insurance Contributions (NICs)

NICs are another consideration. If you are over state retirement age you can forget about NICs; otherwise you are liable for the normal Class 1 contributions. If, as many early retirees do, you work for two or more different employers, you will have to pay Class 1 in respect of each. Should you obtain work through an agency (eg catering, nursing or exhibition work), you are usually regarded as an employee of the agency for NIC purposes, and the agency is responsible for the payment of Class 1 contributions on your behalf. However, this does not apply if you do the work from home, are not subject to anyone's direct supervision, or are in the entertainment business.

If you are over retirement age and have a job, the only requirement is that you obtain an exemption card to give to your employer; see form CF 384 (Certificate of Exception). If you do freelance or other assignment work (unless virtually all your earnings come from one employer, in which case HM Revenue & Customs (HMRC) would argue that you are an employee of the organization), you are officially considered to be self-employed for both NIC and taxation purposes (see Chapter 10, Starting your own business). For further information, consult the **HMRC** website (**www.hmrc.gov.uk** – Self-employed).

Tax rules

HMRC has tightened up the rules in order to clamp down on what it sees as the avoidance of PAYE and Class 1 NIC in respect of the provision of services, including, for example, consultancy and contract work. Those most likely to be affected are individuals who:

offer their services via small limited companies;

work over a period of time for a sole organization; or

work for a client or clients who have the right to control and supervise how the work is performed, as opposed to leaving the initiative to the individual concerned.

If you are thinking of operating in an independent capacity – as opposed to becoming a bona fide employee – it would be sensible to discuss the tax implications with an accountant before determining whether you should operate as self-employed, sole trader, partnership or limited company. See Chapter 10.

Jobseeker's Allowance (JSA)

You can claim JSA provided you:

are under state pension age;

are unemployed or working on average less than 16 hours a week;

have paid, or have been treated as having paid, sufficient NICs; or

have a low income.

To qualify, you must be capable of, available for and actively seeking work, and must enter into a jobseeker's agreement with your local Jobcentre. The essence of the agreement is an action programme aimed at maximizing your chances of finding a job. You will receive help and advice, and there is also a fortnightly Jobsearch review to give you and your adviser an opportunity to assess your progress and to discuss any potential openings that might be suitable.

Claimants are not allowed to turn down a job offered to them via their Jobcentre without good reason. Lower pay would not normally be accepted as a reason although, that said, there is a 'permitted period' up to a maximum of 13 weeks when individuals may be allowed to restrict their job search to openings that take advantage of their skills, experience and reasonable salary expectations. A particularly welcome feature of JSA is that it makes it more worthwhile for recipients to do part-time work. See website: **www.gov.uk** – Jobseeker's Allowance.

Working Tax Credit

If you have a job but are not earning very much, you may be able to boost your income by claiming Working Tax Credit. In certain circumstances, including in particular households with three or more dependent children or where a member of the family has a disability, those with slightly higher incomes could still be eligible to apply. HMRC advises that the easiest way to check is to complete the form listed under 'Tax Credits' on its website. To qualify, you would usually be expected to work at least 30 hours a week. However, those with a disability and/or dependent children are required to work only 16 hours. All recipients now receive the payment direct from HMRC. See: **HMRC** website: **www.hmrc.gov.uk** – Tax Credits.

Redundancy

If you have just been made redundant, or fear this is a possibility, see the information in Chapter 2, Money in general.

Special measures to assist disabled people to work

If you can't work because of illness or disability (and this happened before 27 October 2008) you may be able to get Employment and Support Allowance (which replaced Incapacity Benefit). This is a weekly payment for people who become incapable of work while under state pension age. For details on eligibility go to the website: **www.gov.uk** – Disabled People.

Age discrimination and equality

Age discrimination legislation came into force in October 2006, and The Equality Act was enshrined in 2010. These laws make it illegal for employers to discriminate against older candidates on account of age as regards recruitment, training and promotion. In particular, provided individuals are still physically and mentally capable of doing their job, an employer can no longer oblige them to retire before a 'default' retirement age. Employers also now have a duty to consider requests by employees who want to postpone their retirement and will need to give those they want to retire at least six months' written notice of their decision. The government scrapped 65 as the UK's default retirement age, with effect from April 2011.

Assessing your abilities

Some people know exactly what job they want. They have planned their action campaign for months beforehand, done their research, prepared a CV and followed up selective openings. They are ready, waiting for their present employment to come to an end, to embark on their next career phase. But, if you are not one of those few, having announced your intention to find a job then comes the moment of truth when the big question is: what to do?

Knowing what you have to offer is an essential first step. Make a list of everything you have done, in both your formal career and ordinary life, including your outside interests. In particular, consider adding any practical or other skills, knowledge or contacts that you have acquired over the years. These could now prove especially useful. If, for example, you have done a lot of public speaking, fundraising, committee work or conference organization, these would be excellent transferable skills that would make you attractive to a prospective employer. As a result of writing everything down, most people find that they have far more to offer than they originally realized.

In addition to work skills, you should include your personal attributes and any special assets that would attract an employer. The list might include health, organizing ability, a good telephone manner, communication skills, the ability to work well with other people, use of a car and willingness to do flexible hours. Maturity can also be a positive asset. Many employers prefer older people: they can be more reliable and less likely to be preoccupied with family and social demands. Also, in many newly established companies, run by young directors, a senior person's accumulated experience is often rated as especially valuable.

If you spend some time working on your personal branding, how to market yourself and to whom, you will become much more focused. It will help you form a clearer idea of the sorts of jobs that would suit you. Although it's sensible to keep a fairly open mind and not limit your applications too narrowly, the worst mistake you can make is to answer scores of advertisements indiscriminately – and end up with a sack load of rejections, or worse, no response at all to your applications. As a general rule when job hunting, the more accurate and targeted you can be in the application process, the more likely you are to succeed.

Many people find this extraordinarily difficult. After years of working in one occupation, it takes quite a leap in imagination to picture yourself in another role, even if it is in the same or a related area. If you intend to do something completely different it will be harder still, as your knowledge of what the job entails will probably be second hand. Also, quite apart from the question of what you would enjoy, in many parts of the country the issue may be more a matter of what is available.

Talking to other people helps. Friends, family, work colleagues or business acquaintances may have useful information and moreover will quite likely be able to appraise your abilities more objectively than you can yourself. It could also be sensible to consult outside experts who specialize in adult career counselling and whose advice may be more realistic than that of friends in the context of the current job market. Whatever you decide to do, remember that with age and experience comes wisdom. You have the power to negotiate and you have the power to decide what you want to do next. Make sure you take a job that is right for you.

Jobcentre Plus

Jobcentre Plus brings together the former Benefits Agency and Employment Service to provide a one-stop shop where jobseekers can get help and advice about work and training opportunities and also about any benefits for which they may be eligible. Jobcentre Plus provides a network of offices and telephone contact centres. For your local office or more information, see website: **www.gov.uk** – Job and Skills Search.

Travel to interview scheme

This provides financial assistance in meeting travel costs to long-distance interviews. The scheme is available to people who have been unemployed and are receiving JSA or help with NICs.

Job counselling

This is usually a mixture of helping you to identify your talents in a vocational sense combined with practical advice on successful job-hunting techniques. Counsellors can assist with such essentials as writing a CV, preparing for an interview and locating job vacancies. They can also advise you of suitable training courses. There are numerous companies offering this service; a search on the internet will reveal them. Best advice is to ask for recommendations from other people before signing up with a company. If you want to make really certain they can help, you could ask to speak to one or two of their former clients to find out whether they found the service useful.

Training opportunities

Knowing what you want to do is one thing, but before starting a new job you may want to brush up existing skills or possibly acquire new ones. Most professional bodies have a full programme of training events, ranging from one-day seminars to courses lasting a week or longer. Additionally, adult education institutes run a vast range of courses or, if you are still in your present job, a more practical solution might be to investigate open and flexible learning, which you can do from home.

Open and flexible learning

Open and flexible learning is successfully helping to provide a greater range and flexibility of vocational education and training opportunities for individuals of all ages. In particular, it is designed to increase the scope for participants to learn at a time, place and pace best suited to their own particular circumstances.

The following organizations offer advice and an excellent range of courses:

Adult Education Finder provides information about all adult education centres, education services and online adult educational courses in the UK. Website: **www.adulteducationfinder.co.uk**.

Home Learning College, the UK's leading home study provider, offers a huge range of home study courses. See website: **www.homelearningcollege.com**.

Home Learning Courses offers home learning solutions to its clients, to fit their circumstances and location. See website: **www.homelearningcourses.com**.

Learn Direct courses are flexible; many can be done at local centres, at work or from home. See website: **www.learndirect.co.uk**.

National Extension College (NEC) offers over 150 home study courses and 200 resource titles and has been providing distance learning courses for over 40 years. See website: **www.nec.ac.uk**.

National Institute of Adult Continuing Education (NIACE) aims to encourage all adults to engage in learning of all kinds. See website: **www.niace.org.uk**.

Open and Distance Learning Quality Council (ODLQC) is the UK guardian of quality in open and distance learning. Set up originally by the government in 1968, it is now an independent organization. See website: **www.odlqc.org.uk**.

Open University (OU) is a world leader in modern distance learning, the pioneer of teaching and learning methods that enable people to achieve their career and life goals studying at times and in places to suit them. See website: **www.open.ac.uk**.

IT skills

If you are considering a change in direction, some new qualifications may be advantageous. IT skills are essential, so if you are not confident about your computer literacy and don't have much IT experience or specialist knowledge, here are some useful websites to look at:

Affordable Training is the leading source for affordable IT training and certification. See website: **www.affordabletraining.co.uk**.

Computeach is an IT training company providing a range of courses and IT training to suit all types of people. See website: **www.computeach.co.uk**.

Computer Literacy offers IT training in London and the south-east. See website: **www.computerliteracy.co.uk**.

Computer Training Courses offers a range of courses designed to get you a specific job in the IT industry. See website: **www.computer-courses-uk.co.uk**.

Home and Learn offers a free computer courses and tutorials site. Courses are aimed at beginners: all you do is click on a computer course that interests you and start. See website: **www.homeandlearn.co.uk**.

SkillsTrain is the UK's largest specialist home study and distance learning provider of IT courses. See website: **www.skillstrainuk.com**.

Help with finding a job

If you plan to work in retirement, the best way is to start looking while you still have a job. Prospective employers may prefer applicants who are busy and actively working rather than those who have had a period of non-employment for whatever reason. However, whether you are hoping to go straight from one job to another, or have had an enforced period of not working, this should not affect the way you approach your job search. If you have been retired for some time and want to return to work, you might consider doing some voluntary work in the meantime (see Chapter 12, Voluntary work). This would provide a ready answer to the inevitable interview question 'What have you been doing?'

When starting to look for work, make sure you tell your friends and acquaintances that you are in the market for work, and include your present or recent employer. Some firms encourage consultancy links with former executives, or at least are prepared to respond to a good idea. A greater number are more than happy to take on previous employees over a rush period or during the holiday season.

If you are a member of a professional institute, talk to them and tell them of your availability. Many institutes keep a register of members wanting work and, encouragingly, receive a fair number of enquiries from firms seeking qualified people for projects, part-time or temporary work, interim management or sometimes even permanent employment. Any clubs to which you belong could provide useful leads, as well as any committees you sit on, or any other group with which you are involved. Often someone you know will be the perfect link between you and your next employer.

If you intend to follow up advertisements, selectivity is the name of the game. Limit your applications to those that sound genuinely promising. You will save yourself a lot of time this way. With so many vacancies being advertised online, it pays to have a CV and covering letter ready for submission straight away. Sign on to a select number of sites that will keep you posted about work opportunities. Check out where there are skills shortages and see if any of your transferable skills would help plug that gap. When applying for jobs, remember that enthusiasm counts. Keep in regular contact, by telephone, e-mail or personal visit. Sometimes being on the spot and available at the right time are the keys to success.

A direct approach to likely employers is another possible option. Do your research carefully both on the internet and among your local and personal network. Ask your colleagues, contacts and friends for their advice on which organizations might be interested in employing someone with your abilities. If possible find out the name of the appropriate person to contact and the best method to reach him or her. If someone you know can prepare the ground in advance by way of introduction, and act as referrer, this is far more likely to get you noticed. Some other tips:

- Making the most of previous employment skills is another important point when hunting for retirement jobs.

- Widen the job search: the more employment sources searched, the greater the amount of opportunities and contacts.

- Consider selling employment skills such as accounts experience to small businesses on an independent contractor basis.

- Contact previous employers to enquire about part-time work.

- Search online job boards on sites such as Craigslist and Gumtree.

- Local job centres should provide good results and jobs can be sourced on online job centre websites.

- Contact local colleges and universities who are always looking for teachers with a wide variety of employment skills.

- The internet has become one of the most useful job search tools and should not be underestimated when searching for that perfect retirement job.

The following websites may be useful:

Laterlife. Its job search section will assist you with all the information and services you need. Website: **www.laterlife.com**.

Redundancy Expert was formed to provide comprehensive information and advice on redundancy and a section of its website is dedicated to finding work and getting a job. See: **www.redundancyexpert.co.uk**.

TAEN (Experts in Age & Employment) works to promote an effective labour market that serves the needs of people in mid and later life, employers and the economy. If you are looking for employment, want to change direction, develop your career or undertake training, see website: **www.taen.org.uk**.

Wise Owls provides information about older people and workers alongside a comprehensive one-stop shop for both employers who have vacancies and individuals who are looking for work. See website: **www.wiseowls.co.uk**.

CV writing

Regardless of whether you use contacts, advertisements or agencies – or preferably all three – a prime requirement will be to have a well presented CV. This is your personal sales document and it will be helpful if it can be e-mailed to prospective employers. It should contain:

your name and address;

contact numbers – land line and mobile;

e-mail and website addresses;

key achievements to date;

qualifications and work experience, past employers, positions held and responsibilities;

referees.

Your CV should be no longer than two pages of A4. While some CVs are highly professional, one that is too long is often counterproductive. It should be targeted to the job on offer, emphasizing those elements of your experience and skills that are relevant. There are companies that will professionally produce CVs, and although this can be worthwhile, there will be a fee attached. There are plenty of websites where CV templates can be downloaded for free, with tutorials explaining the entire process. One useful website is **www.businessballs.com**. A well set out CV can make all the difference when it comes to catching an employer's interest. Older workers should concentrate on their main employment skills and employers when updating a CV.

Interview technique

If you have worked for the same employer for a number of years, your interview skills may be a little rusty. It is a good idea to list all the questions you expect to be asked (including those you hope won't be brought up) and then get a friend to rehearse you in your answers. In addition to questions about your previous job, have answers prepared for the following: what you have done since leaving employment; whether your health is good; why you are interested in working for this particular employer; and, given the job requirements, what you think you have of special value to offer. You may also be asked what you know about the organization, so do your research. Obvious mistakes to avoid are claiming skills or knowledge that you do not possess; giving the impression that you have a series of stock answers to problems; and criticizing your former employer.

Be prepared to have an answer to the question: how much money would you expect? With the economy still struggling, you may have to strike a balance between what you would like and what is realistic in the current market.

Useful reading

Preparing the Perfect CV (5th edition), *Preparing the Perfect Job Application* (5th edition) and *Successful Interview Skills* (5th edition), all by Rebecca Corfield and published by Kogan Page; website: **www.koganpage.com**.

Part-time openings

Part-time work may for some people be the ideal solution; others may regard it as second best. With the job market so competitive, many part-time or temporary assignments offer the perfect way into employment that may develop into full-time work in future. This is especially true of small firms, which may be cautious about recruitment while the business is relatively young.

With the average job now lasting between 1.8 and three years, temporary or project-based professional and executive assignments that last a specific time are becoming increasingly common. People with specialist expertise are actively sought, so it is important to be aware of the growth areas in employment. Over a fifth of all new jobs are now on a contract basis, the average being for six months or a year. Mature candidates have everything to gain here because of the greater turnover of jobs. Serial part-time or freelance work can easily develop into a full-time occupation. Many retired business-people take on two or three part-time jobs and then find themselves working as hard as they have ever done in their life.

Employment ideas

Consultancy

A number of retired executives hire themselves back to their former employer in a consultancy guise. As opposed to being paid a regular salary and working full-time, they undertake specific projects for which they are paid a fee. This may be structured as a lump sum or, as many consultants do, they may negotiate a day rate. Consultancy, by definition, is not limited to a single client. By using your contacts judiciously plus a bit of marketing initiative, it is quite possible to build up a steady list of assignments on the basis of your particular expertise.

Marketing and organizational skills are always in demand, as are knowledge of IT, website design, accountancy, HR issues and public relations experience and fundraising. Small firms are often a good bet for consultants, as they normally buy in expertise as and when it is required. Many established consultancies retain a list of reliable associates – a sort of freelance register – whom they call on, on an 'as needed' basis, to handle suitable assignments.

The Institute of Consulting (IC) is the professional body for the consultancy profession. It encompasses the entire profession of consultants and advisers with a membership touching on all areas of the UK economy. For information on organizations seeking professional consultants, see website: **www.iconsulting.org.uk.**

Interim management

Interim managers represent a huge growth area in recruitment over the past few years. An interim manager gives a company instant access to a 'heavyweight yet hands-on executive' with proven track record to meet its needs. Typically hired for three to nine months, interim managers help organizations undergoing major change, implement critical strategies or plug a crucial management gap. Many of the best jobs go to those who have recently taken early retirement or been made redundant. Assignments could be full-time or involve just one or two days' work a week.

The Interim Management Association (IMA) represents the majority of leading and established interim management recruiters currently operating in the UK. See website: **www.interimmanagement.uk.com**

The following organizations could also assist:

Aim Recruitment Ltd, website: **www.aiminterims.co.uk**;

Executives On Line, website: **www.executivesonline.co.uk**;

Interim Partners, website: **www.interimpartners.com**.

Openings via a company or other reference

Secondment from your current employer to another organization is something worth considering. This can be part-time for a few hours a week or full-time for anything from a few weeks to two years. It can also often lead to a new career. Normally only larger employers are willing to consider the idea since, as a rule, the company will continue to pay your salary and other benefits during the period of secondment. If you work for a smaller firm it could still be worth discussing the suggestion, as employers benefit from the favourable publicity the company attracts by being seen to support the local community.

Business in the Community is a business-led charity which works with businesses to build a sustainable future for people and the planet. It has secondment opportunities for both employers and individuals. See website: **www.bitc.org.uk**.

Public appointments

Opportunities regularly arise for individuals to be appointed to a wide range of public bodies, such as tribunals, commissions and consumer consultative councils. Many appointments are to local and regional bodies throughout the country. Some are paid but many offer an opportunity to contribute to the community and gain valuable experience of working in the public sector on a part-time, expenses-only basis. Public appointments vacancies at local and regional levels across UK are found on **www.gov.uk** – Government, citizens and rights.

Non-executive directorships

Many retiring executives see this as the ideal solution; however, these appointments carry heavy responsibilities made more onerous by recent legislation.

If you are able and committed and have the necessary experience, see these websites:

FT Non-Executive Directors' Club, website: **www.non-exec.com**;

First Flight Placements, website: **www.ffplacements.co.uk**;

NED Exchange, website: **www.nedexchange.co.uk**.

Market research

In addition to the normal consultancy openings in marketing, there is scope for those with knowledge of market research techniques. The work covers a very broad spectrum, from street or telephone interviewing to data processing, designing questionnaires, statistical analysis and sample group selection. For more information, contact **The Market Research Society,** website: **www.mrs.org.uk**.

Survey interviewing

National Centre for Social Research (NatCen) is Britain's leading centre for independent social research. Its research covers all aspects of social policy and its findings have direct, practical applications in terms of understanding social behaviour and informing policy. See website: **www.natcen.ac.uk**.

Paid work for charities

Although charities rely to a very large extent on voluntary workers (see Chapter 12), most charitable organizations of any size have a number of paid appointments. Other than particular specialists that some charities may require for their work, the majority of openings are for general managers or administrators, fundraisers and those with financial skills. Salaries have been improving but in general are still considerably below the commercial market rate. Anyone thinking of applying for a job in a charity must be in sympathy with its aims and style.

Agencies specializing in charity recruitment advise that it is a good idea to work as a volunteer before seeking a paid appointment, as this will provide useful experience. The following organizations may help:

CF Appointments, website: **www.cfappointments.com**;

Charity JOB, website: **www.charityjob.co.uk**;

Charity People, website: **www.charitypeople.co.uk**;

Harris Hill, website: **www.harrishill.co.uk**;

ProspectUs, website: **www.prospect-us.co.uk**;

TPP Not for Profit, website: **www.tpp.co.uk**;

Working for a Charity, website: **www.wfac.org.uk**.

Sales

Almost every commercial firm in the country needs good sales staff. Many people who have never thought of sales could be excellent in the job because of their specialist knowledge in a particular field combined with their enthusiasm for the subject. There is always a demand for people to sell advertising space. Also, many firms employ demonstrators in shops or at exhibitions for special promotions. The work is usually temporary or freelance by definition, and while pay is normally good, the big drawback is that you could be standing on your feet for long periods of the day. If the idea of selling fires you with enthusiasm, there are many opportunities to tempt you.

Tourist guide

Tourist guide work is something that will appeal to extroverts, the super-fit with oodles of stamina and a liking for people. It requires an academic mind as well, since you will need to put in some fairly concentrated study. While there are numerous possible qualifications, some are easier than others. Training for the coveted Blue Badge takes 15 months. The Blue Badge itself is no guarantee of steady work, since openings are largely seasonal. In fact most tourist guides are self-employed and the field is highly competitive, but opportunities are greatest in London, especially for those with fluency in one or more foreign languages. See the national membership association for **Blue Badge Tourist Guides** website: **www.britainsbestguides.org**.

You could sign on as a lecturer with one of the growing number of travel companies offering special interest holidays. To be eligible you need real expertise in a subject, the ability to make it interesting and have an easy manner with people. Pay is fairly minimal, although you may receive tips – plus of course the bonus of a free holiday. See Chapter 14, Holidays, for the names of tour operators that may be worth contacting.

Other tourist work

If you live in a popular tourist or heritage area, there is a whole variety of seasonal work, including jobs in hotels, restaurants, shops and local places of interest. Depending on the locality, the list might also include jobs as deckchair attendants, play leaders for children, caravan site staff, extra coach drivers and many others.

Teaching and training skills

If you have been a teacher at any stage of your career, there is a number of part-time possibilities.

Coaching

With examinations becoming more competitive, demand has been increasing for ex-teachers with knowledge of the public examination system to coach youngsters in preparation for A and AS levels, GCSE and common entrance. Contact local schools, search the internet or contact a specialist educational consultancy.

Gabbitas Educational Consultants is one of the UK's leading educational consultancies offering advice and support in all aspects of independent education. It also maintains an extensive register of appointments for teachers and tutors. See website: **www.gabbitas.co.uk**.

Specialist subjects

Teachers are in demand for mathematics, physics, chemistry, technology and modern languages. People with relevant work experience and qualifications may be able to teach or give tuition in these subjects. A formal teaching qualification is required to teach in state-maintained schools. See the **Training and Development Agency for Schools** (TDA) website: **www.tda.gov.uk**.

Before engaging with children, you will need a CRB check (see below). Retired teachers, linguists and others with specialist knowledge can earn good money from tutoring – find more at **www.hometutors.org.uk**.

You could oversee exams as an invigilator. The British Council may have work – check out **www.britishcouncil.org** and **www.fejobs.com**.

English as a foreign language

There is an ongoing demand for people to teach English to foreign students. Opportunities are concentrated in London and the major academic cities such as Oxford, Cambridge, Bath and York. Good English-language schools require teachers to have an initial qualification in teaching English to those who have a different first language. See the following websites for more information: **www.tefl.co.uk** and **www.tefltraining.co.uk**.

Working in developing countries

There are various opportunities for suitably qualified people to work in the developing countries of Africa, Asia, the Caribbean and the Pacific on a semi-voluntary basis. Skills most in demand include civil engineering, mechanical engineering, water engineering, architecture, urban, rural and regional planning, agriculture, forestry, medicine, teaching English as a foreign language, maths and physics training, and economics. All air fares, accommodation costs and insurance are usually covered by the organizing agency, and pay is limited to a 'living allowance' based on local levels. As a general rule, there is an upper age limit of 65 (VSO accepts volunteers up to 75), and you must be willing to work for a minimum of two years.

The following are the major agencies involved in this kind of work (more details are contained in Chapter 12, Voluntary work):

International Service, website: **www.internationalservice.org.uk**;

Progressio, website: **www.progressio.org.uk**;

Skillshare International, website: **www.skillshare.org**;

Voluntary Service Overseas (VSO), website: **www.vso.org.uk**.

Publishing

Publishers regularly use freelance staff with appropriate experience for proofreading, copyediting, design, typography, indexing and similar work as well as for writing specialist copy. For firms that could be interested, see website: **www.thebookseller.com** or the Society for Editors and Proofreaders and The Society of Indexers.

Caring for other people

There is a number of opportunities for paid work in this field. If you are considering working with vulnerable people (young or old), you will be required to have a full Criminal Records Bureau (CRB) check with enhanced disclosure, designed to protect those who need to rely on other people and to ensure that no one unsuitable is appointed to a position of trust who is likely to abuse it. These checks are extremely thorough and can take several weeks or even months to process. Please be patient and as accurate as possible when asked to provide information by prospective employers, charities or not-for-profit organizations. For further information about CRB checks and why they are required, see website: **www.gov.uk** – Employing people (select the 'Recruiting and hiring' link).

Domestic work

A number of private domestic agencies specialize in finding temporary or permanent companions, housekeepers and extra-care help for elderly and disabled people or for those who are convalescent. Pay rates vary depending on which part of the country you live in and the number of hours involved. The following agencies may be of interest:

> Anchor Care, website: **www.anchor.org.uk**;
>
> Consultus Care & Nursing Agency Ltd, website: **www.consultuscare.com**;
>
> Country Cousins, website: **www.country-cousins.co.uk**;
>
> Universal Aunts Ltd, website: **www.universalaunts.co.uk**.

The Lady magazine, published every Wednesday, has classified advertisements for domestic help.

Home helps

Local authorities sometimes have vacancies for home helps, to assist disabled or elderly people in their own home by giving a hand with the cleaning, light cooking and other chores. Ask your local social services department.

Childminding

If you already look after a grandchild during the day, you might consider caring for an additional couple of youngsters. You will need to be registered with the local social services department, which will explain all the requirements including details of any basic training – such as first aid – that you may first need to do. For babysitting services, see **www.childcare.co.uk** and many others.

Busy parents may need someone reliable to meet children at airports, stations or even travel with them. See website **www.universalaunts.co.uk** or enter 'children's escort' in job agency websites.

Nursing

Qualified nurses are in great demand in most parts of the country and stand a good chance of finding work at their local hospital or through one of the many nursing agencies. Those with suitable experience, although not necessarily a formal nursing qualification, could apply to become a care support worker for the newly merged charity **Carers Trust**. Crossroads Care and The Princess Royal Trust for Carers have merged to form the leading carers' charity. See website: **www.carers.org**.

Home sitting

Taking care of someone else's home while they are away on holiday or business trips is something mature, responsible people, usually non-smokers with no children or pets, can do. It is a bit like a paid holiday, and you get paid every week (extra if care of pets is involved), depending on the responsibilities and on the size of the house or flat. Food and travelling expenses are normally also paid. It is useful to have your own car. Firms specializing in this type of work include:

Absentia, website: **www.home-and-pets.co.uk**;

Homesitters Ltd, website: **www.homesitters.co.uk**;

Housesitters Ltd, website: **www.housesitters.co.uk**;

Rest Assured House Sitters, website: **www.restassuredhousesitters.co.uk**;

Universal Aunts Ltd, website: **www.universalaunts.co.uk**.

Cashing in on your home interests

Cooking, gardening, home decorating, dressmaking and DIY skills can all be turned into modest money-spinners.

Bed and breakfast

Tourist areas, in particular, offer scope for taking in B&B visitors. However, unless you want to make a regular business of it, it is advisable to limit the number of guests to a maximum of five, otherwise you will be subject to stringent fire regulation precautions and other health and safety requirements. To be on the safe side, contact the local environmental health officer who will advise you of anything necessary you should do. You should also register with your local tourist information centre. See the section 'Letting rooms in your home' in Chapter 8, Your home (see also 'Paying guests or lodgers' in that chapter).

Cooking

Scope includes catering other people's dinner parties, selling home-made goodies to local shops and cooking for corporate lunches. Other than top-class culinary skills, requirements are a large deep freeze, a car (you will normally be required to do all the necessary shopping) and plenty of stamina. Notify your friends, advertise locally and set up a website.

Gardening

Small shopkeepers and florists sometimes purchase flowers or plants direct from local gardeners, in preference to going to the market. Alternatively, you might consider dried flower arrangements or herbs, for which there has been a growing demand. However, before spending any money, check around to find out what the sales possibilities are. If you are willing to tend someone else's garden, the likelihood is that you will be inundated with enquiries. Spread the word among friends and acquaintances as well as local advertising.

Dressmaking and home decorating

If you are happy to do alterations, the chances are that you could be kept busy from dawn to dusk. Many shops are desperate for people who sew. Likewise, many individuals and families would love to know of someone who could alter clothes, as well as dress-make properly. Perhaps to a slightly lesser extent, the same goes for curtains, chair covers and other soft furnishings. Often a good move is to approach firms selling materials for the home, which might be only too glad to put work out to you.

If you spread the word among neighbours that you are available, or put a card in the newsagent's window, you may be surprised at the response. Do your friends envy your ability to assemble flat-packed furniture, fix things that are broken or decorate your house? Why not start charging for DIY? You can make money from any hobby – but there's more about this in Chapter 10, Starting your own business.

Agencies and other useful organizations

Job hunting through agencies is very much a question of luck. So many vacancies are advertised via the internet, there is no need to be out of work for long if you are proactive. Work for the over-50s and -60s varies and if you are seeking challenging opportunities, it might be worth checking the following organizations:

Executive Stand-By Ltd specializes in placing executives of proven competence in management or similar posts in industry, commerce and voluntary organizations. See website: **www.esbpeople.co.uk.**

Extend runs recreational exercise-to-music classes for the over-60s and for people with disabilities of all ages. The organization is constantly looking for potential group teachers. See website: **www.extend.org.uk.**

Manpower UK is a major supplier of temporary, contract and permanent staff. See website: **www.manpower.co.uk.**

Parity is looking for all types of IT contract and permanent work for project managers, analysts, programmers and network and software engineers. See website: **www.parity.net.**

There are many other websites worth checking out for work opportunities for the over-50s; three of the best are:

www.prime50plus.co.uk;

www.skilledpeople.com;

www.seniorjobbank.com.

Chapter Twelve
Voluntary work

> *A smile is the shortest distance between two people.*
> **VICTOR BORGE**

Volunteers were celebrated last year, after the WRVS launched their nationwide 'Diamond Champions' search, in recognition of their tireless work. Eighty people were chosen from across the country and invited to meet Their Royal Highnesses the Prince of Wales and the Duchess of Cornwall at an event that took place in November 2012. The actress Patricia Routledge CBE, aged 83 and best known for her role in the TV sitcom *Keeping Up Appearances*, supported the campaign to find these volunteering champions. Its purpose was to highlight the role played by the over-60s in communities throughout the UK.

The local WRVS centre is a good first point of contact if you are interested in volunteering, because they can give advice on where the particular kind of help and assistance offered can best be placed. Their oldest active volunteer is aged 102, and she is driven to where she works by her 98-year-old friend. So it's never too late to start, even if you haven't thought of volunteering before now or haven't had time to. So much real value is given to community life by older people who have lived and understand and suffered and lost. Whatever your talents or skills, from helping dyslexic children to read or supporting a lonely member of your community, all volunteers agree that helping others opens up your own life.

A wise man once said, 'It is important to be able to distinguish "involvement" from "commitment". For clarity, just think chicken and pig. While the chicken is involved in the production of an egg, the pig is committed to the making of bacon...' That's quite a good way of defining volunteering.

While many employees/staff are involved in their work, most volunteers are committed to theirs.

The idea that the elderly are a burden on society, simply pushing up the costs of health and social care, was challenged in a study published by the WRVS ('Gold Age Pensioners', March 2011). It found that older people currently provide to their communities a range of formal and informal volunteering services worth over £10 billion per annum to the national economy. The value of this volunteering effort can be expected to grow to just under £15 billion by 2020. The report also revealed that in fact pensioners' net contribution to the UK economy is between £30 billion and £40 billion a year because they pay tax, spend money that creates jobs, deliver billions of pounds of free care to others and contribute to charities and volunteering. These are quite staggering sums and the current 'baby-boom generation' just reaching retirement now is better off than its predecessors and will in turn push up these figures.

Older people are, without doubt, the social glue of most communities. Their acts of neighbourliness and community spirit, sharing of experience and leadership roles in clubs and groups demonstrate how generous a section of society they really are. Research has shown that every year older volunteers each spend an average of over 1,000 hours 'informally' volunteering and more than 55 hours in formal volunteering roles. Most over-60s are primarily motivated by wanting to 'make a difference' to other people's lives. Those who have had professional careers enjoy using their skills in new and valuable ways. Volunteering in the Third Age (VITA) reports that older volunteers are likely to be found providing front-line services to users of charities, at both local and national levels. Feelings of better physical and mental health, as well as enjoyment and the opportunities to continue to use or teach specific skills, were extremely important motivators for the older volunteers.

But as important as their financial contributions are, older people provide other substantial benefits to their communities and neighbourhoods. This is through their support for local activities, and being committed members of social and charitable projects. This wider 'added value' is generated through the volunteering efforts and other community-based activities of older people, and is beyond quantification at this stage. Over-65s are often the linchpins of local clubs, societies, faith groups and other neighbourhood organizations. This includes active participation in democratic institutions such as parish/community councils, and boards of school governors, Neighbourhood Watch, as well as education, sport, culture, leisure, conservation and the environment.

Every once in a while scientists amaze us by coming up with a discovery that is so obvious you feel it is something everyone knew anyway. One such is from the University of Texas, whose scientists concluded (after several months of laboratory controlled tests) that experience makes us wise. They proved that men and women over 60 years of age are better at making decisions than those in their 20s and 30s. Now who would have thought it? Actually we don't need scientists to tell us things like this; we have learned it for ourselves and can all too easily recall some of our past mistakes and cringe-worthy memories.

So it is not surprising that we have another initiative from the WRVS: this time it is their 'Nationwise' campaign, which was launched after their research found that 91 per cent of British pensioners believed they could answer questions younger people struggle with. Younger generations often do not have all that much contact with people over 65, yet the oldies are keen to pass on their wisdom. These tips range from reducing food waste, to making shoes last longer and even having a happy marriage. Often today the older generation is regarded as a problem, rather than an amazing source of inspiration and knowledge. The charity hopes the campaign will help boost the confidence of many over-65s, and offer wisdom and advice to many young people who are struggling to deal with difficult life situations. Over-65s are recognized as some of the happiest people in the country and can help youngsters with suggestions on saving money, relationships, managing when you are not in work, dealing with bereavement, the secrets of a long-lasting relationship and how to get a week's meals out of just one chicken... Anyone who would like to contribute their own tips or wisdom should visit **www.wrvs.org.uk/nationwise**.

It is vital we celebrate and maximize the contributions of older people. Someone who is starting to volunteer at the age of 60 or just over, could have 20 years or more of positive contribution to make. So if this appeals to you, why not give it some thought? Here are some suggestions as to what you might do.

Types of work

Clerical

Any active group is likely to need basic administrative help, from typing and stuffing envelopes to answering the telephone and organizing committees. This may involve a day or so a week or occasional assistance at peak times.

Many smaller charities in particular would also greatly welcome hearing from individuals with IT expertise to assist with setting up databases, a website, etc.

Fundraising

Every voluntary organization needs money, and when donations are static or falling, more creativity and ingenuity are required to help bring in funds. Events are many and varied, but anyone with energy and experience of organizing fundraising events would be welcomed with open arms as a volunteer.

Committee work

This can cover anything from very occasional help to a virtually full-time commitment as branch treasurer or secretary. People with business skills or financial or legal backgrounds are likely to be especially valuable, and those whose skills include minute-taking are always in demand.

Direct work

Driving, delivering 'meals on wheels', counselling, visiting the housebound, working in a charity shop, helping with a playgroup, respite care for carers: the list is endless and the value of the work incalculable. While certain qualifications and experience – financial, legal, nursing and social work – have particular value in some circumstances, there is also a multitude of interesting and useful jobs for those without special training or with abilities like driving or computer skills. Similarly, the time commitment can vary to suit both helper and organization. It is far better to give just one morning a month and be reliable than to promise more time than you can spare and end up cancelling or letting people down. Equally, as with a paid job, before you start you should be absolutely clear about all the terms and conditions:

What sort of work is involved?

Who will be working with you?

What is expected?

When will you be needed?

Are expenses paid? What for? How much?

If you have all this mapped out in the beginning there will be less chance of any misunderstandings. You will find that voluntary work is not only very rewarding in its own right but also allows you to make a real contribution to the community.

You will be required to have a full Criminal Records Bureau (CRB) check with enhanced disclosure if you are considering working with vulnerable people (young or old). This was covered in Chapter 11, Looking for paid work, and applies to many jobs these days, both paid and unpaid. The purpose is to protect those who rely on other people from anyone unsuitable being appointed to a position of trust. These checks are extremely thorough and can take several weeks or even months to process. Patience is needed and the more accurate the information you provide when requested to do so by prospective employers, charities or not-for-profit organizations, the less tedious the process will be. For further information about CRB checks and why they are required, see the **Criminal Records Bureau** website: **www.gov.uk** – Employing people (select the 'Recruiting and hiring' link).

Choosing the right voluntary work

Once you've decided that you might take on some volunteering, the next question is what to do. You will need to find out where the opportunities are in your local area and what particular outlet would suit your talents. You may have friends or neighbours who are already involved in volunteering locally. Asking their advice would be a start, as they may well have some good suggestions or know which organizations are in need of extra pairs of hands. However, if you don't know where to start, the organizations listed here are arranged in broad categories of interest. As there are literally thousands of voluntary groups, national and local, that need help in some way or other, it is impossible to include them all or describe all their activities and volunteering opportunities. The following websites act as signposts to help you learn more about them and how you can get involved:

REACH is the skilled volunteering charity, encouraging people to take on new challenges and make a difference to their community. See website: **www.reachskills.org.uk**.

Volunteer centres. Most towns have a body of this kind that seeks to match up volunteers with local organizations seeking help.

Volunteer Development Scotland for volunteering opportunities anywhere in Scotland. See website: **www.vds.org.uk**.

Volunteering England for volunteering opportunities anywhere in England. See website: **www.volunteering.org.uk**.

Wales Council for Voluntary Action is the umbrella body for voluntary activity in Wales. See website: **www.wcva.org.uk**.

General

The scope of the work of the British Red Cross, WRVS and Citizens Advice Bureau is so broad that they almost justify a category to themselves:

British Red Cross is a volunteer-led humanitarian organization that helps people in crisis, whoever and wherever they are. See website: **www.redcross.org.uk**.

Citizens Advice Bureau provides the advice people need for the problems they face. Last year the CAB helped 2.1 million people with 7.1 million problems. See website: **www.citizensadvice.org.uk**.

Community Service Volunteers (CSV) is the UK's leading volunteering and training charity. Every year CSV involves over 150,000 volunteers in high-quality opportunities that enrich lives and tackle need. See website: **www.csv.org.uk**.

Lions Clubs International is an international network of men and women who work together to answer the needs that challenge communities across the world. See website: **www.lionsmd105.org**.

Toc H is involved in a wide range of good neighbour schemes within their local community. See website: **www.toch-uk.org.uk**.

WRVS believes in making Britain a great place to grow old, delivering personal and practical support through the power of local volunteers to help older people. See website: **www.wrvs.org.uk**.

Animals

The Cinnamon Trust is the only specialist charity for people in their last years and their much-loved and much-needed companion animals. See website: **www.cinnamon.org.uk**.

Guide Dogs for the Blind Association provides mobility and freedom to blind and partially-sighted people. It also campaigns for the rights of people with visual impairment, educates the public about eye care and funds eye disease research. One of its new initiatives is the opportunity to 'Sponsor a Puppy'. For further information see website: **www.guidedogs.org.uk**

PDSA offers veterinary care to the pets of elderly people who are on benefits or a low income and cannot afford their pets' treatment. See website: **www.pdsa.org.uk**.

Pet Fostering Service Scotland provides short-term foster care for the pets of elderly people who, owing to some emergency such as going into hospital, are temporarily unable to manage. See website: **www.pfss.org.uk**.

Pets As Therapy (PAT) is a national charity providing temperament-assessed/vaccinated cats and dogs with volunteers to visit those in hospitals, care homes. See website: **www.petsastherapy.org**.

The Royal Society for the Prevention of Cruelty to Animals (RSPCA) is the leading animal welfare charity and has been working to promote kindness and prevent cruelty to animals since 1824. Its volunteers can help with dog walking, cat grooming, fundraising, office admin or working in one of the charity shops. See website: **www.rspca.org.uk**.

The Wildfowl & Wetlands Trust (WWT) is a leading conservation organization saving wetlands for wildlife and people across the world. WWT is the only UK charity with a national network of specialist wetland visitor centres. See website: **www.wwt.org.uk**.

Bereavement

Cruse Bereavement Care is the UK's largest bereavement charity. Last year it responded to nearly 100,000 requests for assistance; helped 32,700 bereaved people face to face, including 2,500 children, and worked with more than 1,700 people bereaved by suicide. See website: **www.crusebereavementcare.org.uk**.

Children and young people

Action for Sick Children is the UK's leading children's health-care charity, specially formed to ensure that sick children always receive the highest standard of care possible. See website: **www.actionforsickchildren.org**.

Barnardo's believes in children, whoever they are. Whatever the issue: drug misuse, disability, youth crime, mental health, sex abuse, domestic violence, child poverty or homelessness, Barnardo's tries to bring out the best in every child. It runs 417 projects across the UK. See website: **www.barnardos.org.uk**.

Children's Society is committed to helping vulnerable and disadvantaged young people, including children in care and young runaways. With over 75 programmes and children's centres in England, it offers care, support, legal assistance and mentoring schemes. See website: **www.childrenssociety.org.uk**.

The Children's Trust Tadworth provides care, education, therapy and rehabilitation to children with multiple disabilities, complex health needs and acquired brain injury. See website: **www.thechildrenstrust.org.uk**.

Save the Children UK works in more than 120 countries saving children's lives, fighting for their rights, helping them fulfil their potential. Its work reached over 80 million children last year. See website: **www.savethechildren.org.uk**.

Scout Association provides adventurous activities and personal development opportunities for 400,000 young people aged 6–25. Over 28 million young people internationally enjoy the benefits of scouting in 216 countries. See website: **www.scouts.org.uk**.

Sea Cadet Corps celebrates Britain's maritime heritage and actively supports its future by offering young people and professional seafarers educational and developmental opportunities. See website: **www.ms-sc.org**.

Volunteer Reading Help (VRH) has, since 1973, been training and supporting volunteers to help transform the lives of children by giving them the gift of reading, offering one-to-one support for children to improve their literacy skills and increase their confidence. See website: **www.vrh.org.uk**.

Conservation

Architectural Heritage Society of Scotland is concerned with the protection, preservation, study and appreciation of Scotland's buildings. With 1,100 members throughout Scotland and beyond, its six regional groups organize local activities and carry out casework. See website: **www.ahss.org.uk**.

British Trust for Conservation Volunteers (BTCV) encourages volunteers from both town and country to improve the environment, work with local business and young people and enjoy conservation breaks. A reasonable degree of fitness is required. See website: **www.btcv.org.uk**.

Campaign to Protect Rural England (CPRE) stands up for your countryside, and gets involved in issues such as housing and planning, transport, energy and waste, farming and food. See website: **www.cpre.org.uk**.

Friends of the Earth campaigns to solve environmental problems such as getting a grip on climate change, laws to bring recycling to your doorstep, warmer, more energy-efficient homes, protecting the countryside and persuading big companies to behave better. See website: **www.foe.co.uk**.

Greenpeace is an international environmental pressure group that campaigns to protect the natural environment. Today it has a presence in more than 40 countries. See website: **www.greenpeace.org.uk**.

Ramblers' Association is Britain's walking charity, working to safeguard footpaths, the countryside and other places. With 119,000 members in England, Scotland and Wales, it has been working for walkers for over 76 years. See website: **www.ramblers.org.uk**.

Royal Society for the Protection of Birds (RSPB) is an award-winning charity that gives nature a voice by fighting wildlife crime and harmful developments, campaigning against habitat destruction and by lobbying for laws and policies which benefit nature. It has a network of 200 nature reserves around the UK and 175 local groups. See website: **www.rspb.org.uk**.

The elderly

Abbeyfield is a not-for-profit organization dedicated to making the lives of older people easier and more fulfilling. Abbeyfield helps people to live independently by providing a range of services, all of which are linked to the local community. See website: **www.abbeyfield.com**.

Age UK: Age Concern and Help the Aged merged in 2010 to become Age UK, the leading national charity for everyone later in life. It provides life-enhancing services and vital support to over 5 million elderly people each year, with its three national partners, Age NI, Age Scotland and Age Cymru. See website: **www.ageuk.org.uk**.

Carers Trust is the new charity formed from the merger of The Princess Royal Trust for Carers and Crossroads Carers, to form the leading carers' charity. This provides the largest range of support services for carers across the UK. See website: **www.carers.org**.

Carers UK is the voice of carers, who save the UK over £119 billion a year by looking after others. This organization is a mine of information for family, partners or friends who need help because they look after an ill, frail or disabled person at home. See website: **www.carersuk.org**.

Contact the Elderly is the only national charity solely dedicated to tackling loneliness and social isolation among older people. Contact volunteers take isolated elderly people one Sunday afternoon each month to have tea in the home of a volunteer host. See website: **www.contact-the-elderly.org.uk**.

Independent Age is a unique charity offering lifelong support to older people on very low incomes by giving practical and financial support, through regular visits and telephone calls and by offering friendship to alleviate loneliness. See website: **www.independentage.org.uk**.

The family

Marriage Care is a charity operating across England and Wales to provide marriage preparation, relationship counselling and relationship education. It also offers general support and advice to those wishing to marry or enter a long-term relationship. See website: **www.marriagecare.org.uk**.

Relate is a national federated charity with over 70 years' experience of supporting the nation's relationships. As the country's largest provider of relationship support, every year it helps over 150,000 people of all ages through a national network of centres as well as by phone and online. See website: **www.relate.org.uk**.

Health

Attend is a national charity that supports and expands the roles volunteers play in creating healthy communities. This is done in three ways: supporting those already volunteering, running projects themselves and by sharing what they do through training and events. See website: **www.attend.org.uk**.

BackCare is a national charity that aims to reduce the impact of back pain on society by providing information and support, promoting good practice and funding research. BackCare acts as a hub between patients, (health-care) professionals, employers, policy makers, researchers and all others interested in back pain. See website: **www.backcare.org.uk**.

British Heart Foundation (BHF) is the nation's heart charity. Its vision is a world where people don't die prematurely from heart disease. Its mission is to play a leading role in the fight against disease of the heart and circulation. See website: **www.bhf.org.uk**.

Calibre Audio Library is a national charity providing a subscription-free postal service of unabridged audio books for adults and children with sight problems, dyslexia or other disabilities who cannot read print. See website: **www.calibre.org.uk**.

Cancer Research UK is the world's leading charity dedicated to beating cancer through research into the prevention, treatment and cure of the disease. People's chances of surviving cancer have doubled over the last 40 years and this charity has been at the heart of that progress. See website: **www.cancerresearchuk.org**.

Disability Snowsport UK works to make sure that anybody with a disability, be it learning, sensory or physical, can ski or snowboard alongside other people. See website: **www.disabilitysnowsport.org.uk**.

Leonard Cheshire Disability supports thousands of disabled people both in the UK and in more than 50 other countries. Its wide range of services provide support, respite and care to disabled people and their carers. See website: **www.lcdisability.org**.

Mind (The National Association for Mental Health) is the leading mental health charity for England and Wales. It campaigns to create a society that promotes and protects good mental health for all.

Through its national and local network it works with over 250,000 people each year. See website: **www.mind.org.uk**.

RDA (Riding for the Disabled Association) celebrates 40 years of delivering opportunities for therapy, achievement and enjoyment of riding for people with disabilities. RDA now has almost 500 member groups across the UK, helping 23,000 people enjoy riding, carriage driving and vaulting experiences. See website: **www.riding-for-disabled.org.uk**.

Royal National Institute of Blind People (RNIB) is the UK's leading charity offering information, support and advice to almost 2 million people with sight loss. Its pioneering work helps anyone with a sight problem, with imaginative and practical solutions to everyday problems. See website: **www.rnib.org.uk**.

St Dunstans is a charity providing lifelong support to blind and visually impaired ex-service men and women, promoting and enabling them to regain their independence, meet new challenges and achieve a better quality of life. See website: **www.st-dunstans.org.uk**.

St John Ambulance is best known for its first aid role at public events. It teaches people about first aid – about 800,000 last year – so that they can be the difference between a life lost and a life saved. See website: **www.sja.org.uk**.

Scope is a charity that supports disabled people and their families. It works to drive the changes that will make our society the first in which disabled people are able to realize their full civil liberties and human rights. See website: **www.scope.org.uk**.

Thrive is a charity using gardening to change the lives of disabled people. For more than 30 years Thrive has helped a wide variety of people aged from 14 to 85 and from all walks of life, with differing needs. See website: **www.thrive.org.uk**.

Heritage and the arts

There are numerous opportunities if you wish to volunteer in the arts, through community projects, arts centres, local arts councils and other activities associated with special groups, such as the youth services or people with disabilities. All kinds of volunteer abilities are needed, from painting and other creative skills to accounting and clerical know-how. Further information should be obtainable through your local authority, library or local arts centre.

Council for British Archaeology is an educational charity working throughout the UK to involve people in archaeology and promote appreciation and care of the historic environment for the benefit of present and future generations. See website: **www.britarch.ac.uk**.

Creative Choices is the website to look at if you wish to volunteer in the heritage sector. For loads of information and ideas see: **www.creative-choices.co.uk**.

English Heritage champions historic places and helps today's generation get the best out of our heritage and ensure that it is protected for future generations. For volunteering opportunities, see website: **www.english-heritage.org.uk**.

National Trust Volunteering involves many aspects of the work of conservation in the great houses open to the public and on 248,000 hectares of coast and countryside properties. For full details of all opportunities available, see website: **www.nationaltrust.org.uk**.

SPAB (Society for the Protection of Ancient Buildings) fights to save old buildings from decay, demolition and damage. The charity advises, educates and campaigns and represents the practical and positive side of conservation. See website: **www.spab.org.uk**.

The needy

Alexandra Rose Charities, founded in 1912 by Queen Alexandra, work with charities and community organizations across the country helping them to raise funds. More than 250 caring groups benefit from their national profile, expertise and organizational support. See website: **www.alexandrarose.org.uk**.

Elizabeth Finn Care is a national charity that gives direct support to individuals in need and, through Turn2Us, helps millions of people gain access to the money available to them in welfare benefits, charitable grants and other financial help. See website: **www.elizabethfinncare.org.uk**.

Oxfam is a vibrant global movement of passionate dedicated people fighting to overcome poverty and suffering. To have maximum impact, Oxfam concentrates on three main areas: emergency response, development work and campaigning for change. See website: **www.oxfam.org.uk**.

Samaritans provides confidential, non-judgemental emotional support for people experiencing distress or despair, 24 hours a day. The service is provided by telephone, e-mail, letter or face to face in most branches. Training is given; the minimum time commitment is about four hours a week plus one night duty a month. See website: **www.samaritans.org**.

Offenders and the victims of crime

Nacro reduces crime by changing lives. Its work focuses on three areas: before, during and after people are in trouble. Prevention, offender management and resettlement are vital areas of its work. See website: **www.nacro.org.uk**.

New Bridge Foundation, founded in 1956, creates links between the offender and the community. It offers friendship and support to people in prison and on their release, with the aim of giving them the encouragement and practical skills to lead responsible and law-abiding lives in the future. See website: **www.newbridgefoundation.org.uk**.

Supporting Others through Volunteer Action (SOVA) is a leading national volunteer mentoring organization working with those socially and economically disadvantaged in England and Wales. See website: **www.sova.org.uk**.

Victim Support is the independent charity for victims and witnesses of crime in England and Wales. Every year it contacts over 1.5 million people after a crime to offer help. It depends on thousands of specially trained volunteers to deliver its services. See website: **www.victimsupport.org.uk**.

Politics

You may not immediately think of political parties in the context of voluntary work, but all of them use vast numbers of volunteer helpers. Between elections the help is mostly required with fundraising, committee work and staffing the constituency offices. At election time, activity is obviously intense. See the major parties' websites for details:

Conservative Party: **www.conservatives.com**;

Green Party: **www.greenparty.org.uk**;

Labour Party: **www.labour.org.uk**;

Liberal Democrats: **www.libdems.org.uk**;

Plaid Cymru: **www.plaidcymru.org**;

Scottish National Party: **www.snp.org**;

Social Democratic and Labour Party (SDLP): **www.sdlp.ie**;

UKIP: **www.ukip.org.uk**;

Ulster Unionist Party: **www.uup.org**.

Service personnel and veterans

ABF The Soldiers' Charity has been giving lifetime support to serving and retired soldiers and their families for the past 66 years. See website: **www.soldierscharity.org**.

Combat Stress is the leading UK charity specializing in the care of veterans' mental ill health. It supports over 200 veterans who served in the Falklands War and who, 30 years on, are still suffering from post-traumatic stress disorder, anxiety, paranoia or depression. See website: **www.combatstress.org.uk**.

Help for Heroes is a charity founded in 2007 to raise money to support wounded service men and women returning from Iraq and Afghanistan. See website: **www.helpforheroes.org.uk**.

SSAFA helps and supports those who serve in our armed forces and those who used to serve. It also cares for the families of both. Last year alone, its professional staff and trained volunteers provided a reliable, caring and trusted service to more than 50,000 people. See website: **www.ssafa.org.uk**.

The Royal Air Force Benevolent Fund is the RAF's leading welfare charity supporting serving and former members of the RAF, as well as their partners and dependent children. See website: **www.rbf.org**.

The Royal Alfred Seafarers' Society is a maritime charity which for over 130 years has provided support to elderly, sick or disabled seafarers, their widows and dependants. See website: **www.royalalfredseafarers.com**.

The Royal British Legion provides welfare to the whole armed forces family – serving, ex-service and their dependants. It also campaigns on a range of issues affecting service people. As the custodian of remembrance, the Royal British Legion's annual fundraising activity is the Poppy Appeal. See website: **www.britishlegion.org.uk**.

Work after work

British Chambers of Commerce is the national body for a powerful and influential network of accredited chambers of commerce across the UK. These organizations represent the local business community, and are highly active in a wide range of projects to promote local economic development and renewal in the wider community. See website: **www.britishchambers.org.uk**.

National Federation of Enterprise Agencies, the national enterprise network, supports over 100,000 pre-starts, nearly 25,000 start-ups, and 130,000 established businesses across the country. Volunteers advise and help new small firms at the start-up stage and beyond. See website: **www.nfea.com**.

Scottish Business in the Community helps local enterprises in similar ways. See website: **www.sbcscot.com**.

Long-term volunteering

If you are thinking of a long-term, probably residential commitment there is a number of organizations both in the UK and abroad in need of voluntary help for a wide variety of projects. Some require specialist skills, such as engineering or medicine; others essentially need people with practical qualities, common sense and enthusiasm. Each organization has a minimum period of service. General conditions are similar for all of them; travel is paid, plus a living allowance or salary that is based on local levels rather than on expatriate rates. Couples without dependent children are welcome, as long as both have the necessary skills. National Insurance Contributions are provided, and a resettlement grant is paid on completion of the tour.

Overseas

There are four main organizations for overseas volunteering: Voluntary Service Overseas (VSO), Skillshare International, Progressio and International Service, details of which have already been provided in Chapter 11 (Looking for paid work: 'Working in developing countries').

Volunteering abroad for the over-50s is often referred to as 'golden gapping'. It is gaining popularity among many 50–75-year-olds. Thousands of mature people have enjoyed gap years recently and the number is growing. If a life-changing experience and doing some voluntary work abroad before or just after you retire appeal to you, **Gap Year Advice For All** should be able to help; see website: **www.gapadvice.org**. (This is further described in Chapter 14, Holidays.)

In the UK

Although the organizations in this section are primarily concerned with schemes requiring volunteer help for between two weeks and six months, they would also welcome shorter-term help with administration and fundraising:

Sue Ryder Care centres provide hospice and neurological care. They are run as far as possible as family homes in the true sense of the word. Volunteers are always needed. See website: **www.suerydercare.org**.

Vitalise is a national charity providing short breaks (respite care) and other services for people with disabilities, visually impaired people and carers. It offers inspirational opportunities through one of the most diverse volunteer programmes in the UK. See website: **www.vitalise.org.uk**.

Chapter Thirteen
Health

There are only two classes of mankind in the world: doctors and patients. **RUDYARD KIPLING**

Almost before we realize it, we are getting older. We may not feel it, but we are. For some of us it is our teeth that act as an early warning system for health issues in late middle age. For others it is our hair: women fear going grey, men fear going bald. Perhaps some of us have noticed a bit of weight gain, bigger around the middle (what used to be euphemistically called 'the middle-age spread'). Unless you are very unlucky, your body tends to let you down gradually. It is doubtful you will get everything going wrong all at once. We are more likely to acquire some wrinkles, a double chin or nasal or ear hair; such manifestations of decay are all part of the ageing process and not fatal.

But is it too late to start looking after our health, now that we have retired? Are the bad habits of our youth and years of neglecting our bodies (due to the fact that we have all been working so hard) about to catch up with us? Not necessarily, but there is always a 'but'… The biggest single factor that determines how long we spend in poor health towards the end of our lives is how well we have looked after ourselves in the preceding years. But console yourself with this thought: according to Auberon Waugh, 'the young may look prettier than we do, but they are also tremendously boring and talk nothing but rubbish'.

The big myth about getting older is that there's nothing good about it, that it's downhill all the way. But we do have choices. The first baby boomers, who hit 65 last year, released a 'silver tsunami' that is going to keep on coming. It's bad for pension providers but great for us. We are the first generation to be able to choose how well we age (and learning to age well is just as important as learning how to manage your money). One of the best ways of slowing down the ageing process is to keep moving. Exercise is the closest thing to an anti-ageing pill, say the medical professionals. Keeping a positive attitude, doing things you enjoy, learning new things and having a good social life and relationships all add years to life. The choices you can make about how well you are going to age don't just involve diet and exercise. Mind, emotions and sleep also play a big part. Learning simple healthy ageing secrets can add years to your life.

So, if you are approaching retirement, or are in your early 60s, can you – hand on heart – say that you have lived a healthy life? Did you, for example, walk or cycle to work? Was your job physically taxing? Have you always maintained a healthy weight and not overindulged on alcohol? As we are all well aware, obesity rates have shot through the roof over the last few decades and, with them, the incidence of conditions such as diabetes. Heart and circulatory conditions are also rife and often only kept in check by long-term medication. It seems that the age group most affected by such diseases are the younger ones. With so much high-fat fast food being consumed and binge drinking so prevalent among certain groups, it is inevitable that these habits will have an impact. According to Cancer Research, only 13 per cent of people aged over 60 smoke, compared to 30 per cent in the 20–24 age group. While these youngsters may make it to their 80s and 90s, aided by medication, their last years could be spent in very poor health.

Living a very long time could well be on the cards for many of us, statistics seem to predict. Although doctors advise that aches and pains will probably increase with age, this is far less likely if you remain physically and mentally active. The island of Okinawa, off the coast of Japan, is obviously the place to visit. It is nicknamed by the World Health Organization 'the island of long life'. This is because it has so many centenarians, the oldest being 115. The Okinawa lifestyle, it seems, combines a healthy diet (high in fish, wholegrains, vegetables and soy products), strong spiritual beliefs, tight social networks, a relaxed attitude to time, moderate exercise and a firm determination not to be bundled off to a nursing home.

Since people retiring today are often younger in looks and behaviour than previous generations, they should be able to enjoy many healthy years of life if they take some of this 'Okinawa stuff' on board. Remember, bodies do require care and attention if they are to function at their best. Just as you regularly service your car, routine checks for eyes and teeth are obviously sensible. Also, if habits can be moderate rather than excessive, this is generally a wiser policy. It means you can enjoy small vices without paying the penalty for overindulgence. There is no need to get out of shape: you will have time to make changes that help you to look good and keep alert, which should mean you are likely to have a far longer and more enjoyable retirement.

Exercise is most important if you are to keep healthy, whatever age you are. It tones up muscles and improves the circulation, reduces flab, helps ward off illnesses and can be good fun. For those not accustomed to regular exercise, it is essential to build up gradually. Trying to recapture the sporting feats of your youth could be unwise. If you are planning to run a marathon or win the local tennis competition, start gently. Training in a whole range of sports is available around the country, with beginners in their 50s and older especially welcomed. Details of some of the many facilities, together with other keep fit options, are listed in Chapter 9, Leisure activities. In addition to some of the more exotic choices, swimming has long been recognized as one of the best forms of exercise. Some people swear that there is nothing to beat a good brisk walk. Gardening is also to be recommended.

With the explosion in the number of sports clubs, leisure centres and adult keep fit classes run by local authorities and other organizations, opportunities have never been greater. At the top end of the market there are deluxe health clubs located in hotels, sports clubs and other venues. These offer, among other things, facilities such as a fitness centre, swimming pool, massage and beauty salon. They have qualified staff who can advise on – and supervise – personal fitness programmes. However, at a fraction of the price, many local authority leisure centres offer a marvellous range of sports. They also usually run regular classes in everything from self-defence to badminton.

Keep fit

There is evidence that the over-55-year-olds are putting the younger generation to shame when it comes to leading an active lifestyle, though long-term health conditions do hold millions back. But a campaign was launched last year by GlaxoSmithKline and NHS London called 'Your Personal Best', inspired by the London 2012 Olympic and Paralympic Games, and supported by Len Goodman and Arlene Phillips, TV judges and former dancers. It encouraged many over-55s with long-term health conditions to lead more active lifestyles. Activities such as gardening, doing housework or recreational walking can help certain conditions and improve well-being. For more information see website: **www.yourpersonalbestcampaign.co.uk**.

Emphasis on and availability of every type of keep fit activity are on the increase. It is a welcome innovation, as there are a growing number of opportunities for older people, including those with disabilities. Information should be available online, or in your local newspaper or library. The following organizations may be able to help you:

Extend provides gentle exercise classes for older people and anyone of any age who has a disability, throughout the UK. See website: **www.extend.org.uk**.

Fitness League is a well established nationwide exercise network, supported by Sport England. Emphasis is on exercise and movement to music, with special regard to individual ability. See website: **www.thefitnessleague.com**.

Medau Movement encourages the body to move with energy, strength, stamina, suppleness and coordination. Classes are held throughout the country. See website: **www.medau.org.uk**.

Pilates

Pilates is an invigorating form of exercise for your mind and body that can improve your strength, flexibility and overall mobility. It helps restore your body to balance; as a result your posture will change and you will move more efficiently. Pilates is a safe and effective exercise method that will enable you to look and feel your very best. See **The Pilates Foundation** website: **www.pilatesfoundation.com**.

Yoga

Yoga is popular with all ages and is a means of improving fitness and helping relaxation. Classes are provided by many local authorities and there is also a number of specialist organizations:

British Wheel of Yoga is a registered charity and is the largest yoga organization in the country. With over 3,000 qualified teachers it promotes yoga classes, workshops and events for its members and the public. See website: **www.bwy.org.uk**.

Iyengar Yoga Institute runs classes at all levels, including remedial for those with medical conditions. Of special interest is the 59-plus class for people who would like to start gently. See website: **www.iyi.org.uk**.

Yoga for Health and Education Trust (YHET) is a not-for-profit company and charity dedicated to bringing yoga to all whether fit and well or disabled. For more information, see website: **www.yoga-health-education.org.uk.**

Sensible eating

Advice on healthy eating seems to change so fast it's hard to keep up. But a trim, well-kept body is one of the secrets of a youthful appearance, as everyone knows. Excess weight and being out of condition tend to add years to anyone's age. While regular exercise is important, so is sensible eating. With about one in four adults in Britain being obese, it is a worrying trend that so many people are seriously overweight. The more excess weight that you carry, the greater the risks to your health. In particular there is an increased risk of heart attack, as well as surgery being made more difficult. As age increases, there is greater likelihood of restricted mobility.

Please consult your doctor before embarking on serious dieting. But medical advice does not need to be sought should you plan to cut out or cut down on sweets, cakes, sticky buns, deep-fried foods, alcohol and rich sauces. Healthy foods that most people (except, of course, those on a special doctor's diet) can eat in almost unlimited quantities are fruit, salad, vegetables, fish and white meat, such as chicken. There are several food myths, however, and here are a few tips suggested by health experts at AgeUK (**www.ageuk.org.uk/health-wellbeing/healthy-eating**).

Myth: Low-fat foods are best. The reality is that although a low-fat diet can help you control your weight and lower your cholesterol, there's no need to avoid fat altogether. Some fat is needed in our diets. For example, omega fats are great for circulation and can reduce the risk of heart disease. Oily fish such as salmon, mackerel, pilchards and sardines are good sources of omega fats. Use olive or sunflower oil for cooking.

Myth: Fresh fruit and veg are best. Unless you're feeding a family, it can be hard to get through a variety of fresh food and veg before it goes off. Buying tinned or frozen means that you only use what you need and cuts down on waste. Freezing preserves the food's vitamin and mineral content, is a great way to get your recommended five-a-day and there's no wastage from peel, seeds and stalks.

Myth: A cooked breakfast is bad for you. Breakfast is an important meal and a cooked breakfast can be a healthy way to set yourself up for the day.

Eggs are a brilliant source of lean protein, tomatoes are packed with antioxidants and grilled lean bacon is a tasty addition. Instead of a 'fry up' have a 'grill up'.

Myth: Red meat will kill you. Although recent research has linked red meat to an increased risk of death from heart disease and cancer, red meat is good for you. It's an excellent source of protein, vitamin B12, zinc and iron. The Department of Health says it is safe to consume up to 500g per week. Go for leaner cuts and use healthier cooking methods, such as grilling.

Myth: Snacking is bad for you. There's nothing wrong with snacking provided you don't rely on chocolate, crisps, cakes and biscuits to keep you going between meals. As we age, we don't always feel like eating big meals, but eating regularly helps our body maintain a constant source of energy. It's fine to eat every three to four hours throughout the day but make sure you eat good, healthy snacks.

As every health magazine advises, crash diets are no solution for long-term fitness. Many people need a boost to get started, and whatever method you choose is fine as long as it works. So if a short stay at a health spa is what you need to kick-start your new healthier lifestyle, go for it. If nothing else, the experience is relaxing, though not cheap. There are many places to choose from but if you have friends who can give a recommendation, so much the better. Two excellent websites are:

Livestrong.com, which believes that everyone has the power to change their lives, is a daily health, fitness and lifestyle destination. Lance Armstrong has been an inspiration for millions around the world and shares his philosophy throughout the website: **www.livestrong.com**.

Weight Watchers, whose aim is to help members establish a healthy, balanced approach to weight loss, with emphasis on making small, lifetime changes that can be maintained for the long term. See website: **www.weightwatchers.co.uk**.

Sometimes single people tend to get weight problems because they find it a bore to cook for one. It is easy to fall into bad habits by snacking on the wrong kind of foods. Elderly women are often at risk from malnourishment, so not only do they undermine their health but because of their general frailty they are more susceptible to falls and broken bones. Self-help to avoid trouble is one thing, but those who suspect that they could have something wrong with them should not hesitate to consult their doctor.

Keeping healthy in the heat

The older we get the more conscious we need to be of the sun and how it affects us. The NHS warns that anyone over the age of 65 is in the 'high-risk' category for heat-related illness. Too much sun or getting overheated can induce sunstroke and dehydration, while also causing other issues – such as exacerbating existing health problems such as heart disease and high blood pressure. These guidelines should help you keep your cool:

- *Stay hydrated*. One of the most common effects of prolonged periods in the heat is dehydration. The hotter months are definitely the time you should get at least six to eight glasses of fluids a day. Keep a bottle of water with you, especially when on the road, as caffeine and alcohol actually dehydrate you.

- *Wear sunscreen*. The older we get the more susceptible to certain types of skin cancer we are. Find the right sunscreen for you and top up regularly for the best protection.

- *Protect your eyes*. Protecting eyes from the brightness and UV rays of the sun will promote better eyesight and prevent cataracts. Wear wrap-around sunglasses that offer UV protection and a wide-brimmed hat that will shade your eyes while also protecting your ears, nose and head from sunburn.

- *Lower your temperature*. Even when out of direct sunlight your temperature can be too high. If you're feeling too hot, taking a cool shower is an effective way of maintaining a safe temperature. If you often feel discomfort from the heat, aim to spend the warmest parts of the day in air-conditioned areas.

- *Be prepared*. Keep a sunhat in the car, spare water bottles in your fridge and stock up on sunscreen. Our weather is unpredictable, and whether you are a sun worshipper or prefer the shade, it's best not to get caught out.

Food safety

As most readers will know, basic rules on food safety are important. Food poisoning can happen at any age but older people are more at risk because of associated health complications.

Medication such as antibiotics taken by elderly people also increases the risk of food poisoning. People who have long-term chronic illnesses and health problems are also more susceptible. There are a few ways that food poisoning can occur; one of the most common is by consuming food that is past its use-by date. Older people on a budget often buy food that is close to its use-by date in order to save money. Elderly people who are afflicted by food poisoning will suffer much more severe symptoms than younger people. Dehydration can become a serious factor and can lead to decreased blood pressure. This in turn affects the blood supply to vital organs such as the kidneys. It is very important that fluids are replaced as soon as possible should dehydration occur.

There are a number of precautions that should be taken to reduce the risk of food poisoning. These include:

- Not eating food products that are past their sell-by or use-by dates.
- Always make sure food is stored in refrigerators set at the right temperature.
- Follow cooking instructions carefully.
- Do not eat raw or undercooked meat products or eggs.
- Always wash hands and work surfaces that have been used to prepare meat, seafood and eggs.
- Always wash raw vegetables thoroughly, especially vegetables that are not going to be cooked.
- Ensure that frozen foods are completely thawed before cooking and never refreeze thawed foods.
- Never eat undercooked foods in restaurants. Always send undercooked food back to be cooked completely.
- Have two chopping boards: one for meat and one for everything else.
- Cover the food in your fridge with shrink-wrap; this includes leftovers.
- Never keep cooked and uncooked food together, as they can contaminate each other.
- Keep all parts of your kitchen clean.
- Do not reheat food more than once and don't keep cooked food longer than two days.

Drink

Most doctors cheerfully maintain that 'a little bit of what you fancy does you good'. Retirement is no reason for giving up pleasures and in moderate quantities alcohol can be a very effective nightcap and can also help to stimulate a sluggish appetite. However, bear in mind that alcoholism is the third greatest killer after heart disease and cancer. The condition is far more likely among those who are bored or depressed, who drift into the habit of having a drink to cheer themselves up or to pass the time. Because the early symptoms appear fairly innocuous, the danger signs can often go unnoticed.

Whereas most people are sensible enough to be able to control the habit themselves, others may need help. The family doctor will be the first person to check with for medical advice. But additionally, for those who need moral support, the following self-help groups may be the answer:

Al-Anon Family Groups UK & Eire provides support to anyone whose life is, or has been, affected by someone else's drinking. There are over 800 support groups in the UK and Republic of Ireland. See website: **www.al-anonuk.org.uk**.

Alcohol Concern is the national agency on alcohol misuse, campaigning for effective alcohol policy and improved services for people whose lives are affected by alcohol-related problems. See website: **www.alcoholconcern.org.uk**.

Alcoholics Anonymous is a fellowship of men and women who share their experience, strength and hope with each other so that they may solve their common problem and help others recover from alcoholism. See website: **www.alcoholics-anonymous.org.uk**.

Smoking

Any age is a good one to cut back on smoking or preferably to give up altogether. Smokers are 20 times more likely to contract lung cancer; they are at more serious risk of suffering from heart disease and they are more liable to chronic bronchitis and other ailments. Most people agree that it is easier to give up completely than attempt to cut back. Every habitual smoker knows that after the first cigarette of the day you can always think of a thousand excuses for lighting another. Aids to willpower include the ban on smoking in restaurants, bars and pubs and other designated areas.

Many hardened smokers swear by nicotine patches, but working out how much money you could save in a year and promising yourself a holiday or other reward on the proceeds could help. Thinking about your health in years to come should be an even more convincing argument. Dozens of organizations concerned with health publish leaflets about giving up smoking. Here are three of them:

Smokefree offers help and advice to smokers who want to quit, gives information about local services, including nicotine replacement therapy and group support. See website: **www.smokefree.nhs.uk**.

Quit aims to reduce unnecessary suffering and death from smoking-related diseases, and aims towards a smoke-free UK future. See website: **www.quit.org.uk**.

Smokeline (Scotland only) offers free advice, counselling and encouragement to those wishing to give up smoking. See website: **www.canstopsmoking.com**.

Accident prevention

One of the most common causes of mishap is an accident in the home. In particular this is due to falling and incidents involving faulty electrical wiring. The vast majority of these could be avoided by taking normal common-sense precautions, such as repairing or replacing worn carpets and installing better lighting near staircases. For a list of practical suggestions, see 'Safety in the home', in Chapter 8, Your home.

If you are unlucky enough to be injured in an accident, whether in the street or elsewhere, the Law Society offers a free service called the Accident Line to help you decide whether you can make a claim. You will be entitled to a free consultation with a local solicitor specializing in personal injury claims.

Accident Line, website: **www.accidentlinedirect.co.uk**. Alternatively you could consult **National Accident Helpline**, website: **www.national-accident-helpline.co.uk**.

Aches, pains and other abnormalities

There is nothing about becoming 50, 60 or even 70 that makes aches and pains inevitable. Age itself has nothing to do with the vast majority of ailments. Many people ignore the warning signs when something is wrong, yet treatment when a condition is still in its infancy can often cure it altogether, or at least help to delay its advance. The following should always be investigated by a doctor:

any pain that lasts more than a few days;

lumps, however small;

dizziness or fainting;

chest pains, shortness of breath or palpitations;

persistent cough or hoarseness;

unusual bleeding from anywhere;

unnatural tiredness or headaches;

frequent indigestion;

unexplained weight loss.

Health insurance

People with private medical insurance often get a nasty shock when they reach retirement age, particularly if they were previously covered under a company scheme. Their premiums start to rocket – just at the point when their income has been reduced to a pension. However, switching to a cheaper scheme often gets more difficult as we get older. Some policies have maximum age limits, but a more frequent problem is that if you have already claimed for a condition on your current policy, you will lose that cover if you switch insurers. Pre-existing medical conditions, including associated complaints, will normally be excluded when you take out a new policy.

Nevertheless, if your current policy has become unaffordable, you may feel that you have no alternative but to look for something cheaper. Some leading insurers offer lower-cost policies for 'older' people, but these policies aren't necessarily cheaper than those of other companies. Things to watch out for with lower-cost policies are that they provide less cover, such as limited outpatient cover. Other providers, in order to make the premiums affordable, require policyholders to accept far higher excesses (the amount they have to contribute themselves) in order to obtain cover.

The problem is that there is such a wide range of policies available nowadays; some from smaller, less well known companies; some have introductory no-claims discounts which may make their premiums appear deceptively low. All this can make it difficult to decide where to go to get the best value for money. For this reason it may be better to approach a specialist independent adviser from the Association of Medical Insurance Intermediaries (AMII) to help you find a deal that suits you. See website: **www.amii.org.uk**.

Older people sometimes opt out of private medical insurance cover because they are not aware they can reduce their premiums by shopping around, or even staying with their current insurer. Most policies work on a menu basis now so that there are always ways to find suitable cover at an affordable price. The increasing cost of medical care is the main reason behind escalating insurance premiums. But the insurance companies need to come up with innovative ways of making their policies more affordable to older people if they don't want to lose a large proportion of existing customers as they reach retirement and beyond (source: *The Oldie*: Old Money – March 2012).

The NHS has, generally, an excellent record in dealing with urgent conditions and accidents. However, it sometimes has a lengthy waiting list for the less urgent and more routine operations. By using health insurance to pay for private medical care you will probably get faster treatment, as well as greater comfort and privacy in hospital. Here are some organizations that provide cover:

AXA PPP Healthcare, website: **www.axappphealthcare.co.uk**;

BUPA, website: **www.bupa.co.uk**;

Exeter Family Friendly Society, website: **www.exeterfamily.co.uk**;

Saga Services Ltd, website: **www.saga.co.uk**;

SimplyHealth, website: **www.simplyhealth.co.uk**.

Help with choosing a scheme

With so many plans on the market, selecting the one that best suits your needs can be quite a problem. An Independent Financial Adviser (IFA) or specialist insurance broker could advise you, such as:

Association of Medical Insurance Intermediaries (AMII) website: **www.amii.org.uk**;

Medibroker, website: **www.medibroker.co.uk**;

The Private Health Partnership, website: **www.php.co.uk**.

Private patients – without insurance cover

If you do not have private medical insurance but want to go into hospital in the UK as a private patient, there is nothing to stop you, provided your doctor is willing and you are able to pay the bills. The choice if you opt for self-pay lies between the private wings of NHS hospitals or hospitals run by charitable or non-profit-making organizations, such as:

BMI Healthcare, website: **www.bmihealthcare.co.uk**;

Nuffield Health, website: **www.nuffieldhealth.com**.

An interesting alternative – medical tourism

Have you ever thought of taking a holiday and having an operation at the same time? This concept, known as 'medical tourism', is in fact not new. It dates back many thousands of years to the ancient Greeks, who travelled to Epidauria, the sanctuary of the healing god, Asklepios. In the 18th century in England the spa towns sprang up. These were an early form of medical tourism, as people travelled across the country in search of healing mineral waters.

Medical tourism or 'global health care' as it is now known, involves travelling to a foreign country for a medical procedure, and has been growing rapidly over recent years. More than 75,000 people from the UK last year sought faster or cheaper alternatives elsewhere to the health care offered in their home country. While the medical procedures needed can be urgent, the majority are elective treatments such as cosmetic surgery or dental care.

You can usually save over 50 per cent on the fees that you would pay for private treatment in the UK – and have a holiday as well. The destinations are extensive and sometimes exotic. Within the EU some treatments are available on the NHS, as long as you can prove that you are facing 'undue delay'. Leading health tourism destinations outside the EU include the Middle East, India, Malaysia, Singapore, South Korea, Costa Rica and Argentina.

One way to find out about this growing market and to meet some of the providers of such services is to search the following websites:

The Medical Tourist Company: website: **www.themedicaltouristcompany.com**;

The Health Tourism Show, website: **www.healthtourismshow.com**;

Treatment Abroad, website: **www.treatmentabroad.com**.

Long-term care insurance (LTCI)

An emergency operation is one thing; long-term care because an individual can no longer cope unaided is quite another. A number of insurance companies have policies designed to help meet the costs in the event of people needing to stay long term in a nursing home or requiring a carer to look after them in their own home. Increasingly people are having to contribute towards the costs of their own care and many have to support themselves from their savings. (NB: a married couple will not be forced into selling their home if the other partner is still living there.)

Nursing home fees are rising and good homes are increasingly expensive. Care in your own home, if you were ever to become seriously incapacitated, is likely to be at least as expensive. It is advisable, if you can, to make some provision against long-term care. The big advantages of insurance cover of this type are that it buys peace of mind and helps safeguard your savings should care ever become a necessity in the future. Cover normally applies only if an illness is diagnosed after joining and, while some plans cover a wide range of eventualities, others specifically exclude some of the critical illnesses, such as cancer. The premiums, which can be paid on a regular annual basis or as a lump sum, vary considerably. In all cases, the charges are largely determined by the subscriber's age at the time of first joining and, as you would expect, are very much cheaper at 55 than 75.

Although pre-funded insurance is the cheapest way of buying care cover, a disadvantage is that if you never claim you lose all the money you have paid over the years. Some policies link the insurance with an investment, providing a payout on death if no claim has been made. Though initially more expensive, you can take your money out of the plan at any time. However, if the investment growth is poor you could lose some of your capital.

A possible alternative to a conventional long-term care policy is *critical illness insurance*, which pays a lump sum if you are unfortunate enough to suffer from cancer or have a stroke. Rather than pay into a policy ahead of time, an alternative solution that has been growing in popularity is to buy a *care fee annuity* (sometimes known as an 'immediate-needs annuity') as and when the need arises. An advantage is that you buy a care plan only at the time it would actually be useful. Care fee annuities do require you to invest a sizeable chunk of capital, which, depending on your life expectancy, may or may not prove good value in the long term. Also, prices quoted by different companies to provide exactly the same annual income often differ by many thousands of pounds. You are strongly advised to shop around and to read the small print extremely carefully before signing, or you could ask an IFA to recommend what would be your best choice.

However good the advice, only you can decide whether some form of long-term care cover would be a sensible precaution. As with most major items of expenditure, there will inevitably be arguments for and against. All LTCI products and services now come under the compulsory jurisdiction of the Financial Ombudsman Service and the Financial Services Compensation Scheme. If you choose to seek the advice of an IFA, refer to Chapter 6, Financial advisers, where there is more information.

Hospital care cash plans

These are inexpensive insurance policies that provide cover for everyday health-care costs. Claims are made after the customer has paid for the treatment and are reimbursed within a week. See **British Health Care Association** website: **www.bhca.org.uk**.

Permanent health insurance (PHI)

PHI should not be confused with other types of health insurance. It is a replacement-of-earnings policy for people who are still in work and who, because of illness, are unable to continue with their normal occupation for a prolonged period and in consequence suffer loss of earnings. While highly recommended for the self-employed, many employees have some protection under an employer's policy. Either way, if you are close to retirement, PHI is unlikely to feature on your priority list.

Health screening

Prevention is better than cure, and most of the provident associations offer a diagnostic screening service to check general health and to provide advice on diet, drinking and smoking if these are problem areas. These tests show that roughly a quarter of patients aged over 55 have an unsuspected problem that can often be treated quickly and easily. Screening services normally recommend a check-up every two years, and centres are usually available to members of insurance schemes and others alike. See below:

BMI Healthcare, website: **www.bmihealthcare.co.uk**;

BUPA, website: **www.bupa.co.uk**;

National Health Service, website: **www.nhs.uk**.

National Health Service

Choosing a GP

If you move to a new area, the best way to choose your new GP is to ask for a recommendation. Otherwise your local primary care trust or strategic health authority can assist, or you can search the NHS website: **www.nhs.uk**.

Points you may want to consider are: how close the doctor is to your home; whether there is an appointments system; and whether it is a group practice and, if so, how this is organized. All GPs must have practice leaflets, available at their premises, with details about their service. Having selected a doctor, you should take your medical card to the receptionist to have your name registered. This is not automatic as there is a limit to the number of patients any one doctor can accept. Also, some doctors prefer to meet potential patients before accepting them on their list. If you do not have a medical card, you will need to fill in a simple form.

Changing your GP

If you want to change your GP, you go about it in exactly the same way. If you know of a doctor whose list you would like to be on, you can simply turn up at his or her surgery and ask to be registered; or you can ask your local primary care trust, or health board in Scotland, to give you a copy of its directory before making a choice. You do not need to give a reason for wanting to change, and you do not need to ask anyone's permission.

NHS Direct

If you need medical advice when you are on holiday or at some other time when it may not be possible to contact your doctor, NHS Direct offers a 24-hour free health advice service, staffed by trained nurses. See website: **www.nhsdirect.nhs.uk**.

Help with NHS costs

If you or your partner are in receipt of Income Support, income-based Jobseeker's Allowance or the Pension Credit Guarantee Credit, you are both entitled to free NHS prescriptions, NHS dental treatment, NHS wigs and fabric supports and an NHS sight test. You are both equally entitled to the maximum value of an optical voucher to help towards the cost of glasses or contact lenses and payment of travel costs to and from hospital for NHS treatment. You are also entitled to help if you and/or your partner are entitled to, or named on, a current Tax Credit NHS exemption certificate.

Even if you are not automatically entitled to help with the above costs, you and your partner may be entitled to some help on the grounds of low income. Complete claim form HC1 – available at NHS hospitals, dentists, opticians, GPs and chemists. If you are eligible for help, you will be sent a certificate that is valid for up to 12 months according to your circumstances. Depending on your income, you may receive an HC2 certificate, which entitles you to full help with NHS costs, or alternatively an HC3 certificate, which will entitle you to partial help. See website: **www.nhsbsa.nhs.uk** or, if you live in Scotland, **www.scotland.gov.uk/healthcosts**.

Benefits

If you are on Income Support and have a disability, you may be entitled to certain premiums on top of your ordinary allowance. Various social security benefits are also available to those with special problems because of illness (see website: **www.gov.uk**). These include:

Attendance Allowance (see leaflet DS 702);

Disability Living Allowance (see leaflet DS 704);

Employment and Support Allowance (ESA), which replaced Incapacity Benefit in October 2008. ESA is a new integrated contributory and income-related allowance.

Prescriptions

Both men and women aged 60 and over are entitled to free NHS prescriptions. Certain other groups are also entitled to free prescriptions, including those on low income. If you are not sure if you qualify, you should pay for your prescription and ask the pharmacist for an NHS receipt form FP57, which tells you how to claim a refund. For further information, see leaflet HC11, 'Help with health costs', obtainable from some pharmacies and GP surgeries.

People who do not qualify but who require a lot of prescriptions could save money by purchasing a prescription prepayment certificate. A prepayment certificate will work out cheaper if you are likely to need more than four prescription items in three months, or more than 14 items in 12 months, as there is no further charge regardless of how many prescription items you require. See website: **www.nhsbsa.nhs.uk** or, if you live in Scotland, **www.scotland.gov.uk/healthcosts**.

Going into hospital

There are now improved schemes to cut waiting lists for those in need of operations. Many patients are unaware that they can ask their GP to refer them to a consultant at a different NHS trust or even, in certain cases, help make arrangements for them to be treated overseas. Before you can become a patient at another hospital, your GP will need to agree to your being referred. A major consideration will be whether the treatment would be as clinically effective as the treatment you would receive locally.

Those likely to need help on leaving hospital should speak to the hospital social worker, who will help make any necessary arrangements. Help is sometimes available to assist patients with their travel costs to and from hospital. If you receive Income Support, income-based Jobseeker's Allowance or Pension Credit Guarantee Credit, you can ask for repayment of 'necessary travel costs'. See website: **www.nhsbsa.nhs.uk** or, if you live in Scotland, **www.scotland.gov.uk/healthcosts**.

If you go into hospital you will continue to receive your pension as normal. Your pension – as well as Employment and Support Allowance, Severe Disablement Allowance, Income Support and Pension Credit Guarantee Credit – will continue to be paid in full, without any reductions, for the duration of your stay. For further information, see leaflet GL12, 'Going into hospital?', obtainable from your GP, social security or Jobcentre Plus offices and NHS hospitals.

Complaints

The NHS has a complaints procedure if you are unhappy about the treatment you have received. In the first instance, you should speak to someone close to the cause of the problem, such as the doctor, nurse, receptionist or practice manager. If, for whatever reason, you would prefer to speak to someone who was not involved in your care, you can speak to the complaints manager at your local NHS trust or strategic health authority instead; the addresses will be in the telephone directory. In jargon terms, this first stage is known as *local resolution.*

If you are not satisfied with the reply you receive, you can ask the NHS trust or strategic health authority for an *independent review.* The complaints manager will be able to tell you whom to contact about arranging this. If you are still dissatisfied after the independent review, then the Health Service Ombudsman (formerly known as the Health Service Commissioner) may be able to help. The Ombudsman is independent of both government and the NHS and investigates complaints of failure or maladministration across the whole range of services provided by, or for, the NHS, including pharmacists, opticians and dentists, as well as private hospitals and nursing homes if these are paid for by the NHS. The Ombudsman cannot, however, take up legal causes on a patient's behalf.

Contacts are:

Health Service Ombudsman for England,
website: **www.ombudsman.org.uk;**

Health Service Ombudsman for Wales,
website: **www.ombudsman-wales.org.uk;**

Scottish Public Services Ombudsman, website: **www.spso.org.uk.**

If you wish to make a complaint, there is a time limit. You should register complaints within 12 months of the incident or within 12 months of your realizing that you have reason for complaint. If you need further advice on the complaints procedure, see the independent complaints advisory service, **PohWER** website: **www.pohwer.net.**

Rather than proceed through the formal channels described above, an alternative approach is to contact the independent advice centre that offers guidance to patients in the event of a problem with the health service. See the **Patients Association** website: **www.patients-association.com.**

Alternative medicine

Alternative medicine is dismissed by some doctors out of hand, while many patients claim that it is of great benefit. Here are some of the better known organizations:

British Acupuncture Council (BacC) is the home of traditional acupuncture in the UK. With around 3,000 members it is the UK's largest body of professional acupuncturists, where excellence in training, safe practice and professional standards are paramount. To find an acupuncturist in your local area, see website: **www.acupuncture.org.uk.**

British Chiropractic Association practitioners specialize in the diagnosis, treatment and overall management of conditions that are due to problems with the joints, ligament, tendons and nerves, especially related to the spine. See website: **www.chiropractic-uk.co.uk.**

British Homeopathic Association exists to promote homeopathy practised by doctors and other health-care professionals. For a list of practising GPs and pharmacies that stock homeopathic medicines, see website: **www.trusthomeopathy.org.**

British Hypnotherapy Association keeps a register of professionally trained practitioners who are able to treat phobias, emotional problems, anxiety, migraine, psoriasis or relationship difficulties. See website: **www.hypnotherapy-association.org.**

General Osteopathic Council regulates the practice of osteopathy in the UK with over 4,000 registered practitioners. Osteopathy is a system of diagnosis and treatment of a wide range of medical conditions. See website: **www.osteopathy.org.uk.**

Incorporated Society of Registered Naturopaths: naturopathy is concerned with the underlying conditions that may cause illness, including, for example, diet, general fitness, posture, stress and the patient's mental outlook on life. See website: **www.naturecuresociety.org.**

National Institute of Medical Herbalists is the UK's leading professional body representing herbal practitioners. It promotes the benefits, efficacy and safe use of herbal medicine. See website: **www.nimh.org.uk.**

Eyes

It is advisable to have your sight checked at least every two years. Did you know that regular sight tests can pick up conditions such as glaucoma, cataracts, macular degeneration, dry eye and inflammation of the cornea?

They can also detect signs of other diseases including diabetes, hypertension (high blood pressure), thyroidtoxicosis, auto immune disorders, pituitary tumours, raised cholesterol and shingles.

You will qualify for a free NHS sight test if you are aged 60 and over; you live in Scotland; you or your partner receive Income Support, Family Credit, income-based Jobseeker's Allowance, Pension Credit Guarantee Credit and are entitled to or named on a valid NHS Tax Credit exemption certificate or are named on a valid HC2 certificate. For details, see leaflet HC11 – website: **www.gov.uk**. Even if you do not belong to any of these groups but are on a low income, you may be entitled to a free, or reduced-cost, sight test. To find out if you qualify for help, you should fill in claim form HC1, which you can get from social security or Jobcentre Plus offices – website: **www.gov.uk**.

People with mobility problems who are unable to get to an optician can ask for a domiciliary visit to have their eyes examined at home. This is free for those with an HC2 certificate or who are in receipt of one of the benefits listed above. People with a (partial help) HC3 certificate can use this towards the cost of a private home visit by their optician. The going rate for private sight tests if you do have to pay is about £25.

You do not need a doctor's referral to have your eyes tested. Whether you have to pay or not, the optician must either give you a prescription identifying what type of glasses you require or give you a statement confirming that you have no need of spectacles. The prescription is valid for two years. If you do not use it straight away, you should keep it safe so that it is handy when you need to use it. When you do decide to buy spectacles or contact lenses, you are under no obligation to obtain them from the optician who tested your eyes but can buy them where you like.

There is a voucher system for helping with the purchase of glasses or contact lenses. If you or your partner are in receipt of Income Support, income-based Jobseeker's Allowance or Pension Credit Guarantee Credit, you will receive an optical voucher, with a cash value. The amount you get will depend on your optical prescription. If you do not get any of the above benefits but are on a low income, you may still be entitled to help. To find out, fill in claim form HC1, as explained above. The voucher might be sufficient to pay for your contact lenses or spectacles outright, or it may make only a small contribution towards the cost. Part of the equation will depend on the frames you choose. You will not be tied to any particular glasses: you can choose spectacles that cost more than the value of the voucher and pay the difference yourself.

People who are registered blind are entitled to a special tax allowance each year. For 2012/13 it is £2,100. A great deal of practical help can be obtained from the **Royal National Institute of Blind People** (RNIB). In addition to giving general advice and information, it can supply a range of special equipment, details of which can be found on the website: **www.rnib.org.uk**.

Do any of the following apply to you? Are you over 40? Do you have a family history of glaucoma? Are you short-sighted? Do you have diabetes? Are you of African-Caribbean origin? If the answer to any of these is yes, then you could be at risk. There are various types of glaucoma, but the most common is primary open angle glaucoma (POAG). It has no symptoms in the early stages but slowly and painlessly destroys sight if not detected and treated. For more information **The International Glaucoma Association** can help. See website: **www.glaucoma-association.com**.

Many elderly people with failing sight suffer from macular degeneration, which affects their ability to distinguish detail. Although there is no known cure, individuals can be helped to make the most effective use of their sight by special magnifiers and other aids, such as clip-on lenses that fit over normal spectacles. See the **Partially Sighted Society** website: **www.partsight.org.uk**.

British Wireless for the Blind is a national independent charity providing specially modified audio equipment to all UK-registered blind or partially sighted people over the age of 80 and in receipt of means-tested benefits. See website: **www.blind.org.uk**.

It is worth knowing that all the main banks will provide statements in Braille; and Barclaycard now also issues credit card statements in Braille, on request. Additionally, several institutions offer large-print chequebooks or templates for chequebooks, as well as other facilities such as a taped version of their annual report. There is no extra charge for these services.

BT has a free directory enquiry service for customers who cannot read or handle a phone book. To use the service you first need to register with BT, which will issue you with a personal identification number. See website: **www.bt.com/inclusion**.

Feet

Many people forget about their feet until they begin to give trouble. Corns and bunions, if neglected, can become extremely painful, and ideally everyone, especially women who wear high heels, should have podiatry treatment from early middle age or even younger. One of the problems of which podiatrists complain is that because many women wear uncomfortable shoes they become used to having painful feet and do not notice when something is more seriously wrong. The result can sometimes be ingrowing toenails or infections. Podiatry is available on the National Health Service without referral from a doctor being necessary, but facilities tend to be very oversubscribed, so in many areas it is only the very elderly or those with a real problem who can get appointments.

The **Society of Chiropodists and Podiatrists**, the professional association for registered chiropodists and podiatrists, has a list of over 10,000 private practitioners. See website: **www.feetforlife.org**.

Hearing

Like many things in life, we don't really notice our hearing until it starts to go. But when it does, we start to understand what an important sense it is. In the UK alone there are 10 million people living with a hearing loss; and only 2 million of them are wearing hearing aids, even though many more could benefit from them. Often people fail to act because they don't recognize the symptoms or know that treatment is now easily available, affordable and on the high street. Being able to hear properly is important for a number of reasons: for safety and awareness; conversation and interaction; enjoyment and entertainment. Because hearing works 'invisibly' it isn't always given as much attention as it should. Changes happen so gradually, hearing loss can often go undetected. Signs to look out for are:

  not hearing the doorbell or a telephone ring;

  turning up the television too loud for the comfort of others;

  failing to hear people come into the room;

  misunderstanding what has been said in conversation;

  not speaking clearly or speaking in a monotonous tone;

  uncertainty about where sounds are coming from;

  difficulty in hearing at a distance or in public gatherings.

If you have noticed any of these, talk to your GP, who may refer you to an audiologist or hearing care professional. They will be able to advise on the best course of action to help your hearing. You can obtain a hearing aid and batteries free on the NHS or buy them privately. There are many other aids on the market that can make life easier. **BT**, for example, has a variety of special equipment for when a standard phone becomes too difficult to use. See website: **www.bt.com/inclusion**. There are other specialist organizations that can give you a lot of help on hearing aids and on other matters:

Action on Hearing Loss is the new name for RNID (Royal National Institute for the Deaf); it offers a wide range of services including sign language interpreters and other communication support. See website: **www.actiononhearingloss.org.uk**.

AgeUK has teamed up with Boots Hearingcare to provide a unique hearing care package that offers practical and professional advice to help tackle the symptoms of hearing loss early on. For more information see website: **www.ageuk.org.uk** or **www.bootshearingcare.com**.

British Deaf Association (BDA) works to protect the interests of deaf people and also provides an advice service through its regional offices. See website: **www.bda.org.uk**.

British Tinnitus Association (BTA) is a world leader, with a trained team of friendly and experienced advisers for anyone who experiences tinnitus or those simply seeking guidance or information about the condition. See website: **www.tinnitus.org.uk**.

Hearing Link is a voluntary organization providing support and information to people with hearing loss, as well as their families. See website: **www.hearinglink.org**.

Friends and family can do a great deal to help those who are deaf or hard of hearing. One of the essentials is not to shout but to speak slowly and distinctly. You should always face the person, so he or she can see your lips, and avoid speaking with your hand over your mouth or when smoking. Learning British Sign Language is another option. In case of real difficulty, write down your message.

Teeth

People in their 50s, 60s and 70s are much younger looking than their counterparts of a few decades ago, thanks to advances in medicine and a healthier diet and lifestyle. But one thing that can let the older generation down is their smile. Teeth gradually darken with age. Two of life's simplest pleasures – a cup of fresh coffee and a glass of decent red wine – eventually lead to stained teeth; and there are additional penalties if you are a smoker. A natural smile is often a person's best asset, so if your teeth have seen better days it is worth spending some time looking after them as you become older. Everyone knows the importance of having regular dental check-ups. Many adults, however, slip out of the habit, which could result in their having trouble with their teeth as they become older. Dentistry is one of the treatments for which you have to pay under the NHS, unless you have a low income. If you or your partner are in receipt of Income Support, income-based Jobseeker's Allowance or Pension Credit, you are entitled to free NHS dental treatment. You may also receive some help if you are in receipt of the Working Tax Credit; for details, see leaflet HC11.

Even if you do not belong to any of these groups, you may still get some help if you have a low income. To find out if you qualify, fill in claim form HC1 (obtainable from social security or Jobcentre Plus offices, NHS hospitals and NHS dentists). To avoid any nasty surprises when the bill comes along, it is important to confirm with your dentist before he or she treats you whether you are being treated under the NHS. This also applies to the hygienist, should you need to see one. The best advice is to ask in advance what the cost of your treatment is likely to be. Help with the cost is all very well, but for many an even bigger problem than money is actually finding an NHS dentist in their area. The best advice is to call the British Dental Health Foundation's helpline (see below) or, if you are thinking of going private, ask friends and acquaintances for recommendations.

For those who like to be able to budget ahead for any dental bills, **Denplan** is the UK's leading dental payment plan specialist, with over 6,500 member dentists and approximately 1.8 million patients across the UK. For more information on Denplan's hassle-free dental health care, see website: **www.denplan.co.uk**.

Prevention is always better than cure. If you want free, independent and impartial advice on all aspects of oral health and free literature on a wide range of topics, including patients' rights, finding a dentist and dental care for older people, see the **British Dental Health Foundation** website: **www.dentalhealth.org.uk**.

Personal relationships

Retirement, for couples, involves a major lifestyle change. With it come fresh opportunities, and, inevitably, a few compromises are needed. Many women continue to work once their husbands retire. Couples can sometimes find it difficult to adjust to spending longer together while others may feel they have little left in common. There has been a recent increase in the over-60s' divorce rate, so it is important in the early stages of retirement that couples work out the best way of living together in their retirement. Normally, with goodwill and understanding on both sides, difficulties are quickly resolved to allow the relationship to flourish. However, for some couples it does not work out so easily, and it may be helpful to seek skilled guidance:

Albany Trust is a professional therapy service for individuals and couples needing emotional and psychological help. See website: **www.albanytrust.org**.

Marriage Care offers a similar service, plus a confidential telephone helpline, for those who are having problems with their marriage or other close personal relationship. See websites: **www.marriagecare.org.uk**; Scottish Marriage Care: **www.scottishmarriagecare.org**.

Relate, the relationship people, offers advice, relationship counselling, sex therapy, workshops, mediation, consultations and support face to face, by phone and through the website. See **Relate England** website: **www.relate.org.uk**, Relate Scotland: **www.relatescotland.org.uk**.

Help for grandparents

A sad result of today's divorce statistics is the risk to grandparents of losing contact with their grandchildren. While some divorcing parents lean over backwards to avoid this happening, others – maybe through force of circumstance or hurt feelings – deny grandparents access or even sever the relationship completely. Recourse to the law is never a step to be taken lightly and should obviously be avoided if there is the possibility that a more conciliatory approach could be successful. There are a number of organizations that have experience of advising grandparents and offer practical help and support:

Grandparents' Association, website: **www.grandparents-association.org.uk**;

Grandparents Plus, website: **www.grandparentsplus.org.uk**;

Gransnet, website: **www.gransnet.com**.

Depression

Depression is a condition that is often akin to problems in a marriage and other personal crises. A number of retired people find it develops as a result of the lifestyle change from working to having time on their hands. If you are depressed, you find being on your own difficult, or you suffer from loss of self-esteem due to no longer having the status of your job, then boredom or a general lack of purpose can result. Usually people manage to deal with it alone by involving themselves in outside activities. However, if the condition persists for more than a few days, a doctor should always be consulted, as depression can create sleeping difficulties. Another reason for consulting a doctor is that depression may be due to being physically run down. If you've recently suffered from flu, maybe all that is required is a good tonic – or perhaps a holiday. Sometimes, however, depression persists. In these cases it may be that, rather than medicines or the stimulus of a new activity, individuals need to talk to someone. There are several organizations that may be able to help:

Depression Alliance, website: **www.depressionalliance.org**;

Mind, website: **www.mind.org.uk**;

Samaritans, website: **www.samaritans.org**;

Sane, website: **www.sane.org.uk**.

Some common afflictions

You may be one of the lucky ones and the rest of this chapter will be of no further interest to you. It deals with some of the more common afflictions, such as back pain and heart disease, as well as with disability. However, if you are unfortunate enough to be affected, or have a member of your family who is, then knowing which organizations can provide support could make all the difference in helping you to cope.

Aphasia

This condition makes it hard to speak, read or understand language, and affects individuals who have suffered a stroke, a head injury or other neurological damage. **Speakability** (Action for Dysphasic Adults) is the national charity offering information and support to people with aphasia, their families and their carers. See website: **www.speakability.org.uk**.

Arthritis and rheumatism

Although arthritis is often thought of as an older person's complaint, it accounts for the loss of an estimated 70 million working days a year in Britain, and 10 million people suffer from it. You don't have to put up with the pain of arthritis. There are a number of websites to help you:

Arthritic Association is a national charity that promotes ways to increase mobility and lessen the pain of arthritis sufferers. See website: **www.arthriticassociation.org.uk**.

Arthritis Care exists to support people with arthritis. It encourages self-help and has over 400 local branches offering practical support and social activities. See website: **www.arthritiscare.org.uk**.

Arthritis Research UK is the charity leading the fight against arthritis. See website: **www.arthritisresearchuk.org**.

Back pain

Four out of five people suffer from back pain at some stage of their lives. While there are many different causes, doctors agree that much of the trouble could be avoided through correct posture, care in lifting heavy articles, a firm mattress, and chairs that provide support in the right places. The following two organizations could be helpful:

The Back Shop established since 1984, offers the finest back care products in the world, to help prevent back trouble or provide relief for those who suffer. See website: **www.thebackshop.co.uk**.

BackCare is a national charity that aims to reduce the impact of back pain on society. It acts as a hub between patients, (health-care) professionals, employers, policy makers, researchers and all others with an interest in back pain. See website: **www.backcare.org.uk**.

Blood pressure

Unlike most illnesses or diseases, high blood pressure can be symptomless yet it is the leading cause of strokes in the UK and can lead to heart attack and heart failure. One in three adults has high blood pressure but a third of those will be completely unaware of it. Anyone over the age of 50 should keep a check on their blood pressure as it tends to rise with age. Post-menopausal women also see an increase in their blood pressure. The good news is that blood pressure can be successfully managed with medication and some simple lifestyle changes. In brief:

Watch your salt intake.

Eat at least five portions of fruit and vegetables per day.

Watch your weight.

Cut down on alcohol.

Take regular exercise.

Laugh – watch a funny movie.

Be sociable – lonely people often suffer from high blood pressure.

The Blood Pressure Association offers help and information. See website: **www.bpassoc.org.uk**.

Cancer

Cancer is now a subject that is often discussed openly, and with continuing research and improved treatments more people suffering from cancer make a complete recovery. Early diagnosis can make a vital difference. Doctors recommend that all women should undergo regular screening for cervical cancer, and women over 50 are advised to have a routine mammography to screen for breast cancer at least once every three years. Computerized cervical screening systems for women aged 25 to 64 and breast cancer screening units for women aged 50 to 70 are available nationwide. In both cases, older women can have access to the services on request. It also goes without saying that anyone with a lump or swelling, however small, should waste no time in having it investigated by a doctor.

There is so much work being done to cure cancer that now over 300 cancer charities exist to research or focus on a particular variant of the disease. To find a list of all of them consult: **www.charitychoice.co.uk**. There are a number of excellent support groups for cancer sufferers, including:

Bowel Cancer UK aims to save lives by raising awareness of bowel cancer, campaigning for best treatment and care, and providing practical support and advice. See website: **www.bowelcanceruk.org.uk**.

Breast Cancer Care offers practical advice, information and emotional support to women who have, or fear they have, breast cancer or benign breast disease. See website: **www.breastcancercare.org.uk**.

Macmillan Cancer Support improves the lives of people affected by cancer, providing practical, medical and financial support. Cancer affects everyone: Macmillan can help. See website: **www.macmillan.org.uk**.

Chest and heart diseases

The earlier sections on smoking, diet, drink and exercise list some of the most pertinent 'dos and don'ts' that can help prevent heart disease. The advice should be taken seriously. Statistics reveal that UK death rates from coronary heart disease are among the highest in the world, killing almost 120,000 people a year, and coronary heart disease is responsible for one in five of all deaths. Although people tend to think of heart attacks as particularly affecting men, over four times as many women die from heart disease as from breast cancer.

British Heart Foundation's vision is a world where people do not die prematurely from heart disease. It plays a leading role in the fight against diseases of the heart and circulation. See website: **www.bhf.org.uk**.

Diabetes

Diabetes occurs when the amount of glucose in the blood is too high for the body to use properly. It can sometimes be treated by diet alone; sometimes pills or insulin may also be needed. Diabetes can be diagnosed at any age, although it is common in the elderly and especially among individuals who are overweight.

Diabetes UK is the charity that aims to improve the lives of people with diabetes. See website: **www.diabetes.org.uk**.

Insulin Dependent Diabetes Trust is a small charity offering support and information to people with diabetes and their families on the issues that are important to them. See website: **www.iddtinternational.org**.

Migraine

Migraine affects over 10 million people in the UK. It can involve severe head pains, nausea, vomiting, visual disturbances and in some cases temporary paralysis. The leading UK charity that funds and promotes research, holds international symposia and runs an extensive support service is the **Migraine Trust**. See website: **www.migrainetrust.org**.

Osteoporosis and menopause problems

The importance of healthy bones is something AgeUK highlighted last year in their 'Falls Awareness Week'. A diet which is rich in calcium and vitamin D builds and maintains healthy bones. Strong bones help reduce the risk of breaking bones should we fall when we grow older. Over 3 million people over the age of 65 in the UK suffer a fall each year. This represents half of all hospital admissions for accidental injury, with many of these resulting in fractures. Injuries as the result of falls are one of the leading causes of death for the over-75s.

Bone is a living tissue which needs to be kept healthy. It changes throughout our lifetime, with new bone constantly replacing old bone. From the age of 35 our bones begin to weaken gradually. This can lead to osteoporosis. Osteoporosis is a disease affecting bones, which become so fragile that they can break very easily, with injuries most common in the spine, hip and wrist. It affects one in two women (and one in five men) and often develops following the menopause, when body levels of oestrogen naturally decrease.

AgeUK compiled a list of ways to boost bone health:

- Weight-bearing exercise is important to help keep your bones strong. Walking, tennis, aerobics and dancing strengthen your bones.

- Enjoy a balanced diet. Milk, cheese, yoghurt, baked beans, lentils and dried apricots are great sources of calcium.

- Taking a stroll in the summer sun (just 10 minutes will help) is a great way of absorbing vitamin D, which keeps bones healthy.

- Avoid smoking. Smokers lose bone at a faster rate than non-smokers.

- Drink moderately. (Source: **www.ageuk.org.uk/fallsweek**.)

The following websites may be useful:

Menopause Exchange gives independent advice and practical information on a range of topics concerning health issues affecting women in mid-life. See website: **www.menopause-exchange.co.uk**.

National Osteoporosis Society is the only UK-wide charity dedicated to improving the diagnosis, prevention and treatment of osteoporosis. See website: **www.nos.org.uk**.

Women's Health Concern (WHC) provides an independent service to advise, reassure and educate women about their health concerns, to enable them to work in partnership with their own medical practitioners and health advisers. This is a branch of the British Menopause Society. See website: **www.womens-health-concern.org**.

Stroke

Over 130,000 people suffer a stroke every year in England and Wales. A stroke is a brain injury caused by the sudden interruption of blood flow. It is unpredictable in its effects, which may include muscular paralysis or weakness on one side, loss of speech or loss of understanding or language, visual problems or incontinence. Prevention is similar to the prevention of heart disease.

The Stroke Association works to prevent strokes and helps stroke patients and their families. A stroke has a greater disability impact than any other medical condition. The Stroke Association is the only UK-wide charity solely concerned with combating stroke in people of all ages. See website: **www.stroke.org.uk**.

Disability

Disability is mainly covered in Chapter 15, Caring for elderly parents, so if you or someone in your family has a problem you may find the answer you need there. In this section, there are simply one or two points that may be useful for others.

Local authority services

Social services departments (*social work departments* in Scotland) provide many of the services that people with disabilities may need, including:

practical help in the home, perhaps with the support of a home help;

adaptations to your home, such as a ramp for a wheelchair or other special equipment for your safety;

meals on wheels;

provision of day centres, clubs and similar;

the issue of badges for cars driven or used by people with a disability (in some authorities this is handled by the works department or by the residents' parking department);

advice about other transport services or concessions that may be available locally.

In most instances, you should speak to a social worker who will either be able to make the arrangements or point you in the right direction. He or she will also be able to tell you of any special facilities or other help provided by the authority.

Occupational therapists can advise about special equipment and help teach someone with a disability through training and exercise how best to manage. They also come within the orbit of the social services department.

Health care

Services are normally arranged through either a GP or the local authority health centre. Key professional staff include:

health visitors (who are qualified nurses), who, rather like social workers, will be able to put you in touch with whatever specialized services are required;

district nurses, who will visit patients in their home;

physiotherapists, who use exercise and massage to help improve mobility, for example after an operation;

medical social workers, employed in hospitals, who will help with any arrangements before a patient is discharged.

Council tax

If someone in your family has a disability, you may be able to claim a reduction on your council tax. If you have a blue badge on your car, you may get a rebate for a garage. You would normally apply to the housing benefits officer, but different councils employ different officers to deal with this; see website: **www.gov.uk**.

Chapter Fourteen
Holidays

A journey of self-discovery starts with a single step; but so does falling down a flight of stairs. **KATHY LETTE**

The over-50s are very important to the travel market. An ageing population, fitter than previous generations of pensioners, they have more disposable income and free time than ever before. As a result, senior holidaymakers have been expanding their horizons. No longer content just to sit on the beach, the over-50s are choosing skiing, African safaris and white-water rafting as their holiday options. For fit and active older people there really is no limit when it comes to adventure tourism and far-flung continents. But if you are thinking of your carbon footprint, it isn't necessary to go abroad to try out some exciting activities while on holiday. Mountain climbing, skiing and cycling in England, Wales and Scotland are popular holidays for over-50s. Should you be thinking of camping in the sunshine in Devon and Cornwall, or canoeing through the Norfolk Broads, all are available not too far from home. The beauty of an activity holiday in Britain is that it can take the form of a short break over a weekend. These holidays are also great for meeting and staying in touch with other UK holidaymakers.

Let the imagination roam free when considering the options for an active or adventure holiday. Don't just look at the usual holiday brochures; get on the internet and seek out adventure holiday companies. Active holidays can include:

- jungle safaris in Cancun, Mexico;
- touring the wineries and vineyards of Italy, France, Germany and beyond;
- learning to cook in gastronomy tours in France;
- trekking through the Australian outback;

- photographing wildlife in India;
- surfing courses in Newquay, Cornwall;
- trekking through the wilderness in Iceland;
- touring the outback in Australia.

Active holidays can open up a new lease of life in later years. Holidays can be spent learning new sports or acquiring new skills that can then be enjoyed both at home and abroad. The chance to visit far-flung exciting locations is, of course, a bonus. This year perhaps it's time for you to try something different that will provide unforgettable experiences.

Of course, one of the most popular types of holidays for seniors is a cruise. It's not designed to be adventurous, or to provide a white-knuckle experience. But it is a perfectly wonderful way to spend several weeks at sea; you not only get to travel and see any number of places, but you have the bonus of spending the entire time being pampered. For most people, what could be better than that? It's like being in a moving luxury hotel. A number of cruise lines cater specifically to the older market, making sure they offer things like disabled access, special diets and a variety of lectures and entertainment that will appeal to seniors. It's a lucrative market for the holiday industry, with many over-50s having disposable income and plenty of time to enjoy it. Senior cruises also have a doctor on board, and are equipped to take care of most minor medical problems. If you contact the cruise line beforehand about any particular problems you have, they will make sure they have appropriate medication in stock before you set sail.

Many women cruise alone, and some feel vulnerable while at sea. To avoid that, most cruise lines now have what they call gentlemen hosts. These are carefully screened men who are available to escort single women, dance and dine with them and also accompany them on excursions on shore. Having been well vetted, they bring a sense of security, and the knowledge that they're there can bring more unaccompanied women into cruising. For the disabled, many new ships are specially equipped with wheelchair-accessible rooms and all manner of gadgets to make life easier. All these factors add together to make the idea of a cruise a pleasure for older people, making travel easy, without having to deal with luggage in airports, packed flights and getting to and from a resort. Also, there's a chance to travel with people in the same age group. Although that doesn't mean you'll make friends with everyone, there are common bonds and experiences which make things more enjoyable.

So with such a large number of active retired people with time and money to spare, it is hardly surprising that there is need for a wide variety of choice of good-quality resorts and reasonably priced holidays for older adventurous people. The fact that you've retired makes very little difference to what you can do or where you can go. Lots of people combine holidays with a special interest, such as painting or music. There is ample opportunity for you to enrol for summer school, exchange homes with someone in another country or sign on for a working holiday, such as voluntary conservation activity or home and pet sitting, for which you get paid. The choice is enormous. If you wish to go somewhere exotic, it is likely the prices will be high; but if your budget is limited, with a bit of research you will find some holidays that are extremely reasonable in cost. Whether you are fit and active or require special care, there are plenty of options. Retirement is a time for experimentation, so don't think about your age being an issue – it's time to do something different.

For ease of reference, entries are listed under subheadings, for example 'Arts and crafts', 'Sport', 'Self-catering and other low-budget holidays'. To avoid repetition, the majority are featured only once, in the most logical place. There is a general information section with brief details about insurance, concessionary fares and other travel tips at the end of the chapter. Website addresses are up to date at the time of going to press.

Art appreciation

Many tour operators, clubs and other organizations that arrange group holidays include visits to museums, churches and other venues of artistic interest along with their other activities such as walking, bridge and general sightseeing. Alternatively, if you enjoy the performing arts, you could spend several glorious days attending some of the music and drama festivals held in many parts of the country, as well as some of the famous festivals overseas.

Specialtours offers escorted tours for discerning travellers and cultural groups, such as the British Museum, the Royal Academy and the National Art Collections Fund. It is now part of The Ultimate Travel Company. See website: **www.specialtours.co.uk**.

Kirker Holidays began providing carefully crafted tailor-made holidays in 1986, and continues to look after the discerning traveller with luxury hotels in Europe and beyond with private transfers, private tours and well researched itineraries. See website: **www.kirkerholidays.com**.

Festivals

There is a feast of music, drama and the arts. The most famous festivals in the UK are those held at Edinburgh and Aldeburgh. Over the years the number of festivals has been growing, and they are now a regular feature in many parts of the country. To find out what is going on where, in your local area or any other part of the UK, contact the Arts Council or your regional Arts Council office.

There are simply too many to list here, but you will find them advertised in the national and local press, or search the internet for lists of major festivals at home and overseas.

Aldeburgh Music: world-renowned as an outstanding year-round performance centre, Aldeburgh has a varied programme of classical and contemporary music. There are also exhibitions, talks, walks and films. See website: **www.aldeburgh.co.uk**.

Edinburgh International Festival is held every August. Details of music, theatre, dance, opera and other events are available from early April. See website: **www.edinburgh-festivals.com**.

Glyndebourne Festival Opera is an opera house in the Sussex countryside, home to the annual Glyndebourne festival. Its global reputation stems from a passion for artistic excellence. Festival season end May to end August each year. See website: **www.glyndebourne.com**

Three Choirs Festival is the oldest classical music festival in Europe, originating in the early 1700s. It takes place in August each year by rotation in the Cathedral cities of Gloucester, Hereford and Worcester. It is described as choral music at its best, in a quintessentially English setting. See website: **www.3choirs.org**.

Arts and crafts

The focus is on taking courses or just participating for pleasure, rather than viewing the works of others. Further suggestions are also given in Chapter 9, Leisure activities.

Benslow Music offers residential and day courses and summer schools to musicians, choirs, orchestras, chamber groups, soloists, composers and conductors of all standards from beginner to advanced, throughout the year. See website: **www.benslowmusic.org**.

Dartington International Summer School is the biggest and oldest classical music festival and summer school in the south-west. Courses include choir, vocal ensembles and chamber music as well as non-classical and world-music courses. See website: **www.dartington.org/summer-school**

The Crafts Council aims to make the UK the best place to make, see, collect and learn about contemporary craft. This is a growing industry and contributes to the UK's reputation as a world leader in creativity. See website: **www.craftscouncil.org.uk**.

West Dean College, near Chichester, is an internationally renowned centre for study. The college provides MAs and diplomas and short courses in contemporary and traditional crafts, the visual arts, photography, music and gardening. See website: **www.westdean.org.uk**.

Coach holidays

Some coach companies organize holidays, as distinct from simply offering a mode of transport. Before embarking on a lengthy coach tour, try a few shorter excursions to see how you cope with the journey.

National Express is a leading transport provider delivering services in the UK, Spain and North America, to over 1,000 destinations, carrying more than 16 million customers a year. Passengers aged 60-plus, or who are registered disabled, enjoy concessionary rates (but not including hotel costs). See website: **www.nationalexpress.com**.

Other websites which offer good choices of coach holidays include:

www.nationalholidays.com;

www.silvertraveladvisor.com;

www.shearings.com;

www.grandukholidays.com;

www.travel55.co.uk.

Historical holidays

Holidays with a particular focus on history are becoming increasingly popular.

Commonwealth War Graves Commission, established in 1917, pays tribute to the 1,700,000 men and women of the Commonwealth Forces who died in the two world wars. If you are planning to visit a Commission cemetery or memorial, see website: **www.cwgc.org**.

Holts Tours – Battlefields & History offers a choice of over 40 battlefield, historical and archaeological tours throughout the world. All are accompanied by a specialist guide-lecturer, including local experts. See website: **www.holts.co.uk**.

Kentwell in Suffolk offers a glimpse into both past and present of this unique house. Visit during one of the award-winning recreations of Tudor, Victorian or Second World War everyday life. See website: **www.kentwell.co.uk**.

Poppy Travel is the specialist travel division of The Royal British Legion, arranging personalized and memorable journeys of remembrance since 1927. See website: **www.poppytravel.org.uk**.

War Research Society – Battlefield Tours is the battlefield tours specialist, organizing tours and excursions to museums and battlefields of the Great War, the Second World War, and specialist tours. See website: **www.battlefieldtours.co.uk**.

Language courses

If you are hoping to travel more when you retire, being able to speak the language when abroad will greatly add to your enjoyment. The quickest and easiest way to learn is in the country itself. There are attractive opportunities for learning any language, whether you wish to attend a course or via computer, CDs or private tutor; you will find what you need by searching the internet. Should you wish to improve your French, German, Italian, or Spanish, see below.

British Institute of Florence is situated in the historic centre of Florence, city of Dante and the birthplace of the Renaissance. It was the first British cultural institute to operate overseas, and offers courses in the

Italian language, art history and other events. Website:
www.britishinstitute.it.

Goethe-Institut is the Federal Republic of Germany's cultural
institution, offering a variety of German-language courses.
Website: **www.goethe.de**.

Institut-Français was founded in 1910 and is the official French
government centre of language and culture in London, offering
a range of courses for students of all abilities. Website:
www.institut-francais.org.uk.

Instituto Cervantes provides courses for studying Spanish in London
and also discovering the cultures of Spain and Latin America.
See website: **www.londres.cervantes.es**.

Other people's homes

Living in someone else's home free is one of the cheapest ways of enjoying
a holiday. There are two ways of doing this: exchange your home with
another person in this country or abroad, or become a home sitter and mind
someone else's property while they are away.

Home exchange

Exchanges are normally arranged direct between the two parties concerned,
who agree the terms between themselves. Some people even exchange their
cars and pets. Here are some organizations that may be useful:

Guardian Home Exchange helps you swap homes for free
accommodation and unlimited holidays worldwide. See website:
www.guardianhomeexchange.co.uk.

Happy Home Swap is the boutique home-exchange and holiday rental
company catering for beautiful, unique and stylish homes across the
globe: the exchange company with a personal touch. See website:
www.happyhomeswap.com.

Home Base Holidays, established in 1985, helps people arrange
home-exchange vacations, from small city apartments to large
country homes complete with swimming pool. See website:
www.homebase-hols.com.

HomeLink International is the largest UK-based home-exchange holiday organization. With HomeLink there is access to the UK office and a professional team of experienced coordinators in 24 countries. See website: **www.homelink.org.uk**.

Simply Home Exchange is a non-commercial home-exchange and vacation rental site with complete worldwide coverage and unique property vetting system by its members. See website: **www.simplyhomeexchange.com**.

Home sitting

Retired people are generally considered ideal home sitters: you provide a caretaking service and get paid for doing so. Duties variously involve light housework, plant watering, care of pets and sometimes tending the garden. Careful vetting of applicants is essential, as are first-class references.

Absentia sitters offer a holiday care service for home and pets, from one day to several months at a time. See website: **www.home-and-pets.co.uk**.

Homesitters stay in the home and look after everything – pets, garden and security. See website: **www.homesitters.co.uk**.

Trusted House Sitters helps home and pet owners find trusted sitters to care for their home and pets while away. See website: **www.trustedhousesitters.com**.

Universal Aunts is the original and most experienced provider of daily and residential assistance, both in the UK and abroad. See website: **www.universalaunts.co.uk**.

Overseas travel

Many big tour operators make a feature of offering special holidays designed for the over-55s. Also included here are companies that specialize in arranging cruises and packaged motoring holidays, and information on timesharing.

Explore Worldwide specializes in adventure holidays and other activities to over 130 countries across the world. See website: **www.explore.co.uk**.

Relais du Silence was created on the initiative of a few perceptive hoteliers, and provides holidays 'in a natural and peaceful environment, offering rest and recreation in calm and tranquillity'. See website: **www.relaisdusilence.com**.

Saga Holidays are exclusively for people aged 50 and over, including ocean and river cruising, safaris, short- and long-stay resort holidays and multi-centre tours. See website: **www.saga.co.uk/travel**.

Here are some holiday and travel websites that specifically cater for the over-55s:

Easier.com: **www.easier.com**;

Silver Travel Advisor: **www.silvertraveladvisor.com**;

Travel Quest: **www.travel-quest.co.uk**;

Travelsphere: **www.travelsphere.co.uk**.

Cruises

Some 2 million people in the UK take a cruise holiday every year and that figure is rising. Cruise operators have been making cruising more accessible, exciting, varied and affordable. Apart from the traditional routes around the Caribbean and the Mediterranean, smaller companies offer more unusual voyages on compact ships, exploring coasts and ports that big ships cannot visit. Luxury cruises can have a staggering level of opulence, but they come at a price. However, for a special occasion, such as a wedding anniversary, it is wonderfully decadent.

If you are interested in finding out more, visit one of the exhibitions dedicated to help you discover a world of voyages: **The Cruising Show**, sponsored by the *Daily Telegraph*, takes place twice each year, in Glasgow and Birmingham. See website: **www.cruisingshow.co.uk**.

Here are some *top tips* for cruising:

Avoid an inside cabin. It will be cheaper because there is no natural light, but it plays havoc with your body clock.

Don't pay the brochure price. Protect yourself by booking your cruise through an ABTA agent.

Remember that prices usually include extras. If you think the cost is high, remember that food and non-alcoholic drinks are included.

Watch out for on-board credit offers. Cruise lines tempt customers with on-board credit that can only be spent on the ship.

From among the mass of companies offering cruise travel advice and tours, here are just a few websites to look at:

One particularly useful website is Alastair MacKenzie's **Travel Lists,** which is an independent 'expert directory'-style website for British holidaymakers and travellers who want to browse a simple list of only the best and most relevant travel providers for their travel research: **www.travel-lists.co.uk.**

Avalon Waterways: **www.avaloncruises.co.uk.**

Blue Water Holidays: **www.cruisingholidays.co.uk.**

Carnival Magic: **www.carnival.com.**

Celebrity Cruises: **www.celebritycruises.co.uk.**

Cunard: **www.cunard.co.uk.**

Fred Olsen Cruise Lines: **www.fredolsencruises.com.**

Hebridean Island Cruises: **www.hebridean.co.uk.**

Hurtigruten Norwegian Cruises: **www.hurtigruten.co.uk.**

NCL (Norwegian Cruise Line): **www.ncl.co.uk.**

Noble Caledonia: **www.noble-caledonia.co.uk.**

P&O Cruises: **www.pocruises.com.**

Page & Moy: **www.pageandmoy.com.**

Planet Cruise: **www.planetcruise.co.uk.**

Princess Cruises: **www.princess.com.**

Royal Caribbean International: **www.royalcaribbean.co.uk.**

Seabourn: **www.seabourn.com.**

SeaDream Yacht Club: **www.seadream.co.uk.**

Shearings Holidays: **www.shearings.com.**

Silversea: **www.silversea.com.**

Six Star Cruises: **www.sixstarcruises.co.uk.**

Titan HiTours River Cruises: **www.titanhitours.co.uk**.

Viking River Cruises: **www.vikingrivercruises.co.uk**

Voyages of Discovery: **www.voyagesofdiscovery.co.uk**.

Voyages to Antiquity: **www.voyagestoantiquity.com**.

Windstar Cruises: **www.windstarcruises.com**.

Cargo ship cruises

If price is one of the main considerations, travelling via cargo ship could be the solution. Accommodation and facilities (there is often a swimming pool) vary according to the size and type of vessel. A few of the best are:

Andrew Weir Shipping, website: **www.aws.co.uk**;

Cargo Ship Voyages, website: **www.cargoshipvoyages.com**;

Strand Voyages, website: **www.strandtravelltd.co.uk**.

Possibly the most unusual cruise in the world is on board one of the few Royal Mail ships still working. **RMS St Helena** is equipped to provide a relaxing cruise experience to the Island of St Helena, which is just a speck in the Atlantic ocean, south of the equator. The ship sails there from the UK and South Africa, calling at various islands along the way. See website: **www.rms-st-helena.com**.

Motoring holidays abroad

A number of organizations, including in particular some ferry operators, offer packages for the motorist that include ferry crossings, accommodation and insurance. While these often provide very good value, some people prefer to make all their own arrangements in order to get exactly what they want. Here are some of the major operators:

AA for all your motoring needs, at home and abroad, including route planning, maps, AA Five Star Europe Breakdown Assistance and travel service. See website: **www.theaa.com**.

Brittany Ferries, where holidays begin: sail and holiday choices, planning your trip, ferry bookings, holiday bookings, routes and timetables. See website: **www.brittany-ferries.co.uk**.

RAC for overseas single-trip or annual travel insurance, plus international driving permits and roadside assistance. See website: **www.rac.co.uk**.

Here are some *top tips* when motoring abroad, if taking your own vehicle:

Have your car thoroughly serviced before you go.

Make sure your GB sticker is clearly visible.

Check with the FCO for travel advice via their website.

Have headlight converters if driving in Europe.

Get insured for medical and travel purposes for the countries you are visiting.

Invest in a good guide book on your destination that advises on local customs and laws.

Check whether you require a green card for the countries you are visiting.

Make sure your passport is valid and you have necessary visas.

Find out about speed limits and if you require any specific equipment

Does your breakdown cover provide roadside assistance while abroad?

Make sure all documentation is easily available, should you need it.

Take the following with you: a tool kit, the manual for your car, a rented spares kit, a fuel can, a mechanic's light that plugs into the cigarette lighter socket, at least one extra set of keys, and any extras required by local laws such as a reflective tabard and warning triangles.

Always lock your car and park it in a secure place overnight (nearly 75 per cent of luggage thefts abroad are from cars).

Other sources of advice and services are:

Association of British Insurers, website: **www.abi.org.uk**;

Europ Assistance, website: **www.europ-assistance.co.uk**;

Green Flag, website: **www.greenflag.com**.

If instead of taking your own car you plan to hire a vehicle overseas, you will probably have to buy special insurance at the time of hiring the vehicle. Make sure that this is properly comprehensive (check for any excesses or exclusions) or, at the very least, it gives you adequate third-party cover. If in doubt, seek advice from the local motoring organization regarding essential requirements, and do not sign any documents unless you understand them.

How is your driving?

If you've recently travelled in a car and been frightened by a friend's driving, or you think you might be starting to scare others with your driving skills, it is simple enough to get yourself checked. The Institute of Advanced Motorists offers to assess anyone over 55 on their driving skills. It takes about an hour, while you go out with a tactful and helpful examiner. If you pass, you receive a clean bill of driving health. It would be sensible for anyone over 55 to take advantage of this exercise every few years or so. See the **IAM Driving Road Safety** website: **www.iam.org.uk**.

Short breaks

Many organizations offer short-break holidays all year round, with special bargain prices in spring and autumn. British hotels have winter breaks from November to April, and overseas travel operators slash prices during the off-peak seasons. Here are just a few websites to look at:

ACP Shortbreaks: **www.uk-short-break.co.uk**;

City Break Holidays: **www.citiesdirect.co.uk**;

Responsible Travel: **www.responsibletravel.com**;

Shortbreaks.com: **www.short-breaks.com**;

Shortbreak.UK.com: **www.shortbreak.uk.com**;

Superbreak: **www.superbreak.com**.

Timesharing

Timesharing is an investment in long-term holidays. The idea is that you buy the use of a property for a specific number of days each year, either for an agreed term or in perpetuity. Your timeshare can be lent to other people, sublet or left eventually in your will. Most timeshare schemes allow you to swap your week(s) for time in other developments throughout the world for your annual holiday, via one of the exchange companies.

A week's timeshare will vary in price – from £8,000 to over £50,000 depending on the location, the size of the property, the time of year and the facilities of the resort. Maintenance charges could cost another £250-plus a year, and you should always check that these are linked to some form of cost-of-living index such as the RPI. Another useful point to check is that there is an owners' association linked to the property.

While the great majority of people enjoy very happy experiences, there are still stories about unscrupulous operators. You should beware timeshare scratch cards and fraudulent holiday clubs that are not protected by the Timeshare Directive. A new Directive was passed into national law by all countries in the European Union in February 2011, replacing the old European Timeshare Directive. This one goes further by including timeshare exchange, resale and holiday clubs. It also covers fractional ownership. Also be wary of such enticing promotional gifts as a 'free' holiday flight to visit the property.

Most reputable companies belong to one of two worldwide exchange organizations: **RCI Europe**, website: **www.rci.com** or **Interval International Ltd**, website: **www.intervalworld.com**. You might also like to check whether the operator is a member of the **Resort Development Organisation** (RDO), which is the regulatory body dedicated to promoting the interests of all with a legitimate involvement in the industry. It offers potential buyers free advice and information and also has an arbitration scheme, run in conjunction with the Chartered Institute of Arbitrators, to handle complaints that are not resolved through its standard complaints-handling procedure. See website: **www.rdo.org**.

Existing owners wishing to sell their property should be on their guard against unknown resale agents contacting them 'on spec' and offering, in exchange for a registration fee, to act on their behalf. While some may be legitimate, the RDO has received complaints about so-called 'agents' taking money and doing nothing further. A telephone call to the RDO will establish whether the company is a member body. If not, leave well alone.

Holiday Property Bond

Although it has been in existence for more than 25 years, the **Holiday Property Bond** remains one of the best-kept secrets in the holiday industry. It is a uniquely flexible alternative to fixed-week timeshare and villa ownership. The bond is a life assurance bond that invests, after initial charges, in a combination of securities and carefully chosen holiday properties throughout the UK and Europe. By securing a financial interest in HPB's entire portfolio of villas, cottages and apartments, bondholders and their family and friends are entitled to use any bond property at any time – rent free. (It is a privilege that can be passed on, without charge, to holders' children and grandchildren too.) Find out more from the website: **www.hpb.co.uk**.

Rail holidays

You don't have to be a rail enthusiast to enjoy a holiday by train. There are many wonderful routes to travel and here are some useful websites to research:

www.diamondrailholidays.co.uk;

www.greatrail.com;

www.myrailtrip.co.uk;

www.orient-express.com;

www.railholidays.com;

www.seat61.com;

www.planetrail.co.uk .

Retreats

If peace and quiet is what you seek when you are on holiday, a retreat might be the answer. **The Retreat Association** has retreat centres all over Britain and Ireland. For further information see website: **www.retreats.org.uk**.

Self-catering and other low-budget holidays

If your days of managing on a fiver a day are over, you might like to consider some of the suggestions in this section. They may cost a bit more but not much. Camping, caravanning or renting very simple accommodation with friends may suit you if your budget is limited. There are also farm cottages, hostels, university accommodation and other rentals of varying degrees of sparseness or comfort; some suggestions are listed here:

Camping and Caravanning Club, website:
www.campingandcaravanningclub.co.uk.

English Country Cottages, website: **www.english-country-cottages.co.uk**.

Farm Stay UK Ltd, website: **www.farmstayuk.co.uk**.

Holiday Cottages in Scotland, website:
www.holiday-cottages.scotland.org.uk.

Landmark Trust restores historic buildings ranging from castles and moated properties to towers and follies, and lets them for holidays. See website: **www.landmarktrust.org.uk.**

National Trust Holiday Cottages has a wide variety of holiday cottages and flats in many areas of England, Wales and Northern Ireland. See website: **www.nationaltrustcottages.co.uk.**

National Trust for Scotland has a large number of holiday cottages available in all areas, as well as cruises. See website: **www.nts.org.uk.**

Venuemasters is a consortium of university and college venues that let residential accommodation during the vacation periods and other times of the year. See website: **www.venuemasters.co.uk.**

YHA (England and Wales) Ltd welcomes people of all ages. There are over 200 youth hostels in England and Wales and over 4,000 worldwide. See website: **www.yha.org.uk.**

Special interest holidays

This section includes weekend courses and more formal summer schools, between them offering a huge variety of subjects including crafts, computer studies, drama, archaeology, creative writing, photography and many others. It also includes holidays in the more conventional sense, both in Britain and abroad, but with the accent on a hobby such as bridge, dancing, yoga, photography, antiques and other pastimes. Many of the organizations offer a wide range of choices.

Centre for Alternative Technology offers a number of short courses on a variety of subjects including sustainable living, renewable energy, environmentally responsible building and organic gardening. See website: **www.cat.org.uk.**

Denman College, the WI's residential adult education college, runs over 500 short courses on craft, cookery, and lifestyle including art, antiques, IT, dance, drama, literature and aromatherapy. See website: **www.denmancollege.org.uk.**

Field Studies Council (FSC) offers hundreds of fieldwork and cross-curricular courses at its network of 17 centres throughout the UK. See website: **www.field-studies-council.org.**

HF Holidays Ltd is Britain's walking and leisure activity holiday provider with over 50,000 people going on holiday with it each year. See website: **www.hfholidays.co.uk**.

Mercian Travel Centre Ltd specializes in arranging bridge, bowling and special interest holidays to many destinations. See website: **www.merciantravel.co.uk**.

Opera Tours in Italy: experience the opera in the company of experts. Discover stunning Lucca and the Puccini Festival and much more. See website: **www.operatoursitaly.com**.

Painting and Cooking in Italy: holiday destinations include Venice, Florence, Cortona and Pienza. Non-painting and non-cooking partners welcome; a great holiday for people travelling on their own. See website: **www.paintinginitaly.com**.

The Peak District National Park Centre for Environmental Learning at Losehill Hall offers weekend and week-long special interest breaks, including painting and illustration, natural history, bird watching, navigation, photography and rambling. See website: **www.peakdistrict.gov.uk**.

Vegi-Ventures offers amazing natural health holidays in Britain, Turkey, Peru and the Caribbean, with great vegetarian/vegan food cooked especially for the group. Full range of holidays from the relaxing to the challenging. See website: **www.vegiventures.com**.

Sport

Holidays with on-site or nearby sporting facilities exist all over the country. The list that follows is limited to organizations that can advise you about organized residential courses or can offer facilities. For wider information, see Chapter 9, Leisure activities, which lists some of the national sports associations.

Sportscotland is the lead agency for the development of sport in Scotland. It runs three national sports centres that offer courses for all levels in golf, hill walking, skiing, sailing and many others. See website: **www.sportscotland.org.uk**.

Boating

Beautiful Boating Holidays, Europe's No 1 boating holiday company, offers the widest choice of beautiful boating holidays in Europe. See website: **www.leboat.co.uk**.

Blakes offers cruising, yacht and narrow boat holidays throughout all the main waterways of Britain and also in France and Ireland. Basic boating tuition is provided for novices. See website: **www.blakes.co.uk**.

Hoseasons Boating Holidays: choose from the Norfolk Broads, Cambridgeshire waterways, the Thames, and canals of England, Scotland and Wales, as well as waterways in France, Belgium, Holland, Italy and Ireland. See website: **www.hoseasons.co.uk**.

Royal Yachting Association (RYA) can supply a list of recognized schools that offer approved courses in sailing, windsurfing, motor cruising and power boating. See website: **www.rya.org.uk**.

UK Canal Boat Holiday Hire: the waterways of the UK provide some of the most relaxing and rewarding of all holidays. See website: **www.holidaycanalboat.co.uk**.

Cycling

CTC Cycling Holidays organizes cycling tours in Britain and overseas and helps cyclists who wish to arrange their own holiday. CTC offers members free third-party insurance, free legal aid and introductions to local cycling groups. See website: **www.cyclingholidays.org**.

Cycling for Softies. Susi Madron's Cycling Holidays were first to offer holidays on a bike with hotel stays in France. It now offers 12 regions throughout France with hotels including chateaux and Michelin-starred restaurants. See website: **www.cycling-for-softies.co.uk**.

Railways. Cycles are allowed on some trains. However, it is normally necessary to make an advance reservation, and there is usually a small charge to pay. See website: **www.nationalrail.co.uk**.

Golf

Some clubs will allow non-members to play on weekdays when the course is less busy, on payment of a green fee. Many hotels around the country offer special golfing weekends and short-break holidays.

Supertravel is the tour operating division of The Lotus Group, which offers a wide choice of golfing holidays overseas. Favourite destinations include Florida, Spain and the Algarve in Portugal. See website: **www. supertravel.co.uk**.

Rambling

Rambling features on many special interest and other programmes as one of the options on offer. Three organizations that specialize in rambling holidays are:

ATG Oxford: Founded in 1979, on principles of conservation and sustainable tourism, it offers journeys on foot along continuous routes through the most beautiful and interesting parts of Europe. The emphasis is on visiting places of historical, cultural or artistic interest, exploring the scenic highlights and dining out on the best local cuisine. See website: **www.atg-oxford.co.uk**.

Exodus is the original adventure and activity holiday company specializing in walking, cycling, winter activities, photographic and wildlife holidays. See website: **www.exodus.co.uk**.

Ramblers Worldwide Holidays offers a choice of over 250 fantastic walking and trekking holidays in around 65 countries, from sightseeing to adventurous walking holidays. See website: **www.ramblersholidays.co.uk**.

Skiing

Disability Snowsport UK, the skiers' and snowboarders' charity, has a vision that skiers and snowboarders with a disability should be able to ski alongside the able bodied as equals at all facilities and resorts. It aims to increase opportunities, fitness, mobility, freedom, social interaction and independence. See website: **www.disabilitysnowsport.org.uk**.

Ski Club of Great Britain runs skiing holidays in Austria, France, Italy, Switzerland, Canada and the United States. Qualified leaders accompany each group. See website: **www.skiclub.co.uk**.

Tennis

The **Lawn Tennis Association** (LTA) can provide details of residential courses at home and abroad. See website: **www.lta.org.uk**.

For other sporting holidays, see 'Tourist boards', below. Their websites give information on golfing, sailing and fishing holidays, pony trekking in Wales, skiing in Scotland and many others.

Wine tasting

Wine-tasting holidays are popular with many people and ensure plenty of variety with visits, talks, convivial meals, free time for exploring as well as memorable tastings.

Arblaster & Clarke Wine Tours offers the most imaginative and wide-ranging tours throughout the wine world. In 2012, this company celebrated its 25th anniversary. See website: **www.winetours.co.uk**.

Grape Escapes offers specialist wine tours to France and Spain, for all wine lovers. See website: **www.grapeescapes.net**

Winetasting Holidays offers the selective traveller on a limited budget a good range of vineyards and wineries to visit with a range of reasonably priced and convenient places to stay. See website: **www.winetastingholidays.com**

Working holidays

There is scope for volunteers who would like to engage in a worthwhile project during their holidays. Activities vary from helping run play schemes to conservation work. A few are listed here but most are mentioned in Chapter 12, Voluntary work:

British Trust for Conservation Volunteers (BTCV) encourages volunteers from both town and country to improve the environment, work with local business, young people and enjoy conservation breaks. A reasonable degree of fitness is required. See website: **www.btcv.org.uk**.

National Trust Working Holidays organizes around 450 week and weekend working holidays each year on Trust properties in England, Wales and Northern Ireland. Full guidance and instruction are given by Trust wardens, suitable for the reasonably fit and active of all ages. See website: **www.nationaltrust.org.uk**.

Toc H organizes short residential events throughout the year, with scope for volunteers running play schemes, activities with disabled people, conservation and manual work. See website: **www.toch-uk.org.uk**.

Golden gappers

Increasing numbers of middle-aged Britons are taking gap years: this is a popular trend among the baby boomers, with 59 per cent of this age group taking up to a year out. They are known as 'golden gappers' because they have time and money to spare and are willing to spend it trekking across the world. They are making up for lost time, so it seems that 'gapping' is no longer the preserve of the young.

The image for most people is of 'gappers' being young, backpack-laden people hiking around the world, communicating only when their credit card no longer works or their mobile phone has been lost or stolen. But it's now big business for the 50-plus age group. For a lot of people a career break is not as crazy as it sounds. After years of working in a high-pressure environment, taking a year out, rather like a sabbatical, to experience a complete contrast of culture and work ethic can be revitalizing. Leaving a job in the City to work as a volunteer with an AIDS charity in Africa – there's no greater contrast.

There are lots of 'golden gappers', 'denture venturers' or 'Saga louts' – whatever the media may call them: an estimated 200,000 pre-retirement gappers in the UK alone. Some of these people are both wealthy and adventurous. They were hippies in the 1960s and now have good earnings behind them. They have financial security, mortgage-free properties and children who are now adults themselves. Sometimes the younger generation refer to them as SKINs – spending kids' inheritance now.

A retirement gap is an opportunity to take control of your life, rather than drift into old age. If you think escaping on a gap year could be fun and want the latest information and advice, **Gapadvice** can help you. See website: **www.gapadvice.org**.

Holidays for singles

There is a number of people, who, if being completely honest, admit they would rather not go on holiday if it means travelling alone. Many of the special interest holidays listed on previous pages are ideal for those without a partner, as are some of the working holidays. However, there are a few organizations that cater specifically for solo holidaymakers, among others:

Exodus has great holidays for singles, as almost half their clients are solo travellers. They provide safety and security for people travelling on their own, and guaranteed single-room accommodation at very reasonable extra cost. See website: **www.exodus.co.uk**

Just You is the UK's No 1 travel specialist for single travellers. If you want to see the world but not on your own, this company offers singles inspirational holidays and tours. See website: **www.justyou.co.uk**.

One Traveller for singles. The escorted holidays are fully geared to the needs of mature single travellers, and small groups are escorted to Europe, Russia, Thailand and China. See website: **www.onetraveller.co.uk**.

Solo's Holidays specializes in arranging group holidays for single people, both in the UK and abroad. A vast choice of special interests is catered for, including opera, golf, cruises, walking holidays and many others. See website: **www.solosholidays.co.uk**.

Travel One has a wealth of experience in arranging holidays for single travellers who wish to travel with like-minded people, to make friends and enjoy a memorable stay in a destination of their choice. See website: **www.travelone.co.uk**.

Holidays for those needing special care

Over the past few years, facilities for infirm and disabled people have been improving. More hotels are providing wheelchairs and other essential equipment. Transport has become easier. Specially designed self-catering units are more plentiful and of a higher standard. Also, an increasing number of trains and coaches are installing accessible loos. Many people with disabilities can now travel perfectly normally, stay where they please and participate in entertainment and sightseeing without disadvantage.

Travel and other information

If you need help getting on and off a train or plane, inform your travel agent in advance. Arrangements can be made to have staff and a wheelchair available to help you at both departure and arrival points. If you are travelling independently, you should ring the airline and/or local station and explain what assistance you require, together with details of your journey, so that facilities can be arranged at any interim points, should you need to change trains.

Age UK can put individuals in touch with organizations that can assist with transport or that organize special care holidays. See website: **www.ageuk.org.uk**.

Choice Care Assisted Holidays offers a wide variety of holidays designed to be as comfortable and accommodating as possible. From the moment your holiday starts you will be assisted by two qualified helpers. Choice Care Holidays are fully inclusive. See website: **www.choicecareservices.co.uk**.

Tourism for All/Vitalise is the UK voice for accessible tourism. It can provide details about a wide range of suitable accommodation, facilities and services both in the UK and overseas and has information about hiring equipment for holiday use, accessible attractions and respite care centres. See website: **www.tourismforall.org.uk**.

Virgin Holidays has been much recommended, especially for holidays in the United States. It has a department dedicated to assisting passengers with special needs. It provides information and assistance to help with holiday arrangements and much more. Contact the Special Assistance Team; see website: **www.virginholidays.co.uk**.

Another source to contact is your local social services department. Some local authorities arrange holidays or give financial help to those in real need.

Tourist boards

If you plan to holiday within the UK and are looking for hotels and accommodation in Britain, or are simply after UK travel, attractions or event information, you will find everything you need to know at **Visit Britain**, website: **www.visitbritain.com**.

Regional tourist boards

England's regional tourist boards cover the following areas; the boards for Scotland and Wales are also listed:

East of England Tourism: Bedfordshire, Cambridgeshire, Essex, Hertfordshire, Norfolk and Suffolk; website: **www.visiteastofengland.com**.

East Midlands Tourism: Derbyshire, Leicestershire, Lincolnshire, Northamptonshire, Nottinghamshire and Rutland; website: **www.eastmidlandstourism.co.uk**.

Heart of England Tourism: Birmingham, Herefordshire, Shropshire, Staffordshire, Warwickshire, the West Midlands and Worcestershire; website: **www.heartofengland.com**.

North East Tourist Board: Durham, Northumberland, the Tees Valley, and Tyne and Wear; website: **www.visitnortheastengland.com**.

North West Regional Development Agency: Cheshire, Cumbria, Greater Manchester, Lancashire and Merseyside; website: **www.nwda.co.uk**.

South West Tourism: Bath, Bristol, Cornwall, Devon, Dorset, Gloucestershire, the Isles of Scilly, Somerset and Wiltshire; website: **www.swtourism.co.uk**.

Tourism South East: Berkshire, Buckinghamshire, East Sussex, Hampshire, the Isle of Wight, Kent, Oxfordshire, Surrey and West Sussex; website: **www.visitsoutheastengland.com**.

Visit London, website: **www.visitlondon.com**.

Visit Scotland, website: **www.visitscotland.com**.

Visit Wales, website: **www.visitwales.co.uk**.

Yorkshire Tourist Board: Northern Lincolnshire and Yorkshire; website: **www.yorkshire.com**.

Long-haul travel

The specialist organizations listed below can offer a great deal of practical information and help, as well as assist in obtaining low-cost fares, if you are planning to travel independently. Round-the-world air tickets are an excellent buy. Travel agents may also achieve savings by putting together routes using various carriers. Most airlines offer seasonal discounts that sometimes include a couple of nights' concessionary hotel stay, if you want to break your journey or visit another country at minimum extra travel cost.

Trailfinders Travel Centre has 27 local travel centres across the UK and Ireland; its award-winning consultants are on hand seven days a week to offer ideas, inspiration and exceptional value for your next holiday. See website: **www.trailfinders.com**.

Voyages Jules Verne has over 30 years' experience in tours that span the globe, following carefully devised itineraries by air, road, river and rail that capture the true essence of your chosen destination. See website: **www.vjv.com**.

WEXAS is the leading travel club for leisure and business club travellers. Founded in 1970 by Dr Ian Wilson, with distinguished honorary presidents including Sir Ranulph Fiennes, John Simpson and Michael Palin, its members and staff share a passion for travel. See website: **www.wexas.com**.

Visa and passport requirements

All too many people get caught out at the airport by not keeping up to date with the visa and other requirements of the country to which they are travelling. These sometimes change without much warning and, at worst if you get it wrong, can result in your being turned away on arrival.

Don't get caught out at customs when you return from a non-EU trip. You can now bring back up to £390 worth of goods (excluding alcohol and tobacco) without paying import duties or VAT. But you can't split items – you have to pay the full bill on, say, a £500 camera and not just the balance over £390. And you can't share a high-value item with someone else either. See website: **www.hmrc.gov.uk/customs**.

Health and safety advice

This sometimes changes and travel agents are not always as good as they should be about keeping customers informed. The best advice, especially if you are travelling out of Europe, including to the United States, is to check the **Foreign Office** website (**www.fco.gov.uk**) and consult the section on 'travel advice'. The best plan is to do this several weeks before departure, to allow time for any inoculations, and again just before you leave.

Insurance

Holiday insurance, once you are over the age of 65, is not only more difficult to obtain but also tends to be considerably more expensive. However, were you unfortunate enough to fall ill or experience some other mishap, it would almost certainly cost you very much more than paying a bit extra for decent insurance. Age UK offers insurance policies for the over-60s, and other firms that cater for people in their 60s and 70s are American Express and Saga. Another company is **Insurance Choice**, which has a wide variety of policies to choose from. See website: **www.insurancechoice.co.uk**. Alternatively you could look at **Onestop4:Travel Insurance**; see website: **www.onestop4.co.uk**.

Made-to-measure travel insurance for **Motability** customers and supporters is flexible, and you can choose whether you want cover for cancellation and/or winter sports. See website: **www.motability.co.uk/travelinsurance**.

Many tour operators try to insist that, as a condition of booking, you either buy their inclusive insurance package or make private arrangements that are at least as good. While this suggests that they are demanding very high standards, terms and conditions vary greatly. Before signing on the dotted line, you should read the small print carefully. Be sure to check that the package you are being offered meets all the eventualities and provides you with adequate cover should you make a claim.

Although older people may not find it easy to get cover, there is still a range of policies available and some do not employ upper age limits. With travel insurance you will need to disclose any pre-existing medical conditions fully before you can get a quote. If you are travelling independently, it is even more important to be properly insured. Under these circumstances you will not be protected by the normal compensation that the reputable tour operators provide for claims for which they could be held liable in the event of a mishap.

Here are some *top tips* when buying holiday insurance. Your policy should cover you for:

medical expenses, including hospital treatment and the cost of an ambulance, an air ambulance and emergency dental treatment, plus expenses for a companion who may have to remain overseas with you should you become ill;

personal liability cover, should you cause injury to another person or property;

personal accident leading to injury or death (check the small print, as some policies have reduced cover for older travellers);

additional hotel and repatriation costs resulting from injury or illness;

loss of deposit or cancellation (check what emergencies or contingencies this covers);

the cost of having to curtail your holiday, including extra travel expenses, because of serious illness in the family;

compensation for inconvenience caused by flight cancellations or other travel delays;

cover for baggage and personal effects and for emergency purchases should your baggage be delayed;

cover for loss of personal money and documents.

If you are planning to take your car abroad you will need to check your existing car insurance to ensure that you are properly covered. Alternatively, if you are planning to hire a vehicle overseas, you will need to take out fully comprehensive insurance cover (which you may need to purchase while on holiday).

Before purchasing new insurance, check whether any of the above items are already covered under an existing policy. This might well apply to your personal possessions and to medical insurance. Even if the policy is not sufficiently comprehensive for travel purposes, it will be better and cheaper in the long run to pay a small supplement to give you the extra cover you need than to buy a holiday insurance package from a tour operator. A cost-effective plan may be to extend any existing medical insurance to cover you while abroad. Then take out a separate policy (without medical insurance) to cover you for the rest of your travel needs.

The Association of British Insurers suggests the following guidelines in respect of the amount of cover holidaymakers should be looking for in their policy:

Cancellation or curtailment of holiday: the full cost of your holiday, as well as the deposit and any other charges paid in advance, plus cover for any extra costs should you be forced to return early. Depending on the policy, cover is normally limited to a maximum of £5,000 per person.

Money and travel documents: £500. Some companies offer additional cover for lost or stolen documents. Normally there is a limit of £200 to £300 for cash.

Luggage/belongings: £1,500 (NB: check the limit on single articles).

Delayed baggage: £100 for emergency purchases in the event that luggage is lost en route and arrives late.

Delayed departure: policies vary greatly. A number pay around £20 to £30 if departure is delayed by more than a certain number of hours. Some will allow you to cancel your holiday once departure has been delayed by over 12 hours, with cover normally limited to the same as for cancellation. If risk of delay is a serious concern, you should check the detail of your policy carefully.

Personal liability: up to £2 million.

It is essential that you take copies of the insurance documents with you, as losses or other claims must normally be reported immediately. You will also be required to quote the reference number and/or other details given on the docket. Additionally, there may be particular guidelines laid down by the policy. For instance, you may have to ring a helpline before incurring medical expenses. Failure to report a claim within the specified time limit could nullify your right to compensation. The best advice is to check that you have the 24-hour helpline number and to keep it with you at all times.

Be sure to get a receipt for any special expenses you incur – extra hotel bills, medical treatment, long-distance phone calls and so on. You may not get all the costs reimbursed, but if your insurance covers some or all of these contingencies you will need to produce evidence of your expenditure.

The Association of British Insurers has information on holiday insurance and motoring abroad. See website: **www.abi.org.uk**.

The Association of British Travel Agents (ABTA) operates a code of conduct for all travel agents and tour operators that are ABTA members and helps holidaymakers seek redress if they are dissatisfied with their travel company. See website: **www.abta.com**.

Compensation for lost baggage

If the airline on which you are travelling loses or damages your baggage, you should be able to claim compensation up to a maximum value of about £850. (The figure may vary slightly up or down, depending on currency fluctuations.)

Cancelled or overbooked flights

Also useful to know about is the **Denied Boarding Regulation**, which entitles passengers who cannot travel because their flight is overbooked to some immediate cash payment. This applies even if the airline puts them up in a hotel or books them on to an alternative flight a few hours later. To qualify, passengers must have a confirmed reservation and have checked in on time. Also, the airport where they were 'bumped off' must be in an EU country. (It may sometimes also be possible to get compensation in the United States.)

If, as opposed to being overbooked, your flight is cancelled, you are entitled to get a refund if you decide not to travel. Alternatively, you can request to be re-routed. You may get compensation depending on the length of your journey and how long you are delayed. If the delay is more than two hours, you will also be entitled to meals or refreshments plus two free telephone calls, e-mails or faxes. If it is overnight and you have more than five hours' wait, you will be put up in a hotel and given free transfers. Compensation is not, however, obligatory if the cancellation is due to 'extraordinary circumstances which could not have been avoided'. See the **Aviation Consumer Advocacy Panel** website: **www.caa.co.uk**.

If you miss your flight or have to cancel your trip, you may be able to get a refund on at least a small part of the ticket cost. Most airlines will reimburse non-fliers for the air passenger duty and overseas government taxes. This applies even to normal non-refundable tickets. However, you have to make a claim, and in most cases there is an administration charge payable. If you booked through a travel agent, there could be a second administration charge. Even so, especially for long-haul travel and family holidays, the savings could be quite considerable.

Medical insurance

This is one area where you should never skimp on insurance. Although many countries now have reciprocal arrangements with the UK for emergency medical treatment, these vary greatly in both quality and generosity. Some treatments are free, as they are on the National Health Service; others, even in some EU countries, may be charged for as if you were a private patient.

The Department of Health has advice for travellers. In particular you should get a **European Health Insurance Card** (EHIC). This card entitles the holder to free or discounted medical treatment at state-run hospitals and GPs in any EEA (European Economic Area) country plus Iceland, Liechtenstein, Norway and Switzerland. But it is not insurance and will not, for instance, arrange for repatriation, nor pay for a hotel room if you have to extend your stay to look after a sick relative. There is no charge for an EHIC. The EHIC replaced the E111 form in January 2006 and it is completely free and valid for five years. All UK residents are eligible, though residents of the Channel Islands and Isle of May are not. Each person, including members of the same family, requires his or her own individual card. If you already have one, check that your card has not expired, because if it has, it can easily be renewed. To obtain a card, or to renew one, go to the European Health Insurance Card website: **www.ehic.org.uk**, or you can apply by post using the application form available from the Post Office.

However, even the very best reciprocal arrangements may not be adequate in the event of a real emergency. Moreover, they certainly will not cover you for any additional expenses you may incur. In the United States the cost of medical treatment is astronomical. For peace of mind, most experts recommend cover of £1 million for most of the world and up to £2 million for the United States. Some policies offer higher or even unlimited cover. Although theoretically there is no upper age limit if you want to take out medical insurance, some insurance companies are very difficult about insuring older travellers. Many request a note from a qualified medical practitioner stating that you are fit to travel if you are over 75, or require you to confirm that you are not travelling against medical advice.

Another common requirement is that the insured person should undertake not to indulge in any dangerous pursuits, which is fine in theory but in practice (depending on the company's interpretation of 'dangerous') could debar you from any activity that qualifies as 'strenuous'.

Book through a reputable operator

Many of the sad tales of woe one hears could have been avoided, or at least softened by compensation. It is essential that holidaymakers check to ensure that their travel agent or tour operator is affiliated to either ABTA or the Association of Tour Operators (ATO). Both organizations have strict regulations that all member companies must follow, and both run an arbitration scheme in the event of complaints. No one can guarantee you against every mishap, but a recognized travel company plus adequate insurance should go a long way towards giving you at least some measure of protection.

Travel and other concessions

Buses, coaches, some airline companies and especially the railways offer valuable concessions to people of retirement age.

Trains

Some of the best-value savings that are available to anyone aged 60 and over are provided by train companies. These include:

Disabled Persons Railcard: costs £20 for one year or £54 for three years and entitles the holder and one accompanying adult to reduced train fares. See website: **www.disabledpersons-railcard.co.uk**.

Family Friends Railcard: costs £28 for a whole year and entitles up to four adults and four children to travel on one card. Adults get one-third off and children get 60 per cent off the normal child fare. See website: **www.familyandfriends-railcard.co.uk**.

Network Railcard: costs £28 and is valid for 12 months, available only in London and the south-east. It gives a one-third reduction on most standard-class fares after 10 am, Monday to Friday. Up to three adults can travel with you and they will also get a third off their fares, and you can take four children with you and save 60 per cent on their fares. See website: **www.railcard.co.uk**.

Senior Railcard: for those aged 60-plus, costs £28 for one year and entitles you to a third off standard and first-class fares, plus discounts on hotels, restaurants and days out. See website: **www.senior-railcard.co.uk**.

Buses and coaches

Over 11 million people over 60 in the UK use buses for free travel around the country. Make the most of this while you can: it is reported that the government has plans to raise the eligible age gradually to 65:

If you live in **England**, over-60s and disabled people can travel free on local buses anywhere in England between 9.30 am and 11 pm on weekdays and all day weekends and public holidays.

If you live in **Scotland**, over-60s and disabled people can travel free on local buses and scheduled long-distance coach services in Scotland at any time – no time restrictions.

If you live in **Wales**, over-60s and disabled people can travel free on local buses in Wales at any time. People living in Wales can also use their passes to travel free on cross-boundary journeys into and out of England, provided the journey starts or finishes in Wales.

Bus passes are usually issued free by local authorities. **Arriva** has further information; see website: **www.arriva.co.uk**. There are often reduced rates for senior citizens on long-distance buses and coaches. For example, discounts of 33 per cent apply on **National Coaches** on both ordinary and Rapide services. If you are planning to travel by coach, it is worth shopping around to find out what bargains are available.

Airlines

Several of the airlines offer attractive discounts to older travellers. The terms and conditions vary, with some carriers offering across-the-board savings and others limiting them to selected destinations. Likewise, in some cases the qualifying age is 60; in others, it is a couple of years older. A particular bonus is that concessions are often extended to include a companion travelling at the same time. Ask your travel agent or the airline at the time of booking what special discounts, if any, are offered.

Overseas

Many countries offer travel and other reductions to retired holidaymakers including, for example, discounts for entry to museums and galleries, day excursions, sporting events and other entertainment. As in Britain, provisions are liable to change, and for up-to-date information probably the best source to contact is the national tourist office of the country to which you are travelling. All EEA countries – as well as most lines in Switzerland – give 25 per cent reductions on international rail fares. These are available to holders of a Railplus Card who are purchasing international rail travel tickets and are applicable to both first- and second-class travel.

Airport meet-and-greet services

If you hate the hassle of parking your car in the long-term car park and collecting it again on your return after a long journey, **BCP** offers a better choice for parking. It operates a meet-and-greet service at six airports (Heathrow, Gatwick, Stansted, Birmingham, Manchester and Edinburgh). See website: **www.parkbcp.co.uk**.

A number of firms offer a similar service but, at the time of booking, enquire where your car will be parked and, when dropping it off it would be sensible to ask for a 'conditions form' to complete, to avoid disputes if you find any damage on your return.

Health tips for travellers

Remember to pack any regular medicines you require: even familiar branded products can be difficult to obtain in some countries.

Take a mini first-aid kit, including plasters, disinfectant, tummy pills and so on.

If you are going to any developing country, consult your doctor as to what pills (and any special precautions) you should take.

One of the most common ailments among British travellers abroad is an overdose of sun. In some countries it really burns, so take it easy, wear a hat and apply plenty of protective lotion.

The other big travellers' woe is 'Delhi belly', which unhappily can occur in most hot countries, including Italy and Spain. Beware the water, ice, salads, seafood, ice cream and any fruit that you do not peel yourself.

Always wash your hands before eating or handling food, particularly if you are camping or caravanning.

Travelling is tiring and a sudden change of climate more debilitating than most of us admit. Allow plenty of time during the first couple of days to acclimatize before embarking on any activity programme.

Have any inoculations or vaccinations well in advance of your departure date.

When flying, wear loose clothes and above all comfortable shoes, as feet and ankles tend to swell in the air.

To avoid risk of deep vein thrombosis, which can be fatal, medical advice is to do foot exercises and walk around the plane from time to time. For long-haul travel especially, wear compression stockings and, another tip, unless advised otherwise by your doctor, take an aspirin before flying.

On long journeys, it helps to drink plenty of water and remember the warning that 'an alcoholic drink in the air is worth two on the ground'. If you have a special diet, inform whoever makes your booking. Most airlines, especially on long-distance journeys, serve vegetarian food.

Department of Health leaflet T7, 'Health advice for travellers', contains essential information and advice on what precautions to take when you travel abroad and how to cope in an emergency. See website: **www.dh.gov.uk**.

Finally, the old favourite: don't drink and drive.

Chapter Fifteen
Caring for elderly parents

Nothing is more responsible for the good old days than a bad memory. **FRANKLIN PIERCE ADAMS, JOURNALIST**

An extract from a local newsletter, written by a resident:

> Tips for growing older gracefully include not losing touch with friends, even if email is the best way of staying in contact. Should you lose friends, don't be afraid of making new ones, even if they are all younger than you. You should not rely on your family to do everything. Be a good neighbour – it is so important. Don't be too dependent on the TV, it's a fantasy world. Try not to be too grumpy, though it often is tempting. Read everything you can; stimulating the brain keeps the body alive. Don't be afraid of computers – they are easily set up and learnt.

The writer is 90 years old.

If you think back to when the NHS was founded, half the population didn't reach the age of 65. Now we are living much longer, but this is a triumph, not a disaster. Recently an 83-year-old man became Britain's oldest living kidney donor. Last year two British centenarians were officially crowned the oldest sisters in the world, after notching up an astonishing 213 years between them. They entered the *Guinness Book of World Records* and had an emotional reunion to celebrate their landmark achievement. Pensioners have, for years, devoted their time to raising their families, holding generations together, looking after their own parents or other relatives. It is only the older generation who have experienced living through depressions or recessions. They know what it is like not to have a job, to really struggle and manage on very little. The WRVS is one of the leading organizations in the field of social care, with a growing army of volunteers who give positive and practical help to the elderly, to enable them to grow older with 'choice, independence and dignity'. And rightly so: the elderly have made a massive contribution to society which has been either hidden or not recognized, in quantifiable terms. This is the generation that has got community values and community spirit at its heart. Because of the war, they are used to pulling together and helping each other. They didn't give up; they have kept on working hard for Britain. So we should, at least, give them as much emotional help and financial support as possible when they need it.

But how will dutiful, middle-aged couples manage? Many are caring for their parents, while still supporting financially their teenagers or 20-somethings. The demands of Britain's ageing population means the 'coping classes' are increasingly struggling with the responsibility of looking after two generations at once. The economic situation and the government's spending cuts have made matters worse and squeezed this generous generation to breaking point. For many families, caring for elderly parents or relatives is a moral duty. Already one in four women and one in five men in their 50s is a carer. Alarmingly, the number of elderly relatives needing informal care is expected to increase by 90 per cent over the next 25 years.

The results of a recent survey by Age UK on the 'isolation of elderly parents', conducted among over-55s, revealed that 45 per cent of people put the lack of parental visits down to simply being 'too busy', with 29 per cent blaming work commitments. More than four in 10 said they live 'too far away' from their parents to visit regularly. Over a third, however, confessed to feeling guilty that they do not pop in to check on their parents enough. Four out of 10 of the over-55s wished that their own children got in touch more. Yet interestingly, more than a quarter of grown-up children wish their parents made more effort to get in touch with them. The study also revealed that despite the lack of contact, three-quarters of children would be happy to look after their parents, if they needed caring for later in life. Living in isolation and loneliness is a stark reality for many older people. However, family and friends play a crucial role in helping people in their later life stay connected and involved with their community. It is so important that everyone keeps in touch regularly with older friends and family – especially those who may be isolated or unable to leave their home due to mobility issues or illness. With so many different methods of communication available to everyone today, surely it is possible to find a suitable way of keeping in touch with our older relatives?

The undoubted preference for most elderly people is that they remain in their own homes for as long as possible. With a bit of support from friends, relatives or local care organizations, many can and will be able to do this.

The main focus of this chapter is on helping aged parents remain as independent as possible, for as long as possible, until a care home or nursing home becomes necessary. Knowing what facilities are available and what precautions your parents can take against a mishap occurring is an important factor. Being aware of whom they can turn to in an emergency can make all the difference. There is now much greater awareness of the needs of the elderly, mostly in regard to the financial implications of funding older people's care. In line with this, many provisions for the elderly have improved enormously.

It is possible to find out from your local authority what programmes operate in your area that can help. With a bit of research you might discover that there is a scheme such as Your Circle (a website which is a mine of local information – see **www.yourcircle.org.uk**) giving advice and practical help. It is a support network of trusted people, places and services, to assist elderly people in leading an independent life for as long as possible. It is designed to bring together all those things that help older people keep their independence. These include local social clubs, financial advice, volunteering opportunities, support groups, help in the home and much more. It also helps them to get more out of life.

Since everything today depends on computers to a greater or lesser extent, remember that some oldies (the over-80s group in particular) may not have access to the internet at home. These people are fast becoming 'digitally excluded' because so much information is readily available to download. Websites are now the first stop for any research that is needed (whether it involves purchasing a new toaster or going on an exotic cruise). If possible, encourage your relatives to invest in a computer, or buy them one as a present, then help them get connected. Some over-75s become IT savvy very quickly – they may be old but they are still curious – finding the benefits far outweigh the fears they once had. A number really enjoy the ability to Skype, they have visual contact and conversation with friends and relatives across the world. However, should they adamantly refuse to go online themselves, it is sometimes possible, if you are a friend, family member or trusted contact, to invite them over and show them how simple it is to keep up to date and connected with information, events and news of family and friends via your computer. With mobile technology becoming easier and faster, perhaps it is an idea when next visiting to take along your own laptop to show them what they're missing.

It is well worth investing a bit of time finding out where help and support can be accessed and familiarizing yourself (on your parents' behalf) with how to source funding or access equipment and personal aids. A bit of time spent now improving their home to make it easier to cope as they get older, and fine-tuning their social and support network, might make all the difference and help them maintain their independence for longer. Many families face the difficult choice between moving parents in to live with them and allowing them to continue to live on their own. While the decision will depend on individual circumstances, in the early stages at least the majority choice on all sides is usually to 'stay put'. Later in the chapter we cover sheltered housing, which some people see as the best of all worlds. Meanwhile, to postpone moving, the best solution for most elderly people is to adapt their home to make it safer and more convenient.

Ways of adapting a home

Many elderly people will not require anything more complicated than a few general improvements. These could include better lighting, especially near staircases, a non-slip mat and grab rails in the bathroom, and safer heating arrangements. For some, a practical improvement might be to lower kitchen and other units, to place them within easy reach and make cooking less hazardous. Another fairly simple option is to convert a downstairs room into a bedroom and en suite bath or shower, should managing the stairs be proving difficult. These and other common-sense measures are covered in more detail in Chapter 8, Your home. Should such arrangements not really be sufficient, in the case of a physically handicapped or disabled person, more radical changes will usually be needed. This involves accessing help from the GP and local authority.

Local authority help

The state system is designed to support the elderly in their own home for as long as possible. Local authorities have a legal duty to help people with disabilities and, depending on what is required and the individual's ability to pay, may assist with the cost. Best advice is to approach their GP or contact the social services department direct. A sympathetic doctor will be crucial support at this stage, particularly if he or she has known them for some years and is familiar with their circumstances. The GP will be able to advise what is needed and supply any prescriptions, such as for a medical hoist, and will also be able to suggest which unit or department to approach, and make a recommendation to the housing department, should re-housing be desirable. If your parents can afford it, they will have to pay for the services they need themselves. If their income and savings are low, the council may pay part or all of the cost.

Personal budgets

Increasingly, councils no longer provide services themselves. Instead your parents are offered cash so that they can choose and buy in the services they need. The council gives contact details for local providers. Local councils have now put in place a system of 'personal budgets'. Under this system, the cash allocated to your parents is paid into an account in their name. While they choose the services they need, either they or the local authority can commission and pay for them from that account. If they need medical care in their own home, such as visits from the district nurse to change dressings or administer drugs, this is free on the NHS. With budget cuts it is vital that local councils continue to prioritize spending on social care by ring-fencing the funding they have been given. Unless they do, the dignity and independence of older and disabled people will be undermined and more families will be forced to shoulder the responsibility of caring for them.

In *Scotland* free personal care for the elderly has been in place since 2002. Under the policy, over-65s who live at home are not charged for personal care services. Those paying their own way in care homes get a weekly allowance for personal and nursing care.

In *Northern Ireland* a recent survey suggested many elderly people were worried about reduced incomes, higher taxes and cuts in vital services. Pensioners here are at a significant risk of poverty in comparison to their counterparts in Great Britain and the Irish Republic.

In *Wales* the current legislation operates on an England and Wales basis, yet while social care is a devolved matter, the UK benefits system that impacts on charging for care is not. Both the Welsh Assembly government and the UK government have emphasized that any new system must promote independence, choice and control for everyone who uses care and support services, as well as being affordable to government, individuals and families in the long term.

Help with home repair and adaptations

Disabled facilities grant

This is a local council grant to help towards the cost of adapting a home to enable a disabled or elderly person to live there. It can cover a wide range of improvements to help the occupants manage more independently. This includes work to facilitate access either to the property itself or to the main rooms, like the widening of doors or the installation of ramps or a lift; the provision of suitable bathroom or kitchen facilities; the adaptation of heating or lighting controls; improvement of the heating system, and various other works where these would make a home safe for a disabled person. Provided the applicant is eligible, currently a mandatory grant of up to £30,000 in England, £25,000 in Northern Ireland and £36,000 in Wales may be available. See website: **www.gov.uk** – Disabled Facilities Grant.

Home Improvement Agencies (HIAs)

Foundations is the national body for Home Improvement Agencies in **England.** HIAs help older and vulnerable people maintain their independence by providing housing-related support. For more information about how home improvement agencies can help, see website: **www.foundations.uk.com**. If your parents live in **Wales**, see **Care and Repair Cymru: www.careandrepair.org.uk**, or in **Scotland: www.careandrepairscotland.co.uk**.

> **Age UK** (website: **www.ageuk.org.uk**) and the **British Red Cross** (website: **www.redcross.org.uk**) can loan equipment in the short term and may also be able to advise on local stockists. Larger branches of Boots, for example, sell a wide range of special items for people with disabilities, including bath aids, wheelchairs and crutches.

> **Assist UK** leads a UK-wide network of locally situated disabled living centres. Each centre includes a permanent exhibition of products and equipment, giving people opportunities to see and try products and equipment and get information and advice from professional staff. See website: **www.assist-uk.org**.

> **CAE** (Centre for Accessible Environments) offers a range of access consultancy services customized to the needs of clients. See website: **www.cae.org.uk**.

> **DEMAND** (Design & Manufacture for Disability) is an independent charity that transforms the lives of disabled people through the provision of bespoke equipment. It does not charge clients for its services. See website: **www.demand.org.uk**.

> **Disability Wales/Anabledd Cymru** is another helpful source of advice. See website: **www.disabilitywales.org**.

Disabled Living Foundation (DLF) is one of the UK's leading health charities, providing impartial advice and information to people of all ages, to help them find equipment to assist with everyday tasks essential to independent living. See website: **www.dlf.org.uk**.

Hearing and Mobility has a range of mobility aids and equipment that is available online or through a number of outlet stores nationwide. See website: **www.hearingandmobility.co.uk**.

REMAP is a special charity working through volunteers who use their ingenuity and skills to enable people with disabilities to achieve much-desired independence. It has 85 panels across the country, and helps over 3,000 people each year. See website: **www.remap.org.uk**.

Alarm systems

Alarm systems for the elderly are many and varied, but the knowledge that help can be summoned quickly in the event of an emergency is reassuring in its own right to many elderly or disabled people. Having a personal alarm can enable many people to remain independent far longer than would otherwise be sensible. Some alarm systems allow people living in their own homes to be linked to a central control, or have a telephone link, enabling personal contact to be made. Others simply signal that something is wrong. Sometimes a relative or friend who has been nominated will be alerted. Your parents' local authority social services department will have information. See website: **www.gov.uk**.

Commercial firms

A number of firms install and operate alarm systems. Price, installation cost and reliability can vary quite considerably.

DLF (Disabled Living Foundation): see website: **www.dlf.org.uk**.

Contact4me is an identification, next of kin and medical alert notification service. It ensures that if anything should happen to an elderly person, the emergency services on the scene receive fast and secure access to the person's identity, next of kin and vital medical alerts. See website: **www.contact4me.com**.

Helpline Limited: Nationwide monitored personal alarms for the elderly and disabled. See website: **www.helpline.co.uk**.

Community alarms

Telephone alarm systems operated on the public telephone network can be used by anyone with a direct telephone line. The systems link into a 24-hour monitoring centre and the individual has a pendant that enables help to be called even when the owner is some distance from the telephone. Grants may be available in some cases to meet the costs.

Age UK Personal Alarm Service gives independence when you want it, help when you need it. Friends and family are only a button press away. See website: **www.ageuk.org.uk**.

SeniorLinkEldercare provides a combination of equipment and personal intervention that helps people to live safely and independently in their homes. See website: **www.seniorlinkeldercare.com**.

Main local authority services

Quite apart from any assistance with housing, local authorities supply a number of services that can prove invaluable to an elderly person. The two most important are meals on wheels and home helps. Additionally, there are social workers and various specialists concerned with aspects of health. Since the introduction of Community Care, local authority social services departments have taken over all responsibility for helping to assess and coordinate the best arrangements for individuals according to their particular requirements.

Other organizations which may offer home help include the British Red Cross, website: **www.redcross.org.uk**, and Age UK, website: **www.ageuk.org.uk**.

Meals on wheels

The meals on wheels service is sometimes run by local authorities direct and sometimes by voluntary organizations, such as WRVS, acting as their agents. The purpose is to deliver ready-made meals to individuals in their own homes. Different arrangements apply in different areas, and schemes variously operate from two to seven days a week, or possibly less frequently if frozen meals are supplied. For further information, contact the local social services department or see website: **www.gov.uk** – Meals at home services.

The **WRVS** delivers over 6 million meals a year to people who have difficulty with shopping, carrying food home or cooking for themselves. For further information see website: **www.wrvs.org.uk**.

Home helps

Local authorities have a legal obligation to run a home-help service to help frail and housebound elderly people with such basic household chores as shopping, tidying up, a little light cooking and so on. In many areas the service is badly overstretched, so the amount of help actually available varies considerably, as does the method of charging. A health and social care assessment with the social services department of your local council is often the first step towards getting the help and support your parents need. See website: **www.gov.uk** – Disabled people.

Specialist helpers

Local authorities employ a number of specialist helpers, variously based in the social services department or health centre, who are there to assist:

Social workers are normally the first people to contact if your parents need a home help or meals on wheels, or have a housing difficulty or other query. Contact the local social services department or, in Scotland, the social work department.

Occupational therapists have a wide knowledge of disability and can assist individuals via training, exercise or access to aids, equipment or adaptations to the home. Contact the local social services department.

Health visitors are qualified nurses with a broad knowledge of health matters and other available services. Rather like social workers, health visitors can put your parents in touch with whatever specialized facilities are required. Contact is through the local health centre.

District nurses are fully qualified nurses who will visit a patient in the home, change dressings, attend to other routine nursing matters, monitor progress and help with the arrangements if more specialized care is required. Contact is through the health centre.

Physiotherapists use exercise and massage to help improve mobility and strengthen muscles, for example after an operation or to alleviate a crippling condition. They are normally available at both hospitals and health centres.

Medical social workers (MSWs) (previously known as almoners) are available to consult if patients have any problems – whether practical or emotional – on leaving hospital. MSWs can advise on coping with a disablement, as well as such practical matters as transport, after-care and other immediate arrangements. They work in hospitals, and an appointment should be made before the patient is discharged.

Good neighbour schemes

A number of areas of the country have an organized system of good neighbour schemes. In essence, these consist of volunteers agreeing to act as good neighbours to one or several elderly people living close by. Depending on what is required, they may simply pop in on a daily basis to check that everything is all right, or they may give more sustained assistance such as providing help with dressing, bathing, shopping or preparing a light meal. To find out whether such a scheme exists locally, ask social services, your parents' health centre, the Citizens Advice Bureau or look on the internet.

Key voluntary organizations

Voluntary organizations complement the services provided by statutory health and social services in making life easier for elderly people living at home. The range of provision varies from area to area but can include:

lunch clubs;

holidays and short-term placements;

day centres and clubs;

friendly visiting;

aids such as wheelchairs;

transport;

odd jobs and decorating;

gardening;

good neighbour schemes;

prescription collection;

advice and information;

family support schemes.

The particular organization providing these services depends on where your parents live, but the best organization to advise you is the local Citizens Advice Bureau. These are the key agencies:

Age UK, website: **www.ageuk.org.uk**;

Age Scotland, website: **www.agescotland.org.uk**;

Age Wales, website: **www.agecymru.org.uk**;

Age Northern Ireland, website: **www.ageni.org.uk**;

Disability Wales, website: **www.disabilitywales.org**;

Update (Scotland's disability information service), website: **www.update.org.uk**;

Care Information Scotland, website: **www.careinfoscotland.co.uk**;

Centre for Individual Living, Northern Ireland, website: **www.cilbelfast.org**.

British Red Cross supplies some important services to elderly people such as: helping sick, disabled or frail people make essential journeys; loaning medical equipment for short-term use at home and on holiday; providing home-from-hospital support: easing the transition of patients to their own home after discharge; 'signposting' vulnerable people towards the statutory or voluntary services by which their needs may best be met. They make thousands of home care visits to help those struggling after leaving hospital, or managing on their own. See website: **www.redcross.org.uk**.

St John Ambulance has over 45,000 volunteers providing first aid and care services, helping in hospitals and offering practical help in other ways such as shopping, collecting pensions, staying with an elderly person for a few hours or providing transport to and from hospital. See website: **www.sja.org.uk**.

WRVS runs many local projects: books on wheels; social transport; meals on wheels; good neighbour schemes; lunch clubs; a meal delivery service for those not qualifying for meals on wheels. For services available in your area, see website: **www.wrvs.org.uk**.

Other sources of help and advice include:

Civil Service Retirement Fellowship is a charity dedicated to helping former civil servants, their partners, widows, widowers and dependants. See website: **www.csrf.org.uk**.

Counsel and Care is a national charity working with older people, their families and carers to get the best care and support. It provides personalized, in-depth help and advice. See website: **www.counselandcare.org.uk**.

Disability Alliance is a national registered charity that provides help and information including the *Disability Rights Handbook*, which is a mine of information on benefits and rights for the disabled. See website: **www.disabilityalliance.org**.

Jewish Care provides services for elderly Jewish people, including those who are mentally ill, in London and the south-east of England. Principal facilities include: special day-care centres; residential and nursing homes; community centres; a home care service for the housebound; and short-term respite care. See website: **www.jewishcare.org**.

National Centre for Independent Living is run by disabled people for disabled people and recommends reliable local people including 'support brokers'. It can give you details of independent living schemes in your county. See website: **www.ncil.org.uk**.

National Brokerage Network helps you find a support broker to make the most of your personal budget. See website: **www.nationalbrokeragenetwork.org.uk**.

Transport

Difficulty in getting around is often a major problem for elderly and disabled people. In addition to the facilities run by voluntary organizations already mentioned, there are several other very useful services:

Forum of Mobility Centres provides information on a network of independent organizations throughout England, Scotland, Wales and Northern Ireland to help individuals who have a medical condition that may affect their ability to drive. See website: **www.mobility-centres.org.uk**.

London Taxicard provides subsidized door-to-door transport in taxis and private-hire vehicles for people who have serious mobility or visual impairment. See website: **www.taxicard.org.uk**.

Motability is a registered charity set up to assist recipients of the war pensioners' mobility supplement and/or the higher-rate mobility component of Disability Living Allowance to use their allowance to lease or buy a car or a powered wheelchair or scooter. See website: **www.motability.co.uk**.

Driving licence renewal at age 70

All drivers aged 70 are sent a licence renewal form to have their driving licence renewed. The entitlement to drive will need to be renewed by the DVLA; the new licence will normally be valid for three years. See website: **www.gov.uk** – Motoring.

Holidays

Many people in their late 70s and older travel across the world, go on activity holidays and see the great sights in the UK and abroad without any more difficulty than anyone else. They will find plenty of choice in Chapter 14, Holidays, including information about how to obtain assistance at airports and railway stations. However, some elderly people need special facilities if a stay away from home is to be possible. A number of organizations can help:

Able Travel offers accessible adventures including African safaris and worldwide adventure travel advice for wheelchair users and physically disabled people. See website: **www.able-travel.com**.

Accessible Travel and Leisure is a leading accessible and disabled holidays company enabling disabled people to enjoy the holidays they've always dreamed of. See website: **www.accessibletravel.co.uk**.

Can be done specializes in pioneering wheelchair accessible holidays to a widening choice of destinations in over 30 countries. See website: **www.canbedone.co.uk**.

Chalfont Line has been providing holidays for slow walkers and wheelchair users since 1980 with its high-quality, specialist escorted holidays. See website: **www.chalfont-line.co.uk**.

Enable holidays believes that travel for disabled people should involve less work and more play. Each resort, hotel and apartment is carefully assessed to ensure that it is accessible and suitable for travellers with mobility impairments. See website: **www.enableholidays.com**.

Tourism for All for information about a wide range of suitable accommodation, facilities and services both in the UK and overseas, including hiring equipment for holiday use, accessible attractions and respite care centres. See website: **www.tourismforall.org.uk**.

Voluntary organizations

A number of the specialist voluntary organizations run holiday centres or provide specially adapted self-catering accommodation. In some cases, outings and entertainment are offered; in others, individuals plan their own activities and amusement. Guests requiring assistance usually need to be accompanied by a companion, although in a few instances care arrangements are inclusive. Most of the organizations can advise about the possibility of obtaining a grant or other financial assistance.

Holidays for all gives information on organizations providing holidays for disabled people: website: **www.holidaysforall.org.uk**.

Holiday with Help: respite care breaks for disabled people and their carers: website: **www.holidayswithhelp.org.uk**.

Leonard Cheshire: the disability charity has information on holiday accommodation. See website: **www.leonard-cheshire.org**.

Vitalise offers essential breaks for disabled people and their carers: website: **www.vitalise.org.uk**.

The *Disabled Travellers' Guide*, published by the AA, lists a wide choice of holiday venues where disabled travellers can go in the normal way but with the advantage of having special facilities provided. Downloadable in pdf format, it gives information on holiday accommodation suitable for disabled individuals and their families, together with advice on travelling in Europe. See website: **www.theaa.com**.

Power of Attorney

Giving another person Power of Attorney authorizes someone else to take business and other financial decisions on the donor's behalf. A Lasting Power of Attorney continues, regardless of any decline, throughout the individual's life. To protect the donor and the nominated attorney, the law clearly lays down certain principles that must be observed, with both sides signing a declaration that they understand the various rights and duties involved. The law furthermore calls for the power to be formally registered with the Public Trust Office in the event of the donor being, or becoming, mentally incapable.

Lasting Powers of Attorney (LPA) have replaced Enduring Powers of Attorney. This coincided with the implementation of the Mental Capacity Act 2005. LPAs enable individuals to give their attorney power to make decisions about their personal welfare, including health care, and their finances when they lack the capacity to make such decisions themselves. Enduring Powers of Attorney set up before October 2007 are still effective. However, if your parents have not yet set one up but are planning to do so, they will now need to apply for the new LPA.

The right time to give Power of Attorney is when the individual is in full command of his or her faculties, so that potential situations that would require decisions can be properly discussed and the donor's wishes made clear. For the Lasting Power of Attorney to be valid, the donor must in any event be capable of understanding what he or she is agreeing to at the time of making the power. If your parents are considering setting up an LPA, it is advisable that they consult their GP and the family solicitor.

Living-in help

Temporary

Elderly people living alone can be more vulnerable to flu and other winter ailments; they may have a fall; or, for no apparent reason, they may go through a period of being forgetful and neglecting themselves. Equally, as they become older, they may not be able to cope as well with managing their homes or caring for themselves. In the event of an emergency or if you have reason for concern – perhaps because you are going on holiday and will not be around to keep a watchful eye on them – engaging living-in help can be a godsend. Most agencies tend inevitably to be on the expensive side, although in the event of a real problem they often represent excellent value for money. A more unusual and interesting longer-term possibility is to recruit the help of a Community Service Volunteer.

Community Service Volunteers (CSVs)

CSV was founded in 1962 and is the UK's leading training and volunteering charity. CSV trains over 12,000 young people and adults each year. They provide practical assistance in the home and also offer companionship. Usually a care scheme is set up through a social worker, who supervises how the arrangement is working out. Volunteers are placed on a one-month trial basis. For more information contact your parents' local social services department, or see CSV website: **www.csv.org.uk.**

Agencies

The agencies listed specialize in providing temporary help, rather than permanent staff. Charges vary, but in addition to the weekly payment to helpers there is normally an agency booking fee:

Consultus Care & Nursing Agency Ltd, website: **www.consultuscare.com;**

Country Cousins, website: **www.country-cousins.co.uk;**

Universal Aunts Ltd, website: **www.universalaunts.co.uk.**

For a further list of agencies, see *The Lady* magazine, or search the internet under the heading 'Nursing agencies' or 'Care agencies'.

Nursing care

If one of your parents needs regular nursing care, the GP may be able to arrange for a community or district nurse to visit him or her at home. This will not be a sleeping-in arrangement but simply involves a qualified nurse calling round when necessary. If they need more concentrated home nursing you will have to go through a private agency. Some of those listed above can sometimes supply trained nurses. Additionally, there are many specialist agencies that can arrange hourly, daily or live-in nurses on a temporary or longer-term basis.

Fees and services vary considerably. Some nurses undertake nursing duties only – and nothing else – and may even expect to have their meals provided. Others will do light housework and act as nurse-companions. Costs vary throughout the country, with London inevitably being most expensive. Private health insurance can sometimes be claimed against part of the cost, but this is generally only in respect of qualified nurses. Your local health centre or social services department should be able to give you names and addresses of local agencies, or search the internet under the heading 'Nursing agencies'.

Permanent

There may come a time when you feel that it is no longer safe to allow one of your parents to live entirely on his or her own. One possibility is to engage a companion or housekeeper on a permanent basis; such arrangements are normally very expensive. However, if you want to investigate the idea further, many domestic agencies supply housekeeper-companions. Alternatively, you might consider advertising in *The Lady* magazine, which is probably the most widely read publication for these kinds of posts. See website: **www.lady.co.uk**.

Permanent help can also sometimes be provided by agencies, which will supply continuous four-weekly placements. This is an expensive option, and the lack of continuity can at times be distressing for elderly people, particularly at the changeover point. The three agencies listed above may be worth contacting.

Au pairs are cheaper but a drawback is that most au pairs speak inadequate English (at least when they first arrive). As they are technically students living *en famille*, they must by law be given plenty of free time to attend school and study. An alternative solution for some families is to engage a reliable daily help who, in the event of illness or other problem, would be prepared to stay overnight.

Flexible care arrangements

One of the problems for many elderly people is that the amount of care they need is liable to vary according to the state of their health. There are other relevant factors including, for example, the availability of neighbours and family. Whereas after an operation the requirement may be for someone with basic nursing skills, a few weeks later the only need may be for someone to act as a companion. Under normal circumstances it may be as little as simply popping in for the odd hour during the day to cook a hot meal and check all is well. Few agencies cater for all the complex permutations that may be necessary in caring for an elderly person in his or her own home, but here are some that offer a flexible service:

Anchor Care offers care for the elderly in their own home by the hour, or nightly, for temporary or longer periods, or on a more permanent residential basis. See website: **www.anchor.org.uk**.

Christies Care is the largest independent specialist provider of live-in care, providing a professional and dedicated service tailored to clients' individual requirements. See website: **www.christiescare.com**.

Cura Domi – Care at Home is a specialist organization able to provide care and support seven days a week, 52 weeks of the year, as much or as little as required. See website: **www.curadomi.co.uk**.

Miracle Workers agency offers both long- and short-term care. It looks after clients in all sorts of situations. Live-in carers provide practical assistance, support and companionship. See **www.miracle-workers.co.uk**.

UKHCA (United Kingdom Home Care Association) is the professional association for home care providers, which may include specialist nursing care to elderly and/or disabled people in their own home. See website: **www.ukhca.co.uk**.

Although any of these suggestions can work extremely well for a while, with many families it may sooner or later come down to a choice between residential care and inviting a parent to live with you. Sometimes, particularly in the case of an unmarried son or daughter or other relative, it is more practical to move into the parent's (or relative's) home if the accommodation is more suitable.

Emergency care for pets

For many elderly people a pet is a very important part of their lives. It provides companionship and fun as well as stimulating them into taking regular outdoor exercise. But in the event of the owner having to go into hospital or through some other emergency being temporarily unable to care for the pet, there can be real problems. Two organizations that can help under these circumstances are listed here:

The Cinnamon Trust offers permanent care for pets whose owners have died, as well as respite care while the owners are in hospital. Animals either stay at the Trust's havens in Cornwall and Devon or are found alternative loving homes with a new owner. See website: **www.cinnamon.org.uk**.

Pet Fostering Service Scotland focuses on temporary care. The only charges are the cost of the pet's food, litter (in the case of cats) and any veterinary fees that may be incurred during fostering. See website: **www.pfss.org.uk**.

Practical help for carers

If your parent is still fairly active – visits friends, does his or her own shopping, or enjoys some hobby that gets him or her out and about – the strains and difficulties may be fairly minimal. This applies particularly if your parent is moving in with you and your home lends itself to creating a granny flat, so everyone can retain some privacy and your parent can continue to enjoy maximum independence. However, this is not always possible, and in the case of an ill or very frail person far more intensive care may be required. It is important to know what help is available and how to obtain it. The many services provided by local authorities and voluntary agencies, described earlier in the chapter, apply as much to an elderly person living with a family as to one living alone. If there is nothing there that solves a particular problem you may have, it could be that one of the following organizations could help:

Age UK, website: **www.ageuk.org.uk**;

British Red Cross, website: **www.redcross.org.uk**;

Carers Trust (the recently merged charities, Crossroads Care and The Princess Royal Trust for Carers), website: **www.carers.org**;

St John Ambulance, website: **www.sja.org.uk**;

WRVS, website: **www.wrvs.org.uk**.

Most areas have respite care facilities to enable carers to take a break from their dependants from time to time. Depending on the circumstances, this could be for just the odd day or possibly for a week or two to enable carers who need it to have a real rest. A particularly welcome aspect of respite care is that many schemes specially cater for, among others, elderly people with dementia.

Holiday breaks for carers

There are various schemes to enable those with an elderly relative to go on holiday alone or simply to enjoy a respite from their caring responsibilities. A number of local authorities run *fostering schemes*, on similar lines to child fostering. Elderly people are invited to stay in a neighbour's home and live in the household as an ordinary family member. Lasting relationships often develop. There may be a charge, or the service may be run on a voluntary basis (or be paid for by the local authority). Some voluntary organizations arrange *holidays for older people* to give relatives a break. Different charities take responsibility according to the area where you live: the Citizens Advice Bureau, volunteer centre or social services department should know whom you should approach.

Another solution is a *short-stay home*, which is residential accommodation variously run by local authorities, voluntary organizations or private individuals, catering specifically for elderly people. The different types of home are described under the heading 'Residential care homes' further on in this chapter. For information about local authority provision, ask the social services department. If, as opposed to general care, proper medical attention is necessary, you should consult your parent's GP. Many *hospitals and nursing homes* offer short-stay care arrangements as a means of relieving relatives, and a doctor should be able to help organize this for you.

Carers UK was set up to support and campaign for those caring for an ill, frail or disabled relative at home. It has around 80 self-help branches that are run for and by carers. See website: **www.carersuk.org**.

Jewish Care runs a number of carers' groups, mostly in London. See website: **www.jewishcare.org**.

Benefits and allowances

There is a number of benefits or allowances available to those with responsibility for the care of an elderly person and/or to elderly people themselves. If you are caring for someone, **Gov.uk** is the place to turn to for the latest and widest range of online public information. It is the gateway for government advice. There is a section for carers covering support services and assessments, carer's rights, working and caring, carer's allowance and much more. See website: **www.gov.uk** – Caring for Someone.

Gov.uk is also the place to turn to for online public information for *disabled people*. This covers employment, financial support, independent living, disability rights, health and support and much more. See **www.gov.uk** – Disabled people.

Entitlements for carers

Home Responsibilities Protection

This is a means of protecting your state pension if you are unable to work because of the need to care for an elderly person. For further details, see under 'The state pension' at the start of Chapter 3, or ask for leaflet CF411 at any pension centre.

Carer's Allowance

If you spend at least 35 hours a week caring for someone who is getting attendance allowance or the middle or highest rate of the Disability Living Allowance care component, you may be able to claim Carer's Allowance. You cannot get this if you are already getting the state pension or work and earn over £100 per week. See website: **www.gov.uk** – Caring for someone.

Entitlements for elderly or disabled people

Attendance Allowance

This is paid to people aged 65 or over who are severely disabled, either mentally or physically, and have needed almost constant care for at least six months. (They may be able to get the allowance even if no one has actually given them that help.) An exception to the six months' qualifying period is made in the case of those who are terminally ill, who can receive the allowance without having to wait.

There are two rates of allowance: £77.14 a week for those needing 24-hour care, and £51.85 for those needing intensive day- or night-time care. The allowance is tax free and is generally paid regardless of income (although payment might be affected by entering residential care). See website: **www.gov.uk** – Attendance Allowance.

Disability Living Allowance (DLA)

This benefit is paid to people up to the age of 65, inclusive, who become disabled. It has two components: a mobility component and a care component. A person can be entitled either to one or to both components. There are two rates for the mobility component and three rates for the care component. DLA is tax free and is generally paid regardless of income (although payment may be affected by entering residential care). Except in the case of people who are terminally ill, who can receive the higher-rate care component of DLA immediately, there is a normal qualifying period of three months. See website: **www.gov.uk** – Disability Benefits.

From 2013, the Department for Work and Pensions (DWP) will be replacing the Disability Living Allowance (DLA) with a new benefit called Personal Independence Payment (PIP) for eligible people under 65. Whether you are entitled to PIP will affect whether you are entitled to lease a car, scooter or powered wheelchair through the Motability Scheme. PIP will have two components, a daily living component and a mobility component. Each component will have a standard and an enhanced rate. For information on the changes, see the Disability Rights UK fact sheet online at: **www. disabilityalliance.org/f60.htm** or visit **www.dwp.gov.uk/pip**.

Cold Weather Payments

These are designed to give particularly vulnerable people extra help with heating costs during very cold weather. Anyone aged 60 and over who is in receipt of the guaranteed element of Pension Credit, Income Support or income-based Jobseeker's Allowance qualifies automatically. The payment is made by post as soon as the temperature in an area is forecast to drop – or actually drops – to zero degrees Celsius (or below) for seven consecutive days, so people can turn up their heating secure in the knowledge that they will be receiving extra cash help. The amount paid is £25.00. Those eligible should receive it without having to claim. For more information, see website: **www.gov.uk** – Cold Weather Payments.

Winter Fuel Payment

This is a special annual tax-free payment of between £125 to £400, given to all households with a resident aged 60 and over. See website: **www.gov.uk** – Winter Fuel Payments.

Free off-peak bus travel

People over the age of 60 and also disabled people can travel free on any bus service in the country. See Chapter 14, section on 'Travel and other concessions'.

Free TV licence

People aged 75 and older no longer have to pay for their TV licence.

Financial assistance

A number of charities give financial assistance to elderly people in need. These include the following:

Counsel and Care gives advice on ways to fund care, whether this is for nursing or other residential care, or for care in the home. Single needs payments are sometimes available to help towards holidays, special equipment, telephone installations and other priority items. See website: **www.counselandcare.org.uk**.

Elizabeth Finn Care gives grants to enable British and Irish people to remain in their own home and can also provide weekly grants to top up private care home fees. See website: **www.elizabethfinncare.org.uk**.

Guild of Aid for Gentlepeople can assist those 'of gentle birth or good education' who want to stay in their own home and who cannot call on any professional or trade body. See website: **www.turn2us.org.uk**.

Independent Age helps older people to remain independent by providing small lifetime annuities, financial help in times of crisis, and equipment to aid mobility. See website: **www.independentage.org.uk**.

Independent Living Fund (ILF) is a trust fund set up with government backing to assist people aged 16 to 65 with severe disabilities to pay for domestic or personal care to enable them to remain in their own homes. To become eligible, applicants must first approach their local authority for assistance under the Community Care scheme and be successful in obtaining care services. See website: **www.ilf.org.uk**.

Motability is a registered charity set up to assist recipients of the war pensioners' mobility supplement or the higher-rate mobility component of DLA to use their allowance to lease or buy a car, a powered wheelchair or a scooter. See website: **www.motability.co.uk**.

RABI (Royal Agricultural Benevolent Institution) is a grant-making charity that supports members of the farming community and their families facing need, hardship or distress. See website: **www.rabi.org.uk**.

SSAFA Forces Help is restricted to those who have served in the armed forces (including reservists and those who have done National Service) and their families. See website: **www.ssafa.org.uk**.

Wavelength loans TVs and radios on a permanent basis to elderly housebound people who cannot afford sets. Application should be made through a health visitor, social worker or officer of a recognized organization. See website: **www.wavelength.org.uk**.

For many people, one of the main barriers to getting help is knowing which of the many thousands of charities to approach. **Charity Search** delivers a free service which helps older people in genuine financial need receive the support that may be available to them from a variety of charitable sources. See website: **www.charitysearch.org.uk**.

Another organization that helps people to access money that is available to them through charities, welfare grants and benefits is **Turn2Us**, which is part of Elizabeth Finn Care. See website: **www.turn2us.org.uk**.

Useful reading

For other sources of financial help, ask at your library, or search online for *A Guide to Grants for Individuals in Need*, published by the Directory of Social Change (**www.grantsforindividuals.org.uk**).

Independent Age is a unique and growing charity, a support community for thousands of older people across the UK and the Republic of Ireland. It offers a 'helping hand from a trusted friend', tackling older people's poverty and loneliness by offering information, advice and friendship. Their helpful publication, *Wise Guide – Life-improving advice for the over-65s*, is the practical pensioners' handbook. See **www.independentage.org**.

Special accommodation

Elderly parents who no longer feel able to maintain a family home may decide that the time has come to move into accommodation that is smaller, easier and more economic to maintain. Purpose-designed retirement housing, with a high degree of independence and with the option to have a range of support resources as and when required, is a solution that suits increasing numbers of people. There is a wide choice available to meet individual requirements, budgets and tastes. Should their health deteriorate, they may need care in their new home, or at least the chance to call for more support if needed in the future.

Close care housing is another form of care provision that has grown up to bridge the gap between the retirement home and residential care. One of the attractions of this is the provision of domestic and personal services, enabling independent living to be maintained. Often the main reason for choosing a housing development like this is that, should the resident's health decline, he or she can remain on the same site, staying in contact with the social circle he or she has developed there and does not have to face moving.

Retirement living accommodation offers elderly parents the ability to maintain as much of their independence as possible, and a degree of flexibility should their needs change at any time in the future. Retirement villages are gaining in popularity and there is the added luxury of having a ready-made social network for your parents outside their front door, of people of their own age who may have similar interests.

One big bonus is that the community areas can be a real hive of activity; somewhere for residents to meet, hold social events or club meetings and enjoy entertainment. Some developments have in-house restaurants and luxurious leisure facilities, all within a safe and secure environment. There is a wealth of choice of such accommodation covering an enormous spectrum, so anyone considering either of these options should make a point of investigating the market before reaching a decision. Choosing the right accommodation for elderly parents is critically important, as it can make all the difference to independence, lifestyle and general well-being. It can also, of course, lift a great burden off families' shoulders to know that their parents are happy and comfortable, in congenial surroundings and with on-the-spot help, should this be necessary.

Just to sound a note of warning: there have been recent revelations in the press about bad practice in retirement and sheltered housing management, which are little short of disgraceful (for example, adding VAT to electricity bills which already contain VAT, and paying an 'exit fee' to the freeholder if the property is sold, which can be as much as 5 per cent of the sale price). One suggested solution is for flat owners to club together and take over the management. Advice on this can be obtained from the Campaign Against Residential Leasehold Exploitation (**www.carlex.org.uk**) and the Right to Manage Federation (**www.rtmf.org.uk**).

Sheltered housing

Sheltered housing is usually a development of independent, purpose-designed bungalows or flats within easy access of shops and public transport. It generally has a house manager and an alarm system for emergencies, and often some common facilities. These could include a garden, possibly a launderette, a sitting room and a dining room, with meals provided for residents, on an optional basis, either once a day or several days a week.

Residents normally have access to all the usual range of services – home helps, meals on wheels and so on – in the same way as any other elderly people. Sheltered housing is available for sale or rent through private developers, housing associations or local authorities. It is occasionally provided through gifted housing schemes, or on a shared ownership basis.

Sheltered housing for sale

Good developments are always sought after and can require you to join a waiting list. Although this is emphatically not a reason for rushing into a decision you might regret, if you were hoping to move in the fairly near future it could be as well to start looking sooner rather than later. There are many companies offering sheltered housing for sale, with standards and facilities varying enormously. Some also provide personal care services as an adjunct to their retirement home schemes. Flats and houses are usually sold on long leases (99 years or more) for a capital sum, with a weekly or monthly service charge to cover maintenance and resident support services. Should a resident decide to move, the property can usually be sold on the open market, either through an estate agent or through the developer, provided the prospective buyer is over 55 years of age.

Occupiers normally have to enter into a management agreement with the housebuilder, and it is important to establish exactly what the commitment is likely to be before buying into such schemes. Factors that should be considered include: who the managing agent is; the house manager's duties; what the service charge covers; the ground rent; the arrangements for any repairs that might prove necessary; whether there is a residents' association; whether pets are allowed; what the conditions are with regard to reselling the property – and the tenant's rights in the matter. Although the rights of sheltered housing residents have been strengthened over the years, you would nevertheless be strongly recommended to get any contract or agreement vetted by a solicitor before proceeding.

The range of prices is very wide, depending on size, location and type of property. Weekly service charges vary widely too. Additionally, there is usually an annual ground rental – and council tax is normally excluded. The service charge usually covers the cost of the house manager, alarm system, maintenance, repair and renewal of any communal facilities (external and internal) and sometimes the heating and lighting costs. It may also cover insurance on the building (but not the contents). A particular point to watch is that the service charge tends to rise annually, sometimes well above the inflation level. Be wary of service charges that seem uncommonly reasonable in the sales literature, as these are often increased sharply following purchase. Owners of sheltered accommodation have the same rights as other lease-holders, and charges can therefore be challenged by appeal to a leasehold valuation tribunal.

A further safeguard is the Sheltered Housing Code operated by the **NHBC**, which is mandatory for all registered housebuilders selling sheltered homes. The code, which applies to all new sheltered dwellings in England and Wales registered on or after 1 April 1990, has two main requirements. One is that all prospective purchasers should be given a purchaser's information pack (PIP), clearly outlining all essential information that they will need to enable them to decide whether or not to buy. The second is that the builder and manage-ment organization enter into a formal legal agreement giving purchasers the benefit of the legal rights specified in the code. See website: **www.nhbc.co.uk**.

The following organizations can provide information about sheltered housing for sale:

Elderly Accommodation Counsel is a nationwide charity that aims to help older people make informed choices about meeting their housing and care needs. See website: **www.eac.org.uk**.

Retirement Homesearch is Britain's No 1 retirement property specialist, with an extensive nationwide portfolio of over 2,000 properties, including flats, houses and bungalows, in all price ranges. See website: **www.retirementhomesearch.co.uk**.

New developments are constantly under construction. Properties tend to be sold quickly soon after completion, so it pays to find out about future develop-ments and to get on any waiting lists well in advance of a prospective purchase. Firms specializing in this type of property include the following:

Bovis Homes Retirement Living, website: **www.bovishomes.co.uk**;

Churchill Retirement Living, website: **www.churchillretirement.co.uk**;

Cognatum (the merger of Beechcroft and English Courtyard Association), website: **www.cognatum.co.uk**;

McCarthy & Stone Retirement Living, website: **www.mccarthyandstone.co.uk**;

Pegasus Retirement Homes plc, website: **www.pegasus-homes.co.uk**;

Richmond Villages, website: **www.richmond-villages.com**.

Housing associations build sheltered housing for sale and also manage sheltered housing developments on behalf of private construction companies; see:

Anchor, website: **www.anchor.org.uk;**

RLHA Group, website: **www.rlha.org.uk.**

Rented sheltered housing

This is normally provided by local authorities, housing associations and certain benevolent societies. As with accommodation to buy, quality varies.

Local authority housing is usually only available to people who have resided in the area for some time. There is often an upper and lower age limit for admission, and prospective tenants may have to undergo a medical examination, since as a rule only those who are physically fit are accepted. Should a resident become infirm or frail, alternative accommodation will be found. Apply to the local housing or social services department or via a housing advice centre.

Housing associations supply much of the newly built sheltered housing. Both rent and service charges vary around the country. In case of need, Income Support or Housing Benefit may be obtained to help with the cost. Citizens Advice Bureau and housing departments often keep a list of local housing associations. There are hundreds to choose from; here are just a few:

Abbeyfield, website: **www.abbeyfield.com;**

Anchor, website: **www.anchor.org.uk;**

Girlings, website: **www.girlings.co.uk;**

Habinteg Housing Association, website: **www.habinteg.org.uk;**

Hanover, website: **www.hanover.org.uk;**

Jewish Community Housing Association Ltd, website: **www.jcha.org.uk;**

Southern Housing Group, website: **www.shgroup.org.uk.**

Benevolent societies

These all cater for specific professional and other groups:

Housing 21 is a major national provider of housing, care and support services for older people. See website: **www.housing21.co.uk.**

Royal Alfred Seafarers' Society provides quality long-term care for elderly seafarers, their widows and dependants. See website: **www.royalalfredseafarers.com.**

SSAFA Forces Help is restricted to those who have served in the armed forces (including reservists and those who did National Service) and their families. See website: **www.ssafa.org.uk**.

Alternative ways of buying sheltered accommodation

For those who cannot afford to buy into sheltered housing either outright or through a mortgage, there is a variety of alternative payment methods.

Shared ownership and 'Sundowner' schemes

Part-ownership schemes are now offered by a number of developers. Would-be residents, who must be over 55 years, part-buy or part-rent with the amount of rent varying according to the size of the initial lump sum. Residents can sell at any time, but they only recoup that percentage of the sale price that is proportionate to their original capital investment, with no allowance for any rental payments made over the intervening period.

'Investment' and gifted housing schemes

Some charities and housing associations operate these schemes, for which a capital sum is required, to obtain sheltered accommodation.

'Investment' schemes work as follows. The buyer puts in the larger share of the capital, usually 50 to 80 per cent, and the housing association puts in the remainder. The buyer pays rent on the housing association's share of the accommodation and also service charges for the communal facilities.

Gifted housing schemes differ in that an individual donates his or her property to a registered charity, in return for being housed and cared for in his or her own home. The attraction is that the owner can remain in his or her own property with none of the burden of its upkeep. However, it is advisable to consult a solicitor before signing anything, because such schemes have the big negative of reducing the value of the owner's estate, with consequent loss for any beneficiaries.

Age UK offers a free advice and information service about community or residential care and housing options. See website: **www.ageuk.org.uk**.

Almshouses

Most almshouses are endowed by a charity for the benefit of older people of reduced means who live locally or have a connection with a particular trade. There are now over 2,000 groups of almshouses, providing about 35,000 dwellings. Although many are of considerable age, most of them have been modernized and new ones are being built. Rents are not charged, but there will be a maintenance contribution towards upkeep and heating.

A point you should be aware of is that almshouses do not provide the same security of tenure as some other tenancies. You would be well advised to have the proposed letter of appointment checked by a lawyer or other expert to ensure you understand exactly what the beneficiary's rights are. There is no standard way to apply for an almshouse, since each charity has its own qualifications for residence. Some housing departments and advice centres keep lists of local almshouses. An organization that could help is the **Almshouse Association**, which supplies information on almshouses and contact details in the county in which you are interested. See website: **www.almshouses.org**.

Granny flats

A granny flat or annexe is a self-contained unit attached to a family house. A large house can be converted or extended for this purpose, but planning permission is needed. Enquire at your local authority planning department. Some councils, particularly new towns, have houses to rent with granny flats.

Salvation Army homes

The **Salvation Army** has 18 homes for elderly people in various parts of the UK, offering residential care for men and women unable to manage in their own homes. Christian caring is given within a family atmosphere, in pleasant surroundings, but the homes are not nursing homes. See website: **www.saha.org.uk**.

Extra-care schemes

A number of organizations that provide sheltered accommodation also have extra-care sheltered housing, designed for those who can no longer look after themselves without assistance. Although expensive, it is cheaper than most private care homes and often more appropriate than full-scale nursing care. A possible problem is that tenants of some of these schemes do not have security of tenure and, should they become frail, could be asked to leave if more intensive care were required. Among the housing associations that provide these facilities are Housing 21, Hanover Housing Association, Anchor and Abbeyfield (see the details listed earlier in this chapter).

Community Care

Since the start of Community Care in April 1993, anyone needing help in arranging suitable care for an elderly person should contact his or her social services department. Before making suggestions, the department will assess what type of provision would best meet the needs of the individual concerned. This could be services or special equipment to enable the person to stay in his or her own home, residential home accommodation or a nursing home. If residential or nursing home care is necessary, the department will arrange a place in either a local authority or other home, pay the charge and seek reimbursement from the individual according to his or her means.

It is anticipated that nearly 70 per cent of men and some 85 per cent of women over the age of 65 will need care at some time. One in five British adults has elderly parents who require some form of care or assistance. One in four of those aged over 65 will require some form of long-term care. According to the health think tank, the King's Fund, almost everyone in the UK will either need care or become a carer. The state has no responsibility to fund daily care, such as help with washing and dressing. Frailty in old age is quite different from actual illness, where elderly people are entitled to receive free treatment under the National Health Service. While some older people can afford to retire in comfort and others are confident and optimistic about how they will end their days, it is very sad when relatives have to sell their loved ones' property so that they can afford to pay for their growing care needs in their later years.

Care homes

If your parents need to move into a care home, the state may help with the cost. The rules are complex and only a brief outline is given here. For more information, the local council is the point of contact.

If moving into a nursing home is a continuation of NHS treatment that your parents have been having for an illness – for example he or she is discharged from hospital direct to a home – this should be paid for by the NHS. However, this is a grey area and you may have to be persistent to get their costs met in this way.

If they do not qualify for NHS continuing care, they may still qualify for some state help with care home fees, provided their needs assessment found this was the best option for them and their means are low. If their capital (savings and other assets) are above a set threshold, (currently £23,250 in 2012/13) they will have to pay for themselves. If their capital is less, their local council may pay part or, if their capital is below the lower threshold, the full amount.

Moving into a care home is a big decision, whether you are doing it yourself or for a loved one. Here are some suggestions before taking the decision:

- Is a care home really needed? Get advice on the housing options.
- What type of care home is wanted? Some offer accommodation and help with personal care; others care homes offer nursing care as well as the basic help. (This is the crucial difference between residential homes and nursing homes, though they are no longer classed as such.)
- How to find a care home? Think of it like buying a house: you need to get a feel for what is out there before making a decision. Personal recommendations are important. (Lists available from Age UK; Counsel and Care; Elderly Accommodation Counsel.)
- How much will it cost? There is a lot of difference in care home fees. If the local council is paying, it will set a maximum cost that it will contribute. If the costs are higher, a relative or friend will need to top up that amount. If your parents are self-funding, make sure they can afford the fees.

Residential care homes (care homes registered to provide personal care)

There may come a time when it is no longer possible for an elderly person to manage without being in proper residential care. In a residential care home, sometimes known as a 'rest home', the accommodation usually consists of a bedroom plus communal dining rooms, lounges and gardens. All meals are provided, rooms are cleaned, and staff are at hand to give whatever help is needed. Most homes are fully furnished, though it is usually possible to take small items of furniture. Except in some of the more expensive private homes, bathrooms are normally shared. Intensive nursing care is not usually included.

Homes are run by private individuals (or companies), voluntary organizations and local authorities. All homes must be registered with the Commission for Social Care Inspection to ensure minimum standards. *An unregistered home should not be considered.* It is very important that the individual should have a proper chance to visit it and ask any questions. Before reaching a final decision, it is a good idea to arrange a short stay to see whether the facilities are suitable and pleasant.

It could also be sensible to enquire what long-term plans there are for the home. Moving to a new care home can be a highly distressing experience for an elderly person who has become attached to the staff and made friends among the other residents. Though a move can never be totally ruled out, awareness of whether the home is likely to remain a going concern could be a deciding factor when making a choice. Possible clues could include whether the place is short-staffed or in need of decoration. If it is run by a company or charity, you could request to see the latest accounts.

Private homes

Private care homes are often converted houses, taking up to about 30 people. As more companies move into the market, the homes can be purpose-built accommodation and may include a heated swimming pool and luxury facilities. The degree of care varies. If a resident becomes increasingly infirm, a care home will normally continue to look after him or her if possible. It may, however, become necessary at some point to arrange transfer to a nursing home or hospital. Fees vary enormously.

Voluntary care homes

These are run by charities, religious bodies or other voluntary organiza-tions. Eligibility may be determined by age, background or occupation, depending on the criteria of the managing organization. Income may be a factor, as may general fitness, and individuals may be invited to a personal interview before acceptance onto the waiting list. Priority tends to be given to those in greatest need. Homes are often in large converted houses, with accommodation for under 10 people or up to 100. Fees vary depending on locality.

Local authority homes

These are sometimes referred to as 'Part III accommodation', and admission will invariably be arranged by the social services department. If someone does not like the particular accommodation suggested, he or she can turn it down and ask the department what other offers might be available. Weekly charges vary around the country. In practice, individuals are charged only according to their means.

Nursing homes (care homes registered to provide nursing care)

Nursing homes provide medical supervision and fully qualified nurses, 24 hours a day. Most are privately run, with the remainder being supported by voluntary organizations. All nursing homes in England must be registered with the Commission for Social Care Inspection, which keeps a list of what homes are available in the area. In Wales, the inspectorate is called the Care Standards Inspectorate for Wales, and in Scotland it is called the Scottish Commission for the Regulation of Care.

Private

These homes normally accommodate between 15 and 100 patients. Depending on the part of the country, charges vary. Some fees rise depending on how much nursing is required. For information about nursing homes in the UK, contact the following:

Elderly Accommodation Counsel maintains a nationwide database of all types of specialist accommodation for elderly people and gives advice and detailed information to help enquirers choose the support and care most suited to their needs. See website: **www.eac.org.uk**.

NHFA offers free advice to individuals and their families on specialist accommodation and how to pay for care home fees, what state benefits are available to them and other related matters. See website: **www.nhfa.co.uk**.

RNHA (Registered Nursing Home Association) is an organization that provides support for nursing home owners, requiring its members to meet high levels of standards and service. Patients in nursing homes that are members of the RNHA can expect to receive some of the best standards of service available. See website: **www.rnha.co.uk**.

Voluntary organizations

These normally have very long waiting lists, and beds are often reserved for those who have been in the charity's care home. Voluntary organizations that run care homes include:

Careways Trust, website: **www.carewaystrust.org.uk**;

Friends of the Elderly, website: **www.fote.org.uk**;

IndependentAge, website: **www.independentage.org.uk;**

Jewish Care, website: **www.jewishcare.org.**

Costs of care

Free nursing care

Since October 2001, the nursing costs of being in a home have been made free to all patients. This does not include the personal care costs (eg help with bathing, dressing or eating), nor the accommodation costs; individuals will continue to be assessed for both of these under the rules described below. In Scotland, exceptionally, the personal care costs are also free. The provision of free nursing care may make only a fairly limited contribution to the cost of being in a home. Patients are assessed according to their needs and the amount of actual nursing care they require.

Financial assistance for residential and nursing home care

Under the Community Care arrangements, people needing to go into a residential or nursing home may receive help from their local authority social services department. As explained earlier, the department will make the arrangements direct with the home following its assessment procedure and will seek reimbursement from the person towards the cost, according to set means-testing rules.

People who were already in a residential or nursing home before April 1993 used to receive special levels of Income Support. This arrangement, known as 'preserved rights', ended in April 2002, and instead the full cost of residential care is now met by the individual's local authority.

People who had been or are currently paying for themselves but can no longer afford to do so may have the right to claim help, now or in the future, if they qualify on grounds of financial need. Help is provided on a sliding scale for those with assets. Even those on a very low income are required to make some contribution towards the cost of being in a home.

For further information, see following organizations:

Citizens Advice Bureau, website: **www.citizensadvice.org.uk;**

Elderly Accommodation Counsel, website: **www.eac.org.uk;**

NHFA, website: **www.nhfa.co.uk.**

Funding care

A major worry for many people going into residential care is the requirement to sell their home to cover the costs. While this may still eventually be necessary, the rules have been made slightly more flexible to allow a short breathing space for making decisions. Under the rules introduced in April 2001, the value of a person's home is disregarded from the means-testing procedure in assessing their ability to pay for the first 12 weeks of their going into care. Also, instead of selling, they may be able to borrow the money (secured against their home) from the local council, which will eventually reclaim the loan at a later stage or from their estate.

But if you are thinking about funding care for your parents in future, you are ahead of the game. Most people leave it until it is needed and then have to sort things out in a hurry. Planning for care is a new sphere for most people and there are different types of care to consider: in the home, in residential care and then in nursing care. The funding aspect is always difficult. The starting point is to see what the local authority can provide. Beyond that, careful planning is required so that best use is made of your parents' income and assets.

Obtaining and paying for care is a complex area. An organization that provides support and advice to seniors as well as an information service for carers is **Equity Care**. See website: **www.equitycare.co.uk**. Other useful organizations are:

Care & Quality Commission, website: **www.cqc.org.uk**;

Home Instead Senior Care, website: **www.homeinstead.co.uk**;

Solicitors for the Elderly, website: **www.solicitorsfortheelderly.com**.

Further information

Key sources of information about voluntary and private homes are: the *Charities Digest* (available in libraries, housing aid centres and Citizens Advice Bureaus) and the *Directory of Independent Hospitals and Health Services* (available in libraries). The *Charities Digest* also includes information about hospices. Here are some other sources of advice:

Action on Elder Abuse was founded to help prevent physical, psychological or financial exploitation and other types of abuse of elderly people. An estimated 340,000 older people are abused every year in this country in their own homes – and only 10 per cent of cases are acted upon. As well as providing guidance and training for professionals engaged in the care of vulnerable older people, it also runs a free confidential helpline offering advice and support to individuals who feel that they are the victims of abuse as well as to other members of the public who have grounds for concern about someone's welfare. See website: **www.elderabuse.org.uk**.

Age UK offers a free advice and information service, available throughout the UK for older people and their carers. See website: **www.ageuk.org.uk**.

Elderly Accommodation Counsel maintains a nationwide database of all types of specialist accommodation for elderly people and gives advice and detailed information to help enquirers choose the support and care most suited to their needs. See website: **www.eac.org.uk**.

NHFA runs a free helpline that offers advice to individuals and their families on specialist accommodation and how to pay for care home fees, what state benefits are available to them and other related matters. See website: **www.nhfa.co.uk**.

R&RA (Relatives & Residents Association) offers a support service to families and friends of older people in, or considering, long-term care. It gives advice on most questions, from finding a home to concerns about the standard of care. See website: **www.relres.org**.

Useful reading

Finding Care Home Accommodation, a free fact sheet downloadable from Age UK website: **www.ageuk.org.uk**.

Some special problems

A minority of people, as they become older, suffer from special problems that can cause great distress. Because families do not like to talk about these problems, they may be unaware of what services are available and so may be missing out on practical help and sometimes also on financial assistance.

Hypothermia

Elderly people tend to be more vulnerable to the cold. If the body drops below a certain temperature, this can be dangerous, because one of the symptoms of hypothermia is that sufferers no longer actually feel cold. Instead, they may lose their appetite and vitality and may become mentally confused. Instead of doing all the sensible things like getting a hot drink and putting on an extra sweater, they are liable to neglect themselves further and can put themselves at real risk. Although heating costs are often blamed, quite wealthy people can also be victims by allowing their home to become too cold or not wearing sufficient clothing. For this reason, during a cold snap it is very important to check up regularly on an elderly person living alone.

British Gas, electricity companies and the Solid Fuel Association are all willing to give advice on how heating systems can be used more efficiently and economically. It also is worth checking that elderly parents are on the correct tariff when it comes to utility bills. Some utility providers have reduced charges for elderly, vulnerable people who are in receipt of certain benefits. It could make the difference between them staying warm and feeling obliged to turn off their heating. Insulation can also play a very large part in keeping a home warmer and cheaper to heat. It may be possible to obtain a grant from the local authority, although normally this would only be likely on grounds of real need.

Elderly and disabled people in receipt of Income Support may receive a Cold Weather Payment to help with heating costs during a particularly cold spell – that is, when the temperature is forecast to drop to zero degrees Celsius (or below) for seven consecutive days. Those eligible should receive the money automatically. In the event of any problem, ask at your social security office. In an emergency, such as a power cut, contact the Citizens Advice Bureau or Age UK.

Finally, every household with someone aged 60 or older will get an annual tax-free Winter Fuel Payment of £250, while those with a resident aged 80 or older will receive £400. See website: **www.gov.uk** – Winter Fuel Payment.

Incontinence

Bladder or bowel problems can cause deep embarrassment to sufferers as well as inconvenience to relatives. The problem can occur in an elderly person for all sorts of reasons, and a doctor should always be consulted, as it can often be cured or at least alleviated by proper treatment. To assist with the practical problems, some local authorities operate a laundry service that collects soiled linen, sometimes several times a week. Talk to the health visitor or district nurse (at their local health centre), who will be able to advise about this and other facilities.

B&BF (Bladder and Bowel Foundation) is the charity for people with bladder and bowel dysfunction. The charity offers advice from its specially trained nurses. See website: **www.bladderandbowelfoundation.org**.

Dementia

Sometimes an elderly person can become confused or forgetful, suffer severe loss of memory or have violent mood swings and at times be abnormally aggressive. It is important to consult a doctor as soon as possible, as the cause may be depression, stress or even vitamin deficiency. All of these can be treated and often completely cured. If dementia is diagnosed, there are ways of helping a sufferer to cope better with acute forgetfulness and other symptoms. Arguably the hardest aspect is the thought that there is no cure for a progressive disease that gradually erodes the personality of the person one loves. But there is ongoing research into finding a cure and there are some treatments that can delay the progression of some forms of dementia. Meanwhile there are many ways to make life for people with dementia more manageable and enjoyable.

The most common type of dementia is Alzheimer's disease, which is usually found in people aged over 65. Approximately 24 million people worldwide have dementia, of which the majority of cases (over 60 per cent) are due to Alzheimer's. Clinical signs are characterized by progressive cognitive deterioration, together with a decline in the ability to carry out common daily tasks, and behavioural changes. The first readily identifiable symptoms of Alzheimer's disease are usually short-term memory loss and visual-spatial confusion. These initial symptoms progress from seemingly simple and fluctuating to a more pervasive loss of memory, including difficulty navigating familiar areas such as the local neighbourhood. This advances to loss of other familiar and well known skills, as well as recognition of objects and people.

Since family members are often the first to notice changes that might indicate the onset of Alzheimer's (or other forms of dementia) they should learn the early warning signs. They should serve as informants during initial clinical evaluation of patients. It is important to consult your doctor as soon as you have concerns. It is also a good idea to talk to the health visitor, as he or she will know about any helpful facilities that may be available locally. The health visitor is also able to arrange appointments with other professionals, such as the community psychiatric nurse and the occupational therapist.

It is important to remember that people with dementia are still people. The Alzheimer's Society recommends the following tips. Always treat the person with respect and dignity; be a good listener; be a good communicator; remember that little things mean a lot. Staying in touch shows that you care; offer practical help; organize a treat; and find out more about the condition so that you understand and feel comfortable spending time with the person with dementia.

Sources of help and support for people with dementia and their carers are:

Alzheimer Scotland, website: **www.alzscot.org**;

Alzheimer's Society, website: **www.alzheimers.org.uk**;

Mind, website: **www.mind.org.uk**.

Useful reading

Caring for the Person with Dementia, published by the Alzheimer's Society, see website: **www.alzheimers.org.uk**, and *Understanding Dementia*, available from Mind, see website: **www.mind.org.uk**.

Chapter Sixteen
No one is immortal

I was dead billions of years before I was born and suffered not the slightest inconvenience. **MARK TWAIN**

Old people are different. They are special, even fortunate. Who else can understand the pleasure of sitting on a bench for hours in the shade of a tree, doing nothing, gazing into the distance, silent, motionless, their hands folded? This was the opinion of the late Francois Mitterand, 21st president of France, who died in 1996. He, who had been so active in his life, understood in his old age the virtues of 'non-action'. When we are younger, we seem to regard doing nothing as a defect or a failure. But in old age, *being* becomes far more important than *doing*. Those of us who cling on to things that are past, that we can no longer do, are demonstrating an inability to let go. If we don't learn to embrace the future, that of a tranquil and passive old age, we are likely to feel unhappy and frustrated. As we grow old, newness comes from the inside, since the outer body naturally ages and slows down. We must learn to rely more on our senses and not on our physical strength.

Being prepared for old age and learning to let go are most important. Woody Allen once remarked that he had 'nothing against growing old since nobody has yet found a better way of not dying young'. At the beginning of life, when we are totally dependent on others, we allow ourselves to be fed, carried and cared for trustingly. So it is at the end of our lives: some of us find ourselves in the same condition again, partially or totally dependent on other human beings. Yet this time we are aware of it. If we have the opportunity, we should try to live out our old age without fear. If we are prepared for death, the result should be liberating, allowing us to experience the final stage of life with confidence. Before we get too old, it is important to think for a moment about the practicalities.

We all know that we should write a will, but it is one of those things that many of us never seem to get around to. It is estimated that 53 per cent of people die without having made a will. But not writing a will can mean chaos and financial worry for your family or dependants after you've gone. A great deal of heartbreak and real financial worry could be avoided if people were more open about the subject of dying. At the earliest and most appropriate moment, if you can bring yourself and your relatives to have an honest and open discussion about mortality, it could potentially save huge amounts of trouble later on.

Wills

Planning what will happen to your money and possessions after your death helps ensure your survivors are financially secure and that the people you want to inherit from you do so. When you retire, there are often big changes to your finances as well as to the rest of your life. It is at this stage that it is important to review how your survivors would manage financially if you were to die. Would, in fact, your money and possessions (your 'estate') be passed on as you would wish? (Your estate is everything you own at the time you die, including your share of any joint possessions, less everything you owe.)

Three out of 10 people aged 65 and over die without having made a will. This is called dying 'intestate'. A will is, in its simplest form, a set of instructions about how your estate should be passed on. If you don't have a will, the law makes these decisions for you. This could mean that the wrong people inherit, your home might have to be sold to split the proceeds and your survivors could have extra work and stress.

There are five rules of will making:

1 The person making the will must be of sound mind.

2 The will must be properly executed.

3 The will must be correctly witnessed.

4 Be clear about what or how much you want to leave and to whom.

5 Remember to update your will as your life circumstances change.

Having a will is especially important if you live with an unmarried partner, have remarried, need to provide for someone with a disability, own a business, own property abroad, or your estate is large (ie over the inheritance tax threshold). A will is a legal document that needs to be drawn up precisely and set out your wishes clearly and unambiguously. Although you can write your own will, it is safer to get a solicitor to do it.

Laws of intestacy

Under the intestacy laws:

- your husband, wife or civil partner and your own children are favoured; this includes a former partner if you are only separated rather than divorced;

- an unmarried partner and stepchildren have no rights;

- your husband, wife or civil partner does not automatically get the whole of your estate;

- possessions, including your home, may have to be sold to split the proceeds between your heirs;

- if you have no partner or children, more distant relatives inherit;

- if you have no relatives, the state gets the lot.

Making a will

You have three choices: you can do it yourself, you can ask your bank to help you, or you can use a solicitor or a specialist will-writing practitioner.

Doing it yourself

Home-made wills are not generally recommended. People often use ambiguous wording which, while perfectly clear to the individual who has written it, may be less obvious to others. This could result in the donor's wishes being misinterpreted and could also cause considerable delay in settling the estate. Wills forms are available from good stationers. They are not perfect and still leave considerable margin for error if the estate is complicated.

Two witnesses are needed, and an essential point to remember is that beneficiaries cannot witness a will, nor can the spouses of any beneficiaries. In certain circumstances, a will can be rendered invalid. A sensible precaution for those doing it themselves is to have it checked by a solicitor or by a legal expert from the Citizens Advice Bureau.

For individuals with sight problems, **RNIB** has produced a comprehensive guide to making or changing a will that is available in large print size, in Braille and on tape, as well as in standard print size. See website: **www.rnib.org.uk**.

Banks

Advice on wills and the administration of estates is given by the trustee companies of most of the major high street banks. In particular, the services they offer are to provide general guidance, to act as executor and to administer the estate. They will also introduce clients to a solicitor and keep a copy of the will – plus other important documents – in their safe, to avoid the risk of theirs being mislaid. Additionally, banks (as solicitors) can give tax planning and other financial guidance, including advice on inheritance tax. Some banks will draw up a will for you.

Solicitors and will-writing specialists

Solicitors may offer to draw up a will, act as executors and administer the estate. Like banks, they will also retain a copy of your will in safekeeping (most will not charge for storing a will). If you do not have a solicitor, your friends may be able to recommend one, or ask at the Citizens Advice Bureau. The **Law Society** can also provide you with names and addresses; see website: **www.lawsociety.org.uk**.

Alternatively, if you simply want help in writing a will, you could consult a specialist will-writing practitioner. The best approach is to contact one of the following organizations:

The Society of Will Writers, website: **www.willwriters.com**;

Trust Inheritance Limited, website: **www.trustinheritance.com**;

The Will Bureau, website: **www.twb.org.uk**.

Charges

A basic will could cost around £120 or just under. However, if your affairs are more complicated, the cost could be considerably more. Always ask for an estimate before proceeding. Remember too that professional fees normally carry VAT. Some solicitors charge according to the time they spend on a job so, although the actual work may not take very long, if you spend hours discussing your will or changing it every few months the costs can escalate very considerably. However, many solicitors will give you a fixed-fee estimate for a will. The fees for will-writing practitioners are broadly in line with those of solicitors.

Community Legal Service funding (Legal Aid)

Financial assistance for legal help and advice is available to certain groups of people for making a will. These include people aged over 70, disabled people, and a parent of a disabled person whom the parent wishes to provide for in his or her will. Additionally, to qualify, the people will need to satisfy the financial eligibility criteria. For further information enquire at your Citizens Advice Bureau or other advice centre.

Executors

Making a will at some stage in your life is a normal event. But appointing an executor is not a decision to be made without some serious consideration.

The duties of an executor are many, including dealing with the financial wishes made by the testator. An executor may have to settle debts, create trusts and distribute the testator's assets among nominated individuals. Executors may also have to inform the next of kin of the death, register the death, deal with house sales and tax if required. The testator, when appointing an executor, should be sure of the intended person's ability to carry out these duties when making their choice.

Practically anyone over 18 can become an executor. In some families the eldest child will be chosen for the task. Maybe another member of the family or a friend is financially minded, and has had experience in dealing with this type of situation. More than one person can be named as an executor, and it is possible for a solicitor or accountant to take on this responsibility. Family squabbles over the appointment of an executor are not uncommon. Often only the executor and the testator of the will know who has been nominated.

Family disagreements over how the assets of the deceased are distributed can be commonplace. One of the duties of the executor should be to play peacemaker. The executor should have the capability to stay calm when dealing with disgruntled family members over the contents of a will. They should remember that the death of a loved one may lead to dependants not acting as reasonably as they would normally.

The person named as an executor should be trustworthy and reliable. He or she should also be financially minded and, if possible, have previous experience in dealing with financial matters of this nature. However, an inexperienced person can be appointed executor, but in this case it will be helpful for that person to be able to liaise with the family solicitor on the matter.

When choosing an executor of a will, the following points are worth bearing in mind:

- A spouse as a sole executor is not the best choice, especially if both husband and wife are elderly.

- It is advisable not to appoint benefactors as an executor in case others claim there is a conflict of interests.

- The chosen person should be informed of the decision in order to agree to the role.

- Legally, the executor must be over 18, of sound mind and not in prison when the executor decision is made.

- If conflicts within the family are likely to be a factor, it may be worthwhile appointing more than one executor, or even hiring a professional executor.

- If a family member is chosen, he or she should have the time to carry out all the duties. This can be difficult if the executor does not live in the same part of the country.

Other points

Wills should always be kept in a safe place – and their whereabouts known. The most sensible arrangement is for the solicitor to keep the original and for both you and the bank to have a copy.

A helpful initiative devised by the Law Society is a mini-form, known as a personal assets log. This is for individuals drawing up a will to give to their executor or close relatives. It is, quite simply, a four-sided leaflet with space to record essential information: name and address of solicitor; where the will and other important documents, for example share certificates and insurance policies, are kept; the date of any codicils and so on. Logs should be obtainable from most solicitors.

Wills may need updating in the event of an important change of circum-stances, for example a divorce, a remarriage or the birth of a grandchild. An existing will normally becomes invalid in the event of marriage or remarriage and should be replaced. Any changes must be by codicil (for minor alterations) or by a new will, and must be properly witnessed.

Another reason why you may need, or wish, to change your will is in consequence of changes in the inheritance tax rules. The Law Society had been advising all owners of homes and other assets worth more than the nil-rate band (£325,000 for the 2012/13 tax year – frozen until 2015) to review their wills. Partners who wish to leave all their possessions to each other should consider including a 'survivorship clause' in their wills, as an insurance against the intestacy rules being applied were they both, for example, involved in the same fatal accident. Legal advice is strongly recommended here.

If you have views about your funeral, it is sensible to write a letter to your executors explaining your wishes and to lodge it with your will. If you have any pets, you may equally wish to leave a letter filed with your will explaining what arrangements you have made for their immediate and long-term welfare. Over the years there has been increased interest in advance decision making. For those who would like more information, **Dignity in Dying** is very helpful and can supply you with forms and advice. See website: **www.dignityindying.org.uk**.

If you would be willing to donate an organ that might help save someone else's life, you could indicate this in your will or alternatively obtain an organ donor card. These are available from most hospitals, GP surgeries and chemists.

Age UK can help with information on locally based wills and legacy advisers who provide confidential, impartial advice to older people in their own homes about all aspects of making or revising a will. The advice service is available free of charge to anyone of retirement age.

Inheritance tax points

Inheritance tax (IHT) is a tax on money or possessions you leave behind when you die, and on some gifts you make during your lifetime. (See Chapter Four, Tax). There are two main aims to planning inheritance: to make sure your estate is divided as you wish; and to minimize the amount of tax paid on the estate. The particular inheritance planning strategies you adopt will depend largely on your personal intentions and circumstances.

Some ways of reducing IHT include: making tax-free gifts in your will. Bequests to charity and whatever you leave to your spouse or civil partner are tax free. Nearly 75 per cent of people give to charity during their lifetime, but only 7 per cent include a charitable legacy in their will. Last April the government changed the tax law reducing the inheritance tax payable on estates that give at least 10 per cent to charity. It is called Legacy 10, and anyone who does this will have the remainder of their estate taxed at 36 per cent instead of the usual 40 per cent IHT tax rate.

Charities have welcomed the move, as have many will-writers. Existing wills can be amended by codicil to include the 10 per cent provision providing the wording is precise enough to make the donor's wishes clear, yet not mention exact amounts because they won't know the size of their eventual estate. There is, however, no advantage to people with estates below the inheritance tax threshold.

Examples of IHT-free gifts:

Gifts you make during your lifetime:

up to £3,000 a year of any gifts (or £6,000 if you did not use last year's allowance);

£250 a year to any number of people;

gifts on marriage up to £5,000 if you are a parent of the bride or groom and smaller sums for anyone else;

gifts that form a regular pattern of spending from your income;

gifts for the maintenance of your family;

gifts to any person, provided you survive for seven years after making the gift.

Gifts you make during your lifetime or on death:

gifts to your husband, wife or civil partner (in most cases);

gifts to charities.

Useful reading

Will Information Pack, from Age UK; see website: **www.ageuk.org.uk**. *How to Write Your Will* (the complete guide to structuring your will, inheritance tax planning, probate and administering an estate), by Marlene Garsia, published by Kogan Page; see website: **www.koganpage.com**.

Provision for dependent adult children

A particular concern for parents with a physically or mentally dependent son or daughter is what plans they can make to ensure his or her care when they are no longer in a position to manage. There is no easy answer, as each case varies according to the severity of the disability or illness, the range of helpful voluntary or statutory facilities locally, and the extent to which they, as parents, can provide for their child's financial security long term.

While social services may be able to advise, parents thinking ahead might do better to consult a specialist organization experienced in helping carers in this situation to explore the possible options available to them. Useful addresses are:

Carers UK, website: **www.carersuk.org**;

Carers Trust, website: **www.carers.org**.

Parents concerned about financial matters such as setting up a trust or making alternative provision in their will would also be advised to consult a solicitor or accountant.

Money and other worries – and how to minimize them

Many people say that the first time they really think about death, in terms of what would happen to their nearest and dearest, is after the birth of their first baby. As children grow up, requirements change, but key points that anyone with a family should consider – and review from time to time – include life insurance and mortgage protection. Both husbands and wives should have life insurance cover. If either were to die, not only would the partner lose the financial benefit of the other's earnings, but the partner would also lose immeasurably in other ways. Most banks and building societies urge home owners to take out mortgage protection schemes. If you die, the loan is paid off automatically and the family home will not be repossessed. Banks also offer insurance to cover any personal or other loans. This could be a vital safeguard to avoid leaving the family with debts.

Funeral plans

Many people worry about funeral costs. Burial service costs can vary, according to different parts of the country. The costs are rising fast, not just because of funeral directors' fees but more because disbursements – payments to third parties including church, grave or crematorium – have soared in the past few years. Since January 2002, prepaid funeral plans have been regulated, although companies can avoid being regulated directly by the Financial Services Authority if they keep clients' money in either a trust or a life insurance policy. Then they can choose to be regulated by the voluntary Funeral Planning Authority, although not all have done so. Before handing over any money, make sure the company has signed up with the Funeral Planning Authority.

Prepaid schemes are usually linked to a particular funeral director, which you might, or might not, be able to choose. The funeral director must then carry out your funeral with whatever money is available in the trust or insurance policy. If that is less than they are charging at the time, that is their loss. You can also buy small-premium life insurance policies that pay out when you die. Those targeted at the over-50s are sometimes called funeral plans, although the money can be used for any purpose. But your relatives will still have to make your funeral arrangements. They are whole-of-life policies, which means you have to continue paying premiums until you die – and quite possibly will pay more in premiums than the fixed present pay-out allowed. If you stop paying premiums you won't get any money back.

It is a subject most of us would prefer not to discuss, but we all have to face eventually. There is enough sadness when someone dies without adding to the stress and upset with the cost of the funeral. Your family and friends will have enough difficult decisions and arrangements to make without having to pay for the funeral too.

The charity Age UK offers a Guaranteed Funeral Plan that will take care of funeral expenses and arrangements in advance. It is easy to understand and straightforward to arrange. The plan means that you can pay towards your own funeral at today's prices – thereby beating the effects of inflation. With Age UK's plan there will be no bill left for anyone to pay for the services covered. There are three plans on offer which can be tailored to suit your requirements, including requests for your favourite hymn or reading. As you save towards your plan, the funds are expertly managed and held in an Independent Trust Fund. The plan is made in association with Dignity – a leading and well established provider of funeral plans. **Age UK Funeral Plan,** website: **www.ageuk.org.uk**

Funeral plans are also offered by the following:

Co-operative Funeralcare, website: **www.co-operativefuneralcare.co.uk;**

Dignity Caring Funeral Services, website: **www.dignityfuneralplans.co.uk;**

Golden Charter, website: **www.golden-charter.co.uk;**

Perfect Choice Funeral Plans, website: **www.nafd.org.uk.**

As with insurance policies, a point to check is whether there are any exclusions. Because of the large increases in fees being charged by some cemeteries and crematoria, as well as the rising cost of other disbursements, a number of funeral plan providers are now restricting their guarantee on price to those services within the control of the funeral director. This does not necessarily mean that there would be an excess to pay. If you are considering this type of scheme, as with any other important purchase it is sensible to compare the different plans on the market to ensure that you are choosing the one that best suits your requirements.

Before making any advance payment you would be wise to investigate the following points:

- whether your money will be put into an insurance policy or trust fund or, if not, whether the plan provider is authorized by the Financial Services Authority;
- what fees are deducted from the investment;
- what exact expenses the plan covers;
- what freedom you have if you subsequently want to change any of the details of the plan;
- if you cancel the plan, whether you can get all your money back – or only a part.

Before paying, you should receive a letter confirming the terms and conditions together with full details of the arrangements you have specified. It is important to check this carefully and inform your next of kin where the letter is filed.

For further information see:

Funeral Planning Authority, website: **www.funeralplanningauthority.com**;

National Association of Funeral Directors, website: **www.nafd.org.uk**;

National Society of Allied and Independent Funeral Directors, website: **www.saif.org.uk**.

Those in receipt of Income Support, Pension Credit, Housing Benefit or Council Tax Benefit may qualify for a payment from the Social Fund to help with funeral costs. For details of eligibility and how you claim, see website: **www.gov.uk** – Bereavement benefits.

Dealing with a death

A very real crisis for some families is the need for immediate money while waiting for the estate to be settled. At least part of the problem can be overcome by couples having a joint bank account, with both partners having drawing rights without the signature of the other being required. Sole-name bank accounts and joint accounts requiring both signatures are frozen. For the same reason, it may also be a good idea for any savings or investments to be held in the joint name of the couple. However, couples who have recently made any changes – or were planning to do so – as a result of independent taxation could be advised to discuss this point with a solicitor or qualified financial adviser.

Additionally, an essential practical point for all couples is that any financial and other important documents should be discussed together and understood by both parties. Even today, an all-too-common situation is for widows to come across insurance policies and other papers that they have never seen before and do not understand, often causing quite unnecessary anxiety. A further common-sense 'must' is for both partners to know where important papers are kept. The best idea is either to lock them, filed together, in a home safe, or to give them to the bank to look after.

When someone dies, the bank manager should be notified as soon as possible so he or she can assist with the problems of unpaid bills and help work out a solution until the estate is settled. The same goes for the suppliers of essential services: gas, electricity, telephone and so on. Unless they know the situation, there is a risk of services being cut off if there is a delay in paying the bill. Add, too, any credit card companies, where if bills lie neglected the additional interest could mount up alarmingly.

Normally, you must register the death within the first five days (eight in Scotland). Your local registrar can be found on the government website: **www.gov.uk**. You will need to take to the registrar's office the medical certificate issued by the doctor who attended the death, and if possible, the deceased's medical card, birth certificate and any marriage or civil partnership certificate. The registrar will give you:

a certificate allowing cremation or burial to go ahead; give this to the funeral director you appoint;

a certificate to give to the Jobcentre Plus or the Pension Service, if the deceased had been getting state benefits or pensions;

a leaflet with details of bereavement benefits you may be able to claim;

one or more death certificates, for which there is a fee. You normally need to send a death certificate to each provider of pensions, life insurance, savings and investments that the deceased had. It is cheaper to buy extra certificates straight away than later.

For more information on what to do after a death, see the government website: **www.gov.uk**.

Registering a death is upsetting, and dealing with a death involves more paperwork and phone calls than a family wants to deal with at such a time. With exceptional common sense, the government has introduced a simple scheme that takes away a lot of this effort. The **Tell Us Once** service was launched last year in collaboration with local authorities across England, Wales and Scotland. Most have been offering this service since March 2012. It means people need make just one appointment with their local registrar, who can then advise 28 different services of the changed circumstances, including all state pensions and benefits through the Department for Work and Pensions, and HMRC, passports, driving licences, council tax, local library, Blue Badge and social services.

Another organization that may be able to help you after a loved one has died is the **Bereavement Register**. This organization has one aim: to reduce the amount of direct mail to those who are deceased. Originally launched in the UK in 2000, this service has since expanded into France and Canada. Coming to terms with the loss of a loved one takes time; receiving direct mail bearing the name of the deceased is often painful and unnecessary. The Bereavement Register puts an end to such occurrences. See website: **www.the-bereavement-register.org.uk**.

Useful reading

What to Do after a Death, a free booklet, from any social security office, and *Planning for a Funeral*, a free fact sheet from Age UK, website: **www.ageuk.org.uk**.

State benefits and tax

Several extra financial benefits are given to widowed people. Most take the form of a cash payment. However, there are one or two tax and other points that it may be useful to know.

Benefits paid in cash form

There are three important cash benefits to which widowed people may be entitled: Bereavement Benefit, Bereavement Allowance and Widowed Parent's Allowance. These have replaced the former widow's benefits, as all benefits are now payable on equal terms to men and women alike. To find out more information see website: **www.gov.uk** – Bereavement benefits.

You will be given a questionnaire (BD8) by the registrar when you register the death. It is important that you complete this, as it acts as a trigger to speed up payment of your benefits.

Bereavement Benefit

This is a tax-free lump sum of £2,000, paid as soon as people are widowed, provided that: the widowed person's spouse had paid sufficient NI Contributions; the widowed person is under state retirement age; or if over state retirement age, the widowed person's husband or wife had not been entitled to retirement pension.

Bereavement Allowance

Bereavement Allowance is for those aged between 45 and state pension age who do not receive Widowed Parent's Allowance. It is payable for 52 weeks and, as with widow's pension before, there are various levels of payment: the full rate and age-related allowance. Receipt in all cases is dependent on sufficient NI Contributions having been paid.

Full-rate Bereavement Allowance is paid to widowed people between the ages of 55 and 59 inclusive. The weekly amount is £105.95 (2012/13), which is the same as the current pension for a single person. Age-related Bereavement Allowance is for younger widows or widowers who do not qualify for the full rate. It is payable to those who are aged between 45 and 54 inclusive when their partner dies. Rates depend on age and vary from £31.79 for 45-year-olds to £98.53 (2012/13) for those aged 54.

Bereavement Allowance is normally paid automatically once you have sent off your completed form BB1, so if for any reason you do not receive it you should enquire at your social security office. In the event of your being ineligible, owing to insufficient NICs having been paid, you may still be entitled to receive Income Support, Housing Benefit or a grant or loan from the Social Fund. See website: **www.gov.uk** – Bereavement benefits.

Widowed Parent's Allowance

This is paid to widowed parents with at least one child for whom they receive Child Benefit. The current value (2012/13) is £105.95 per week. The allowance is usually paid automatically. If for some reason, although eligible, you do not receive the money, you should inform your social security office.

Retirement pension

Once a widowed person reaches state retirement age, he or she should receive a state pension in the normal way. An important point to remember is that a widow or widower may be able to use the late spouse's NICs to boost the amount he or she receives. See leaflet RM1, *Retirement – A Guide to Benefits for People Who Are Retiring or Have Retired.*

Problems

Both pension payments and bereavement benefits are dependent on sufficient NICs having been paid. Your social security office will inform you if you are not eligible. If this should turn out to be the case, you may still be entitled to receive Income Support, Housing Benefit, Council Tax Benefit or a grant or loan from the Social Fund – so ask. If you are unsure of your position or have difficulties, ask at your Citizens Advice Bureau, which will at least be able to help you work out the sums and inform you of your rights. See website: **www.citizensadvice.org.uk.**

Particular points to note

Most widowed people's benefits are taxable. However, the £2,000 Bereavement Benefit is tax free, as are pensions paid to the widows or widowers of armed forces personnel. Widowed people will normally be able to inherit their spouse's additional pension rights if they contributed to SERPS (see the note below) and/or the Second State Pension (S2P), or at least half their guaranteed minimum pension, if their spouse was in a contracted-out scheme. Additionally, where applicable, all widowed people are entitled on retirement to half the graduated pension earned by their husband or wife.

NB: SERPS benefits paid to surviving spouses are due to be halved over the coming years. Anyone over state pension age before 6 October 2002 is exempt from any cuts and will keep the right to pass on his or her SERPS pension in full to a bereaved spouse. Equally, any younger widower or widow who inherited his or her late spouse's SERPS entitlement before 6 October 2002 will not be affected and will continue to receive the full amount.

Women in receipt of widow's pension who remarry, or live with a man as his wife, lose their entitlement to the payment unless the cohabitation ends, in which case they can claim it again. If a woman is aged over 60, the fact that she is living with a man will not affect her entitlement to a retirement pension based on her late husband's contribution record. Widows and widowers of armed forces personnel whose deaths were a direct result of their service are now entitled to keep their armed forces attributable pension for life, regardless of whether they remarry or cohabit.

Tax allowances

Widows and widowers receive the normal single person's tax allowance of £8,105 and, if in receipt of Married Couple's Allowance, are also entitled to any unused portion of the allowance in the year of their partner's death.

Advice

Many people have difficulty in working out exactly what they are entitled to and how to claim it. The Citizens Advice Bureau is always very helpful. Additionally, Cruse and the National Association of Widows (see below) can assist you.

Organizations that can help

Problems vary. For some, the hardest thing to bear is the loneliness of returning to an empty house. For others, money problems seem to dominate everything else. For many older women, in particular, who have not got a job, widowhood creates a great gulf where for a while there is no real sense of purpose. Many widowed men and women go through a spell of feeling enraged against their partner for dying. Most are baffled and hurt by the seeming indifference of friends, who appear more embarrassed than sympathetic.

In time, problems diminish and individuals are able to recapture some of their joy for living with all its many pleasures. Talking to other people who know the difficulties from their own experience can be a tremendous help.

The following organizations not only offer opportunities for companionship but also provide an advisory and support service:

Cruse Bereavement Care offers free help to anyone who has been bereaved by providing both one-to-one and group support through its 150 local branches throughout the UK. See website: **www.crusebereavementcare.org.uk.**

The National Association of Widows is a national voluntary organization. Its many branches provide a supportive social network for widows throughout the UK. See website: **www.widows.uk.net.**

Many professional and other groups offer a range of services for widows and widowers associated with them. These include:

The Civil Service Retirement Fellowship, website: **www.csrf.org.uk;**

The War Widows Association of Great Britain, website: **www.warwidows.org.uk.**

Many local Age UK groups offer a counselling service. Trade unions are often particularly supportive, as are Rotary Clubs, all the armed forces organizations and most benevolent societies.

Directory of useful organizations and contacts

Benefits advice

Age UK (formerly Age Concern and Help The Aged), Tavis House, 1-6 Tavistock Square, London WC1H 9NA, tel: 0800 169 6565, website: **www.ageuk.org.uk**

Citizens Advice Bureau (England, Wales and Northern Ireland), for free independent advice about State Benefits, website: **www.citizensadvice.co.uk; www.adviceguide.org.uk**

Citizens Advice Scotland, website: **www.cas.org.uk**

Community Legal Advice (England and Wales), tel: 0845 345 4345, website: **www.communitylegaladvice.org.uk**

Money Advice Scotland, tel: 0141 572 0237, website: **www.moneyadvicescotland.org.uk**

Advice NI (Northern Ireland), tel: 029 9064 5919, website: **www.adviceni.net**

Government benefits adviser tool, website: **www.gov.uk** – Benefits adviser

Turn2us, to identify potential sources of funding for those facing financial difficulty, website: **www.turn2us.org.uk**

Debt

Citizens Advice Bureau, free independent debt advice in England, Wales and Northern Ireland, website: **www.citizensadvice.org.uk**

Citizens Advice Scotland, website: **www.cas.org.uk**

Community Legal Advice (England and Wales), tel: 0845 345 4345, website: **www.communitylegaladvice.org.uk**

National Debtline, tel: 0808 808 4000, website: **www.nationaldebtline.co.uk**

Debtline NI (Northern Ireland), tel: 0800 0287 4990, website: **www.debtlineni.org**

Money Advice Scotland, tel: 0141 572 0237, website: **www.moneyadvicescotland.org.uk**

Consumer Credit Counselling Service, Wade House, Merrion Centre, Leeds, LS2 8NG, tel: 0800 138 1111, website: **www.cccs.co.uk**

Debt test, Money Advice Service: **www.moneyadviceservice.org.uk/ debt_test**

Pay Plan, tel: 0800 280 2816, website: **www.payplan.com**

Disabilities

Age UK, tel: 0800 169 6565, website: **www.ageuk.org.uk**

Attendance Allowance and Disability Living Allowance, tel: 0845 712 3456

Benefits Enquiry Line (for general enquiries and claim forms for disability and carer benefits), tel: 0800 88 22 00 (textphone 0800 24 33 55)

Carer's Allowance, call the Disability Living and Attendance Allowance Help Line for information, tel: 0845 608 4321 (textphone 0845 604 5312)

Free Tax Disc, tel: 0845 712 3456

Pensions, Disability and Carers Service for Disability Living Allowance and Attendance Allowance (existing claims), tel: 0845 712 3456

Pension Credit (The Pension Service), tel: 0800 991 234, website: **www.gov.uk** – State pensions

Social Fund grants and loans, Jobcentre Plus (Great Britain), tel: 0800 055 6688, website: **www.gov.uk** – Jobseeker's Allowance; Local Jobs and Benefits Office or Social Security Office (Northern Ireland) website: **www.dsdni.gov.uk/index/ssa.htm**

Winter Fuel Payment Helpline, tel: 0845 915 1515, website: **www.gov.uk** – Heating and housing benefits

Energy-saving advice and grants

ACT ON CO_2 Advice Line, tel: 0800 512 012

Energy Saving Trust, tel: 0800 512 012, website: **www.energysavingtrust.org.uk**

Warm Front (England), tel: 0800 316 2805, website: **www.gov.uk** – Heating and housing benefits

Warm Zone (England), website: **www.warmzone.co.uk**

NEST (replaced Wales – Home Energy Efficiency Scheme), tel: 0800 512 012, website: **www.nestwales.org.uk**

Scotland – Energy Assistance Package (replaced Warm Deal – Scotland), tel: 0800 512 012, website: **www.energyassistanepackage.com**

Warm Homes Scheme (Northern Ireland), tel: 0800 988 0559, website: **www.warm-homes.com**

To compare fuel deals, website: **www.consumerfocus.org.uk** (UK); **www.cheapestoil.co.uk** (Northern Ireland)

Funeral and inheritance tax planning

Bereavement Register, tel: 0845 300 3900, website:
  www.the-bereavement-register.com

Funeral Planning Authority Ltd, Knellstone House, Udimore, Rye,
  East Sussex TN31 6AR, tel: 0845 601 9619, website:
  www.funeralplanningauthority.co.uk

HM Revenue & Customs (England and Wales) Ferrers House, PO Box 38,
  Nottingham NG2 1BB; Northern Ireland: Level 5, Millennium
  House, 17-25 Great Victoria Street, Belfast BT2 7BN; Scotland:
  Meldrum House, 15 Drumsheugh Gardens, Edinburgh EH3 7UG

Probate and IHT, tel: 0845 302 0900, website: **www.hmrc.gov.uk**
  – Inheritance Tax

For inheritance tax advice

Society of Trust and Estate Practitioners (STEP), Artillery House
  (South), 11-19 Artillery Road, London SW1P 1RT,
  tel: 020 7340 0506, website: **www.step.org**

To register a death

General Register Office (England and Wales), website: **www.gro.gov.uk**;
  Scotland: **www.gro-scotland.gov.uk**; Northern Ireland:
  www.groni.gov.uk

To obtain a copy of the government booklet: 'What to do after a death':
  England and Wales: website: **www.gov.uk** – Death and bereavement;
  Scotland: **www.scotland.gov.uk**; Northern Ireland:
  www.nidirect.gov.uk

Health and health care

Free prescriptions and other health benefits in UK, free booklet: HC11
  Help with Health Costs from your GP or pharmacies, tel: 0845 850
  1166, website: **www.nhsbsa.nhs.uk/HealthCosts/1558.aspx**. For
  Scotland: free booklet HCS2 'Help with health costs', tel: 0131 244
  2529, website: **www.scotland.gov.uk/healthcosts**

Prescription pre-payment certificates (England), tel: 0845 850 0030;
website: **www.nhsbsa.nhs.uk/1127.aspx**; Scotland:
www.psd.scot.nhs.uk/doctors/prepayment-certificates.html

In Northern Ireland and Wales prescriptions are free.

Holidays

To apply for a European Health Insurance Card (EHIC) Pick up a form
at the Post Office or tel: 0845 605 0707, website: **www.ehic.org.uk**

House and home

For details about local Domestic Energy Assessors see **EPC Register;**
website: **www.epcregister.com**

For a free and impartial home energy check visit **Energy Saving Trust;**
website: **www.energysavingtrust.org.uk**

To find an independent surveyor/valuer

Royal Institute of Chartered Surveyors, tel: 0870 333 1600,
website: **www.rics.org**

For help with property

The **National Association of Estate Agents (NAEA)** runs a service
called 'PropertyLive', a network of estate agents providing access
to a professional, friendly property service. See website:
www.Propertylive.co.uk

For protection

The **Property Ombudsman** scheme provides an independent review
service for buyers or sellers of UK residential property in the event of
a complaint. See website: **www.tpos.co.uk**

Help for the elderly

Elderly Accommodation Counsel, Third Floor, 89 Albert Embankment, London SE1 7TP, tel: 0800 377 7070, website: **www.housingcare.org**

Home improvement agencies

England – Foundations, tel: 0145 789 1909,
website: **www.foundations.uk.com**

Wales – Care & Repair Cymru, tel: 029 2057 6286,
website: **www.careandrepair.org.uk**

Scotland – Care & Repair Forum Scotland, tel: 0141 221 9879,
website: **www.careandrepairscotland.co.uk**

Northern Ireland – Fold Housing Association, tel: 028 9042 8314,
website: **www.foldgroup.co.uk**

Help for tenants

The Leasehold Advisory Service; see website: **www.lease-advice.org**

Landmark Leasehold Advisory Services specializes in providing legal services to residential leaseholders of England and Wales; see website: **www.landmarklease.com**

Department for Communities and Local Government for advice on leasehold legislation and policy, website: **www.communities.gov.uk**

Independent financial advice

To find an Independent Financial Adviser

IFA Promotion/Unbiased.co.uk, website: **www.unbiased.co.uk**

Institute of Financial Planning, Whitefriars Centre, Lewins Mean, Bristol BS1 2NT. Website: **www.financialplanning.org.uk**

Personal Finance Society (PFS), 20 Aldermanbury, London EC2V 7HY, website: **www.findanadviser.org**

Financial Services Authority (FSA Register), 25 The North Colonnade, London E14 5HS, tel: 0845 606 1234, website: **www.fsa.gov.uk**

Financial Ombudsman Service, South Quay Plaza, 183 Marsh Wall, London E14 9SR, tel: 0845 080 1800 or 0800 0234 567. website: **www.financial-ombudsman.org.uk**

Financial Services Compensation Scheme, 7th Floor, Lloyds Chambers, Portsoken Street, London E1 8BN, tel: 020 7741 4100 or 0800 678 1100, website: **www.fscs.org.uk**

Ethical Investment Research Service (EIRIS): **www.yourethicalmoney.org**. Information about product providers and other sources that provide ethical investments

MyLocalAdviser: **www.mylocaladviser.co.uk**. For financial advisers in your area

Society of Later Life Advisers – see website: **www.societyoflaterlifeadvisers.co.uk**

To find a stockbroker

See London Stock Exchange website: **www.londonstockexchange.com**, or the Association of Private Client Investment Managers and Stockbrokers (APCIMS) website: **www.apcims.co.uk**

To find equity release providers

Equity Release Council is a trade body for equity release. (Its members abide by a code of conduct, formerly **SHIP**) 3rd Floor, Bush House, North West Wing, Aldwych, London WC2B 4PJ, tel: 0844 669 7085. Website: **www.equityreleasecouncil.com**

To find a tax adviser

Chartered Institute of Taxation, tel: 020 7235 9381, website: **www.tax.org.uk**

Insurance

Association of British Insurers, for advice and information on insurance: website: **www.abi.org.uk**

Association of Medical Insurance Intermediaries (AMII), Suites 21-24, The North Colchester Business Centre, 340 The Crescent, Colchester CO4 9AD, tel: 01206 848 443. Website: **www.amii.org.uk**

To check whether you have enough buildings insurance, Buildings Insurance Cost Calculator, tel: 020 7695 1500, website: **www.bcis.co.uk**

To check a car's insurance group, www.carpages.co.uk, www.checkthatcar.com

British Insurance Brokers Association (BIBA), to find an insurance broker, Consumer Helpline: 0870 950 1790, website: **www.biba.org.uk**

Legal

To find a solicitor

Law Society, 113 Chancery Lane, London WC2A 1PL, tel: 0870 606 2555, website: **www.lawsociety.org.uk**

Law Society of Scotland, 26 Drumsheugh Gardens, Edinburgh EH3 7YR, tel: 0131 226 7411, website: **www.lawscot.org.uk**

Law Society of Northern Ireland, 96 Victoria Street, Belfast BT1 3GN, tel: 028 9023 1614, website: **www.lawsoc-ni.org**

Community Legal Advice (CLA). People living on a low income or benefits may be eligible for legal aid to get free specialist advice from qualified legal advisers. See website: **www.legalservices.gov.uk**

Solicitors for Independent Financial Advice (SIFA), is the trade body for solicitor financial advisers. Its membership now also includes accountancy IFAs as members; see website: **www.sifa.co.uk**

For Complaints about a legal services adviser: see **Legal Services Ombudsman** website: **www.legalombudsman.org.uk**

Making a will

Institute of Professional Willwriters, Trinity Point, New Road, Halesowen, West Midlands, B63 3HY, tel: 0345 257 2570, website: **www.ipw.org.uk**

Power of Attorney

Office of the Public Guardian, England and Wales, tel: 0300 456 0300, website: **www.publicguardian.gov.uk**. Scotland, tel: 0132 467 8300, website: **www.publicguardian-scotland.gov.uk**

Office of Care and Protection, Northern Ireland, tel: 028 9072 4733, website: **www.courtsni.gov.uk**

Leisure

Free digital TV channels

Freeview, website: **www.freeview.co.uk/Services/Freeview2**

Freesat, PO Box 6296, London W1A 3FF, tel: 0845 313 0052, website: **www.freesat.co.uk**

Free bus travel

England and Wales, your local council or website: **www.gov.uk** – Blue badge parking, local travel and the environment

Scotland, your local council or Strathclyde Partnership for Transport, tel: 0141 332 6811, website: **www.spt.co.uk**

Northern Ireland, Translink, tel: 028 9066 6630 or bus and rail stations, see website: **www.translink.co.uk**

Cheap rail and coach travel

Rail travel in the UK, buy a Senior Railcard in UK from rail stations or some travel agents, or tel: 0845 748 4950, website: **www.senior-railcard.co.uk/online**

Rail travel in Europe: **Rail Europe Ltd**, Rail Europe House, 34 Tower View, Kings Hill, West Malling, Kent ME19 4ED, tel: 0870 584 8848

For cheap coach travel: **National Express**, tel: 0871 781 8181, website: **www.nationalexpress.com**

For free swimming

Your local council, or website: **www.direct.gov.uk** – Local Councils

Money

For information and advice on money matters: **Money Advice Service**, Money Advice Line: 0300 500 5000, website: **www.moneyadviceservice.org.uk**

To trace lost savings: Get a claim form from any bank or building society, library or Citizens Advice, see website: **www.mylostaccount.org.uk**

To trace lost investments: **Unclaimed Assets Register**, tel: 0870 241 1713, website: **www.uar.co.uk**

Internet comparison sites: **www.comparethemarket.com**; **www. confused.com**; **www.moneyfacts.com**; **www.moneysupermarket.com**; **www.which.co.uk/switch**; **www.uswitch.com**

Pensions

State Pension Forecasting Team, The Future Pension Centre, Tyneview Park, Whitley Road, Newcastle upon Tyne NE98 1BA, tel: 0845 300 0168, website: **www.gov.uk**, if you want to get a forecast of your State Pension

The Pension Service for any query regarding State Pension, if you live in the UK, tel: 0845 606 0265. If you are within four months of your State Pension age and have not received your claim pack and you live in the UK: tel: 0800 731 7898

If you live abroad, **The International Pension Centre**, Tyneview Park, Whitley Road, Newcastle upon Tyne NE98 1BA, tel: 0191 218 7777, website: **www.gov.uk** – State pension

To check your State Pension age: website: **www.gov.uk** – State pension

Pension Tracing Service, Tyneview Park, Whitley Road, Newcastle upon Tyne NE98 1BA, tel: 0845 600 2537, website: **www.gov.uk** – Workplace and personal pensions

Pensions Advisory Service for any help understanding your pension rights, tel: 0845 601 2923, website: **www.pensionsadvisoryservice.org.uk**

Pensions Ombudsman website: **www.pensions-ombudsman.org.uk**

Pension Protection Fund (PPF) website: **www.pensionprotectionfund.org.uk**

Money Advice Service has comparison tables, if you wish to shop around for an annuity, website: **www.moneyadviceservice.org.uk/tables**

Service Personnel & Veterans Agency Service to claim a war widow or widower's pension, tel: 0800 169 2277, website: **www.veterans-uk.info**

Society of Later Life Advisers, tel: 0845 303 2909, website: **www.societyoflaterlifeadvisers.co.uk**

Age UK Annuity Service, tel: 0845 600 9267, website: **www.ageuk.org.uk**

Savings and investments

To find a credit union

Association of British Credit Unions Ltd (ABCUL), tel: 0161 832 3694, website: **www.abcul.org**

Ace Credit Union Services, tel: 0191 224 4061, website: **www.aceus.org**

Scottish League of Credit Unions, website: **www.scottishcu.org**

UK Credit Unions, tel: 01706 215 082, website: **www.ukcu.co.uk**

To compare savings accounts

Money Advice Service, tel: 0300 500 5000, website:
www.moneyadviceservice.org.uk/tables

To find out about investment funds

Unit trusts and open-ended investment companies: Investment
Management Association (IMA), tel: 020 7269 4639,
website: **www.investmentfunds.org.uk**

Investment trusts: Association of Investment Companies,
tel: 0800 085 8520, website: **www.itsonline.co.uk**

Life insurance funds: Association of British Insurers,
website: **www.abi.org.uk**

Ethical investments: Ethical Investment Research Service,
website: **www.eiris.org**

To report suspected investment scams

Any scam: Action Fraud, tel: 0300 123 2040, website:
www.actionfraud.org.uk

Scams involving unauthorized overseas firms: website:
www.fsa.gov.uk/Pages/Doing/Regulated/Law/Alerts/form.shtml

'Boiler Room' fraud (national reporting system): City of London Police's
Operating Archway, tel: 020 7601 2222, website: **www.cityoflondon.
police.uk** – Boiler Room

Tax

Free help with tax problems if your income is low

Tax Aid, Room 304, Linton House, 164-180 Union Street, London SE1
0LH, tel: 0845 120 3779, website: **www.taxaid.org.uk**

Tax Help for Older People (TOP), Pineapple Business Park, Salway Ash,
Bridport, Dorset DT6 5DB, tel: 0845 601 3321, or 0130 848 8066,
website: **www.taxvol.org.uk**

For tax help and advice

Association of Taxation Technicians, 1st Floor, Artillery House, 11–19 Artillery Row, London SW1P 1RT, tel: 0844 251 0830, website: **www.att.org.uk**

Chartered Institute of Taxation, 1st Floor, Artillery House, 11–19 Artillery Row, London SW1P 1RT, tel: 0844 579 6700, website: **www.tax.org.uk**

Association of Chartered Certified Accountants, 29 Lincoln's Inn Fields, London WC2A 3EE, tel: 020 7059 5000, website: **www.acca.co.uk**

Institute of Chartered Accountants in England and Wales, PO Box 433, Chartered Accountants' Hall, Moorgate Place, London EC2R 6EA, tel: 020 7920 8100, website: **www.icaew.co.uk**

Institute of Chartered Accountants in Ireland, Chartered Accountants House, 47–49 Pearse Street, Dublin 2, Republic of Ireland, tel: 00353 1 637 7200, website: **www.icae.ie**

Institute of Chartered Accountants of Scotland, CA House, 21 Haymarket Yards, Edinburgh EH12 5BH, tel: 0131 347 0100, website: **www.icas.org.uk**

HM Revenue & Customs for local enquiry centres, see website **www.hmrc.gov.uk**. For your local tax office, see your tax return, other tax correspondence or check with your employer or scheme paying you a pension

Contact the Adjudicator's Office for information about referring a complaint. The Adjudicator acts as a fair and unbiased referee looking into complaints about HMRC, including the Tax Credit Office, the Valuation Office and the Office of the Public Guardian and the Insolvency Service. See website: **www.adjudicatorsoffice.gov.uk**

HMRC Helplines

Claiming back tax on savings income: tel: 0845 366 7850

Registering for gross interest on savings: tel: 0845 980 0645

Self-assessment: tel: 0845 900 0444

Tax Credit Helpline: tel: 0845 300 3900

Volunteering

To find out about how to volunteering across UK

REACH is the skilled volunteering charity, encouraging people to take on new challenges, and make a difference to their community. See website: **www.reachskills.org.uk**

Volunteer centres. Most towns have a body of this kind that seeks to match up volunteers with local organizations seeking help

Volunteer Development Scotland for volunteering opportunities anywhere in Scotland. See website: **www.vds.org.uk**

Volunteering England for volunteering opportunities anywhere in England. See website: **www.volunteering.org.uk**

Wales Council for Voluntary Action is the umbrella body for voluntary activity in Wales. See website: **www.wcva.org.uk**

Leading volunteering organizations

British Red Cross is a volunteer-led humanitarian organization that helps people in crisis, whoever and wherever they are. See website: **www.redcross.org.uk**

Citizens Advice Bureau provides the advice people need for the problems they face. Last year the CAB helped 2.1 million people with 7.1 million problems. See website: **www.citizensadvice.org.uk**

Community Service Volunteers (CSV) is the UK's leading volunteering and training charity. Every year CSV involves over 150,000 volunteers in high quality opportunities that enrich lives and tackle need. See website: **www.csv.org.uk**

Lions Clubs International are an international network of men and women who work together to answer the needs that challenge communities across the world. See website: **www.lionsmd105.org**

Toc H is involved in a wide range of good neighbour schemes within each local community. See website: **www.toch-uk.org.uk**

WRVS believes in making Britain a great place to grow old, delivering personal and practical support through the power of local volunteers to help older people. See website: **www.wrvs.org.uk**

Work

To find out about rights at work

Advisory, Conciliation and Arbitration Service (ACAS) Great Britain, tel: 0845 747 4747, website: **www.acas.org.uk**

Labour Relations Service (Northern Ireland), tel: 028 9032 1442, website: **www.lra.org.uk**

Jobcentre Plus (Great Britain), tel: 0800 055 6688, website: **www.gov.uk** – Finding a job

Local Jobs and Benefits Office (Northern Ireland), website: **www.dsdni.gov.uk**

Careers Advice Service (UK), tel: 0800 100 900, **https://nationalcareersservice.direct.gov.uk**

Skills Development Scotland, tel: 0141 285 6000, website: **www.skillsdevelopmentscotland.co.uk**

Careers Wales, tel: 0800 100 900, website: **www.careerswales.com**

LearnDirect UK (except Scotland), PO Box 900, Leicester LE1 6XJ, tel: 0800 101 901, website: **www.learndirect.co.uk**

Recruitment and Employment Confederation, 15 Welbeck Street, London W1G 9XT, tel: 020 7009 2100, website: **www.rec.uk.com**

To register a new business

HM Revenue & Customs (HMRC), Newly Self-employed Helpline, tel: 0845 915 4515, website: **www.hmrc.gov.uk/startingup**

Companies House, tel: 0303 1234 500, website: **www.companieshouse.gov.uk**

Index

NB: page numbers in *italic* indicate tables